INWARD HUNGER

INWARD HUNGER

The Education of
a Prime Minister

ERIC WILLIAMS

with a new introduction by
Colin Palmer

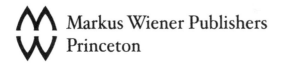

Markus Wiener Publishers
Princeton

Second Printing, 2017.
First Markus Wiener Publishers edition, 2006.
Copyright © 2006 for the introduction by Colin Palmer.

For information, write to: Markus Wiener Publishers
231 Nassau Street, Princeton, NJ 08542
www.markuswiener.com

Book design by Wangden Kelsang

Library of Congress Cataloging-in-Publication Data

Williams, Eric Eustace, 1911.
     Inward hunger : the education of a prime minister / Eric Williams; with a
new introduction by Colin Palmer. —1st Markus Wiener publishers ed.
     p. cm.
     Includes index.
     ISBN-13: 978-1-55876-387-6 (pbk.)
     1. Williams, Eric Eustace, 1911-2. Trinidad and Tobago—Politics and
government—20th century. I. Palmer, Colin A., 1942–   . II. Title.
F2122.W5A3 2006
972.983'03092—dc22

                                                          2006000864
                                                          CIP

To My Daughter Erica

CONTENTS

Introduction by Colin Palmer   I

PART 1   THE STUDENT

1 Portrait of a Colonial Society: Trinidad in 1911   II
2 Life with Father   26
3 Education of a Young Colonial   30
4 A Colonial at Oxford   40

PART 2   THE TEACHER

5 'Negro Oxford'   57
6 West Indian Travel   63
7 Research in West Indian History   68
8 West Indian and American Affairs   73
9 The Anglo-American Caribbean Commission   81
10 The West Indian University   96
11 Colonial Problems   100

PART 3   THE INTERNATIONAL CIVIL SERVANT

12 The Caribbean Commission   105
13 Intellectual Pursuits   108
14 The Nationalist Backlash   112
15 Colonialism! There's the Enemy   118

PART 4   THE PRIME MINISTER

(a) THE FIRST MANDATE

16   I cast down my bucket   131
17   Adviser to the Workers   138
18   The Birth of the P.N.M.   144
19   The 1956 General Election   161
20   Constitution Reform   168
21   Federation   173
22   Chaguaramas   204
        (i)   *The Federal Capital Site*   204
        (ii) *The London Conference*   206
        (iii) *The Chaguaramas Joint Commission*   207
        (iv) *The 1941 Agreement*   209
        (v)   *The Legal Aspect of the Agreement*   211
        (vi) *The Public Campaign*   213
        (vii) *April 22, 1960*   225
        (viii) *The Tobago Conference*   235
23   Member of the Legislative Council   246
24   The Party Organisation   260
25   Intellectual Pursuits   269

(b) THE SECOND MANDATE

26   The 1961 General Election   274
27   Independence   277
28   External Affairs   289
29   Direct Democracy   304
30   Member of Parliament   311
31   The Party in the Era of Independence   319
32   Intellectual Pursuits   327

(c) THE THIRD MANDATE

33   The 1966 General Election   332
34   The Reality of Independence   338

Index   344

INTRODUCTION

"Some are born great, some achieve greatness, some have greatness thrust upon them. Greatness, Trinidad style, was thrust upon me from the cradle," Eric Williams wrote in his memoir, *Inward Hunger*.[1] As the most distinguished son of Trinidad and Tobago in the twentieth century, the prime minister was recalling the extraordinary expectations that his parents had of him. As a young boy, he was "never allowed to forget that I was the rising hope of my stern, unbending relatives."[2] As the embodiment of familial dreams for success, Eric was the most favored child, pampered and showered with privileges. But as the eldest of twelve children, he assumed major responsibilities for the care of his siblings, becoming the first among equals and serving as a surrogate parent. He grew into manhood conditioned always to being the exemplar, and one committed to the welfare of others and willing to embrace their burdens.

Eric Eustace Williams was born in Port of Spain on September 25, 1911. Intellectually gifted, he was the child of economically challenged parents. The size of his family increased every two years, exacerbating "the steady and inexorable disproportion between population and resources."[3] His mother was a housewife and his father a junior civil servant with only a primary school education. In a white-dominated colonial society, Eric said his father lacked the "social qualifications" to reach his human possibilities. As he observed: "The necessary social qualifications were colour, money, and education, in that order of importance. My father lacked all three."[4]

Eric Williams, by dint of his superior intellectual gifts and discipline, was one of the fortunate Trinidadians of his time to realize their human potential. He won the prestigious and highly coveted island scholarship in 1931 and left for Oxford University the following year. In accordance with the high value placed on the study of medicine and the law at the time, Eric's father wanted him to become a physician. But the independent young man followed his own drummer, deciding to read for a degree in history instead. Undaunted by the racism that he confronted at

Oxford, Williams excelled in his undergraduate and postgradu-
ate studies. In December 1938, the university awarded him the
doctorate for a dissertation entitled "The Economic Aspect of
the Abolition of the West Indian Slave Trade and Slavery." The
following year he accepted a professorship at Howard University in Washington, D.C. After 1942 Williams also worked for
the Anglo-American Caribbean Commission and its successor,
the Caribbean Commission. The two Commissions had been
created to promote the social and economic development of
the Caribbean region.

Eric Williams recalled that while he was in Howard's em-
ploy he "concentrated on my work, and I soon came to be regarded as a worker doing his work and minding his own business."⁵ His business included teaching and an energetic program
of research and writing on the Caribbean. In 1940, Williams
received a fellowship from the Julius Rosenwald Foundation
to advance his research on the region, and received a second
two years later. In 1942, the Trinidadian scholar published *The
Negro in the Caribbean*, a trenchant analysis of the deleterious
effects of colonialism on the Caribbean area and an articula-
tion of his vision of a different and better future for it. Williams
concluded that "[t]he Negro's right to decide his own affairs
and his own life is not a question for argument."⁶ The book was
not well received by his superiors at the Commission or by the
colonial authorities. He rejected any suggestion that he should
repudiate it to save the Commission embarrassment. Williams
recalled that he was "prepared to give no quarter and ask for
none. I knew that if I yielded, they would wipe the floor with
me forever after." ⁷

Williams's second book, *Capitalism and Slavery*, an expansion of his Ph.D. dissertation, appeared in 1944 and has become
one of the most brilliant, controversial, and important books
in the historiography of slavery. In his highly original thesis,
Williams maintained that "The commercial capitalism of the
eighteenth century developed the wealth of Europe by means
of slavery and monopoly."⁸ The West Indian scholar argued
that British economic self-interest rather than humanitarian-
ism constituted the motive force for the emancipation of the
slaves. The book's publication marked an important watershed

in the writing of Caribbean history. The young scholar had challenged and undermined the prevailing historical view that the
African-descended peoples of the Caribbean were more the recipients of British benevolence and less the architects of British prosperity in spite of their unpaid labor as slaves for two
hundred years. D.A. Farnie, a British scholar, dismissed *Capitalism and Slavery* as providing Williams's "own community with
the sustaining myth that 'capitalism' was responsible for their
condition, a view that has not found favour in western Europe,
where history has been separated from its tap-root in myth, but
has been found highly acceptable to the educated *élites* of Africa
and Asia."[9] In all, Eric Williams wrote seven books, edited an
eighth, and coedited a ninth.

Eric Williams's formal entry into the difficult and turbu-
lent world of politics occurred in 1956, about a year after his
ties with the Caribbean Commission were severed. Sensing
a paucity of strong, visionary, and enlightened leadership in
Trinidad and Tobago, Williams founded the People's National
Movement in January 1956, leading it to its first electoral victory in September of that year. He became the chief minister
shortly thereafter and remained the head of government until
his death in 1981. Williams was the principal architect of Trinidad and Tobago's independence in August 1962, becoming the
prime minister, dominating the political stage for the next two
decades, and dazzling his compatriots with his brilliance and
his unparalleled command of the issues of the moment.

Published in 1969, *Inward Hunger* is essentially a political
autobiography. It was completed in July 1968, twelve years after
Williams assumed the reins of government in Trinidad and Tobago. The autobiography provided him with an opportunity to
reflect on his achievements in office and to continue imagining
his nation's future. The scholar-politician loved to write, steal-
ing moments from his numerous tasks to research and compose.
An indefatigable worker, Williams wrote his own speeches, and
the official papers of his government bear his stylistic imprimatur. There is no doubt that he wrote his government's most
significant policy statements and closely monitored those he
delegated to others. But it was the writing of history that most
energized him. As he confessed in *Inward Hunger*, he identified

with other leaders who sought refuge from the "pressures from
individual citizens and sectional interests." He had to "make
do with my private study upstairs, turning off the lights downstairs, taking the telephone off the hook. Achieving peace at
the price of air and sunlight, I deliberately leave the files and
reports and grievances and read and write as a private citizen,
maintaining his sanity and seeing the daily chores, stresses and
strains in clearer perspective, determined to prove that, like
Dante's Ulysses, I

> Could conquer the inward hunger that I had
> To master earth's experience, and to attain
> Knowledge of man's mind, both good and bad."[10]

Inward Hunger, however, does not entirely capture the essence of Eric Williams: his joys, dreams, hopes, fears, and vul-
nerabilities. He does provide, in some of the earlier chapters,
glimpses of his childhood and formative experiences. But the
autobiography is not a flesh-and-blood portrait of the charis-
matic leader who intrigued his fellow citizens and who was the
recipient of the trust, loyalty, and adulation of many. He remains
distant in the autobiography, a tantalizing isolation that adds to
his mystique and his image of inscrutability. But political au-
tobiographies are generally designed to justify and explain the
subject's behavior and reveal as much, or as little, as the author
intends. The authors have their optic on the historical record,
writing for their contemporaries as well as for posterity.

That said, *Inward Hunger* is a very important historical
document. Eric Williams, the historian, remains scrupulously
faithful to the extant evidence as he recounts his life and times.
He supports his narrative with copious quotations, obviously
delighting on occasion with exposing the follies of his opponents. Williams occupies center stage in the story he tells but
this is, after all, *his* memoir. The carefully crafted and readable
book reflects the talents of a gifted historian and is the best and
most detailed memoir yet written by an Anglophone Caribbean
statesman.

Eric Williams stood at the center of the major issues that
animated the Anglophone Caribbean in the 1950s and the 1960s.

His denunciation of colonialism in his speeches and writing was harsh and unrelenting. Williams maintained that colonialism was primarily responsible for the ills of the Caribbean peoples and dedicated his life to their mental regeneration. But he was under no illusion that the task would be an easy one. "It is one thing to get rid of colonialism," he said. "there will be joy before the angels of heaven for every imperialist sinner that repents, but if you colonial nationalists think that it is as easy as that, I am afraid they have another thought coming to them. I go a little further than that. A lot of the colonial attitudes are not dead at all."[11] In 1961 Williams proclaimed Massa Day Done in a speech that represented one of the strongest indictments of the psychological impact of colonialism ever made by a head of government. The slavish mentality that Massa inculcated in the colonial citizenry had ended. "Massa Day Done, Sahib Day Done, Yes Suh Boss Day Done," he exulted.[12]

As Williams recounts in *Inward Hunger*, he was particularly outraged by the American occupation of Trinidadian soil at the Chaguaramas Naval Station. Acting on its own volition in 1941, and without the approval of the government and peoples of Trinidad and Tobago, the United Kingdom had leased the land to the Americans for ninety-nine years. When he became aware of the circumstances under which the lease was signed, Williams unleashed an aggressive campaign to effect an evacuation of the base by the outsiders. In the process, he alienated the Americans, the Colonial Office, and some of his countrymen and other West Indians. An incensed, arrogant, and uncomprehending American consul general recommended to the Department of State that steps should be taken to remove the pugnacious leader from office. But the "tough little terrier at the top," as Norman Costar, the first British high commissioner, once called him, prevailed.[13] It was a classic David-and-Goliath–like struggle and Eric Williams emerged with the greatest foreign policy triumph of his political career.

Inward Hunger is faithful to Williams's commitment to the political and economic integration of the Caribbean. He took second place to no one in the advocacy of his positions, first stated publicly in 1940. In 1942 he urged "a political federation of the various units according to nationality" as well as "an

economic federation of all the Caribbean areas."[14] In time, he
would play a major role in the construction of the West Indies
Federation that came into being in 1958, and in its brief history. In order to contain the centrifugal forces that defined the
islands, Williams urged a strong federal center, a position that
the Jamaican leaders Norman Manley and Alexander Bustamante opposed most vigorously. *Inward Hunger* details the politics of this question with admirable balance. Faced with the
prospect of the Federation's collapse, Williams was willing to
compromise, but his efforts were unsuccessful, as reflected in
Jamaica's decision to secede. He sought, in succeeding years, to
revive the question of economic integration of the islands. He
was significantly more successful in this effort as the Caribbean
Free Trade Association was founded in 1968 and its successor,
the Caribbean Community, in 1972.

Inward Hunger gives ample testimony to the variety of roles
that Williams played on the Trinidadian, Caribbean, and international stages. He founded Trinidad and Tobago's first modern political party, and played an unprecedented role in raising
the political consciousness of his peoples through his written
and spoken words. He renamed a public park in Port of Spain
the University of Woodford Square, and delivered thoughtful lectures to the "students" on a variety of subjects. As Williams stated: "Somebody once said that all that was needed for
a university was a book and the branch of a tree; someone else
went further and said that a university should be a university in
overalls. With a bandstand, a microphone, a large audience and
slacks and hot shirts, a topical subject for discussion, the open
air and a beautifully tropical night, we have all the essentials of
a university."[15] The "university" was an unparalleled and extraordinary exercise in the education of a people and in the shaping
of their sense of self and their national purpose.

The restless and energetic head of government also introduced programs to improve the quality of life of his people.
Inward Hunger gives a full account of those initiatives and the
challenges they confronted. Williams had no precedents of
note to follow, no maps with clearly defined pathways. The government over which he presided in the 1950s and the 1960s
was bold and imaginative in its planning and refreshingly effec-

tive in its promotion of the gospel of hope and change. Few remained unaffected by the brilliant scholar-politician's rhetoric and his charge to his people to achieve their potential and take their place in the world as a confident, independent, productive, and proud people. "Hold up your heads high," he ordered; "all of you, the disinherited and dispossessed, brought here in the lowest states of degradation to work on a sugar plantation or cocoa estate for Massa. All of you, don't hang your heads in shame. You are today taking over this country from the Massa's hand."[16] Williams was, in those heady days, the enabler of a people's dreams, the articulate exponent and champion of their human and national possibilities.

Inward Hunger appeared at the midpoint of Williams's political career. He was obviously proud of his achievements in office but remained energized by the continuing challenges. At the apogee of his political power in 1969, Williams was a colossus in the political arena. The "tough little terrier" had accomplished much but he was never one to rest on his laurels. The challenges that the new nation confronted would change and the resilient systemic obstacles had to be addressed, but Eric Williams did not lose his resolve to leave Trinidad and Tobago in a better condition than that into which he was born. That he succeeded is indisputable. *Inward Hunger* is at once his political testament, his account of his career in office, and yet another gift to his people.

Princeton, January 2006

NOTES

1. Page 30.
2. *Inward Hunger,* 31.
3. Ibid., 27.
4. Ibid., 26.
5. Ibid., 62.
6. Eric Williams, *The Negro in the Caribbean* (1942; repr., Brooklyn, N.Y.: A + B Books, 1994), 102.

7. Selwyn Cudjoe, ed., *Eric E. Williams Speaks: Essays on Colonialism and Independence* (Wellesley, Mass: Calaloux Publications; Amherst: Distributed by the University of Massachusetts Press, 1933), 120.

8. Eric Williams, *Capitalism and Slavery* (1944; repr., Chapel Hill: University of North Carolina Press, 1994), 210.

9. D.A. Farnie, "The Commercial Empire of the Atlantic, 1607–1783," *Economic History Review,* 2nd ser., 15 (1962): 212.

10. *Inward Hunger*, 343.

11. Eric Williams, lecture on "Intellectual Decolonisation," Howard University, Washington, D.C., April 29, 1964. The lecture is located in The University of the West Indies, St. Augustine, Eric Williams Memorial Collection, Folder 638.

12. Selwyn Cudjoe, ed., *Eric E. Williams Speaks*, 252.

13. N.E. Costar to Duncan Sandys, May 6, 1964. Records of the Dominions Office and of the Commonwealth Relations and Commonwealth Offices, Public Record Offices, London.

14. Eric Williams, *The Negro in the Caribbean*, 104.

15. Ivar Oxaal, *Black Intellectuals and the Dilemmas of Race and Class in Trinidad* (Cambridge, Mass.: Schenkman, 1982), 113.

16. Selwyn D. Ryan, *Race and Nationalism in Trinidad and Tobago: A Study of Decolonization in a Multiracial Society* (Toronto: University of Toronto Press, 1972), 280.

PART 1
THE STUDENT

I

PORTRAIT OF
A COLONIAL SOCIETY
TRINIDAD IN 1911

The religious outlook which had prompted Christopher Columbus to baptise the territories he discovered with such names as San Salvador, Navidad, Santa Maria de la Concepcion, led him to bequeath the name Trinidad, the Trinity, to the first land he sighted in his third voyage to the New World in 1498. In 1911 Trinidad's trinity connoted the mundane rather than the religious. This was a government unrepresentative of the people and not responsible to it; an economy almost exclusively in non-native hands; and a native population which were hewers of wood and drawers of water for its foreign overlords.

The centre of gravity was Sir George Ruthven le Hunte, K.C.M.G., Governor of the Island and Commander-in-Chief. Himself a trinity, King's representative, head of the Government and president of the Legislative Council, he joined together the executive, administrative and legislative functions which the eighteenth-century democrats had put asunder. The King of England reigned but did not govern; the President of the United States of America governed but did not reign; the President of the French Republic before de Gaulle neither reigned nor governed; it was left for the Governor of Trinidad both to reign and to govern. He united in himself the prestige of the King of England and the power of the President of the United States of America. His decisive advantage over both was his relationship with the legislature.

Legislation passed by Parliament, elected on the basis of adult male suffrage, required, even though a pure formality, a constitutional convention, the assent of the King of England. The Congress of the United States, elected by universal adult suffrage, could override the President's veto. The Governor of Trinidad, on the contrary, could withhold assent from legislation, his veto could be overridden only by the Secretary of State for the Colonies in England, to whom he was solely responsible, and he controlled his legislature as neither the King nor the President could ever hope to do. Trinidad's Legislative Council was wholly nominated by the Secretary of State for the Colonies on the recommendation of the Governor.

Under the crown colony system Trinidad's 190,000 inhabitants of voting age, irrespective of colour, were unrepresented in the legislature, and even at the municipal level the representative principle and elections were more honoured in the breach than the observance. The nominated legislative council was the symbol of the island's arrested development. Its composition was the antithesis of democratic theory; its impotence the negation of democratic practice.

The Council comprised two types of members – official and 'unofficial'. The Governor's top civil servants were *ex officio* members; in the absence of any one on leave, his deputy replaced him. There was an equal number of 'unofficial' members, three of whom in 1911 represented the sugar industry, two the cocoa industry and three commerce; three were lawyers, two physicians.

The Council was no more a legislature (in the democratic sense of the word) *de jure* than it was *de facto*. It was impotent before its two masters: the Governor, locally; the Secretary of State for the Colonies, abroad. The Governor was required to withhold his assent from specified bills, and could do so of his own accord in the case of all others; the former were reserved for His Majesty's signification, the latter were simply inoperative. To make assurance doubly sure, the Governor was entrusted with a dual vote – an original deliberative vote as a member of the Council, and a casting vote as President in case of a tie.

'Be British', urged the Senior Unofficial Member, himself an Englishman, quoting the captain of the *Titanic* in support of his arguments for reciprocal trade relations with Canada. Legislation in Trinidad had a local habitation – the Council Chamber in the Red House, the Government Buildings – and a name – the Honourable the Legislative Council of Trinidad and Tobago. The unofficial Trinidadian members were airy nothing. But, for the rest, the Council was British. The predominance of Englishmen gave a pronounced English tone to the discussions which the unofficials, English by birth or English-educated, could readily appreciate and not infrequently duplicate.

The intellectual justification of the nominated Council and the crown colony system was the paucity of local talent and its incapacity for the art of government.

Puerto Rico, with half of its population Negro, had a fully elected bicameral legislature, restricted by the right of the Federal Congress to veto its measures, and the power of the President to make appointments to the island's chief offices. The French West Indies, almost entirely Negro or mulatto, had universal suffrage in purely local affairs, and sent representatives to the Parliament in Paris. Barbados had an assembly elected on a severely restricted franchise, which ensured the domination of the white planters. Jamaica, like Trinidad a crown colony, had a minority of elected members in its house of assembly. Trinidad's constitution in 1911 marked the nadir of political development in the Caribbean.

Trinidad, then, in 1911, was still *in statu pupillari*, and there seemed little prospect of its ever graduating, far less graduating with honours. An Oxford professor had inquired in exasperation in 1860 whether Britain was retaining the colonies for the mere pleasure of governing them. He ignored one important aspect of the colonial system – imperialism was a vast system of outdoor relief for the British middle classes.

But important issues other than jobs were at stake. The crown colony system in Trinidad was designed to promote and maintain British economic ascendancy over the island. In 1911 it was doing exactly this, and doing it well.

The island's agricultural economy was based on cocoa, sugar, coconuts, and peasant cultivation of food crops and rearing of livestock, in that order of importance. Sugar was pre-eminently a British interest; the others were emphatically Trinidadian. In 1911 cocoa was the queen of Trinidad's economy. Sugar and its by-products, rum and molasses, ran a bad second. The small farmer was the Cinderella of Trinidad.

In industry, unlike agriculture, the balance was in favour of British interests and against the local. Angostura bitters had earned Trinidad an international reputation. The hub of the island's industry in 1911, however, was its world-famous Pitch Lake. But the year 1911 is memorable in the economic history of Trinidad for one portentous fact – the first commercial shipment of Trinidad oil on April 28. The year's production amounted to 125,000 barrels, of which over seven million gallons, worth £33,000, were exported, and the industry gave employment to 1,200 workers.

Cocoa the reigning queen, sugar the ex-king, oil the future emperor – dynasties might come and dynasties might go, but the merchant adventurer, kingmaker or kingbreaker, went on forever. Cocoa estate, sugar plantation, oil well – the centre of gravity of them all was the harbour, and dominating the harbour were the four hundred merchants of the island, principally English, with the Chinese, Portuguese and Indian retail shopkeepers and Syrian pedlars bringing up the rear. Merchant capital found outlets in cocoa, sugar and oil – the pioneer

of Trinidad's oil industry was one of the most prominent English
merchants, a well-known Canadian firm owned a sugar plantation, a
West Indian merchant (from Grenada) was one of the principal cocoa
planters of the island. The Cocoa Planters Association, the Usine Ste.
Madeleine, the Trinidad Lake Petroleum Company – none of the parts
could be greater than the whole, the Chamber of Commerce. Its
Secretary in 1911 bore the most famous name in the annals of political
economy, Adam Smith.

Agriculture and industry formed the basis of the third branch of
Trinidad's economic activity, commerce. The island's dependence on
exports made it necessary to import its essential requirements.

This, then, was Trinidad's economy in 1911, dependent on external
trade, extrovert rather than introvert, emphatically British in its
commercial and industrial aspects, with a powerful British interest in
the sugar industry. The crown colony legislature fostered and promoted British interests at the expense of Trinidadian. It did this either
positively, as in its vigorous support of the sugar and oil industries,
or negatively, as in its subordination of the cocoa industry or its
passive indifference or active hostility to the small farmer.

Priority in the defence and support of British economic interests in
Trinidad in 1911 went naturally to the sugar industry. The whole
paraphernalia of crown colony rule was brought to the support of the
demands of the sugar industry as presented by its representatives
among the unofficial members of the Legislative Council of Trinidad
or by the West India Committee in London direct to the Secretary of
State for the Colonies. The only voices raised in opposition were those
of Trinidadian unofficial members.

The Trinidad Government not only gave general support, by its
policy of Indian immigration, to the sugar industry, at the expense of
the public. It specifically supported sugar against cocoa and took the
side of the sugar planter against the small farmer.

In 1911 the battle between sugar and cocoa was in full swing. The
casus belli was Canadian reciprocity. The issues were the relative importance of cocoa and sugar to the economy of Trinidad, and the relative importance of the United States market for the former and the
Canadian market for the latter. There could be no doubt whatsoever
as to where Trinidad's interests lay. Canadian reciprocity benefiting
sugar endangered the United States market for cocoa.

The Legislative Council would not hear of it. Sugar, sugar, nothing
but sugar – that was its attitude. The cocoa planters were suffering
from 'funkitis americana', the United States would never be guilty of

such international indecency as would be implied in retaliation, etc. Sugar remained the spoilt child of the Council; on Canadian reciprocity, as on Indian immigration, the Council was quite ready to neglect the community as a whole and the other industries of the island in order to bestow precious gifts on its pampered child.

The small farmer could not hope to accomplish what cocoa had failed to achieve. What he wanted was land in small plots on easy terms and roads to get his produce to market. There was no shortage of Crown Lands. Yet the Crown Colony Legislature did the exact opposite of what had been recommended: it raised the cost of Crown Lands – from £1 10s. an acre at the beginning of the century to £2 10s. in 1911. The result was a decline in grants and in the acreage sold.

The protection of British interests involved not only sugar but also oil. In 1910 the First Lord of the Admiralty, Winston Churchill, against a background of growing concern with the exhaustion of the British coalfields, started the conversion of the British Navy from coal to oil firing. With Burma as the only other major source of British Empire oil, Trinidad's resources became a prominent imperial interest, and 'oil for the Empire from the Empire' was the catchword of the day. At a dinner given by the West India Club in London during the Coronation festivities of King George V in 1911, the Prime Minister, Mr. Asquith – motivated partly no doubt by his family connections with the leading absentee sugar interests in Trinidad, according to a local newspaper – stressed the need for developing Trinidad's resources, especially its oilfields, which were being watched with the closest attention by the British Government.

The paramountcy of imperial interests was reflected in the inducements held out by the Trinidad Government to British investors. First it granted leases for 50 years, with options for renewal for a further 30 years. These periods were extravagantly long and were likely to outlast the life of the oilfields covered by them, as was stated by an expert appointed by the government some years later. They were associated, furthermore, with rates of royalty distinctly favourable to the lessees, declining on a sliding scale as production increased; the rates in Trinidad were half those in Burma, where no one had questioned their fairness.

The system of taxation further weighted the scales in favour of the absentee interests and the well-to-do local people against the masses. Customs duties represented almost half of the Island's revenue for 1911. A considerable proportion of the duties came from the foodstuffs consumed by the masses.

The wealthier classes objected to direct taxes – for there was wealth in the West Indies. $100,000 houses existed in Port-of-Spain in 1911, houses with plunge baths capable of holding 1,000 or 2,000 gallons each, where the water was never turned off, so that it should be always fresh; one such house consumed 8,170 gallons of water a day. But the owners objected strongly to meters. The salaries of expatriate civil servants represented an additional source of revenue from income tax which no colonial government could have afforded in 1911 to sneer at. But this was out of the question. A 'committee of representative gentlemen' in Trinidad advised the Governor in 1911 that it was opposed to a graduated income tax owing to the inquisitorial character of its proper assessment and the technical difficulties incidental to it. The Governor concurred in this view. The sugar industry was foremost in its opposition to increased taxation, and the Legislative Council was there to support it.

The people did not receive adequate medical and educational advantages in return for their contributions and sacrifices to crown colony government and absentee property.

For two out of every three adults in Trinidad in 1911 their orbit was the plantation, the kitchen, the washtub, the shop counter, the sewing machine, the corner pavement, the roads or the tradeshop.

If there was dignity in their labour, there was indignity in their wages. The Trinidad society of 1911 was dominated by cheap labour, the legacy of slavery, strengthened by the 25-cent wage of indenture. Poverty was widespread and indigence considerable. There were nearly 16,000 applications for poor relief in 1911. The poverty of the masses was strikingly brought out in the evidence before the commission on trade relations between Canada and the West Indies in 1911.

The low standard of living was further depressed by the high fertility of the population and the high birth rate. In the decade before 1911 the population of the island increased by 57,655. Where there were five people in 1901, there were six in 1911; where there were 100 mouths to feed in 1901, there were 102 ten years later. One out of every three people in Trinidad in 1911 was under fifteen. Add to these the population aged 15 to 20 and the population over 55, and for every breadwinner there was one dependant.

Low wages, the high cost of living and the number of dependants made it difficult for the masses to accumulate capital. Two forms of savings predominated. The first was the government savings bank, opened on instructions from the British Government as a part of the campaign to ameliorate the conditions of the slaves in 1823. The second was the Friendly or Benevolent Society, a people's organisation, which, by weekly dues, aimed principally at providing sickness and death benefits for its members. The assets and situation of both savings banks and friendly societies in 1911 emphasised the poverty of the people and the difficulty of accumulating capital. Depositors in Savings Banks and members of Friendly Societies combined totalled 35,000. Excluding the almost certain duplication, this represented less than one-quarter of the able-bodied population aged 20 to 55.

For those for whom even these limited opportunities of accumulating capital were impossible, the 'susu' afforded a means of putting aside small sums for a brief period. Of West African origin, the susu was a sort of informal bank, organised by a number of people, to which each contributed a fixed weekly sum, the total being drawn by each member in turn. It was particularly popular at those seasons when larger sums of money than usual were needed – Christmas, carnival, Easter, first communion of a child, and so on. Let us assume that there were twenty members and each agreed to contribute two shillings a week. Each person in turn would draw during each of the twenty weeks forty shillings, or $9·60. A 'commission' to the 'banker' – say one shilling – and each person had over nine dollars and the 'banker' almost five for his – or her – 'trouble'.

The housing of the masses accorded with their menial status. The island contained 48,000 houses with 108,000 rooms, whilst there were a further 45,000 rooms in divided dwelling and barrack rooms for its people. Overcrowding was inevitably more characteristic of the barrack room than of the detached house.

The barrack room itself bore mute testimony to the condition of the people. A relic of slavery, it was essentially a feature of the urban areas; four-tenths of the total number of rooms in Port-of-Spain, for example, were of this type. The cesspit was the rule, the water closet the exception.

Its primitive furnishings reflected the all-pervading poverty. The bed of boards without mattress, the box substitutes for chairs, the tin cup, the absence of knives and forks, the oil lamp or candle, the coal pot – the trade statistics and the census figures indirectly reflected these physical limitations of the family ménage.

West Indian society has inherited a tradition of immorality from the slave system. The housing system and particularly the barrack room combined with the general struggle for survival to perpetuate this tradition. Of the adults in the community, 73 out of every 100 males

and 64 out of every 100 females were unmarried; of the children, two
out of every three were illegitimate.

The excess of females over males in Port-of-Spain combined with
the excess of males over females among its non-Trinidadian inhabitants aggravated this general situation. What song the sirens sang is not
beyond all conjecture. Two out of five of all the seamstresses and
domestic servants in the island, half of the washerwomen and female
cooks lived in Port-of-Spain. One-seventh of the unmarried males,
one-fifth of the unmarried females, one-third of the widows lived in
the capital. Port-of-Spain was the city of the gay caballero, the bachelor
girl, and the merry widow. To make matters worse, the female of the
species was increasing more rapidly than the male.

Variety added to the spice of life. The Negro woman concerned
with lighter skinned children with good hair – 'good grass' rather than
the 'tic tic' variety, or the texture which local malice compared in
patois with goat dung – had a wide range of racial and colour types
with which to experiment. The Portuguese rumshop keeper or the
Chinese shopkeeper with his black partner was as familiar and notorious
in Port-of-Spain as the sun at noonday, there was abundant opportunity for occasional nonconformity, and the staid married man could
have his *de jure* wife and *de facto* woman. 'It (the child) isn't for me it is
for stinking Potegee (Portuguese)'; 'Chinee children calling me daddy',
'Sly mongoose . . . mongoose went in de madam kitchen run out
with she big fat chicken' (relations of the white man with the Negro
cook); 'the blacker the woman, the sweeter she be' – the Trinidad
calypso has immortalised the efficiency of the permutations and the
fecundity of the combinations which swelled the island's illegitimacy
statistics and bequeathed to later generations that exasperating colour
complex which became for so long one of the most powerful centrifugal forces in the life of the island.

Ill-fed, ill-housed, and ill-clothed, the population was exposed to all
the ravages of tropical diseases. Deaths during the fiscal year 1911–1912
numbered 7,870, or 23 per thousand. Water-borne diseases – diarrhœa,
enteritis and dysentery – constituted the chief cause of death. The milk
supply was also an important factor in disease.

Malaria and ankylostomiasis affected principally the rural areas,
while tuberculosis was essentially an urban scourge. An infant mortality rate of 149 per 1,000 live births (a large proportion during the
first month of life) and a still-births rate of 76 per 1,000 of all births
further underlined the cheapness of life. Officialdom excused this
lamentable waste of life with the plea that 'so many diverse and intri-

cate problems are indissolubly bound up with this subject in the shape of contributory causes, local and other conditions, that only a most careful and exhaustive study of its protean ramifications can be expected to indicate measures that might effect any amelioration. . . .' One thing was certain: exuberant verbosity would not.

The public mind in 1911 was agitated by three additional threats to the health of the population – plague, rabies and leprosy.

Low wages and poor housing bred not only disease but also crime. Convictions for all offences during the year totalled 16,280. Major crimes were represented by 25 convictions for murder, 3 for manslaughter, 7 for rape, 9 for arson. There were, in addition, 7 convictions for forgery, 8 for embezzlement, 3 for counterfeiting, 2 for swindling, 10 for false pretences, 2 for uttering a forged note.

One of every four offences involved breaches of ordinances and regulations, of which, apart from breaches of indenture, the most numerous were breaches of the traffic regulations and of the weights and measures ordinance. One in eight involved keeping dogs without licence. Thus the criminal population in 1911 was engaged in petty crime.

Bad as social conditions were generally, they were most deplorable among the Indian immigrants, the lowest paid, most poorly fed and worst housed section of the population. Of Trinidad's inhabitants in 1911, 50,000 – one-sixth of the total population – had been born in India. A further 58,000 – nearly one-fifth of the total – were Indians born in Trinidad of Indian parents. One out of every three people in Trinidad in 1911 was an Indian.

The Indians were predominantly a rural group; only four out of every 100 people in Port-of-Spain were Indian, and only three out of every 100 Indians lived in the capital. The mass lived in destitution, squalor and degradation, represented by the barrack room.

The indentured population was a sick population. Less than 10,000 in number, the number of cases of sickness treated in 1911 was over 24,000. Malaria and ankylostomiasis were the chief scourges. Introduced for sugar, the Indians lived and died by sugar. Much of this disease was directly traceable to the barrack system.

Approximately 9 out of 10 Indian births were illegitimate. Officialdom sought to palliate this by pleading the persistence in the new environment of the polygamous habits of the race. But those habits found a congenial breeding ground in the system of indenture and in the milieu of the barrack. Among the population of the island born in India males exceeded females by 100 to 55. Herein lay the root of the social problem among the Indians. Less than one-seventh of the males over 15 were married, less than one-fifth of the females. Unmarried males outnumbered the females 2 to 1. The barrack room and the sexual precociousness developed by it and in it did the rest. Some allowance must undoubtedly be made, however, for the probability that all Indian marriages, performed according to Hindu or Muslim rites, were not registered, which automatically invalidated them and bastardised their issue.

On June 24, 1911, Coronation night, whilst his wife and servant were in Port-of-Spain enjoying the festivities, a Chinese shopkeeper in a rural area was murdered and his shop burned. Seven Indians were subsequently charged with the murder, and three were convicted and hanged.

The brutal murder was one of sixteen committed by Indians, who also accounted for one of the three persons convicted of manslaughter and four of the six persons convicted for shooting with intent to murder. The Governor, in an address to the Legislative Council and with pointed reference to the Indian population, condemned the serious number of crimes of violence with apparently little or no reason or excuse, and deplored the fact that trifling quarrels which Englishmen would settle with their fists had ended in Trinidad in a sudden resort to the cutlass or fatal weapon.

There was the rub. Trinidad was not England. The English agricultural worker was a man with the vote, protected by law. The Indian agricultural worker in Trinidad was a man with the cutlass, oppressed by the law which, instead of being his protector, was his principal enemy. Those who erected the cutlass into a system of agriculture found that they had made it a way of life. The cutlass was useful not only for cutting cane but also for slicing its owner's loaf or slitting his wife's lover's throat.

The Indians figured prominently not only in major crimes but also in petty ones. Two out of every five crimes in the year were committed by a section of the community which comprised one-sixth of the population. But what was the nature of these crimes? Almost half the convictions against Indians comprised breaches of indenture, the keeping of unlicensed dogs, and traffic violations.

Indian illiteracy was not the principal factor in the crime situation. In 1911 only four out of every hundred Indians were literate; but 26 out of every 100 prisoners were able to read and write. The Indians were no more culpable from the point of view of religion than they were from that of nationality or literacy. Half of the prisoners in 1911 were

Hindus or Muslims; the proportion for the preceding decade was three-fifths. Correspondingly crime in Trinidad was becoming more Christian and more Trinidadian.

There was no question that the Indian occupied the lowest rung of the ladder in Trinidad. Cribb'd, cabin'd and confin'd in the sugar plantation economy, from which other racial groups had succeeded in large part in escaping, the few who did escape to the Mecca of Port-of-Spain were concentrated on the outskirts of the town in a sort of ghetto popularly known as 'Coolie-Town' – today St. James, a bustling suburb of the capital – which tourists interested in Oriental scenes and ceremonies were advised to visit in order to see 'the Son of India in all his phases of Oriental primitiveness'.

Imperialism and the crown colony system subordinated the 'civilising mission' to the maintenance of law and order. British democracy in the nineteenth century had expanded to the slogans of 'We must educate our masters' and 'Open a school and close a jail'. British rule in Trinidad, on the other hand, was marked by the denial of education to the masses and the priority of jails and their appurtenances over schools.

Of a total expenditure of just under a million pounds in 1911, Trinidad spent £62,000 on education and £66,000 on the police force. To the latter must be added a further £18,000 on prisons, reformatories and industrial schools, and approximately £4,000 on the military – the local volunteer force. For every ten pounds spent on schools, therefore, fourteen were spent on jails. It was worse than this. A considerable proportion of the revenue was devoted to the very system of indentured immigration which filled the jails and kept the police busy. Government expenditure on immigration amounted to £87,606, of which approximately half was returned by the sugar and other industries in the form of immigration taxes; but a considerable share of the £21,000 spent on the Medical Department and the £51,000 spent on hospitals and asylums was also to be credited to the cost of immigration.

Nineteenth-century European democracy had taken charge of education and left labour relations to the interplay of employers' associations and labour unions. The colonial government of Trinidad, however, assumed responsibility for labour relations and disclaimed it for education. Fifty-five out of every 100 males and females were literate; a further three men and four women were able to read but not to write. To be an Indian born in India was to say, in fact, that one was illiterate.

In 1911 of the children under 15, one out of every two boys, three out of every five girls were not at school. The Indians, as usual, depressed still further the low standards: only one boy in ten and one girl in fourteen were at school. The Government left education almost entirely in the hands of the Christian churches.

Three enormous consequences for the future of Trinidad followed from this abdication by the government of its responsibility. The first was the total absence of uniformity in the school system. Instead of the school helping to obliterate the differences of race, religion and nationality inherent in the demographic structure of Trinidad, it helped to accentuate them. The obvious centripetal force in theory, it was a centrifugal force in practice.

The second consequence of denominational control of the schools was the injustice visited on a large number of children. The greatest injustice fell on the Hindus and Muslims. The government recognised only Christian sects.

The third feature of the denominational school was that the standard of the teachers, low in all schools, was lower in the denominational schools.

If the concept of free primary education as the right of every child in Trinidad had thus signally failed to penetrate the consciousness of the Trinidad community in 1911, the attitude to secondary education was inevitably ultra-conservative. There were four secondary schools in the island. Secondary education was exclusively urban. It was also very expensive. Secondary education was thus severely aristocratic. The total enrolment in 1911 was 796, of whom 194 were girls – that is to say, of the 46,838 children in primary school, three in two hundred could expect to proceed to a secondary school. The exclusion of illegitimate children from the secondary school in the earlier days added a social to the financial disability.

The government provided a bridge from the primary to the secondary school in the form of four exhibitions for the duration of the secondary school course, exempting the recipients from tuition fees and giving them textbooks free. Another bridge led from the secondary school in Trinidad to the university outside. Two scholarships to a recognised university in Great Britain or Ireland were afforded, tenable for three years; the value of the scholarship was £150. The number was raised to four in 1870, but reduced to three in 1904, when their value was increased to £200 a year. Sir Hubert Jerningham, Governor of the island, awarded in 1897, a silver medal and a gold medal for competition between the secondary schools. The silver medal, based on the Cambridge Junior Certificate examination, was the property of the winner; the gold medal, based on the School Certificate, was kept by the principal of the winning school until it was won by a pupil of a rival school. The gold medallist was the first of the Island Scholars. Silver and gold medallists had their names inscribed on a wall in the college hall, leaving behind them as they departed a reminder to those who followed that they, too, could make their lives sublime, for the gold medal, with its prestige, plus the material value of the scholarship, was the sublimation of intellectual life in Trinidad.

The purpose of the secondary school in Trinidad was to ensure the Anglicanisation of the colony. It consciously took the English public school as its model. The external examinations of Oxford and Cambridge, in which Trinidad was the first colony to participate, strengthened the prevailing English influence.

The secondary curriculum was indistinguishable from that of an English public school. The standard of work in classics and mathematics came in for high praise in 1911. The good students held their own with their colleagues in England and the Empire. One of the island scholars of 1911 was placed first among 57 candidates in the British Empire in Agricultural Science; second in History of the British Empire among 314 candidates; fifth in Geography among 5,361 candidates; fourteenth in French among 2,778; thirty-first in Mathematics among 2,862. He gained distinction in five subjects, as did four other students in the Empire, one in Ceylon, three in England. Of 23 candidates who gained distinction in history, four were from Trinidad. This was no flash in the pan, no happy accident. At the 1910 examinations one island scholar from Queen's Royal College was placed first in the Senior Cambridge examinations throughout the Empire whilst another from St. Mary's College topped the candidates in the entrance examination to St. Bartholomew's Hospital in London. Thus Queen's Royal College and St. Mary's College were not only English grammar schools in the tropics, they were also excellent grammar schools.

The illiteracy of the masses, the semi-literacy of numbers of the literate, the numbers of children excluded from the primary school, the exclusiveness of the secondary school, the predominance of the English influence and the subordination of all things Trinidadian – all these necessarily determined the cultural life of the island and influenced its literary tastes.

The literary and scientific style of the day was affected, pompous, high-flown and ponderous, with a pronounced tendency to the archaic, hyperbole, and Johnsonese. Men were 'the sterner sex', women 'the fair sex'; 'thusly' was preferred to 'thus'. The newspaper's report of a police dance gave the assurance that 'with a well prepared floor, the devotees of Terpsichore did ample justice to the select programme which was rendered'. Could the Trinidad oilfields be exhausted? The following answer was given by a local author: 'We must answer in the beautiful form of sentence to be found in a certain book: No, the Trinidad oilfields will not be exhausted till the Arctic and Antarctic lines bisect at an Equatorial point, and when human energy shall reach a stopping place, the point from which man shall recede.'

The 'small island pride' of Trinidadians was bolstered by the assertion that the enchanting views of their lovely island, where nature showed herself 'in her variform dicta of mixed humanology and separate nationalistic environments', could not be surpassed in natural grandeur even by the picturesqueness of the sunny hills of Italy, the inviting woody resorts of Canada, the scenic beauty of Killarney. The exhortation to the tourists reads: 'The cosmopolitanism of the place awakens in his locomotive breast the love of mankind – God's handiwork – and an enthralling wonder at the various never-to-be-forgotten scenes which meet his gaze. In Trinidad nature seems always to be in her most beatific mood, and every living thing seems to steal forth from its seclusion as if to listen to the diapason of the spirit of Ierean enchantment'. As an example of English influence in the island, the literary style bore as great a resemblance to English literature as the Legislative Council did to the House of Commons.

The public lecture was the principal form of literary and scientific intercourse and enjoyed great vogue. The topics were abstract and alien. Lectures were given in 1911 on 'Times' (whatever that may mean), reading, compulsory education, trips to Morocco and the Southern Pacific, and the rubbish heaps of Egypt.

This was Trinidad in 1911, in every sense – politically, economically, socially, educationally, culturally – literally a British Colony. To what could a boy born in that year, the son of a junior civil servant of the coloured lower middle class, reasonably aspire, assuming that he had talent, 'brains' to use the Trinidad expression?

There were two openings – the civil service or the professions. For the former a secondary school education was desirable, for the latter indispensable. The open sesame to the secondary school, in the case of a family without means, was the government exhibition, and to the professions the island scholarship. The competition for both was naturally very severe.

Supposing the boy did successfully overcome the hurdles of the exhibition, the scholarship, and the university qualifying examination, what then? The opportunities for a successful professional man of colour returning to Trinidad in 1911 were extremely limited. Not being white, he could not aspire to the positions in the civil service which were held by local whites – English or French creoles – whom the British, up to a point, associated with them in the administration of the island.

The professions illustrated not only the poverty of the people but the prejudices of the slavery period. The doctors and lawyers in the island in 1911 were for the most part white or light-skinned. But there were men of colour in both professions, and neither was overcrowded. The census indicated 67 doctors and 41 lawyers.

On the surface the situation in Trinidad seemed fixed for all time. Its beneficiaries no doubt thought so. But below the surface rumblings could be detected by those who had ears to hear. The lamps nearly went out all over Europe in 1911. The portents were internal also. In 1912, a British member of Parliament visited Trinidad to inquire into labour conditions and the suffrage, whilst an unofficial member of the Council served notice of a motion for the restoration of municipal government in Port-of-Spain.

The effectiveness of popular pressure on the British-dominated administration was not merely a question of future probability in Trinidad. Concrete evidence existed in 1911. The Water Riots of 1903 had immediately been followed by the appointment of two non-white Trinidadians to positions until then reserved for whites, the principal-ship of the Government Training School for male teachers and a magistracy. In the very year 1911 Prudhomme David, the most feared of the unofficial members of the Legislative Council, was appointed Commissioner of the District Court of Port-of-Spain.

Opportunity, then, was knocking at the door. Trinidad in 1911 would move only in one direction – forward.

2

LIFE WITH FATHER

In 1911 a young man in the civil service was denied the promotion he deserved and expected because, in the opinion of the head of his department, he lacked 'social qualifications'. The *Port-of-Spain Gazette* protested against the injustice. But the lack of social qualifications was an impediment to the progress of thousands of Trinidadians, inside and outside the civil service. My father was one of them.

The necessary social qualifications were colour, money, and education, in that order of importance. My father lacked all three. In colour he was dark brown. His three great expectations of money failed him. Unfortunate in his colour, disappointed in his hopes of a legacy, he had no more than a primary school training.

In the absence of social qualifications, my father necessarily had to depend on pulling himself up by his own bootstraps. He did not get very far. He joined the Post Office at the age of 17; he acted for two years without pay and then was put on the daily paid staff until his definite appointment in 1899. From this humble beginning he had ascended to a salary of $56 a month in 1910, when he decided to get married at the age of 32. Between 1911 and 1931 his salary rose to $160; during the same period twelve children were born, of whom the eldest girl died at the age of nine months. On his retirement in 1935, tired and disillusioned, his monthly salary was $180. He received $4,000 and a monthly pension of $90 until his death in 1946, whereafter my mother drew a monthly annuity of $38·10, subsequently raised to $49, under the widows and orphans fund of officers in the public service.

Our family existence thus entailed, on the one hand, a search for additional sources of income, and, on the other, husbanding the total resources. As far as the former was concerned, both my father and my mother put their shoulders to the wheel. As the eldest child I was their principal assistant. My father took to auditing the books of Friendly

Societies. My facility at figures made me a valuable aide to him. The gratuities which he handed over on receipt of his fees were my first earnings.

My mother's contribution to the family budget was typical of the Trinidad housewife. Excellent in the kitchen, she made bread and cakes not only for home consumption but for sale on a small scale to regular customers. I found myself drawn into the arrangement in two ways. In the first place I was my mother's assistant in baking. In the second place I was seller of the produce. With a servant boy or girl carrying the basket, I walked around to the various houses filling orders or getting new ones.

It would have been necessary for my father to audit the accounts of all the Friendly Societies in the island and my mother to supply cakes and bread to the entire population of Port-of-Spain in order to meet the fundamental family problem – the steady and inexorable disproportion between population and resources. The salary of a postal clerk, auditing fees and cake sales were simply inadequate. Birth control was not practised by my parents. Not only were they Catholic, but my father was one of the leading figures in the erection of a new church in Woodbrook, St. Theresa's, after whom he named one of his daughters, and his last rites testified to the position he held in the church.

The failure to control births meant an increasing inability to provide for the children after birth. This was my parents' dilemma – to be faithful children of the Church or not to be poor parents. On my father's salary they couldn't be both. Saving and the accumulation of capital were entirely out of the question; the susu was the only form of planning possible.

The first struggle for survival, the daily problem of making both ends meet dogged the family as a whole and determined the fate and fortune of individual members. Their manifold manifestations and cumulative effect were the ineluctable consequences of a large number of dependants on a single breadwinner drawing a sub-standard salary.

The housing problem was first in the list of evils which afflicted the family. We disputed our way all over Port-of-Spain, seeking living space at low rentals. In my first twenty-one years in Trinidad we changed houses eight times, and it is possible to identify members of the family not only by name or by sex or by age but also by the house in which each was born. The descending family fortunes were reflected in the descent from the water closet to the cesspit and in one bad case the bailiff appeared.

The ordeal of removal, the horror of the cesspit, the dread of eviction were only the external aspects of the increasing gravity of our housing problem. The domestic aspects were no less nagging. The overcrowding, for example.

The family diet, whilst not inadequate, betrayed the general financial strain. The Christmas table was incomplete without its imported delicacies. Our Sunday table was also good, its variety of meats and vegetables again proving us good Trinidadians. But for the rest of the week the meat supply was supplemented by beef bones for soup, salt fish, corned beef, and, not infrequently, our meat was bought in the afternoons when it was cheaper. I was brought up on cheap red butter, as seldom were we able to afford a tin of 'fresh' butter from New Zealand or Australia. We children seldom drank milk. Like Trinidadians in general, we bought goods not in terms of weight but in terms of cents at the corner shop.

Clothing put a severe strain on the family's limited resources. The bed of boards could be made to last a long time, the broken chair might be kept at the back and used only *en famille*, but after a certain point, long trousers had to be substituted for short pants, shoes simply could not fit if they were too small, and decency alone required a longer dress for a girl.

Rent, food, clothing, all were curtailed, in one way or another, by the exiguous family resources. Medical expenses could also be curtailed, and they were, but the consequences were not so obvious or rather were not immediately obvious.

They could be curtailed, that is to say, except in the case of my mother. The midwife for example, could not be dispensed with. Nor could one ignore the effects of repeated childbirths on her health. She became prematurely old, fat, and querulous, a constant victim of headaches. She called more and more for dental care and protective foods (milk, drunk almost exclusively by her in the family, Ovaltine, eggs and so on), each birth bringing her closer and closer to the edge.

Attention to my mother's needs left little for the remainder of the family, and medical care for us had to be restricted to the barest essentials. Serious illness – for example, my father's prolonged attack of colitis – demanded prompt attention, even though it set everything back – my father was for months on half-pay. But wherever money could be saved, it had to be saved. I paid my first visit to a dentist when I was sixteen.

A serious fall in my youth whilst playing football reflects the general outlook of Trinidad families in such matters and the inability of mine to afford medical expenses. No doctor was called in, and I was not laid up for any length of time. But twenty years ago, I could no longer ignore the fact that something was seriously wrong with my hearing; audiograph tests having indicated a fairly serious loss in my right ear, which has since extended to my left, I have been using a hearing aid for years. No organic defect has been found by the various specialists I have consulted, and all of them have fallen back upon the alternative explanations, either hereditary deafness which was ruled out or a serious fall. I have grown more and more convinced that that fall over forty years ago had something to do with the deterioration of my hearing. Not that I regret it – a hearing aid is a powerful weapon against an Opposition in Parliament; one can always turn it off.

The family's cultural life reflected in part the pervading financial stringency, in part also the absence of learned leisure and liberal recreations in the community. The silent pictures were beyond our means, and I never saw one. The family's entertainment was bounded by the Police Band Concert in the Botanic Gardens on Sunday afternoons, the only form of music, that is to say, apart from Carnival, the Trinidad *fête par excellence*, to which I was exposed. The prayer book and the school textbook represented the sum total of the literature in the home, with the exception of mail order catalogues and a condensed version of the report of the commission of inquiry on the Water Riots and the evidence taken by it. For the newspaper we depended most of the time on friends and neighbours. My younger brother and I, however, read a great deal, outside of our textbooks.

3

EDUCATION OF
A YOUNG COLONIAL

Some are born great, some achieve greatness, some have greatness thrust upon them. Greatness, Trinidad style, was thrust upon me from the cradle. My father knew that what he had never been given an opportunity to achieve with his brains, he might with his loins. The island scholarship for his son became the dream of his life.

The first hurdle to be overcome was the government exhibition from the primary to the secondary school. In 1922 the number was increased from four to eight; at the same time, however, their duration was reduced from the entire secondary school course of nine years to five. To compensate for this, four House Scholarships were awarded on the basis of the Junior Cambridge Examination, entitling the winners to a stipend of $24 a term, adequate for tuition and books. The House Scholarship thus constituted the second hurdle.

The third hurdle was the island scholarship. This goal, the *summum bonum* which the Trinidadian could hope to attain, was made both more difficult and more limited. In 1917 the Cambridge School Certificate, on which the scholarships were awarded, was replaced by the Oxford and Cambridge Higher Certificate, at least three times as difficult. In 1919 the number of scholarships was reduced from three to one, but a separate agricultural scholarship, changed in 1925 to a science scholarship, was instituted.

The young Trinidadian thus had eight chances of getting an exhibition, four of a House Scholarship, and one of an island scholarship, either in the field of classics or modern studies or mathematics or in the field of science. The age limits were twelve for the exhibition, sixteen for the house scholarship, twenty for the island scholarship.

I won a college exhibition in June 1922, when I was not yet eleven. I would thus have had yet another try at it had I needed one. My September 25 birthdate meant similarly that I had two tries instead of one at the house scholarship and three tries instead of two at the island scholarship. I won the former on the second try and the latter on the third.

My father took the steps necessary for the realisation of the pious hope he shared with the majority of Trinidadians. The first was an unrelenting domestic pressure. It began in the cradle. He had read in a magazine about a nurse teaching a young child the alphabet and nursery rhymes. He promptly bought an alphabet card and began to put me through my paces. When I could recite the alphabet I received a tricycle.

I was never allowed to forget that I was the rising hope of my stern, unbending relatives. How my father sneered, for example, when, on the occasion of one prize-giving day at the elementary school, he read out the title of the prize I had been given for having come third – *Great Expectations*! I should have come first. Poor man! Little did he suspect then how often I would come third before I came first, or what hard times would have to precede the realisation of his great expectations. In my final try at the crucial scholarship his concern over my performance in each paper, the rest of the family listening the while, was such an intolerable strain that I refused point blank to answer any question and remained silent; at the end of the examination he asked me, not unkindly, whether I wished to discuss the prospects, and I told him that I did not.

The second step necessary to translate the father's dream into the son's reality was appropriate schools. My father allowed neither religion nor finance to stand in his way. It was the Catholic's bounden duty to send his child to a Catholic school. My father, however, drew a distinction between religion and education. The crucial moment came when I was to enter the secondary school. For my own part I preferred Queen's Royal College, the state school. So did my father, and he was warmly supported by my mother.

The third step which my father thought necessary for the attainment of the goal he had marked out for me involved only his purse and not his soul. It was the 'private lessons', one of the principal articles of the educational faith of the Trinidad parent, then as now. It was a system of cramming, designed to supplement the formal training given in the schools. A financial sacrifice was involved; private tuition in the primary school cost a dollar a month. But my father paid cheerfully.

The intellectual discipline to which I was exposed at Tranquillity emphasised English grammar, spelling, dictation, arithmetic and geography, the subjects in which the college exhibitions were awarded.

I received a firm foundation in grammar, vocabulary and spelling. The core of the secondary curriculum was languages – classical and modern – and history.

From my very first day at Queen's Royal College – auspiciously enough, my eleventh birthday – it was not difficult to discern in what direction my future talents and interests would lie. The first day in the 'special class' we were given our textbooks, and requested to learn for the next afternoon a few tenses of *amo*. Within a short period at home that night I had learned not only all the tenses of *amo*, but of *moneo*, *rego* and *audio*, that is to say, all the conjugations; I was fully conversant with the cases of nouns, and had made my first acquaintance with the ablative absolute. I walked up and down the house, reciting all the tenses, beginning with *amo, amas, amat, amamus, amatis, amant*, my father beaming indulgently the while.

It was the first evidence of the peculiar fascination which Latin exercised over me throughout my secondary school career. I became, in the words of my teacher, the best Latin student the College had produced up to that day, gained distinctions in the subject in the Junior Cambridge and School Certificate, set a school record by winning the special prize for Latin in the highest form of the school three years in succession.

I took to French and Spanish with a zest second only to that I displayed for Latin, and in my final year won the class prizes in those subjects. I can only say of my training in these three languages at Queen's Royal College that, when I reached the University, I took the Latin and French part of the first examination in my stride; two years later, notwithstanding total inattention to them, offered French and Spanish for my bachelor's degree; and have since read, written and spoken both languages with reasonable fluency in connection with my historical research.

In contrast to my early flair for languages, I found myself in history relatively late. Thereafter distinctions came easily and without fail, the high watermark being reached with a distinction in the Higher Certificate in my third try.

As compared with languages and history, I was never particularly good at or interested in geography or advanced mathematics. With the sciences I had no problem whatsoever; I was a failure.

I had a distinguished record at Queen's Royal College, both in the classroom and on the playing field. I topped the third form in my first year at the school, but then did nothing meritorious until the Junior Certificate three years later. Knowing that I had a second try at the

House Scholarship and Silver Medal, I did not exert myself in the first attempt, and the College authorities approved. I was placed seventh in the island as a whole, but got a distinction in Latin. For the next five years my examinations provided the island with one of the most extraordinary patterns they have ever taken in their long history; whilst I topped the students in respect of the number of distinctions, I was always placed third in the order of merit until I won the 1931 scholarship. I gained both cricket and football colours at school and was the football captain. My colleagues indicated their respect for my combination of scholarship and sport by awarding me the Gerald Doorly Prize, awarded on the votes of teachers and students to the boy who, in their opinion, had been the best example to the college during the year.

It was a day of jubilation that, October 19, 1931, when the news of my scholarship victory was brought to me as I was struggling, as a temporary master replacing one who had gone on leave, with the louts of the lower sixth. Jubilation, particularly for my father, who arrived home for lunch bewildered by the congratulations from people on the way. His twenty-year-old dream had come true. Underpaid, tired, demoralised by the sight of younger people promoted out of turn over his head, because he lacked the necessary pliancy to ingratiate himself with the powers who controlled his destiny, he looked upon my victory as a decisive proof of his manhood. His bearing was more erect thereafter, his confidence in himself restored, and he often told me that, whatever his rivals had, they had not an Island scholar as their son. When he sailed with me to England in 1932 on holiday, it was as if he wanted to emphasise that what he had lost on the swings, he had more than gained on the roundabouts.

The intellectual equipment with which I was endowed by the Trinidad school system had two principal characteristics – quantitatively, it was rich; qualitatively, it was British. 'Be British' was the slogan not only of the Legislature but also of the school. If there was a difference between the English public school and its Trinidad imitation, it was this, that the Trinidad school provided a more thorough preparation for the university than the average English school, partly because the students stayed to the age of twenty rather than eighteen and took a higher examination, partly also because it was not even the cream of the crop, but the top individual from Trinidad, who found himself competing with a large number of English students of varying ability. When I arrived at Oxford, the principal of my college introduced me to my history tutor as a man to be watched, who had all sorts of qualifications, he said, which the English students did not have.

Evidence of this was soon forthcoming. In our first class in Latin, the lecturer, an ascetic, irascible man, gave us, as a test of our ability, a long passage, about forty lines, of Latin unprepared translation; he told us that, as we almost certainly lacked the ability to complete the passage in the forty or so minutes at our disposal, we should do only the first twenty lines. The passage – from Ovid, I believe – was of School Certificate standard, and child's play as far as I was concerned I finished the entire passage in twenty minutes, turned in my paper, and walked out of the class.

I was standing at the notice board when my colleagues came out. At their head was a tall English chap with a long nose and an air the quintessence of superciliousness, who inquired maliciously whether I could not make the grade. I said nothing, but continued to read the notices. On seeing an announcement of a soccer practice, I turned to one of the students whom I knew, and said that I thought I would turn out for the practice, whereupon Mr Supercilious turned round and, having heard that I was from Trinidad, said in astonishment, 'Oh, you do speak English in Trinidad, do you?' I walked away, smarting, as a good colonial should, under the insult.

The next morning our Latin papers were returned, all marked, in Latin fashion, S (for *satis*, passed), NS (*non satis*, failed) VS (*vix satis*, borderline case). As we compared notes, we noticed that the majority of these, including my supercilious friend's, were NS. Mine carried no notation at all; instead it bore a note asking me to see the lecturer at the end of the class. The lecturer told me that I could take the examination standing on my head; he wanted me, therefore, to study one textbook on my own whilst I did the other with the rest of the class, so that I would take the examination at the end of one term instead of two. I refused, seeing no reason for the hurry, and though he bawled me out, I stuck to my guns.

My colleagues were waiting for me outside, led by my long-nosed friend, and the following dialogue ensued:

He: What happened, poor chap?

I: He told me not to return to the class.

He: Dear, dear, are you that bad?

I: No, I am that good.

He: I don't understand.

I: He says that I can pass the examination standing on my head, and so he wants me to take it at the end of this term.

He: I don't believe it.

I: You see, we speak Latin in Trinidad.

To say that my equipment was British, is only another way of saying that it was un-West Indian. My training was divorced from anything remotely suggestive of Trinidad and the West Indies. The divorce began in the primary school. My arithmetical problems dealt with pounds, shillings and pence in the classroom, but I had to reckon in dollars and cents when I went shopping for my mother.

The total disregard of the environment was naturally pronounced in the secondary school with a staff English by birth, training, sympathy, or all three. In my special subject, British Colonial history, there were some references to the West Indies, but they were in terms of European diplomacy and European war. What I knew of slavery and the plantation economy came from Roman history. I could discuss quite learnedly the Latin dictum, the plantation economy ruined Italy, but I had not the slightest idea of how it had ruined the West Indies and was even then ruining Trinidad.

It was not until 1939 that West Indian history was included in the secondary curriculum. Even so, it was only at School Certificate level, and I have been told by teachers that it was studied only by the 'weaker boys'; a 'stronger' boy would, it was claimed, be distracted by it from the improvement of his foundation in English History preparatory to the more advanced history of the island scholarship class.

If anything is needed to underline the inferiority and disparagement of things West Indian it is that the West Indian environment should, if studied at all, be studied by weaker boys. There was no problem in my day. The British education of the young colonial was not distracted by the West Indian environment. What is more, this was fully endorsed by the community. What the school disparaged, the society despised. The island scholar, around whom the entire school system revolved, regarded himself and was regarded as 'a superior soul . . . cut out to play a superior role in the goddam bourgeoisie'. The coloured bourgeoisie, that is, but not to be despised socially, with the public awe of the doctor, the 'my learned friend' salutation of the lawyer, the deference of the social climber, the salutes of the policeman. The superiority consisted in the public eye precisely of the British culture and the disparagement of the West Indian. Twenty years ago, I requested one of Trinidad's best-known politicians under the crown colony system to give me his views on a manuscript of mine on British West Indian education, in which I criticised its unsuitability for the preparation of students for life in the West Indies. He accused me of doing insufficient justice to a system of which I had been the most distinguished product.

The two teachers whose influence over me was most decisive were J. J. Mitchell at Tranquillity and W. D. ('Billy') Inniss at Queen's Royal College.

If what astonishes in retrospect is not how bad the pupil teacher system, or lack of system, was, those who could not see leading the blind, but how much was achieved despite it, the explanation lies in men like J. J. Mitchell. For some forty or more years he was one of the old brigade of primary school teachers whose dominant personalities could not be circumscribed by the humble social position they filled and who, unhonoured and unsung, helped to mould thousands of young Trinidad boys, many of whom achieved distinction in one form or another. In his own way, as an assistant teacher at Tranquillity, as the conductor of private classes after school hours, and in later years as the principal of Tranquillity – belated recognition which he fully deserved – he became a veritable institution. He was a stern taskmaster if there ever was one. He firmly believed the old adage, 'spare the rod and spoil the child'. He was apt to be somewhat coarse in some of his expressions.

W. D. Inniss was more dainty. As an assistant master, he made no direct use of the cane; his prerogative was limited to recommending it to the principal. But he would not have used it had it been in his power to do so, and he rarely sent up a boy for punishment. In his quiet unobtrusive way, he was the soul of Queen's Royal College, the secretary-general, the chief administrative officer, of the institution. It was he who, of his own volition, conducted the special form for exhibitioners; he organised and conducted the school library, giving cheerfully of his own time to this end; he supervised the ordering of textbooks and their sale to the students; he above all was the local secretary for the external examinations.

In one way or another, directly or indirectly, every student at the college was touched by W.D., as he was affectionately called – Pepin the Short, we called him when we wished to be rude. Not all the students came in direct contact with him in the classroom. He was the form master of the fifth form, and taught mostly that form and the two sixth forms, too vulnerable, perhaps, to the rather more raucous and obstreperous ages. His specialities were Latin and English Literature throughout the three upper forms, and History in the fifth. But he could teach any subject. More than any other teacher in Queen's Royal College, he shaped my destiny.

He always took particular pride in my annexation of the island scholarship – and well he might, for he had contributed to it more than any other individual except myself – and in my proficiency in Latin, his pet subject. He followed my subsequent career with great interest. His ambition for me was that I should produce others as he had produced me. He was a little surprised when I elected to emphasise historical research and transfer to university teaching, but he was very proud of my doctor's thesis, was instrumental in placing a large order for it in Trinidad when it was published, and was overjoyed when he listened to one of my lectures on a visit to Howard University – where he was highly regarded because of years of service to them in evaluating British certificates in terms of the confusing hours and points of the United States system.

Three other West Indian teachers played an important part in my development – C. E. Bradshaw, G. E. Pilgrim and Stokely Doorly. Among the English teachers the one I respected most was the principal of the college when I entered, A. M. Low; the one I liked most was Achilles Daunt; the one I knew best was a much younger man who joined the staff when I was in the Upper Sixth, A. M. Wilkinson.

One other Englishman played an important part in my life, though negative rather than positive. He was J. O. Cutteridge, who was appointed principal of Tranquillity in my last year at that institution. Nothing reveals more clearly Britain's control of Trinidadian life in all its forms, its domination of the civil service, than the appointment, by the Secretary of State for the Colonies more than forty years ago, of an Englishman as principal of an elementary school. If a Trinidadian was not qualified for such a post, then what was he qualified for? Cutteridge was not a university graduate. His policy at Tranquillity was openly designed to make the school more English in its outlook.

Cutteridge regarded my success in the exhibition examination in his first year as a personal victory, as if the foundations had not been laid in the five preceding years and in Mitchell's private lessons. My father was pleased. I had found a patron, one not to be sneered at. For Cutteridge, within some seven years of his arrival in Trinidad, had become Director of Education, much to the wrath of the teachers at Queen's Royal College who, outside of his jurisdiction, never hesitated to show what they thought of him. Cutteridge's meteoric rise only confirmed that, provided one was white, there was no real obstacle to advancement in the colonial West Indies, whatever one's shortcomings.

As Director of Education Cutteridge was responsible for one of the greatest innovations in the history of education in Trinidad. He published textbooks called West Indian Readers and West Indian Geographies. The idea was, pedagogically, irreproachable. But West Indian public opinion, and not only in Trinidad, considered that the books presented West Indian life in a disparaging light. Cutteridge's successor at Tranquillity and later in the Education Department, another Englishman, but with a bachelor's degree, E. W. Daniel, also published textbooks, this time on West Indian history; these texts, admirable though they are as accounts of the annexation of the West Indies by various European powers, are everything or anything but West Indian histories. It is regrettable that so necessary an educational development as the introduction of study materials related to the West Indian environment should have been exposed to legitimate criticism.

All that Trinidad had to offer had been placed before me. Society and school, father and teachers and classmates, all had contributed to my intellectual discipline. One question remained, the supreme question; what profession should I elect to follow? On this question the disagreement between my father and myself was sharp, profound, persistent, and destined to strain our relations almost to breaking point.

The product of an authoritarian society in which everyone's life was determined by the Secretary of State for the Colonies, through the Governor, my father looked upon his family circle as his domain, and his relations to it that of a crown colony Governor. As it was sedition to question what the Governor could do, so was it blasphemy to question what the father could do. He was to plan, we to obey. His conception of the *patria potestas* was nowhere more clearly indicated than in his attitude to the profession I should choose.

His wish was that I should study medicine or law, preferably the former. He wanted me to have 'independence', as he put it. From a very early age, my point of view diverged from his. I was determined to be a teacher.

Why? The early decision was undoubtedly, at least in part, a childish whim. By the time I had won the scholarship it had become the firm decision of a man, based on a careful analysis of my attitudes and interests and on the material prospects for the future. The decision to become a teacher was further influenced by my admiration and respect for Mitchell, Pilgrim, Bradshaw, and, above all, for W. D. Inniss. I had also been fortunate in gaining a fairly wide experience of the profession before I finally made up my mind as a private tutor of younger secondary school students and by two formal teaching appointments in the year after I left school. Inniss was on leave for one term, and I was appointed to take his place. Then in February, 1932, Cutteridge rushed into Queen's Royal College where I was serving without pay, insisting that I assume immediately the duties of lecturer in English and History at the Government Training College.

Apart from the question of personal interest, there was the important consideration of material prospects. Everything in 1931 pointed to the fact that one could earn a livelihood as a teacher. The appointment of Inniss in 1915 and of Pilgrim in 1920 represented two breaches in the citadel hitherto occupied exclusively by Englishmen or whites. The appointment in 1927 of Arthur Farrell, another Trinidadian, was even more significant. He was a graduate of Codrington College in Barbados, affiliated to Durham University. He represented therefore a breach with the Oxford-Cambridge tradition.

I decided therefore to proceed to Oxford to read for an honours degree in history. I consulted Inniss. He was delighted. I had selected not only his *alma mater* but his profession. I consulted also two coloured nominated members of both the Legislative and Executive Councils of the Island, one a physician, the other a lawyer. Both thought my decision a very sound one.

I was thus ready for the showdown with my father. Aptitudes, my interest, my personal experience, the advice of others, the signs of the times, all cried out in support of my choice. But he was one of those people in Trinidad who cannot draw a distinction between past, present and future. Obsessed by past injustices, Inniss' difficulty in entering the charmed circle before 1915 was a weighty argument to him in 1932, and impressed him more than Farrell's victory in 1927. To him British domination of the teaching profession, British control over the destinies of Trinidadians were eternal verities, the laws of nature imposed on colonials.

He was accordingly very angry with me. He protested and remonstrated, argued and sneered, cajoled and persuaded. It was all in vain; I had made up my mind. He gave in with poor grace. When I saw him in 1944, after twelve years, having got not only the bachelor's degree but the doctorate in philosophy, he greeted me with: 'So you *are* a doctor after all!'

4

A COLONIAL AT OXFORD

The history and literature I had studied in Trinidad assumed new meaning at Oxford. Gladstone and Peel took on a new form – double firsts at Christ Church. My studies of the French Revolution and England after Waterloo received a new slant as I trod the colleges which had sheltered as undergraduates Charles James Fox and Canning, Salisbury and Rosebery, Cecil Rhodes and Lord Birkenhead. I retraced my private study of British colonial history from 1700 to 1763 and the general development of the British Empire after 1763 with the ghosts of William Penn, who had been expelled from Christ Church, Oglethorpe, who left Corpus Christi to found Georgia, George Whitfield who stalked Pembroke, Christopher Codrington, who endowed Codrington Library in All Souls, Chatham and North who, after leaving Trinity, were, the former to win America for Britain and the latter to lose most of it. Addison, Dr Samuel Johnson, Swift, Collins and Shelley, all came to life in Oxford. I heard not only the clash of arms and the battles of the books but also the throb of the Reformation.

The intellectual discipline was gentleness itself. One was left free to sink or swim, as one could or pleased. The most onerous obligation was the weekly tutorial, the core of the Oxford system.

The hurdles in one's way were not high. I elected to read the honour school of modern history. This involved the First Public examination at the end of my second term, in four subjects; I offered Latin, French, European history from 700 to 1789, and Political Economy. I took it in my stride. Three years after matriculation came the Final examination, a gruelling ordeal of eleven papers lasting three hours each for five and a half days – three in English political history, one on general constitutional history of England and another on special texts and cases, one on a special period of European history (I selected the period 1789–1878), one in English economic history, one in prescribed texts in political science (in my time Aristotle's *Politics*, Hobbes' *Leviathan* and Rosseau's *Social Contract*); students aiming at a First or Second Class degree were also required to offer unprepared translations from foreign languages (I chose French and Spanish), and a special period of history studied on their own – I offered British Colonial History from 1830 to 1860, on which there was one paper, together with another on prescribed texts which included Durham's report on Canada, Wakefield's *View of the Art of Colonization*, and Merivale's *Lectures on Colonies and Colonization*.

For my history I depended on my tutor, R. Trevor Davies, a Welsh clergyman, who had himself obtained a first-class degree, and whose special interest was the golden age of Spanish history. He was my guide, philosopher and friend during my three undergraduate years. The tutorial system I found very much to my taste. I read assiduously the books he recommended, discovered others for myself, took extensive notes when he commented, wrote long essays, and took a very independent line. We used to argue heatedly over my views that Aristotle was a dyed-in-the-wool reactionary, that Hobbes had a fascist mentality, that the French revolution was inevitable and had nothing to do with the character of Louis XVI, that Acton's 'repentant monarchy' was unrepentant rubbish, that only a Briton could see democracy in the Witenagemot, that there was far more to the American Revolution than the Boston Tea Party. The tutorial system, expensive though it was, admirably suited my temperament. It was an adult method of dealing with students. The tutor gave the general directions, the student found his own way among the underbrush. I covered my entire history course, except the special subject, in tutorials.

Only two series of lectures was I able to stomach; one, out of personal interest, based very largely on the lecturer's command of language, on the revolutionary tradition in France by Godfrey – later Lord – Elton; the other, at Trevor Davies' insistence, on the constitutional textbooks because the lecturer was one of the five examiners. For the rest I kept far from the lecture room. My weekly tutorial hour at noon on Fridays – which grew longer and longer until it ran to nearly two – represented my sole connection as an undergraduate with the Oxford dons.

In aiming at a First I had two advantages over and above my sound history foundations at Queen's Royal College. The first was the necessary personal discipline, for which the ordeal of the island scholarship was an admirable preparation. My second advantage was a

growing appreciation of literature, and then of art, as sources for the
understanding and appraisal of historical development – or, to put it
differently, a growing realisation that history was not a record of
battles and politicians, dates and events, or even of the follies and
foibles of mankind, but rather a record of the development of humanity, of life and of society, in all their various manifestations.

Thus I found it easier to appreciate the divine right of kings from
Shakespeare's *Richard II* than from Figgis' entire treatise, and all the
texts on the Civil War, for or against Charles I, for or against Cromwell, never gave me that succinct view of the fundamentals of the
struggle contained in a single stanza of Marvell's ode to Cromwell.
Wordsworth's 'Bliss was it in that dawn' helped me to understand
Britain's policy to the French Revolution far better than all the
scholastic dicta about the French Revolution making Pitt a Tory; Brown-
ing's 'God's in his heaven, all's well with the world', Tennyson's
'Parliament of man, the federation of the world', Matthew Arnold's
'the sea of faith was once, too, at the full' afforded an insight into the
essence of nineteenth-century British democracy for the most part lost
in the mass of details in the academic historians.

I understood Britain's Irish policy and the Irish 'colonial' better
after I had read Swift, Shaw and Joyce; Hamlet's dilemma succinctly
summed up the breakdown of the feudal order and the upsurge of
individualism; the struggle for Greek independence took on a new
form in *Childe Harold's Pilgrimage*; the suffering unleashed by the
Industrial Revolution found poetic expression in Shelley's 'Song to the
Men of England' and Thomas Hood's 'The Song of the Shirt'. The
social content of bourgeois democracy after 1688 and John Locke's
treatise on civil government were ruthlessly exposed in G. K. Chester-
ton's contrast between the Commons with a large C and the commons
with a small one.

As with literature, so with art. The Louvre, the National Gallery,
the Tate, the Wallace Collection taught me as much history as I
learned in the Radcliffe Camera, and I have often regretted that circumstances prevented me from visiting Italy, Germany and Holland,
as well as France, until after my graduation in 1935. The difference
between Plato's *Republic* and Aristotle's *Politics* is there in Raphael's
'School of Athens' – Plato pointing to heaven, symbolising his speculative philosophy, Aristotle pointing to the earth, implying the deriva-
tion of philosophy from investigation and experience. I looked at
Rembrandt and Hals and saw the Dutch bourgeoisie; the Spanish
feudal lord and the Spanish church, chivalry and the Inquisition came

to life in the canvases of El Greco. Goya's *Disasters of the War* illuminated the struggle against Bonaparte, and his portrait of the Spanish monarchy helped me to appreciate, as nothing else ever has, the full implications of the revolutionaries' description of the French royal family as the baker, the baker's wife and the baker's boy. Louis Bonaparte's Mexican fiasco was dismissed by Manet's work with a contempt it seldom received from the historian's pen. Canterbury Cathedral, Hastings Castle, and the little houses in between symbolised for me in architecture the peasantry caught between the feudal lord and the feudal church. To see Versailles was to see *Le Roi Soleil*; it was also to feel the deluge which came after him. To stand before the Arc de Triomphe was to see Jéna, Austerlitz and Wagram pass before my eyes; to stand in the Place de la Bastille was like receiving a *lettre de cachet*.

It was with this equipment that I entered my Finals. I was awarded a First Class degree, being placed – with two other students – first in the First Class. I had a broad hint of my success before the results were pinned up on the notice board. The ordeal included a *viva voce* examination. The chairman of the board of examiners – the lecturer on the constitutional textbooks – asked me where I came from, and then what subject had interested me most in my course. I replied that it was my special subject in colonial history. He stated that that was borne out by my marks and asked me why; I answered, in some surprise, 'Well, I am a colonial.' He then asked me something about whether I meant that there was a connection between one's study and one's environment, and I replied that I could not see the value of study unless there was that connection with the environment. On behalf of the board he then congratulated me on my excellent performance in the examination, commented on the regularity of my handwriting and the speed with which I could obviously write, and wished me success in my future career.

I had come, seen and conquered – at Oxford! What next? My tutor and my college principal, enormously pleased and vastly impressed – it was the first college First in history over a long period of years – were agreed that for me to proceed to a diploma in education as preparation for a secondary school career in Trinidad was a sheer waste of time. The principal gave me a testimonial for the Trinidad Government which read as follows:

'Mr E. E. Williams, who came to Oxford with a Trinidad Government scholarship in 1932, has just crowned a successful career there

by getting a brilliant First Class in Modern History. The competition in that examination is very severe but I have been told by one
of the examiners that he was one of the best three men in. The
examiners openly congratulated him on his work.

That is a very distinguished performance, and the more so in that
Mr Williams has from time to time had trouble with his eyes, and
also in that he has not been a mere book-worm, but has distinguished
himself both in cricket and football. He plainly must be an exceptionally able man.

I understand that the terms of his scholarship require that he
should now proceed to the Diploma in Education. In my opinion,
it would be a mistake if he were to do so, in that it would be rather
a waste of his ability.

He is plainly a man who is capable of advanced academic work,
such as teaching teachers, not boys, and I strongly feel that, if it is
at all possible, he should be encouraged to fit himself for that sort
of work, either by taking another Honour School in Oxford or by
taking a research degree there. Plainly, there may be difficulties
about this from the point of view of the Government of Trinidad –
but I think that if the matter is discussed, the Government ought
to be apprised of the views of the Authorities in Oxford, that Mr
Williams is an exceptional man who deserves if possible exceptional treatment.'

The principal thought I should proceed to historical research and the
doctor's degree. My tutor, however, was of the opinion that I should
repeat the bachelor's degree in another field – the university's rule
allowed me two years if I did this – and aim at a fellowship at one
of the colleges, preferably All Souls College. This immediately
raised to my mind the question of racial prejudice. I asked both
very frankly what they thought. My tutor pooh-poohed the idea;
the principal advised me that, if I were after a 'social' fellowship,
one involving principally tutoring, my race would be against me,
but that I would be eligible for a fellowship based on merit. They
both suggested that I think the matter over during the remainder of
the vacation.

The first phase of my educational career had thus come to a dramatic
close. My twenty-four years' preparation for an English University
had ended by unfitting me totally, in the eyes of those best qualified to
judge, for life in Trinidad! The Trinidad people's investment in me
was to bring dividends to England!

I returned to Oxford in the fall of 1935 with my mind fully made up. I had decided to follow my tutor's advice – to read for a second Honour School, the School of Philosophy, Politics and Economics (called familiarly PPE), and to have a try at the All Souls Fellowship Examination in October of that year, not, Heaven forbid! in the hope of winning it, but to get some valuable experience in preparation for another try in the following year when my history training would have been strengthened by the knowledge acquired in my PPE course. The decision was a hopeless mistake, from both angles. Both the Fellowship plan and the PPE course turned out to be fiascos.

My own personal doubts of the fellowship plan were confirmed several times over during the examination. I was physically unfit for so great a strain a second time in the same year, four months after my finals. Presumably, however, it was an equal strain for my colleagues. The real strain was mental rather than physical. I simply did not belong. No 'native', however detribalised, could fit socially into All Souls. What, for example, could I say, in the very midst of the Ethiopian War, shortly after the announcement of the infamous Hoare–Laval peace plan, in reply to a question as to whether advanced peoples have any right to assume tutelage over backward peoples?

If I was ill at ease in the classroom, I was not at home in the dining-room. The aspirants to the fellowship were invited individually to dinner. Gruesome stories circulated about the method of selecting fellows. One was to the effect that the decision was once based on the method of disposing of cherry stones. Of the three most likely candidates, one spat them into his hand, the second made decorous use of his fork, while the third simply swallowed them. The story was that the fellowship went to the man who swallowed them. It seemed to me, on entering the dining-room, uncomfortable in my first dinner jacket and the stiff shirts and collars then fashionable – on arrival four years later in the United States I encountered the soft shirt, but I would have been flunked at sight had I thus departed from the canons of good taste at All Souls – that the fellowship depended on correct choice at the right time of the knife, fork or spoon which one should take up – there were so many of them. The medieval verdict of trial by water seemed child's play compared with the trial by dinner at All Souls. After that came the ordeal of chatter in the Common Room. It was difficult to be polite to the author of one of the wretched textbooks I had used in Trinidad when he defended the Hoare–Laval peace plan. It was not easy to show one's erudition in a discussion of signposts. I have always lacked the social graces, and had never cultivated – as

good colonials must and do – the elegant art of balancing the coffee –
or tea-cup whilst one's legs were crossed.

Gaucherie in the common room, incompatibility in the examination
room. Either would have been sufficient to disqualify me; together
they blackballed me. The Warden of the College took me aside later
in the evening, complimented me on my performance in the written
examination – it seemed rather strange, as I had been told confiden-
tially some hours before by a white aspirant whom I knew well and
who had got the order of merit from an older colleague who was a
Fellow, that I had been placed ninth out of some sixteen candidates –
and advised me, in a paternal tone, that the greatest service I could
render to my people who stood so sorely in need of it was to return to
Trinidad. The entire episode, capped by the Warden's advice, convinced me that I would never get an All Souls Fellowship, and that the
racial factor would dispose of me in 1936 as the examination factor
had in 1935. I was very angry. It was not that I felt that I had won the
fellowship. I knew I had not.

But I knew that I could never win one.

This is one of these difficulties that whites can never understand.
Only Negroes and other racial groups exposed to racial prejudice can.
The principal of my college, when I taxed him with the racial issue,
assured me that I was wrong. I accused him of trying to shield the All
Souls crowd. Two incidents convinced me that I was not wrong, if I
needed – which I did not – any additional proof after the Warden's
advice.

The first incident occurred in the examination room. The examination included an oral translation from a foreign language. I chose
French, Spanish not being available. The student had to enter a long
room, in which he found some forty Fellows seated around a table.
In the course of translation, I made a horrible mistake. The crowd
roared. I received the distinct impression that the roar was aimed at
me and not at the mistake. It sobered me at once, I lost all my nervous-
ness, I looked all around the room, at one individual member after
the other, until quiet had been restored. I felt like a schoolmaster up-
braiding by looks a group of unruly pupils; some began to pick at their
nails, one looked out of the window, one twiddled with a book in
front of him. When there was absolute quiet I resumed translation in a
cold, unemotional voice. At the end I came to a passage of which I
could not make head or tail. I declined to translate. The warden pressed
me three times to have a go at it. I refused. To set the matter at rest,
I told him on the final occasion that I did not wish to give rise to

another such guffaw as I had already listened to. He thanked me for coming, and I took my leave.

Some days later I passed one of the Fellows in the street. He was one of Britain's then leading author-politicians, a household name in certain British circles. He eyed me so curiously when he passed, without speaking, that I glanced back. I found that he was standing still, looking at me; on seeing me turn around, he went his way. For the fun of it I looked back a few yards further on. There he was again, standing still, looking at me. I thereupon stopped, turned around, and looked at him. No one passing in the street realised what was going on; if I had told them, they would not have understood. The distinguished professor, unable to face my stare, continued on his way. As he reached the College gate he turned to look at me again, but seeing me still standing where he had last seen me, he ducked inside. He went in, no doubt, to continue his championship of liberalism, but he will always remind me of those children in my first Christmas vacation in London who used to touch me as they passed me in the street and say 'First luck'.

The blasting of my English career even before it had started was an inauspicious beginning to the second Honour School on which that career had been predicated. I made the further mistake of not abandoning the course immediately. Instead I found myself getting deeper and deeper into abstract discussions on hedonism, utilitarianism and the like. My tutor was a man of my own age, who had got the best first in Philosophy the very year I had got the best first in History. Being white, however, he had landed a Fellowship even without an examination. Philosophy included both moral and political. He had no use for political philosophy, I had no use for moral. He called me a materialist and lectured me that political philosophy dealt not with things as they are but things as they should be. I called it Kantian cant, reminded him that there were more things on earth than were dreamed of in his philosophy, told him that if political philosophy was what he defined it to be, then, it was not for the likes of me. I walked out of the tutorial and never saw him again.

So much for philosophy. Economics was equally unsatisfactory, though here, happily, a friendship developed between the tutor, E. M. Hugh Jones of Keble, and myself which was noticeably absent from the personal relations in philosophy. Hugh Jones was very interested in the problems of the United States economy, and around the time of my connection with him had published, in collaboration with a colleague, a book on the Depression, I believe, which was quite well received in England. One of his good friends was a Negro professor of Economics at Howard University, and that helped to smooth our relations immensely. It was the subject that I clashed with, not the man. I persisted in relating economic concepts and their authors to the historical and economic development of society. I saw, for example, the ideas of Adam Smith and Ricardo as the weapons of one class against another, or one section of one class against another, which could not be taken out of the context of the American and Industrial Revolutions, the First Reform Bill and the Repeal of the Corn Laws. I was the historian studying economics; the course seemed to require that I present myself as a clean slate for economic jargon to be written on it. I refused. Hugh Jones fully appreciated the psychological problem involved, and advised me to give up the course.

By contrast with the futility of philosophy and the inadequacy of economics, I found politics very digestible, and I established contact with one of Oxford's leading thinkers and scholars, D. W. Brogan, who was later annexed by Cambridge. Here it was not only the course that was interesting, but also the tutor. My knowledge of history was also something not to repel or reject but to welcome. My study of Cabinet Government in England, for example, was facilitated by my knowledge of the development of the House of Commons; the French Constitution of 1875 was easier to understand in the light of my knowledge of French history from 1789; my introduction to Swiss democracy brought back pleasant memories of medieval Swiss history and the victors of Morgarten. Most important of all, my course brought me into close contact with United States democracy, hampered though I was by the neglect of American history in my purely British course – the Civil War, for example, had been given no more treatment than the Alabama Case, the Trent Affair and John Bright's support of the North notwithstanding Lancashire's dependence on Southern cotton. As Brogan was the leading English authority on United States democracy – more solid though less popular than Harold Laski of the London School of Economics – I had a very important advantage.

The comparison of the British, French, Swiss and United States democratic systems, the conflict between Second and Third Internationals, the Fascist philosophy and my introduction to Nietzsche and Spengler – unfortunately Hitler's speeches were then not available as they now are – the Stalin–Trotsky split; this was international education with a vengeance, and I responded to Brogan as I responded to no other tutor at Oxford. He had a most disconcerting facility for knowing more than you did and for challenging your most reasoned and logical arguments. I owe a great deal to Brogan, not only for the amount of knowledge he put my way, but also for the intellectual attitude he helped me to cultivate and develop. Two years under his guidance would have been invaluable to me, but one could not do PPE and emphasise only politics. At the end of the academic year, 1936, I decided to abandon PPE and to switch to historical research.

It was, after my decision to proceed to Oxford and read history for a teaching career, the most important decision I had made in my life. It meant a decisive break with the brief dream of an English university career. I could not see myself doing a learned thesis on the Exchequer in the reign of Henry II or on whether Queen Elizabeth I was really a man in disguise. I lacked both the necessary interest and the necessary identification with the environment of which Henry II and Elizabeth I had been products. The textbooks of Cutteridge and Daniel, the total omission of anything pertaining to the West Indies in my study of English history, the acquaintance with slavery, the plantation, and the sugar trade which I had made in my special subject, British colonial history from 1830 to 1860, the interest in government I had gained under Brogan, the political education I had acquired from my international contacts in England – all combined to delimit my field of historical research to research on the West Indies. I chose as my theme the very beginnings of modern society in the West Indies, the abolition of the British West Indian slave system.

My tutor was a relatively young man who was, as so few in Oxford really were, a genuine scholar, Vincent Harlow. Notwithstanding the general contempt for research into colonial history – I could not believe it when I first heard it among the dons – Harlow had already done some very valuable work on seventeenth-century West Indian history. He had published a history of Barbados, from 1625 to 1685, and a biography of Christopher Codrington. As Warden of Rhodes House, he was the premier colonial scholar at Oxford, with Richard Pares at All Souls – later at Edinburgh – a close second. But Harlow's position either at Oxford or in England generally did not reflect this. Reginald Coupland held the Professorship in colonial history at Oxford, A. P. Newton at London. Both were better known than Harlow.

The subject I had selected was, of all the chapters in British colonial history, the least known. No work of any scholarly importance had been done in England. The view was that a band of humanitarians – The Saints, they had been nicknamed – had got together to abolish slavery, and had after many years succeeded in arousing the conscience

of the British people against man's greatest inhumanity to man. Britain
had repented and given an earnest of her contribution by voting
twenty million pounds sterling to the slave-owners for the redemption
of their slaves. It was the thesis propounded by Coupland from his
professorial chair and had behind it all the authority of the British
Government's special representative on commissions of inquiry in
India, Palestine and East Africa. It was the view popularised by W. L.
Mathieson in a series of books which had appeared in the preceding
decade. It was a general British view.

That view could claim no support from the historical records. The
monumental study of a United States scholar like Lowell Ragatz,
while it endorsed the idealistic interpretation of abolition, indicated
powerful economic factors which had been ignored by the British
writers, and Vincent Harlow's book, as well as that of Frank Pitman
of the United States, on the earlier period of British West Indian
history, confirmed the powerful impression left by Ragatz – that the
last word on emancipation had not been written. The abolition of
slavery by Britain – by France and other European countries also, as I
was later to learn – was one of the most important subjects on which
historical research remained to be undertaken. It seemed to me, as I
got down to the problems, that some kindly Providence had reserved
that subject for my especial attention.

The second important factor involved in the traditional view was
fundamentally political. The traditional view not only involved large
conclusions from no evidence at all; it also proceeded to draw still
larger conclusions for imperialism in the twentieth century from its
unsupported large conclusions about imperialism in the nineteenth.
Coupland, in a lecture at Oxford, stated that 'The British will do
justice to Africa because they are heirs and guardians of a great tradition'. As it was clear to me that they had not and were not doing
justice to the West Indians, as the Hoare–Laval peace plan seemed to
me irreconcilable with justice to Ethiopia, it became imperative to
analyse the great tradition.

There followed two years of valuable research work in which I was
guided conscientiously and sympathetically by Vincent Harlow. My
working life in these two years was spent in the Public Record
Office, among the Additional Manuscripts of the British Museum, and
among the Parliamentary Papers and the records of Hansard. I probed
diligently into the Colonial Office Papers, the Foreign Office Papers,
the Chatham Papers, and the Customs Records in the Public Record
Office; the unpublished manuscripts of Liverpool, Clarkson, Wind-

ham, Melville, Huskisson in the British Museum as well as the minute books of the Committee for the abolition of the slave trade; the published manuscripts, correspondence, despatches and memoranda of Canning, Castlereagh, Wellington, Auckland, Bathurst and Fortescue; used all the voluminous Parliamentary debates and blue books of the period.

When I was finished, my thesis, *The Economic Aspect of the Abolition of the West Indian Slave Trade and Slavery*, was an important contribution to research on the subject. Coupland himself, who was one of my examiners, admitted to me that, if he had to revise his own work, he would have to make fundamental changes. My thesis was awarded the Doctor of Philosophy degree, which was conferred on me in December 1938.

I was severely handicapped in my research by my lack of money. The extra year of the Trinidad scholarship was only enough to cover one year of my research work. And so I was continually on the search for more funds. I was turned down everywhere I tried. When I could not take it any longer and could not ignore the racial factor involved, I blazed out to my principal in a letter of January 25, 1936. I wrote:

'But what increasingly strikes me is the vast difference between those professions of one empire, one king, loyalty to the Throne, etc., which I heard almost *ad nauseam* at home and still hear in England, and the actual practice. I have lived in the colonies, and I have no hesitation in saying that an Englishman in the colonies, not only has every opportunity that a local man has, but indeed many more. Any British subject who has attended a secondary school for three years is eligible for the Trinidad scholarship. No West Indian would dream of making any distinction between Englishmen and local West Indians, or even for that matter Chinese and Japanese.

I have come to Oxford, a British subject, by law suffering no disadvantages; yet on arrival I found I could not qualify for an Exhibition at St. Catherine's because my income was too large (!); in any case the Exhibitions were meant for poor undergraduates. I had great difficulty in even getting a grant at all, and now I am told bluntly that money which in the last analysis comes from the English taxpayer cannot be used to subsidise a colonial. I am told to pack up and go home. Outside of St. Catherine's I meet hemming and hawing, shilly-shallying and excuses which would not deceive a babe in arms.

I resent all this in principle. I feel strongly on the question, for I
have played my part – and no mean one – in College and University life – this the testimonial you gave to me last August confirms
eloquently – and I think I should have as fair a chance at any opportunities, financial or otherwise, which are open to English students,
more particularly because of my results last June and because my
sole aim is to further my studies.'

Shortly afterwards I was awarded a Senior University Studentship,
which helped considerably but I found it necessary to combine my
research work with tutorial work. I got a job coaching Siamese students
at Oxford who were having difficulty with the English language and
their foreign studies. This assignment also has its place in my intellectual
development, if only because it introduced me to the poetry of Victor
Hugo, Alfred de Musset and Alfred de Vigny.

My research degree immediately faced me with the problem of a
job. England was clearly out of the question; there were too many
senior people at Oxford, including the Dean of my College who was
so impressed with my Latin background, who, on seeing me would
say: 'Are you still here? You had better go back home. You West
Indians are too keen on trying to get posts here which take jobs away
from Englishmen'. There was no misunderstanding such frankness.
So early in 1938 I applied to the Japanese Ambassador who gave me
an interview in which he was very interested in the prospect of increased Japanese trade, and the Siamese Minister asking for an appointment in a University in Japan or Siam. I also wrote to Professor
Radhakrishnan about a job in India, and I wrote to Gandhi personally
about this. In the meantime the Colonial Office, interviewing me for
a job at my old school in Trinidad, came to the conclusion that my
qualifications were too high for the job. As the war clouds began to
gather more ominously, I turned to the USA, where by mid-1939 I
landed a job as an Assistant Professor of Social and Political Science at
Howard University in Washington DC.

I spent my eight months between my doctorate and my departure
for Washington doing some more private research in the field of my
thesis. I took a trip North and visited Liverpool and the Wilberforce
Museum in Hull in search of more data. And I did a private study on
current West Indian developments for a seminar that Harlow was
holding on the West Indies; the information gathered from the library
resources in Oxford was of great value later for my *The Negro in the
Caribbean*. I tried to get my thesis published. No one would buy.

Britain's most revolutionary publisher, Warburg, who would publish all of Stalin and Trotsky, told me: 'Mr. Williams, are you trying to tell me that the slave trade and slavery were abolished for economic and not for humanitarian reasons? I would never publish such a book, for it would be contrary to the British tradition.'

My stay at Oxford contributed to my intellectual development in yet another direction – foreign travel. The Munich crisis of 1938 found me among the wonders of Italy. Before Italy I had had six weeks in Munich, at the height of Hitlerism; I can still recall my bravado in standing up with hands in my pocket at the tomb of Hitler's martyrs of 1923, refusing to give the Hitler salute. I visited Paris and Brussels on several occasions, even taking in the absurdities of the Ostend tourist season.

And there was the general education that came from merely living in an advanced metropolitan country – the Italian restaurants of Soho, the performances of Gielgud, the visits to the Old Vic and Sadlers Wells, the exhibitions of Epstein and Degas and Chinese art and African art, the discovery of Marcel Proust, the Proms, the ladies who moved from beside me when I went to the communion rail and knelt elsewhere. And it was quite exciting to live through the abdication crisis when Englishmen who would never otherwise open their mouths wanted to know what a colonial thought of it all.

Years after I relived all this experience in an article I wrote in our party paper in Trinidad, *The Nation*. I wrote on March 27, 1959, in my weekly column, my article being entitled 'My University Generation':

'My university generation has taken over not only in the West Indies but also in many of the countries emerging from colonialism. Take the case of India. The only society whose meetings I attended regularly at Oxford was the Indian Majliss, the centre of colonial nationalism in Oxford. . . . Through the Indian Majliss, I heard Pandit Nehru in a memorable speech way back in the thirties. As a University graduate I was one of the many students who listened to a brilliant lecture on "The World's Unborn Soul" by a newly appointed Visiting Professor in Comparative Religion and Philosophy; today, as Sir S. Radhakrishnan, he is Vice-President of the Indian Republic. Consider now Africa. Many West African friends in my university days are today in politics, some on the side of the Opposition, others holding high office in the new Ghana and the new Nigeria. . . .

Not all of my colleagues in the nationalist movement are around today. . . . One such was my closest friend at Oxford, Chamkad Balankura of Siam, a student at Balliol, with whom I toured Germany and other parts of Europe. . . . Chamkad died in the early days of the Japanese invasion, one of the heroes of the Siamese Resistance Movement.

Our PNM Movement is part of the world movement against colonialism. Those who oppose PNM's intellectualism seem ignorant of the fact that the leaders of colonialism the world over are the very colonials who formed part of the university generation of the thirties, who saw the rise of Hitler, the rape of Ethiopia, the trampling of Spanish democracy, and who heard the Oxford Union refuse to fight for King and Country.'

PART 2
THE TEACHER

5
'NEGRO OXFORD'

I saw the Statue of Liberty and landed on American soil on August 7, 1939. One of my young cousins met me on arrival. They lived – inevitably as I soon came to understand – in Harlem, and this became my first acquaintance with the congestion, dilapidation and squalor to which Negroes are subjected. In the infernal heat of August it was an achievement to survive.

I went from New York straight to Howard University. The novelty – for me – of a University comprising different faculties as against constituent, virtually autonomous colleges, defined the visible differences between White Oxford in England on the banks of the Isis and 'Negro Oxford' in America suitably far, in a Jim Crow milieu, from the banks of the Potomac. I spent the month or so before the beginning of the term browsing in the University Library.

My principal responsibility at Howard was to direct a new course in the social sciences compulsory for all freshman students. This was a new departure in Howard's history and reflected the spread and popularity of the idea of orientation courses for freshmen identified particularly with Columbia University.

From the start the course made sense to me only as a survey of the evolution of civilisation and the development of humanity. The academic world in 1939, especially against the background of Oxford, was still dominated by its articulate major premise – that civilisation was the product of the white races and the Western world, and that the non-White world came into its orbit only with the intervention of the Europeans, as in West Africa, in Japan, in India. Knowledge of these earlier civilisations, as in Ghana and Songhay, was for the most part less accessible than it is today, with the work of Davidson and others; a little personal knowledge of Frobenius, Delafosse and Torday, Leo Africanus and Ibn Batuta, Mungo Park and Marco Polo was about all that I could boast of and there was little time, before the

commencement of term, to do any effective research. Du Bois'
book on *Africa and World Peace* only appeared in 1945. One had to
be satisfied with the more accessible data on Egypt and Mesopotamia,
with the Pharaohs and the Code of Hammurabi, with a limited
amount of data on ancient Persia, to correct the inevitable distortion
that would arise from a survey of humanity beginning essentially
with the Greeks and Romans. Fortunately, however, I knew something of Latin American civilisation, the Aztecs and Incas, and even
the tribal patterns of Caribs and Arawaks in the Caribbean and the
northern regions of South America.

For the rest my Oxford education and its Trinidad foundations
served me in good stead. Whilst ignorant of Greek, my knowledge of
Greek history, literature and mythology came to my rescue. With
Rome and the Latin background I was even more at home. Oxford
had filled the medieval gap left by Trinidad. Thereafter I was like a
duck taking to water, but I was somewhat less strong on the twentieth
century. Here life in America helped immensely. I was living with
the New Deal and the appraisal of America's resources just before it
became the arsenal of democracy. I was at the very centre of dollar
diplomacy and intervention by the Marines before the inauguration
of the good neighbour policy. Garveyism had left its mark on the
American Negro. National Socialism and Fascism had their votaries
in America as in Britain. The Third International with its collectivisa-
tion and five-year plans, its liquidation of kulaks and its purges, its
world revolution and its statistics on the class front, was beginning to
agitate American conservatism. Civil war in Spain and civil dis-
obedience in India, nationalisation in Mexico and national resistance
in Ethiopia – the world was headed for World War II, American
supremacy, and the emergence of the colonial peoples.

This was the type of course that I interpreted my assignment to
involve. It was the best thing for the students. I showed the evolution
of humanity through recognised historical periods. The student was
able to see American democracy against the background of the city
state of the ancients with its direct democracy. The descendants of
Negro slaves saw American slavery, reconstruction and Jim Crow in
the context of the Aristotelian rationalisation of slavery and the
detached, non-racial observations of Cato, Varro and Columella. The
evolution of ideas, the growth of the scientific spirit, the role of religion,
literature and society, science and technology, the interaction of social
sciences and humanities – the students were able to see something
precise, definite, concrete, of the evolution of civilisation.

The difficulty was to find a suitable textbook. I soon gave up my search and substituted mimeographed documents selected by myself. I was particularly concerned with exposing the students to original documents contemporary with the period being studied rather than with somebody's wishy-washy analysis of the Code of Hammurabi, Aristotelian doctrines of the state and education, or the communist and fascist philosophies. I wanted them to read the Code itself, to read Aristotle's own words rationalising slavery as based on the slave's lack of a deliberative faculty (any student from the Southern States understood such rationalisation), to see for themselves the doctrine of Lenin or Stalin, Hitler and Mussolini.

The upshot was, after seven years of experimentation and selection, a three-volume anthology of documents beginning with Homer and stopping at the end of World War II. Why three volumes? I was preparing for the school year beginning in September and I began the text in July. There was no time to plan the entire year's work. I had therefore to spend the summer vacation getting Volume One ready, the Christmas vacation on Volume Two, and the Easter vacation on Volume Three.

In each period I dealt separately with economic structure and organisation, political forms, the world of ideas, everyday life and problems; wherever possible the literary life of the society was presented, either for its own sake – e.g. the Romantic Movement – or as basic source material – e.g. Lawrence's poems on the bourgeoisie, Walt Whitman's vistas of American democracy, Shakespeare's defence of the Jews. I tried to build as much as possible on the students' interests. Their interest in sex was notorious. Thus in every period I inserted a section on romantic love and life with father.

As Negroes they were concerned principally with the question of race. So I let them have it wherever possible – Stephen Douglas' black Republican creed, Booker T. Washington's vision of Tuskegee, Lord Acton's contempt for passive races, Gobineau's repudiation of the Negro race, Carlyle's admonition that they should be whipped back into the slavery from which they should never have been emancipated, Hitler's relentless pogrom against the Jews. They were interested in the world Negro movement, so I introduced them to Africa and the West Indies and Latin America.

The compilation was deficient in two important particulars. In the first place, it was too western in its orientation, and I have given a lot of thought to the rectification of this in my private reading and my travel since it was completed. In the second place I gave inadequate attention to scientific development and thought and little or no attention to music and painting.

But I regarded the anthology, with some justification, as a major accomplishment. It was the product of nine years' labouring in the vineyard, and was a far more comprehensive effort than the readings, limited in scope and time, and tending to emphasise later analysis rather than original documents, essayed by others in other places.

My opportunity to make a speciality out of this innovation came in 1946 when the University advised me that it wished me to return from my wartime assignment with the Anglo-American Caribbean Commission to accept a professorship. I discussed with the Dean of the College the possibility of setting up a Department of Social Studies. In a formal memorandum I proposed as follows:

> 'The programme will trace the relationship between the techno-logical base of the society, economic structure and organisation, scientific knowledge, political development, social conditions, family organisation, ideology, philosophy, religion, literature, art, music, even the manners of characteristic periods of Western Civilisation. . . .
>
> The emphasis is not on the accumulation of new facts but on the meaning and interrelation of the facts already acquired; not on knowledge but on interpretation. . . .
>
> A programme of this sort has two important functions to fulfil in the University curriculum: (a) it will permit the student to see his speciality in relation to the entire field of knowledge; (b) it will give the student a broader grasp of the entire field of knowledge than it is now possible for him to fit into four years of college work. . . .'

Nothing came of this initiative, no doubt because it interfered with vested interests. So I tried another direction. I went so far as to seek, tentatively and without too much effort, some publisher's sanction for my ideas, in a brief memorandum I prepared on May 10, 1948, setting out my views of the scope of the work proposed. I had no success. I ended my memorandum as follows:

> 'If I can sum up in a phrase what I propose to do, it is to show that the problems of contemporary life are merely the climax of the problems which the distinctive ages of previous history have always had to face . . . what is aimed at is the sifting of past historical

development which will present the material in such a way that it will be absorbed by an audience apparently superficial and mercurial, but which has given abundant evidence that it is intensely interested in the past, *but only in so far as the past can be related to the present, and in a manner which does not burden it.*'

The Social Science orientation course was assessed at three-quarters of my University schedule of fifteen teaching hours per week. The other quarter of my time was spent in the Department of Political Science, and for this I was responsible to Ralph Bunche. He encouraged me to diversify the departmental programme by giving priority to Latin America, whilst I was assigned the course in comparative government. For the latter Brogan's training was of particular value.

As a lecturer I was popular with my classes. My relations with both colleagues and students were cordial, even though few friendships were developed. Among my colleagues there was the inevitable jealousy of the outsider, particularly one from Oxford. With my older colleagues my relations were possibly more successful; men of some distinction in their own right, they perhaps felt that there was no challenge from a younger outsider. Dr. Bunche, for example, had made some reputation for himself both in the external and the domestic field.

Then there were Abe Harris, the economist with a special interest in Thorstein Veblen, and Franklin Frazier, the sociologist, his massive knowledge of the American Negro fortified by his contact with Brazil; both are now dead. Rayford Logan, the historian, still alive, specialist on Haiti and a known Negro nationalist with a special interest in Africa generally, was another senior colleague for whom I developed a great respect. Sterling Brown in literature, with at least as good a national reputation as the others, was inclined to be less reserved and more friendly than some of the others in the Division of Social Sciences. With William Hastie, dean of the Law School, a good relationship developed based on our mutual interest in West Indian affairs.

But the senior colleague who maintained the closest relations with me was the late Alain Locke, the professor of philosophy. An old Oxford man himself, who tended as a result to regard me as his protégé, with his cultural interests in art and music he was a widely travelled man who reminded me forcibly of W. D. Inniss. With his direct contacts with such people as Eleanor Roosevelt and Adolf Berle, Locke was by no means a man to be despised.

There were the inevitable campus feuds and politics – the big shots competing one with the other for national prestige, the younger men and juniors tending to attack the seniors. For the most part I kept out of these feuds and took no sides. I did not join in the conventional faculty attacks on the President or his Deans. I took no part in the union activity that was then developing seeking better salaries and conditions of employment. The thirties were the great decade of the fellow travellers in American Universities, and the last dying embers were still visible at Howard when I arrived. If they had left me cold in Oxford, there was nothing about them to warm me in Washington, and I left them alone. I maintained correct and even friendly relations with many of them, but I concentrated on my work, and I soon came to be regarded as a worker doing his work and minding his own business.

With the West Indians, both faculty and students, I necessarily developed close contacts and was on good terms. For the West Indian students I had a special responsibility. I helped out with the soccer coaching. I encouraged them to form an association and helped to ease relations on the campus. I advised the university in the field of evaluation of the multiplicity and variety of certificates which the West Indians offered in their applications for admission or for credit exempting them from this, that or the other requirement. This was really a national problem and ultimately my advice was extended informally to the Office of Education of the Federal Government.

The University regarded me as its very special representative in West Indian matters. I prepared a memorandum for the President on September 21, 1944, on the popular attitude in the Caribbean to Howard University. The upshot was the appointment of a Faculty Caribbean Committee of which I was a member. Through the Committee representatives of the University were appointed in Bermuda, Jamaica, Trinidad, British Guiana and the United States Virgin Islands. My recommendation that an honorary degree be awarded to Dr. Fernando Ortiz of Cuba failed, for one reason or another, to materialise, but an honorary degree was conferred on Norman Manley of Jamaica in a ceremony that did much to boost West Indian pride and improve relations between West Indians and Americans.

6

WEST INDIAN TRAVEL

Teaching at Howard was only one aspect of my life in Washington from 1939 to 1948. I developed five other major fields of activity – research in West Indian history; a lecture programme on West Indian Affairs; work with an international organisation dealing with the Caribbean; proposals for a West Indian University; research in colonial questions generally.

Priority went to research in West Indian history, my starting point being my doctoral dissertation at Oxford on the abolition of the West Indian slave system. One of my first concerns on arrival in Washington was to get in direct contact with the two principal scholars on the history of the British West Indies prior to emancipation – Lowell Ragatz who was at George Washington University in Washington, and Frank Pitman who was at Pomona College in California. Our meetings were profitable on both sides and they both encouraged me mightily to proceed with my studies.

The first victory came with my achievement of a $2,000 Julius Rosenwald Fellowship on April 17, 1940, within a few months of my arrival at Howard. Powerfully backed by Bunche, Harris, Locke, Ragatz, Vincent Harlow and my former principal at St. Catherine's and fortified by my Oxford research in an area of great concern to America and Americans, the battle was not too difficult. The title of my proposed research project was 'the rise of capitalism in Europe and America and the institution of slavery'. I intended it as an expansion and amplification of my doctoral research to cover non-British areas. On April 18, 1942 I was awarded another Rosenwald grant of $1,800 to continue my research in West Indian history in Washington.

Thus it was that in early June 1940, I sailed from New York for Havana. Fortified by the Cuban study of the Foreign Policy Association and Leland Jenks' analysis of American imperialism in Cuba, I arrived in Cuba as the third year of its Three Year Plan was drawing to its close. My arrival coincided with the adoption of the Constituent Assembly on June 8, 1940, of the Cuban Constitution of 1940 which came into effect on October 10. The Constitution, on paper, was a model one, with all the conventional guarantees.

Bliss was it in that Batista dawn to be alive, but to be young, was very heaven! I spent some eight weeks in Cuba, principally in Havana, about the most valuable weeks in my career. Most of my day was spent in the *Archivo Nacional* in Havana and in the *Biblioteca Nacional*. Reading Spanish easily, no problem was posed. I collected valuable data on Cuban history in the eighteenth and nineteenth centuries (slavery having been finally abolished only in 1884). There were three important aspects in the data I unearthed and collected: first, the diplomatic relations between Britain and Spain over the abolition of the slave trade, involving constant British interference with the Cuban government; second, United States interest in the island, either to acquire it by purchase or to prevent its acquisition by another European power; third, the astonishing development of the Cuban sugar industry after the adoption of free trade by Britain in 1846.

Of equal importance with my scholarly research to my future development was my personal contact with Cuban scholars. Prince of these was Don Fernando Ortiz, whom I had met in Washington in May 1940. He spoke little English but my Spanish was reasonably adequate. We became firm friends, and his own extensive research into Cuban history and society has over the years been one of the greatest stimuli and one of the most valuable aids to my own intellectual development and my own scholarly research. Ortiz was monumental. He had studied the role of sugar and tobacco in Cuba's history – a masterpiece of Caribbean literature later made available in an excellent English translation – race relations in its philosophical aspect and with special reference to Marti, the African contribution to Cuban music and folklore. He had produced a glossary of 'Afro-Negrismos', and a study of Cuban slavery and the slave trade, *Hampa Afrocubana*. The Acton of Cuba in a sense, he was the editor of a most valuable series of volumes entitled *Colección de Libros Cubanos*.

Through Ortiz I was able to establish contact with Cuba's leading historian, Herminio Portell Vila, professor at the University of Havana, author of the excellent work in several volumes on Cuba's relations with the United States up to 1898. I met also Ramiro Guerra y Sanchez, who had a useful one-volume history of Cuba and a valuable study of the Ten Years War, 1868–1878, who had also written valuable monographs on sugar and society in the Antilles. Guerra also edited the review *Trimestre*. I met above all Cuba's great sculptor, Ramos Blanco, whose bust of Antonio Maceo was later presented to Howard University. I met briefly Nicolas Guillén, and this was my introduction to some of the best poetry which has ever come out of the Caribbean. Cuba meant to me a most valuable accession to my Caribbean library.

I left Cuba with the Cuban Government participating in the second conference of the Ministers of Foreign Affairs of the American Republics held in Havana from July 21–30, 1940, to consider a trusteeship over the European possessions in the Caribbean.

And so I arrived in Haiti, the country of Toussaint Louverture, Dessalines and Christophe, which I knew so well through James' *Black Jacobins*; I knew the history of the American occupation and I had read the 1930 report of the United States Commission on education in Haiti. My principal target was the famous Haitian sociologist, Jean Price Mars, with his *Ainsi Parla l'Oncle*. We met, my French serving as go-between in the face of his almost total inability with English.

Lack of both funds and time forced me to restrict my visit to the capital, Port-au-Prince. But there one saw more than enough. It sufficed to see the Presidential Palace and the well-to-do middle-class houses against the background of the peasantry who seemed to be everywhere, tattered, barefooted, eternal *marchands* selling their vegetables and fruit and their astonishingly good handicraft for a pittance. Other things stood out – the intellectual poverty reflected in the bookshops (such a contrast with Havana) and the ubiquity of the army.

The American policy of intervention in 1916 was still in evidence during my visit. In my search for data on Haitian economic conditions, I found myself in the office of the Fiscal Representative, who supervised the collection of the Haitian customs and the distribution of the Haitian revenues between foreign bondholders and domestic needs. It was an unforgettable sight, that – an office completely black and coloured with one solitary white American. Few white Americans have shown such pleasure on seeing me. This one was elated – it had just been announced, he told me, that Churchill had agreed to concede to Roosevelt bases rights in Trinidad.

Was this, I asked myself, the manifest destiny of Trinidad and Tobago? If Haiti's isolation, poverty and tyranny after independence represented one lesson to West Indian colonials, did the land of Toussaint Louverture pose yet another lesson – that West Indian colonials were destined to graduate from European colonialism to American? Was there an answer to these questions?

Santo Domingo provided one – a native dictatorship that, for sheer corruption and viciousness, could hold its own with the worst of European fascism. In 1940 Trujillo reigned supreme – the boss both political and economic. The capital city was renamed after him, his giant obelisk, modelled on the Washington monument, symbolised his monolithic presence, the neon lights which blazed 'Trujillo and God' made me feel, like Sancho Panza, that I preferred to go to hell than to go to heaven as a governor after Trujillo's fashion.

Ciudad Trujillo was as beautiful as Hitler's Munich had been with its gleaming white new buildings – as if it were a whited sepulchre. The silence of the tomb reigned everywhere, disturbed only by the sound of army boots – there was no one to talk to, little data to collect, no books to buy. The land that Columbus loved had become the land that the descendants of the population introduced by Columbus had grown to hate. In 1940, it was clear, tyranny would end only in one way; then all hell would break loose and confusion reign supreme.

I shook the dust of Dominican dictatorship off my feet and wended my way by steamship to Puerto Rico. Puerto Rico in 1940 was 'a land of beggars and millionaires, of flattering statistics and distressing realities. . . . Uncle Sam's second largest sweatshop' – as the then young Muñoz Marin had expostulated. But it was alive, this American colony, as the Dominican Republic was not under the dead hand of dictatorship. Its life, such as it was, pulsated in the University of Puerto Rico, which I made virtually my home during my stay in the island. It was there that I encountered a number of young intellectuals who were later to become good friends of mine – Rafael Picó in economic geography, Morales Otero with his studies in rural health conditions, Sol Descartes who became an expert on the land question, Jaime Benitez subsequently chancellor of the University, Rafael Cordero in education, José Rosario who wrote feelingly about the *jibaro* and his attitude towards society.

Outside the university circle there was the medical man, Tomás Blanco, obsessed with American colonialism and with the fear of racial prejudice in his writings. And there was the poetry of Pales Matos. There was the faint beginning of that interest in Puerto Rican history which has become a dominant note in the last decade or so.

The rest was depressing – unmitigated poverty: prostitution worse than in Havana; Americans everywhere; Spanish subordinated to English, through an American Commissioner of Education; Puerto

Rican nationalism vainly pointing to the liberal constitution extracted from Spain in 1897 only to be suborned by the most unambiguous American colonialism. One felt the backwash of Albizu Campos and the nationalists shot down on March 21, 1937, in Ponce; and in such a man as Gilberto Concepción on the one hand and Muñoz Marin's new party, the *Populares*, which had just won its first election, on the other, one saw possibilities that seemed remote from the seemingly eternal darkness of Trinidad and Jamaica which did not even enjoy universal suffrage. Bread, land and liberty, the *Populares* preached; but Toussaint Louverture, nearly a century and a half before, had offered the alternatives of liberty or death – and I had myself seen the consequences in Haiti.

The intellectual climate in Cuba, Haiti and Puerto Rico as I encountered it in 1940 I analysed a few years later, in a lecture to the Trinidad and Tobago League of Cultural and Debating Clubs on April 4, 1952, entitled 'Four Poets of the Greater Antilles' – Guillén, Roumain and Brierre of Haiti, Pales Matos.

7

RESEARCH IN
WEST INDIAN HISTORY

This most valuable summer expedition had widened my Caribbean democratic vistas, expanded my knowledge, and laid the foundations for my emergence as intellectual spokesman of the Caribbean peoples. I was in 1940 a West Indian who had more direct and closer contact, historically and actually, with the Caribbean area as a whole than any other. The subsequent years were to emphasise the flowering of a truly Caribbean vision which, in 1932 in Trinidad, had been limited to Trinidad and Tobago, and in 1939 had expanded at Oxford to embrace the British West Indies.

The immediate result of my 1940 Caribbean trip was *The Negro in the Caribbean*, the preparation of the book which Alain Locke had asked me to write as one of his series of Bronze Booklets on the Negro in America which had already covered art, race, economics, American fiction, poetry and drama. Beginning with an introductory description of the islands and their historical background of slavery, I dealt with the sugar industry, the Negro wage-earner, the land problem and the peasantry, the middle class, the racial problem, education, the political system, American intervention and trade, and I called for the future for rational arrangements for Caribbean sugar and a British West Indian Federation. As such the book dealt with Caribbean society and not solely with the Negro.

The book established my reputation. Appearing in 1942, a little over two years after my first appointment, there was nothing like it in any language. It was an out-and-out attack on colonialism in the Caribbean, and I learned later that one of the best single purchasers was the State Department. The Caribbean was in the world news with the bottling up of the French fleet in the harbour of Fort de France in Martinique and was especially in the American news with the Pan-American Havana declaration on the European colonies and the Anglo-American destroyer-base deal.

American Negroes warmly welcomed this analysis of the Negro problem in the West Indies, West Indians in America were overjoyed, West Indian sugar planters (at the level of the West India Committee and especially in Antigua) were in danger of apoplexy such was their rage, and my friend George Padmore brought out an English edition.

The congratulations poured in. Lowell Ragatz congratulated me on a scholarly and interesting piece of work. Lewis Hanke of the Library of Congress expressed amazement at 'the tremendous amount of factual material that you have been able to compress within the limits of a relatively small book'. Arthur Lewis sent me his warmest congratulations on the 'tremendous amount of research' and recommended it – unsuccessfully – to Penguin Books. The Cuban Ambassador to Washington called it 'interesting' and found that it made 'very absorbing reading'. Puerto Rico's Resident Commissioner in Washington, Bolivar Pagan, read it 'with profound interest' and complimented me on 'a very useful and enlightening job'. George Padmore, in a foreword to the English edition, described it as 'the best over-all survey of the Colonial Problem in the West Indies which has appeared in this country'. The Negro journals were enthusiastic.

This was too much for reactionary West Indian vested interests. The West India Committee wrote a blistering attack accusing me, in effect, of *ex parte* quotations from a mass of official commissions. The *pièce de résistance* came from the *Antigua Star*. In two articles it accused me of 'misstatements, exaggerations and one-sided arguments'; I should have known, it said, that 'the conditions he pictures as existing today might have existed at some long bygone day . . . but surely not TODAY, not TODAY'. It accused me of seeking, 'by an ingenious mixture of facts and propaganda', to make the sugar industry 'the creator of all the ills, social, economic and political, that exist in the islands'.

The stage was set for my major work – *Capitalism and Slavery*, the elaboration and expansion of my thesis on the British abolition movement. Having demonstrated the fall of slavery as a part of the movement of mature British capitalism, I proceeded to trace the association of slavery in its heyday with the rise of British capitalism.

American scholarship in this field was quite remarkable. Pride of place went to Elizabeth Donnan's monumental anthology of documents illustrative of the slave trade to America. Leo Stock had edited an equally valuable anthology of debates in the British Parliament regarding North America up to the 1800's. There was also the vast and useful American literature on the indentured servants in the mainland colonies which was one of the foundations on which the trade in Negro slaves was subsequently erected. My Cuban sojourn gave me an insight into one other foundation, the aboriginal *encomienda*. Ultimately the first half of *Capitalism and Slavery* was entirely new research on the period antecedent to that selected for my doctoral dissertation.

The question of finding an appropriate publisher was not particularly difficult, largely because of Lowell Ragatz, to whom, as the master in the field, I dedicated the book. He wrote to me on December 18, 1944:

'First of all, let me congratulate you upon a corking good volume, one which makes a great and very real contribution to the literature of Colonial History.

Second, most sincere thanks for dedicating it to me and for the nice things you have to say. You are very generous in your praise and I deeply appreciate it.

You have, I think, struck a rich vein of historical research and I hope that you will keep on working it. There is certainly no one in the world better qualified than you and you have rare ability both as an investigator and as a writer.'

I turned to the University of North Carolina, one of the outstanding strongholds of American intellectual liberalism, especially in the field of Negro studies. The press had quite recently published two excellent studies on slavery. Their acceptance was soon forthcoming. The University requested a subsidy of $700, repayable on certain conditions; the money was advanced by four West Indian friends of mine. It will suffice here that the subsidy was repaid within less than twelve months, that a second printing appeared within one year of the first, and that, year after year until the second printing was exhausted, every six-months period I received a royalty payment. Thereafter the rights were sold to another publisher, Russell and Russell, who brought out a new edition in 1961 and a second printing in 1967, whilst a paperback appeared in 1966 in Capricorn Books. The book appeared in England in 1964, published by André Deutsch. Russian, Japanese and French editions are now available.

The book was published in November 1944 and was an instantaneous success. Gerald W. Johnson of the *New York Herald Tribune* was the first in the field, on December 7, 1944, describing the work as 'this extraordinarily lucid study, which is a valuable addition to the literature of the subject'; what he stressed most was that 'to the layman, however, the most interesting thing about the book is the strict objectivity of its approach to a question with a certain emotional charge'.

Here and there there was a discordant, querulous note. Wilson Gee in the *American Sociological Review* of August 1945 opined that 'the civilisation of everyone of these areas would today be much more healthful if there had never been a slave in them, and the pace at which the Industrial Revolution proceeded would have been slackened little, if at all.' Elizabeth Donnan in the *American Historical Review* of July 1945 thought that 'Mr. Williams in his zeal to establish the primacy of the economic forces is somewhat less than fair to the humanitarians whose voices were raised against the slave trade and later against slavery.'

The West Indian press was favourably disposed. The *Gleaner* of Jamaica commended the book 'both for the excellence of its manner and the importance of its matter'. The *Port-of-Spain Gazette* described it as 'a notable contribution to Caribbean history in general, and to its economic history in particular'. *The Barbados Advocate* said that it was a 'monumental work and must be regarded as nothing short of a masterpiece'. The West India Committee and the *Antigua Star* maintained a discreet silence.

Only one British review appeared: that being *The Times Literary Supplement* – by my former tutor, D. W. Brogan, I was given to understand – no other was needed. It appeared on May 26, 1945. He ended a long and sympathetic review with the sentence, 'But this is an admirably written, argued and original piece of work'.

Carter Woodson, in the *Negro History Bulletin* of April 1945, advanced me 'to front rank in modern historiography'. And Henry Steele Commager, in the *New York Herald Tribune*, capped it all with this tribute:

> 'This is the most lucid, the most penetrating and the most original monograph that has appeared in this field of history. It would be cause for gratification if he were to turn his attention now to the economics of American abolitionism.'

Selecting some of my material from the Cuban archives, I wrote up a short essay in 1944 on one of the most curious aspects of Anglo-Spanish relations – the persistent interference of the British Government, through their consul in Havana, Richard Turnbull, with the

Spanish authorities in Cuba in relation to Spanish performance of treaties on the prohibition of the slave trade. To my complete astonishment this study of a totally unknown subject, based on archival material hitherto unused in Havana, was rejected by Duke University Press on grounds that I would have more readily associated with England, that it departed from the conventional view of the subject. The article remained unpublished until, on my return to Trinidad, I inaugurated the *Caribbean Historical Review* and in the very first number published my unconventional view.

The *Political Science Quarterly* associated with Columbia University had, before the appearance of *Capitalism and Slavery*, published in March 1943 an essay of mine entitled 'Laisser Faire, Sugar and Slavery', a preview of the eleventh chapter of *Capitalism and Slavery*. In March 1946 the *Quarterly* carried an article by Professor Frank Tannenbaum on the Negro migration to the Western Hemisphere, entitled 'The Destiny of the Negro in the Western Hemisphere'. Little did I imagine that this romanticising was a preview of Tannenbaum's future work on *Slave and Citizen: The Negro in the Americas*. I left it severely alone.

But the following issue of the *Quarterly*, June 1946, carried an attack by Tannenbaum on *Capitalism and Slavery*, entitled 'A Note on the Economic Interpretation of History', opposing my historical method and challenging the validity of my conclusions. Fair enough. I composed a reply and sent it to the *Quarterly* which declined to publish it. When Tannenbaum's book appeared, I wrote a review of it, opposing *his* historical method, repudiating many of his facts and assumptions, and challenging the validity of *his* conclusions. The *Quarterly* declined to publish it. So my reply to Tannenbaum remained without seeing the light of day, until the publication of my *British Historians and the West Indies* provided me with the opportunity, very belatedly through no fault of mine, for dealing with his misrepresentations and distortions.

8

WEST INDIAN
AND AMERICAN AFFAIRS

The publication of *The Negro in the Caribbean* and *Capitalism and Slavery* opened wide the door to lectures and writings and book reviews on West Indian and American affairs. The door had in fact been opened to me within eight months of my arrival at Howard University. The American Council of Learned Societies convened a conference on Negro Studies and their interdisciplinary aspects at Howard on March 29–30, 1940. In my own humble contribution to the conference, in emphasising the research priorities as far as the West Indies were concerned, I stated the problems as 'first, Africa, and the rise of capitalism; secondly, the abolition of the slave system; and third, the Negro in Latin America'.

The conference on Negro studies was followed by a series of public lectures by the Division of Social Sciences at Howard University in May, 1940. I was requested to open the series with a lecture on the Negro in the British West Indies. The Division followed this up by a series of lectures in the following year on 'Minorities in the Present International Crisis'. I led the discussion on the paper on the Caribbean.

The 1943 series of lectures was devoted exclusively to the Caribbean. As Chairman of the Programme Committee I had a very special responsibility for the series, in addition to which I read a paper on the economic development of the Caribbean up to the present. The lectures and the discussion were subsequently published by Howard University Press under the title *The Economic Future of the Caribbean*.

Through my lecture programme I broadened my contacts and saw more of the country than I would otherwise have seen. It took me to Boston where I lectured to the Jamaica Progressive League on the Four Freedoms for Jamaica and made my first real contact with the Jamaican nationalist movement and, through its American wing, with Norman Manley. I was called in on another occasion in New

York in 1943 to lecture on the economic problems of the Caribbean
to a conference sponsored jointly by the Latin American Economic
Institute and the American Committee of the International Women's
League for Peace and Freedom. I went to Chicago in July 1943 to
speak on Philip Randolph's March-on-Washington platform and to
encounter, for the first time, his 'non-violent mass action'. The theme
of the conference was 'The Negro in Peace and Post-War Planning;
Africa, the Caribbean and the United States'. At a Convocation at
West Virginia University on February 21, 1947, during Negro History
Week I spoke on 'The Negro in a World of Crumbling Empires'. At
the Annual Meeting of the Association for the Study of Negro Life
and History, held at Columbus, Ohio, in October 1945, my theme
was education in the British West Indies. I went to New York for an
international conference on the Church and Land Tenure in May 1946,
held under the auspices of the Farm Foundation. I spoke on problems
and prospects in the Caribbean area at the Schomburg Collection's
series in 1945 entitled 'World View of the Negro Question'.

Where scholarly writings were concerned, the *Journal of Negro
History* published by Carter Woodson, and the *Journal of Negro
Education* published at Howard by Dean Charles Thompson could
never have too much of my work. In the July 1941 issue of the *Journal
of Negro Education* I wrote an article on 'The Impact of the International Crisis upon the Negro in the Caribbean'. I stressed the role
of sugar in Caribbean history and I saw in a Pan-Antillean Federation
the long-term solution of Caribbean problems.

In 1946 I accepted an invitation to contribute to a symposium on
'The Problem of Education in Dependent Territories' to be published in that year's yearbook of the *Journal of Negro Education*. The
symposium was divided into general problems, Africa, America, Asia,
and a general critical appraisal. I concluded my analysis of the three
proposals on America as follows:

> 'I must, however, take issue with Dr. Einaar on his sweeping state-
> ment that any attempt to alienate the "natives" from their own
> traditions is destructive and undemocratic. I believe that here he
> gives insufficient credit to the European system that has been
> transplanted. As a result of this system, the first stage of colonial
> development was not an obscurantist defence of their own back-
> wardness but an education as modern as was then possible. With
> all its limitations, this enabled them, in due course, driven by
> nationalistic aspirations, to turn back to their own neglected indi-

genous culture and seek to adapt it to the inescapable integration with the modern world. But if Dr. Einaar means that any further attempt to transmit the metropolitan heritage and to postpone the beginnings of the creation of an indigenous culture is destructive and undemocratic, then I am in complete accord with him.

In this there is no narrow nationalistic bias. Our one world is made up of diverse cultures. European literature is European, but there is the French school, the English school, the Russian school, each with its own distinctive characteristics. In seeking to develop an indigenous West Indian culture, the West Indian dependencies will have to seek inspiration and stimulus abroad. But the process is not one-sided. The specific application and interpretation of the philosophy and concepts of the modern world, in relation to the problems, history and experiences of the West Indies, go back into the general stream of the intellectual development of our one world, and become themselves a contributing factor to the elaboration of the general principles on a broader, higher, more complex, more diversified, and, therefore, more concrete level. I believe that, with such a vision, the educational system of the dependent areas will make not only a distinctive contribution to the lives of the West Indian people, but also a genuine contribution to the stream of that broad intellectual culture which, the more diversified it is, yet expresses the common humanity of our one world. . . .'

Another valuable opportunity came my way when Alain Locke invited my co-operation in a multiple undertaking for *Survey Graphic*. It was the seventh in the 'Calling America' series, published in November 1942 under the title of *Colour, The Unfinished Business of Democracy*. I ended up my article as follows:

'As long as there is truly democratic government, there will be little or no race prejudice. Unduly emphasized, race will create more difficulties in the economic sphere. Only the extension of democratic rights and constitutions, by which the masses can increasingly control their own destiny, promises to improve peacefully conditions in the Caribbean. Just now, it is an important area, for though not so prosperous, it has a rich contribution to make to democracy as an example of how many different races can live amicably side by side.'

On June 19, 1944, the editor of *Foreign Affairs*, Hamilton Fish Armstrong, wrote to me seeking my opinion on the most important problems facing the Negro population in Puerto Rico and the Virgin Islands. The invitation came as I was about to undertake visits to both areas as well as to Jamaica.

The highlight of my visit was my first meeting with Muñoz Marin. I was impressed with him from the start. After all, at that time he was the outstanding nationalist in the Caribbean, and with one electoral victory behind him and other just ahead of him, he was obviously a man to be reckoned with. As a poet and a chain-smoker, he was additionally attractive. We got on well together and I shall always remember his profound simplicity when, after a long discussion, in reply to my question as to the solution of the race problem, he answered: 'More democracy.'

My specific interest in the race problem gave me a deeper insight into the Puerto Rican reality. In the Virgin Islands I made contact with the Chachas, the depressed, originally white, fishermen, despised by the local population who would comment contemptuously in respect of a coloured girl 'She married a Chacha.'

I returned to Washington and wrote my article which duly appeared in *Foreign Affairs* in January 1945. Extracts were included in the Report of the Committee on Insular Affairs of the House of Representatives.

I dealt, in respect of Puerto Rico, with racial discrimination at various levels – restaurants, clubs, etc., – and quoted from reputable studies reactions of Puerto Rican university students: for example, 'God made the Negro so that animals can rest'. But I emphasized that there was no political discrimination, that Puerto Rico in 1943 had passed a Civil Rights Act against discrimination in public places, and that the popular view of a man was such that 'white' denotes class and status rather than colour and race. If by virtue of his position or his wealth he moves about in white society, he automatically becomes 'white'.

The high watermark of my reputation at Howard was the invitation from the American Historical Association that I should read a paper at their annual meeting on slavery and contract labour in nineteenth-century colonial systems. After *Capitalism and Slavery* this was a wonderful opportunity to get down to Indian immigration into the Caribbean in the context of the competition between the British West Indian sugar industry based on indenture and the Cuban sugar industry based on slavery, on the one hand, and, on the other, the conflict between Caribbean cane and European beet. This was virgin territory as far as historical scholarship in America was concerned.

Two Negro University contacts of first-rate significance for my career and my development emerged, the first at Fisk University in Nashville, Tennessee, and the second at Atlanta University in Atlanta, Georgia.

The Fisk contact involved the Institute of Race Relations inaugurated by Charles S. Johnson, President of the University, and one of America's leading scholars. The initial contact at the Third Annual Institute in 1946 proved so satisfactory both to him and to me that I went down in 1947 as well. The enrolment was about 125 students. My theme in 1946 was the Caribbean: my first lecture dealt with the problems of the Caribbean and my second with current trends in the Caribbean towards improvement; and I wrote an article on race relations in the Caribbean for the Institute's journal. In 1947, however, I asked to be allowed to make a change and to deal with Africa instead. Johnson agreed and my two lectures dealt with the dilemma of British imperialism in Africa and the nationalist movement in Africa.

My success at Fisk can be measured by Johnson's offer to me of a post at Fisk involving in his words 'research, some teaching, and perhaps a bit of administration'. This was a wonderful offer for a young man and would have involved, what Commager had wanted me to undertake, research in American slavery. It was with the deepest regret that I felt myself compelled to decline. Fisk was a good school and Johnson was a fine man.

But I had already made my decision about my future. I would stick to the West Indies. West Indians had traditionally deserted the West Indies – Padmore for Africa, James for the absurdities of world revolution, the majority of West Indians for the traditional medicine and law. I would cultivate the West Indian garden, from Cuba to French Guiana. And I had already made up my mind that, when the West Indian University came, as come it must, I would be prepared to play my part and leave Washington. So I declined the offer and have never regretted my decision.

One serious difference emerged between Johnson and myself. It arose out of his book *Bitter Canaan*, a study of Liberia; my opinion on its merits was solicited by the University of Chicago Press. Johnson's study put me in a real quandary. I admired the man, I disliked his book intensely.

The press wished to know how well did the author accomplish his purpose. I replied as follows:

'He does not bring out the basic problem of Liberia: that is that the
Americo-Liberians have had a special problem such as has been
faced by no other representative of Western civilisation in Africa.
They have had to contend with the native populations and the
impact upon them of Western civilisation, and particularly Western
economy. But whereas other colonizers have had the support of
powerful imperialist powers, the Americo-Liberians have been
faced with the necessity of protecting themselves against these very
imperialist powers without the economic basis for so doing. In my
opinion, this is the central problem around which revolves all the
difficulties of the Liberian Governments; and unless this is brought
out very clearly, the reader is likely to draw conclusions about the
organic incompetence and subjective deficiencies of the Negroes
who have tried to rule Liberia.'

The Press inquired whether I had any suggestions for improving the
manuscript or any additional remarks. With the utmost frankness I
replied:

'At the present moment, the great problem of the relationship
between Western civilisation and the African people is the problem
of the adjustment between modern capitalist production, the interests of the native Africans, and what appears to be the almost
inevitable results in the combination of European and American
capital and native wage labour. . . . Unfortunately, this book
does not seem to be aware of the problem at all. The question of
questions in regard to Liberia (as in regard to the rest of Africa) is
and has always been, what are the effects upon the African people
themselves of the introduction of modern capital for the formation
of plantation economies in Africa? There are not five lines in this
book which deal with what ought to be dealt with in, at the very
least, one of the most substantial chapters.

Furthermore, at this time the Truman doctrine has merely
brought to a head what has always been an underlying problem
in the political relations between the wealthy metropolitan powers
and those colonies, territories, protectorates – or whatever you
will – which come under the orbit of economic assistance, investments, exploitation – the actual term is of no significance. This
problem receives no treatment in the volume under consideration.
The author advocates United States assistance under the United
Nations. But that is the very problem which today is occupying

the attention of the civilised world, as to precisely how a powerful economic power, with or without the guidance of the United Nations, can economically assist, not only a backward but sometimes a very advanced country, without laying itself open to the charge of imperialist domination. The author seems unaware of the fact that it is inevitable that a book of this kind will expose him to the accusation of preparing the way for creating a basis for United states imperialism in Africa, and, by virtue of his race, of mitigating the hostility of the Negroes in the United States and elsewhere to the Government of the United States.'

My Atlanta excursion was the result of an invitation from Ira Reid, Professor of Sociology, well known for his work on the West Indian immigrant in the United States. He wanted me to do a seminar in three sessions on some aspect of history in the context of their study of 'Foundations of Social Sciences', as well as a public lecture on a general subject in which I was definitely interested. I went down in April 1946. For the seminar I chose as my subject 'British Historical Writing and the West Indies'. An enormous amount of research was involved, but it was very profitable research, which suitably amplified and expanded, was published by me in Trinidad in February 1964 under the title of *British Historians and the West Indies*. For my public lecture at Atlanta, I chose as my theme the then projected British West Indian University.

The broad scope available to a Negro Professor in the United States in the forties was brought out in an invitation to me from the American Council of Learned Societies on February 19, 1947, to comment on 'tentative suggestions' advanced by Professor Kenneth W. Porter of Vassar College for studies in American Negro History. This was quite a serious matter. I seemed, against my will, to be drawn more and more into the vortex of the history of American slavery, as Commager and Johnson wished me to be.

I drafted a long reply to the Council which I sent to them on June 24, 1947. I wrote:

'Professor Porter's proposal is that the Committee on Negro Studies should encourage the writing of a definitive history of the Negro in the United States, with a view to the integration of the Negro into the general history of the United States to the same extent as has already been done for other minority groups. I do not see my way to accept this initial conception. It is possible to write

monographs about all the minority groups in the United States and
then incorporate them into the general history of the country. It
is impossible to do this with the Negro. In my view, the Negro
has been for so many generations the labour force in basic industries
of the United States that he is inextricably linked with the history
of the United States.'

I then took up Professor Porter's ten specific suggestions, *seriatim*. His
fourth suggestion was biographies of little-known Negroes. He
opposed the tendency to concentrate on 'a few outstanding and dramatic figures, such as Frederick Douglass, Harriet Tubman, Sojourner
Truth'. I disagreed. There was no serious biography of Douglass. I
continued:

'There are two outstanding gaps in Negro history in the modern
United States – (*a*) a study of the Populist Movement and the role
played by the Southern Tenant Farmers Association, which embraced one and one-quarter million Negroes; (*b*) a study of the
Garvey movement. . . . It appears that it was the instinctive
rejection of United States society by the masses of Negroes from
the South which Garvey formulated in the Back-To-Africa movement, one of the most remarkable phenomena not only in Negro
history, but in the history of the United States in modern world
economy. It offers scope both for serious monographic studies and
for general treatment.'

His last suggestion, Negroes in American economic life, the history of
individual business, I thought of little value and suggested instead:

'The history of Negro labour from the days of slavery, the particular
industries towards which Negroes were projected from their low
status in society, the role those industries played in the economic
life of the country, the gradual changes in the social importance of
these industries, with the correspondingly increasing significance
of the Negro in the social life of the country – this is of extraordinary
importance for estimating the development of the history of the
United States and the changing social role of the Negro.'

I don't believe, however, that anything came of Professor Porter's
proposals; at least, I heard nothing further of them.

9
THE ANGLO-AMERICAN
CARIBBEAN COMMISSION

On September 2, 1940, the American and British Governments reached an agreement by which, in return for fifty over-age American destroyers, the British Government ceded certain bases in the Western Hemisphere to the United States, free of charge, for 99 years. One of the first fruits of this collaboration was the announcement on March 9, 1942 of the Anglo-American Caribbean Commission, for the purpose of encouraging and strengthening social and economic co-operation in the Caribbean and to avoid unnecessary duplication of research in these fields.

In November I offered my services to the British representative in Washington, Sir John Huggins, transferred to Washington from the post of Colonial Secretary in Trinidad. He promised to keep me in mind but was pessimistic in his estimate of the prospects. I enlisted the help of Brogan and Harlow in England and of Professor R. H. Tawney who was then in Washington.

And then I met the live wire of the Commission, Charles W. Taussig. As one of Roosevelt's brain trusters, close adviser of the New Deal with special reference to Cuba in particular and Latin America in general, an expert on the practical side in sugar and molasses, conventionally regarded as one of the principal advisers in respect of the President's fireside chats and as enjoying the right of entrance to the White House through the back door, Taussig was a power in wartime Washington. He was also a man of great personality, and withal was a very pleasant and likeable person. Taussig, who knew all about *The Negro in the Caribbean*, decided that I was to be associated with the Anglo-American Caribbean Commission.

And then the fun began. Huggins' pessimism notwithstanding, I was soon called in to do a part-time job; as Huggins explained it, it would require one afternoon of four hours a week, and my job would be to bring West Indian laws up to date (noting amendments to the basic law) and keep a check on price movements on the basis of price lists sent in by the British colonies. Taussig took a personal interest in the study, saw to it that it was expedited and expanded.

The fact of the matter was that the British never wanted to have me associated with the Commission at all, whilst Taussig, for the Americans, was determined that I should be. There was open conflict over this matter between the two sections of the Commission. The test came over my selective service classification. Under American pressure I was given a deferred classification.

On March 1, 1944, I received my appointment, the terms of which were themselves the cause of long dispute – I could not understand why the British seemed to be so concerned to reduce my salary and, in fixing my salary with the Commission, which was paid jointly by the British and the Americans, to take into account my emoluments from night school at Howard, to make sure that my total income would not exceed a particular figure. At the last moment, also, they tried to change our agreement so that my headquarters would be in Barbados, the headquarters of the British Development and Welfare Organisation, whose chairman was British co-chairman of the Commission. I resisted the proposal, whereupon the British representative in Washington was quick to assure me that it was nothing 'immediate' and we would 'discuss it more fully when it comes up later'. I immediately got in touch with an American member of the Commission, and the British manœuvre was promptly squashed.

The difficulty that next emerged in my relations with the Anglo-American Caribbean Commission related to my writings and lectures. It had been clearly established when I took the appointment that I would be free to continue these, and I of my own accord, to protect myself from misreporting and distortion, submitted what I wrote or proposed to say to both sections of the Commission for prior approval. Both sides sought to control and edit my statements where they considered their own interests involved. The results were ludicrous in the extreme.

I submitted the text of my proposed speech on the Jamaican Conference in Boston on the four freedoms for Jamaica. It was approved by the Americans. To my complete astonishment Sir John Huggins initiated a long argument with me, in which at times he became quite heated, about the difference between Puerto Rico and Jamaica. What was this difference? That Puerto Rico had achieved its independence from Spain in 1897 which the Americans had taken away, whilst there was no such question where Jamaica was concerned. What the devil did that have to do with the four freedoms for Jamaica in 1943 anyway? And Huggins was of course quite wrong. As I pointed out to him, Jamaica in 1943 merely wished to recover the self-government Britain had taken away in 1865 in order to prevent black people from qualifying for a franchise which was at the time reserved exclusively for whites.

I resented this interference with my academic freedom from a Colonial office official, and even more the attempt to put British words into my West Indian mouth. As the West Indies were to learn a few years later there were West Indians galore ready to be colonial stooges. I was not one of them. I let Huggins know that, and thereafter I was always on the warpath to defend my academic freedom and constitutional rights. To ask me to delete something was one thing; to ask me to read their speech was a horse of a different colour.

When I told the Americans, they laughed their heads off. They almost died of laughter when I told them of my second encounter with Huggins. It took place in Jamaica in August 1944; Huggins had by then been promoted Governor. A new constitution for Jamaica had just been announced conceding universal suffrage – a mere year after his fuss about my advocacy of the four freedoms for Jamaica (what fools these colonialist mortals be!). I thought it singularly appropriate, therefore, to give a lecture in Jamaica on Representative Government. I sent a copy of my text to Sir John Huggins 'out of courtesy', as I had been advised in Washington. It was a thoroughly academic lecture, tracing the progress of representative government from the direct democracy of the Greeks – after all I was a teacher of political science.

Huggins was livid with rage. He stated quite frankly that he would have preferred me not to speak on that subject, 'in view of the forthcoming general election'. What he wanted, he said, was 'to see me continue my efforts to educate the people of the West Indies along the lines of Federation' – the same policy at work again, I was to speak on what they wanted me to speak; they were to determine the content and priorities of West Indian education. I offered to cancel the lecture. Huggins, one of the most bureaucratic of the colonial office breed I have so far encountered, thought that that might lead to awkward questions; I was quick to point out that there would be nothing awkward as far as I was concerned, as I would refer all queries to his office. He suggested therefore that I should proceed with the lecture as scheduled.

To my surprise he thereupon challenged a statement of mine about the powers of the royal governor in the thirteen mainland colonies in the early eighteenth century. I was flabbergasted. Here was a colonial official who quite obviously did not read. He knew nothing of the subject but was challenging me – on what? On something, as Holmes would have chided Watson, that was elementary. I offered to send to the Institute of Jamaica Library for any book on the eighteenth century to verify my statement. Huggins backed down. Then he requested me to delete a paragraph – something, as far as I recall, from John Stuart Mill, ending with the quotation, 'The price of liberty is eternal vigilance.' If one could not lecture on representative government and quote John Stuart Mill in 1944 Jamaica, when I had only just given evidence before the British Government Commission on higher education in the West Indies, what *could* one talk about and what sort of four freedoms was envisaged for Jamaica?

But the time came when the Americans didn't laugh. That time was when I submitted my article on race relations in Puerto Rico and the Virgin Islands for clearance. What was the problem? The Americans just did not want to acknowledge that there was a race problem in their possessions. They could see the mote in other people's eyes but would not see the beam in theirs. They had run into serious and quite unnecessary trouble in Jamaica when I was there and were getting into even hotter water in Trinidad. They wanted me to abandon the article. I refused. I was opposed to racialism and colonialism everywhere in the Caribbean, and I did not know then what I got to know later about the background to the Chaguaramas Agreement of 1941.

The specific objection taken to my article – apart from its content and general tone – related to the following passage: 'In the leading hotel in Puerto Rico the patronage is almost wholly composed of whites from the United States. Coloured people are never seen in the dining-room or at the bar unless they are foreigners travelling on government missions.' This was queried, but it had happened to me. I explained my experience at one hotel. Everytime I was sent there, it did not matter with how many others, I was given the same room – 'Annex No. 5', outside of the hotel. Once when the reception clerk was checking my reservations, I embarrassed him by saying, 'Annex No. 5'. He looked up in astonishment and asked me how on earth I knew. I explained. He was a Puerto Rican and his confusion was pathetic.

All this was guerrilla warfare, potshots at me, compared with the full-scale frontal assault launched on me in July 1945 as a result of the attack by the *Antigua Star* on *The Negro in the Caribbean*. The *Antigua*

Star had pointedly stated: 'It is more unfortunate that the book should have been written by one who holds a position as Secretary of the Caribbean Research Council, an affiliate of the Anglo-American Caribbean Commission.'

Fortunately for me, on October 16, 1944, on learning in April that George Padmore was proceeding with the English edition of the book having obtained the necessary permission from the American publishers to whom I had sold the book outright, I had written to both sections of the Commission formally as follows:

'As requested I am putting in writing the substance of the conversation I had with you last week with reference to an English edition of *The Negro in the Caribbean*. A long time ago, before my full-time connection with the Anglo-American Caribbean Commission commenced, I was approached by the African Bureau in London for permission to bring out an English edition of *The Negro in the Caribbean*. Owing to the paper shortage, nothing happened until a few months ago when I was notified that the Bureau was going ahead and wanted my consent to necessary changes in statistics that would be appropriate for an English public.

The African Bureau is well-known in London as an anti-imperialist organisation. I have never been identified with the group though I know many of its members personally, and they once asked me to read over a publication of theirs on the West Indies. I feel that, in view of my present position with the Commission, the publication of my book under such auspices might give rise to embarrassment.

Above all, I did not wish the publication to take you by surprise.

It was for these reasons that I spoke to you and asked your advice. In accordance with your suggestions, I am writing immediately to the Bureau to request that a prefatory note be inserted to the effect that I am not, and never have been, a member of the Bureau, nor do I subscribe to its views and policies.'

Two days later, with the experience of Huggins in Jamaica in mind, and perhaps anticipating trouble with the *Foreign Affairs* article, I, of my own volition, proposed a clarification and tightening of the arrangements governing my extra-curricular academic activities. I wrote:

'In these activities I have been guided by three considerations:

(a) that they are essentially subordinate to, and must in no way interfere with, my official duties;

(b) that the occasion or subject should be of importance for the education of public opinion;

(c) that no statement of mine must be made under auspices which would be embarrassing to the Commission.

Thus guided, I have refused several invitations both to write and to speak.

I feel now, however, that I should go further and notify you of the organ, subject and occasion of the article or speech, before accepting any invitation.'

By the time the storm broke in July 1945, I was more vulnerable in that my dual loyalty had been terminated and I was entirely on the British payroll, and was discussing with them an increment in salary and a contract for eighteen months instead of one year. By May 1945 it was imperative that I should have an answer as Howard had invited me to return in September as a full Professor – skipping the inter-mediate grade of Associate Professor – to head a new department of Social Sciences which would specially be created for me. I had so advised the British authorities who had referred the question to the Colonial Office on June 18, 1945.

When the matter was taken up in July, I suddenly found myself faced with the *Antigua Star's* vapourings and what was tantamount to a request for my resignation. I wrote the following letter to the British official in charge, Sir John Macpherson, and sent a copy to Taussig – I was ready for a showdown.

'We have now had three conversations revolving around what is a virtual request for my resignation. I have taken exceptional care not to come to any hasty judgment or opinion on this matter. Yet, after viewing it as soberly as possible, from every conceivable point of view, I have come to the conclusion that this virtual request, the circumstances under which it is made, the grounds that are given for it, and its probable effects are such as to constitute a procedure not only in itself profoundly disturbing but with such implications as make it imperative for me to make known my views to you and to seek some clarifications.

The main points of your communications to me are as follows:

(a) that I, as the author of *The Negro in the Caribbean*, am the subject of controversy which is embarrassing, or potentially embarrassing, to the Anglo-American Caribbean Commission. There is not a single subject in the West Indies today which is not the subject of controversy. A statement of this kind, therefore, made to me in July 1945, is incomprehensible to me except in the light of certain pressures which I shall make clearer later. In addition I should like to state:

(1) The book was published in 1942.

(2) I was appointed to my position after the book was published, and when its existence and point of view were well known in official circles both in Great Britain and the United States.

(3) When I learned that the English edition was due to appear, I gave notice in advance to the Commission. I explained carefully the circumstances: how control of the manuscript was not in my hands, my consent as author had been given when I was a private citizen, publication had been delayed owing to the paper shortage in England, the publishers were a radical, anti-imperialist group with whom I was not affiliated. You asked me for a memorandum which you could send to England so that the Colonial Office would not be taken by surprise and lose confidence in me. Mr. Taussig advised me that the thing above all which I was not to do was to attempt to prevent publication at that date. No one in my situation could fail to interpret this not as an endorsement of the views presented in the book, but as the unmistakable recognition by the heads of the Commission in Washington of the honesty, sincerity, seriousness and importance of the views which I had put forward.

(4) On your visit to England last November you took up with the Colonial Office the question of my writing and speaking whilst I was employed with the Commission. The occasion was my article for *Foreign Affairs*. The Colonial Office agreed with my contention that I was not a civil servant. I cannot quote Mr. Lloyd's letter to you directly as I was not given a copy of it or of the relevant passages. But you gave me to understand that it was agreed that I should have full liberty to write and speak, except that in the West Indies a copy of the talk should be submitted in advance to the Colonial Secretary. I find myself unable to reconcile freedom of speech and expression given me in 1945 with retrospective criticism of what I wrote in 1942.

(5) In the course of my connection with the Commission I have had occasion to make visits to several colonies. Governors were,

as usual, informed in advance. They replied that I was welcome, and there was never any hint that my presence would be embarrassing either to the local governments, the Commission, or the metropolitan countries.

(b) My qualifications are too high for the position I hold. On this point I have to state:

(1) My qualifications today are the same as when I applied for the position and was appointed. The Minutes of the Provisional Committee on Agriculture on the occasion of the meeting held in Washington on November 10, 1943, read as follows: "The Committee also decided to recommend to the Commission that research assistance be provided for the Agricultural Committee. Members of the Committee, believing that Dr. Eric Williams would be well qualified for such an assignment, have approached him informally as to his possible interest in the matter." Sir Frank Stockdale's telegram to London recommending that I be appointed, spoke of my "excellent qualifications".

(2) My qualifications were fully stated in public announcements of my appointment: for example, the *Barbados Advocate* of March 28, 1944, *The Times* of March 28, 1944, the *West Indian Crusader* of St. Lucia, March 29, 1944. All these papers emphasised that I had made a special study of economic problems in the British West Indies. Governors in the West Indies were fully informed of these qualifications by circular letter of Sir Frank's. The little pamphlet on "The Caribbean Research Council" distributed to delegates and advisers at the West Indian Conference, mentioned those qualifications. At the Conference both Dr. Englund and Sir Lennox O'Reilly spoke of the appointment and my qualifications for the post with approval.

That is, so far, the official record on the question of my qualifications. The fact that the issue is raised now that they are too high implies either (a) that the work I have to do in the future is of such a commonplace routine nature that will require a person of no qualifications whatever, and that in consequence the status and salary of the post are going to be reduced – no such suggestion has been made to me; or (b) that experience has shown that my qualifications unfit me, in some manner or other, for carrying out the tasks which I have to perform or those which are likely to be assigned to me.

There has been no hint whatever that my work has been unsatisfactorily performed. As late as June 18, 1945, you stated in your telegram to the Secretary of State for the Colonies that "we hope to retain his services indefinitely in connection with research body of Commission. . . ." The only reason that you give for your present attitude is a letter which presumably represents the hostility of vested interests to my writings. The representative of those interests whom you bring to my attention has not even read the book. You will pardon me if I draw the only conclusion which you leave open to me. It is that in June my work was in every way satisfactory, or, to put it as moderately as possible, I was rendering satisfactory service to an organisation as important politically as the Anglo-American Caribbean Commission. In July, however, as a result of pressure, unofficial, anonymous, and, if you will allow me, with no visible basis either for criticism or positive statement, at the first hint of this I become a liability and am asked not only by you, the British Co-Chairman of the Commission, but, according to your statement, by the entire Commission, to consider retirement from the work to which I have given, as far as possible, devoted service.

I, for my part, would have expected from you, and I am certain that any other subordinate in a department would expect, not a request which virtually amounts to pressure in my opinion absolutely unwarranted, but a vigorous defence of my rights as a satisfactory servant of the Commission. I would remind you that the opinions I have expressed of the vested interests in the West Indies have been expressed in various forms by government commission after commission. It is largely upon the opinions of these commissions that I have based the ideas that I now hold of the past, present and future of the West Indies. Every step that has been taken in the West Indies during the last ten years has been in the direction of the strengthening of the freedom of opinion and free discussion so as to develop the masses of the people in the practice of democracy and to enable them to express their views, and if possible implement them, against the wishes of many of these very vested interests. There is not a single person in the West Indies who does not, for instance, interpret the constitution that has been granted to Jamaica in that way. It seems to me that not only in the West Indies but even in Great Britain itself, the recent elections show precisely the same tendency. I am pained to have to say that the situation in which you now place me leads me to believe that, in this instance at any rate, your request and the circumstances surrounding it represent a complete reversal of what I and, I am

certain, many others have understood to be the recent trend in West
Indian government, stated repeatedly by some of the highest
officials whom there is no necessity for me to quote, and what I
have considered to be a guiding principle of the Anglo-American
Caribbean Commission.

In view of these facts I see no alternative but to inform you that
under no circumstances will I entertain any request for my resignation. I consider myself, in accordance with my letter to you of
February 28, 1945, to be under an eighteen months' contract beginning March 1, 1945, with the understanding that from September 1, 1946, we shall revert to annual contracts. I may also add that I
expect to be appointed Secretary of the general Research Council in
accordance with the various discussions that we have had since the
recommendations at St. Thomas last year. If, through the pressure
of vested interests, I am to be removed from the Commission, it
will be done not only without any assistance from me, but against
every effort which I can make. I have discussed with you very freely,
and in as honest a manner as possible, my personal hopes for the
future and the pros and cons of the post at Howard. But I could
not now consider a post at Howard, whatever the personal
consequences to myself. I do not propose to seek a post at
that University as a refuge from the hostility of West Indian
planters.'

The British backed down, and in defence of my position – after explaining the matter fully to the President of Howard who supported
me one hundred per cent – I declined the University offer and took
another year's leave of absence, knowing full well that the professorial
vacancy would be filled before I returned in 1946.

In 1946 the Commission was expanded to include France and the
Netherlands. The four-power Commission decided to establish its
headquarters in Trinidad. They set up a cumbersome administrative
machinery designed to illustrate the four-power structure. For the
four top posts they chose representatives of the metropolitan countries.
Research went to the British, in the form of head of the Caribbean
Research Council. The British, getting even with me, passed me over
for a retired man, E. S. Pembleton, who had been for years a district
officer in the Nigerian Services. Knowing nothing whatsoever of
research, he was a safe man and could be trusted to do no research –
the Commission lived in mortal fear that someday somebody would
do something in accordance with its terms of reference. A number of

other top positions went to expatriates – one because he had been a Dutch prisoner in a Japanese concentration camp.

This was the expatriate band that the expatriate Caribbean Commission inflicted on the long-suffering West Indian people within the framework of a cumbersome international agreement in four languages signed in Washington by representatives of the four governments on October 30, 1946. The Commission's terms of reference reiterated the subjects agreed to by the British and American Governments in 1942, with minor modifications. The Caribbean Republics continued to be divorced from the Caribbean agreement. The United States linked them with Latin American, with which it was about to work out and sign the Charter of the Organisation of American States at Bogota in 1948.

I decided that the time had come to sever my connection with this collective colonialism. I did so on August 6, 1946, indicating that I had become 'increasingly convinced that my abilities and qualifications, such as they are, would be better suited and bear more fruitful results in scholastic work than in the particular administrative field in which I now find myself.'

The difficulty was that the Commission – at least the American Secretary-General, Cramer – would not release me. He probably foresaw what he was up against. The former Japanese war prisoner died shortly after he took up his post. Pembleton soon retired, ignorant of research and medically unfit, and he too died shortly after. Cramer himself retired at the end of his five-year term and soon became seriously ill. Metropolitan imperialism was the sick man of the Caribbean in 1946.

Within the context of the Caribbean Commission's definition of 'research', a considerable volume of work was in train at the time of my retirement. I was editing a number of studies, reports and surveys which the Commission had directed. It wasn't much, but it had to be done. Cramer considered that I should complete what I had begun. Pembleton readily agreed. So before the termination of my contract, I found myself with a new contract to continue to do part-time research work for the Commission in an office in Washington which I was authorised to open.

There was the usual rumpus, the British, as always, opposing; but the Americans supported Cramer, who had the backing not only of the Puerto Ricans but also of Manley who was a member of the British section of the Commission. Cramer kept piling on the work, quite frequently on Pembleton's recommendation, and an office set up to enable me to complete work in progress continued for nearly two years with much new and additional responsibility added. I found myself, from my Washington post, travelling frequently to Commission headquarters in Trinidad to assist the director of research, for whom I had been passed over on racial grounds and because of political antipathy, in carrying out the research which he was unable to do or to organise himself.

The travel and field work associated with the Commission was the most attractive and valuable aspect of my connection with it. I had to attend the first West Indian Conference – the section of the Commission's work with which politicians, generally handpicked, were associated – in Barbados in 1944, and this allowed me to pay my first visit to Trinidad since I had sailed from its shores in 1932. I was allowed, after the Barbados Conference, to spend a few days in Trinidad, and then I was sent to make contact with British Guiana – my first visit to that colony. My work with the Caribbean Research Council took me to Puerto Rico later in the same year for a meeting of the Council and a land tenure symposium; and I was allowed to visit Jamaica and the Virgin Islands – from St. Thomas I made my first contact with the British Virgins. In connection with the new assignments Cramer imposed on me I was able to visit, for the first time, the Leeward Islands – Antigua, St. Kitts, Montserrat; I also visited Curacao and Aruba, Martinique and Guadeloupe.

The travel broadened my West Indian vision, enhanced my historical research, and widened my political contacts. The highlight was my return to my native land in 1944. I gave two public lectures. The first was to the Literary Society of my old school, Queen's Royal College, which was packed to capacity; Inniss presided. It was a difficult moment this, my remembrance of things past and former classmates. The lecture, on April 3, 1944, went well – but any lecture would have gone well with that audience. My subject was 'The University of the British West Indies'. I was completely objective in my approach, but a personal touch was obviously demanded of me. I gave it in my opening statement which read as follows:

'Let me assure you, my friends, I am not only glad to see you in a personal way. I am also glad to remember that what you gave to me proved not only adequate but rich for understanding and grasping the possibilities, opportunities and ideas of a world much greater than ours. I think it is something of which we can, as old boys of this institution, be proud. You, Mr. Chairman, have spoken kind words of me, and it is idle to deny that I have had some successes in my chosen profession. But I want to emphasise that whatever I have done, I have done it as one of you, and could do it only because I was one of you and had been able to enjoy the benefits of the education and associations which this island in general provided and which were expressed particularly in the schools, boys and masters of my generation.'

My second lecture was given at the Trinidad Public Library on April 19, after my return from British Guiana and I decided to give a preview of *Capitalism and Slavery*. It was entitled 'The British West Indies in World History', and was printed and widely distributed by the Library's secretary, my old friend, Carlton Comma. The pandemonium was unbelievable. A hall, under repair, meant to accommodate 300, had perhaps two persons in every space intended for one. They stood on the stairs, they listened outside the building. The Acting Governor – whose substantive post was Colonial Secretary – was in the chair. All hell broke loose when he introduced me as follows:

'Dr. Williams has come home, and he has brought with him scholarship and learning of which any one, anywhere, however talented, might be proud. Seldom can a Government investment be so well placed. He has passed from the field of study to the field of action, as Secretary of the Caribbean Research Council.'

These people were my own flesh and blood. I had been to school with them, played cricket and football with them, shared their sufferings, enjoyed carnival with them. We had grown up on the same food, the same drink, the same experiences. I had gone away, they had stayed home. I had come back with a University education, they had none. Now I, their former classmate, was their teacher, I who had shared their sufferings was explaining their sufferings, I who had been with them passive objects of British imperial history was telling them of their history, I who had suffered with them the tribulations of colonialism had come back as, so one called me, 'the philosopher of West Indian nationalism.'

How they lapped up the lecture! 'Britain, let go the West Indies', one calypsonian had put it. Now I was telling them how we in the West Indies, against our will, had built up the Britain that would not let us go. The atmosphere was electric. When I interpreted slavery as

the occasion on which 'for the only time in history the black man
emerged as a superior being', they roared their sardonic appreciation.
When I quoted an eighteenth-century political economist that 'the
British Empire is a magnificent superstructure of American commerce
and naval power on an African foundation', they were listening to the
intellectual expression of their own basic convictions. And when,
quoting the English play, *The West Indian*, so popular in Drury Lane
in 1771, I illustrated the wealth of West Indian planters by the statement of the servant, 'They say he has rum and sugar belonging to him
to make all the water in the Thames into punch', they brought the
house down. And, when, tracing the movement from Britain's appreciation to Britain's denigration of its West Indian connections, I
quoted the radical free trader, Roebuck, in the House of Commons in
1844, 'Jamaica to the bottom of the sea and all the Antilles after it', they,
who knew as I did how we had been the object of negotiation for
barter in payment of war debts or in acquisition of destroyers, reacted
in such a way that I knew then that the nationalist historian, unlike
the prophet, had his greatest honour among his own people. All
their pent-up nationalist pride and West Indian dignity were caught
up in my phrase, 'Two hundred years ago we were sugar plantations.
Today we are naval bases.' One day, I knew, they too would assert
the rights of man and rewrite the history it was my privilege to teach
them.

The hostility of vested interests pursued me everywhere I went.
The real confrontation came in Antigua. The Acting Governor, a
white British Guianese, invited me to be his guest at Government
House. It was a little embarrassing, but I accepted the invitation
because I understood it to mean that he was dissociating himself from
the intemperance of the *Antigua Star*. I moved around all the cocktail
parties and then one day a newspaper reporter barged in on a conversation I was having with a number of bigshots at one of the parties:
'My *dear* Doctor Williams, how happy I am to see you! I never
thought I would live to see this day. Perhaps you do not know that
when *The Negro in the Caribbean* appeared, it was threatened that if you
came to Antigua, you would not be allowed to land.' I was really
going places.

Wherever I went I did my homework. In Guadeloupe I discovered
Moreau de Saint Mery's monumental six-volume collection of laws of
the French West Indies, one of the world's rarest books in the field of
Caribbeana. Later, through the courtesy of a delightful French Consul
in Trinidad, I was able to borrow it in order to make photostatic copies.

I worked in the Antigua Public Library. In Antigua and in Trinidad I discovered that colonial contempt for history was about to express itself in the dumping and burning of a lot of 'old papers'. I asked for permission to see them and take what I wanted. Officialdom just could not understand what interest I would have in 'old papers'. Thanks to these outings, I found in Antigua one of my most valuable possessions, the complete list of slave compensation claims in all slave colonies in 1838, and I was able to salvage some valuable documentary material. I worked in the Library of the Jamaica Institute and in the Barbados Public Library. In Jamaica I secured valuable 'old papers' relating to the Jamaica Rebellion of 1865. Thus is colonial nationalism built upon imperialist vandalism.

10

THE WEST INDIAN
UNIVERSITY

In 1944 the British Government announced the appointment of a
Commission to consider the needs of higher education in the colonies.
The Commission established two committees – one for Africa, the
other for the West Indies. Chairman of the West Indies Committee
was Sir James Irvine of St. Andrew's University. Its members were
Margery Perham of Oxford, Raymond Priestley of Birmingham, and
two West Indian friends of mine – Hugh Springer and Philip Sherlock.
The Committee, after visiting the West Indies, passed through the
United States, desirous specifically of seeing Howard University.

Things had obviously begun to move – American bases in 1941,
Anglo-American Caribbean Commission in 1942, universal suffrage
in Jamaica in 1944, and now a West Indian University. I requested
an opportunity to give evidence before the Committee, which I met
on May 29, 1944, in Washington.

I prepared my notes very carefully. They advocated an independent,
unitary, non-residential university working closely with the Imperial
College of Tropical Agriculture in Trinidad, with a modified tutorial
system and a two-year compulsory course for all freshmen, paying
particular attention to history, education, agricultural education, social
work and the training of civil servants.

The Committee was not impressed. Springer himself spoke lugu-
briously of the dangers of having young girls living in rooms off the
campus, and was all for a residential university. Sir James Irvine, with
typical British arrogance, seemed to have already reached his conclusions on the subject. He obviously disliked me and I reciprocated the
feeling. After he had listened to my exposition, he buttonholed me for
a private chat, which went in this fashion:

He: You are a West Indian, aren't you?
I: Yes.

He: You would like to see the West Indies' status improved, wouldn't you?

I: Yes.

He: You agree therefore that the West Indies must have a University, don't you?

I: Yes.

He: You agree that it must be a good university, don't you?

I: Yes.

He: Therefore you agree that the West Indian University must be affiliated to a British University, don't you?

I: No.

I requested his permission to submit a formal memorandum to him setting out in detail my conception of the University. He agreed – obviously to get rid of me; perhaps he thought I would never submit the memorandum. What I wanted, however, was his agreement, so that the Caribbean Commission could hardly interfere with my activity in this field. I was convinced that I could never be too careful where the Commission was concerned.

On this basis, I set to work – that is to study the historical development of university education in the world, with particular reference to colonial or former colonial areas, and in this context, and against the background of primary and secondary education in the West Indies, to propose a University to suit the needs and aspirations of their people.

After a considerable amount of research, I played my trump card. I wrote requesting an interview to John Dewey, still a power in the United States, notwithstanding his advanced age. I said in my letter of October 23, 1944:

'There is a wonderful opportunity of establishing a really worthwhile University which will draw on the best of both English and American experience, and at the same time look to Latin America and the non-British Caribbean territories. . . . In my view this University, wisely planned, could make a double contribution – both to the immediate problems of the Caribbean people and to university education of the larger world.'

I met Professor Dewey on Sunday, November 5, 1944, in New York. I liked him instantly, as a man; I already knew of his work, for which I had developed a profound respect. He was a quite remarkable man, and carried his more than eighty years very well indeed. He was lucid and in total control of all his faculties. His vast erudition was manifest at every turn.

Encouraged by Professor Dewey to proceed, I redoubled my efforts. I unearthed a vast literature of Commissions and committees which I studied relating to Britain, the Dominions and the colonies. I obtained information on the Hebrew University of Jerusalem from its American Friends in New York and on the University of Puerto Rico. I studied the report of the League of Nations Mission of Educational Experts on the reorganisation of education in China in 1931.

I submitted the memorandum to the Committee on March 7, 1945. It was an 80-page memorandum with a bibliography. I poked fun at Trinity College, Dublin, in 1907, whose absurdities can very simply be explained – Ireland had no government of its own.

Knowing my West Indians and their inveterate parochialism, I was concerned to warn about the importance of a unitary university and the danger of proliferation. I took as my examples the incorporation of Newcastle units into Durham University, the duplication of university facilities at professional level in New Zealand and South Africa. I made great play of a famous statement by the University Grants Committee of 1935: 'Such a survey as we contemplate should disregard both the Welsh Marches and the Scottish Border. Where the Universities are concerned, any rigid demarcation of frontiers is strongly to be deprecated.'

I rigidly opposed the idea of affiliation to a foreign university, taking as my principal witness the nationalist movement in Ceylon and its opposition to external London examinations. I leaned heavily for this on what the Royal Commission on University Education in London, headed by Lord Haldane, had advised London University in 1913 – to abandon 'once for all the pernicious theory underlying its present practice that the kind of education it thinks best for its own students must be the best for all people who owe allegiance to the British flag'. This provided me with an opportunity to attack the external British examinations.

John Dewey was delighted with the memorandum; he expressed himself as being in 'cordial agreement' with my views.

I sent the memorandum to both sections of the Anglo–American Caribbean Commission. The British comment was: 'very thoughtful, prepared with burning enthusiasm, showing evidence of deep thought and results of consulting the right authorities. Arguments well marshalled and presented. . . . I feel that in general he goes too far too fast. Wants human material to run, swim, and fly before it can walk. Sights set too high.' It was astonishing how, time and again, whatever I was involved in with the British, this comment appeared – 'too high'. I asked myself whether it ever occurred to them that the problem was that their sights were 'too low'.

I proceeded, with Dewey's encouragement and Irvine's approval, to expand the memorandum and prepare it for publication. I chose the title, *Education in the British West Indies*. I sent the manuscript to a number of people for their comments, including West Indians. The book was honoured with a foreword by John Dewey, in which he described it as 'a case study of a world problem in which this country is now involved'.

The book in its expanded form covered a much wider field than the memorandum – elementary and secondary education in colonial areas, the education revolution in Mexico, recommendations for primary and secondary education, the twentieth-century universities in metropolitan and colonial areas; in an appendix I analysed the official report on the British West Indian University.

But no one was really interested in the British West Indies, and it proved impossible to find a publisher. Kandel's view was that since the various Commissions on Higher Education in West Africa and the West Indies had published their reports, 'the most effective contribution' that I could make would be either a long article or a pamphlet with such criticisms as I could offer of the official report. The Anglo-American Caribbean Commission threw out broad hints that my ideas were not approved by some of the key advisers.

I tried the University of North Carolina, the University of Chicago, Columbia University, even Howard itself. I wrote previews in *School and Society* and the *Harvard Educational Review*. All to no avail. The American firms took the view that the book fell more within the purview of a British publisher. The University of Chicago, for example, deemed it 'an exceptionally competent piece of scholarship and analysis', but doubted that a 'book on this subject will sell sufficiently well in the United States to cover the cost of manufacture'. It was not until 1950 that the book saw the light of day. It was published in Trinidad in a limited edition, sponsored by the Teachers' Economic and Cultural Association. An American edition was published in 1968.

11

COLONIAL PROBLEMS

In all of this literary activity and public-speaking engagements I had emerged as one of the best-known spokesmen of colonial peoples everywhere and the champion of colonial nationalism, utilising the Caribbean – and not merely the British West Indies – as the exemplification of my thesis. I deliberately sought to go outside the narrow British West Indian boundaries.

So that I fairly jumped at the opportunity that presented itself in 1947 for me to do part-time research on British Empire problems with one of the organisations that mushroomed after the war, calling itself the Foundation for International Research. I saw here an opportunity to cultivate a wider field. The proprietor wanted the conventional research on the Caribbean – Caribbean Commission, Development and Welfare, etc. Wearisome though it was, I agreed to do it, but on condition that I would submit articles also on Africa.

I turned my attention to two areas in particular – Nigeria and Kenya. The first article I entitled 'Nigeria, African Spearhead', the second 'Kenya, African Tinderbox'. I stirred up thereby a veritable hornet's nest, and the articles never saw the light of day. So with the clock pointing inexorably to African Independence, a research foundation started in 1947, close to the State Department, with a section on the British Empire, preferred the Caribbean Commission to Nigeria and political developments in the West Indies to political developments in Kenya.

Nothing was generally known about either country. My Nigerian article was written around Azikiwe, and was based on a thorough analysis of his many newspapers. All the best studies on Kenya were utilised – McGregor Ross and Norman Leys, Hailey and Frankel, report of the Kenya Land Commission of 1933, University of Pennsylvania's *African Transcripts*, studies of the Labour Party. I analysed the Nigerian economy, the government of Nigeria and the Nigerian

nationalist movement as centred in Azikiwe. I ended my brief essay
thus:

> 'He gives no indication as to whether his vision is limited to Nigeria
> or extends to the whole of West Africa, British and French. No-
> where in his programme does there appear any systematic, well-
> organised proposals for a comprehensive scheme of economic
> development for West Africa. Not even the advent to power in
> Britain of a Socialist government with capital at its disposal has
> stimulated any such proposal from Azikiwe, whose nationalism
> remains on a political and agitational plane.'

In Kenya I was dealing with British proposals to establish a military
base. I analysed the background of British occupation, the economic
problems of Kenya, the crown colony government of Kenya, and the
absurd argument, *bradyphisis*, advanced by two Kenya doctors to
substantiate the alleged myth of the inferiority of the Kenya people.
I warned of impending trouble. The British Government with its
military base found itself between two fires – the Africans and the
settlers. The predicament was exemplified by Mr. Creech Jones,
Labour Secretary of State for the Colonies, who sought to balance
between opposition to racial discrimination and protection of British
interests, between establishment of a multiracial society and the security
of British settlement. I ended my essay with this warning to the
British militarists:

> 'The new strategic significance of Kenya must ultimately involve
> the Colony and all interested in it in a complete revaluation of all
> its economic, social and political problems. Industrialisation, man-
> power, technical education, a minimum of satisfactory relationships
> between the races – these are the indispensable necessities for a
> stable military base.'

All this culminated in a proposal which, after discussions with Dr.
Azikiwe, I submitted to President Johnson of Howard in May 1947 for
the establishment of an Institute of Colonial Affairs with three main
functions: (1) the publication of a quarterly Journal of Colonial
Affairs; (2) the publication of a series of monographs on colonial
questions; (3) an annual seminar on colonial questions. I was emphatic
that the Institute should, from the very beginning, make every effort
to see that the products of its research reached all centres of learning

and research in every part of the world, and, above all, in the English-speaking countries. But I saw the Institute as going further than this. It should aim, wherever possible, at the publication of outstanding articles and monographs in foreign languages.

If the Institute was established, I recommended that immediate contact should be made with such universities and colleges as the Universities of the Philippines, Hawaii, Puerto Rico, Ceylon, Rangoon, the better-known Indian Universities, Raffles College in Malaya, Achimota and Yaba Colleges in West Africa, Makerere College in East Africa, and when established the West Indian University College in Jamaica.

President Johnson acknowledged my memorandum and thanked me for it. That was the last I heard of the matter.

PART 3
THE INTERNATIONAL CIVIL SERVANT

12

THE CARIBBEAN COMMISSION

I arrived in Trinidad from Washington in June 1948 to act as Deputy Chairman of the Caribbean Research Council of the Caribbean Commission. I was subsequently confirmed in the post after much pressure from the West Indians connected with the Commission.

I was in charge of the research services of the Secretariat. In that capacity I worked principally on conferences and special studies. Most of the conference papers were prepared in the research section of the Secretariat. The conferences held during my tenure of office included trade statistics, industrial development, timbers, fisheries, housing, trade promotion, education, small-scale farming.

These conferences tended to call on the Caribbean Commission to produce more statistics and disseminate more information. They invited the territorial governments to take steps to improve conditions in their area and to facilitate increased trade within the area. They called for standardisation of products or customs terminology and classification. They advised shipping and air services.

The Education and Small Scale Farming Conference, for which I was responsible, made a number of far-reaching recommendations. In the field of education these related to the inclusion of practical subjects in the curriculum of all schools and training colleges; the use of textbooks and reading materials related to the local environment; the improvement of the pupil teacher system; the revision of teacher-training courses; experimentation with interlocking and double enrolment systems to cope with the slender financial resources available; concentration on primary education but side by side with 'such development of other forms of education as the economic and social progress dictates'.

In the field of small-scale farming, the Conference placed emphasis on credit facilities; more comprehensive extension programmes; grading of produce; purchasing depots established by producers and/or government sponsored enterprises; a comprehensive study and appraisal of existing land use legislation; research; study of existing land settlements.

In the field of community development, the Conference called for the establishment of National or Regional Advisory Committees, the appointment of a UNESCO consultant on education to the staff of the Commission, and the convening of a conferedce on library development in the area by the Commission.

The Secretariat published a variety of publications through its research section. There were the trade series and the crop series initiated by me in the Washington office, a number of bulletins on trade in various commodities and surveys of various crops. In 1948 we published a yearbook of Caribbean research. A consultant published a study on population movements. With the aid of two American technicians we paid some attention to housing; in 1951 the research section put out a study on aspects of vocational education in the area. In 1949 I initiated the *Caribbean Economic Review*, published once or twice a year up to 1953.

The Secretariat published also a Monthly Information Bulletin. This was the responsibility of the information section, but I was a member of the Editorial Board which approved its contents. The paper became eventually so poor in quality that it had to be virtually taken over by the Research Branch. In the November–December issue for 1954, I wrote an article, 'In support of Textbooks with a Caribbean Flavour'. Compiling a list of such textbooks in use in various schools, I analysed their content and quality. They were not in fact related to the Caribbean environment and contained information far too difficult for the age groups for which they were intended.

The Research Branch was also responsible for a number of special studies. For example, we published a regular statistical digest. We made a digest of labour legislation in the area. For the fifth session of the West Indian Conference, I made a study of existing trade in agricultural and forestry processed products. We sought to study customs barriers and trade liberalisation in the area. One of my most important assignments at the Commission was a survey for the West Indian Conference with a view to appraising the progress made.

My staff comprised four executive secretaries for agricultural economics, economics, market analysis, health; two research secretaries and a research assistant; a statistician and a small statistical unit. I tried, as far as possible, to get West Indian staff. They could work – unlike the expatriate who told me over his third gin and tonic at lunchtime that the climate made it difficult for him to work after noon – and they shared the West Indian aspirations. I opposed the emphasis on 'transient, temporary, commuting experts, who lack elementary knowledge of the Caribbean background, and who carry away with them at the end of their assignment, such experience, in the main valuable, as they may accumulate during their Caribbean peregrinations'.

But when I was given a 'permanent' expatriate 'expert', my executive secretary for market analysis, the situation really became intolerable. He was Dutch, and wrote miserable English. He knew nothing of his subject. Worse still, he had a *herrenvolk* mentality, and the junior staff consistently accused him of race prejudice, which was rampant at the Commission in terms of selection of French Creoles and Chinese. It was absolutely unbearable that I should have to do such a man's work for him, as I was frequently required to do; eventually under pressure from me he was repatriated.

The most satisfactory aspect of my work at the Commission was the opportunity it provided for foreign travel. On one occasion I had a ten-week tour taking in Puerto Rico, Dominican Republic, Haiti, USA, Jamaica, Curacao. I went to Europe on furlough in 1953. I attended as the Secretariat's representative a conference of the International Institute of Differing Civilisations (INCIDI) in the Hague, and I held discussions with UNESCO in Paris relating to their collaboration in our conference on education and small-scale farming. I visited the Fundamental Education Centre of UNESCO (CREFAL) at Patzcuaro in Mexico and recommended that we should try to get a similar Caribbean centre. I went from Mexico to Cuba for further discussions with UNESCO on our education conference.

But the perennial conflict between West Indians and expatriates remained, with the metropolitan governments fully on the side of the latter. On May 22, 1954, the Commission, faced with a conflict between the Dutch Secretary-General and myself, put me on a year's probation.

13

INTELLECTUAL PURSUITS

I took refuge from official boredom and metropolitan hostility at the Caribbean Commission in my intellectual pursuits and in adult education and community development.

Pride of place went to the history of the Caribbean. I set out to do two things – (1) write a general narrative history from 1492; (2) supplement this with a collection of documents covering the entire area in terms of the speeches and writings of those concerned in the various periods and the pertinent legislation. My basic objectives were facilitated by three bits of good fortune that came my way: (1) I had six months long leave at the end of 1950 which I spent in the USA in various libraries; (2) I entered into a working arrangement with the Social Science Research Centre of the University of Puerto Rico by which the Centre made small grants to assist in the typing and translating of documents which I had selected, copies of each document in return being given to the Centre; (3) I received from the Carnegie Corporation a grant of $2,000 to assist me in making a trip to Europe on my long leave in 1953 in my search for further historical materials.

Thus by the time I parted company with the Commission in 1955, I had two major works in draft to show for my seven years of ineffectiveness and frustration as an international civil servant. The first was a typed draft of the first forty chapters of a history of the Caribbean which reached as far as 1898, the Spanish-American War. The second was a precise outline of the first three volumes of documents, some two thousand documents in all, organised by chapters within a prescribed frame of reference (economic, political, social development, international rivalry, etc.), the first volume from 1492 to 1655; the second from 1656 to 1789; the third from 1789 to 1898.

And I had another advantage – six months' travel in Europe. I spent most of my time in Spain, where I got into contact for the first time with the Spanish materials. I spent some time also in France and

Holland, and I even got in a few days' work in the Royal Archives in Copenhagen, which turned out to have some useful materials in English on the former Danish Virgin Islands.

Determined not to pursue an ivory tower existence with my history of the Caribbean, I set about popularising it. I accepted the presidency of the Historical Society of Trinidad and Tobago. Within a year or two I had started off a *Caribbean Historical Review* of which three numbers appeared. I published two sets of documents on West Indian history – one from the Public Record Office, the other from Hansard. I made plans for the establishment of a West Indian History Book Club, to reprint famous classics on the West Indies; my first choice was *The Ordeal of Free Labour in the British West Indies*, the classic account some thirty years after emancipation of an American journalist on the staff of the *New York Herald Tribune*, W. J. Sewell. I sought also to get local support from the country's leading Indian figures of a doctoral dissertation by Professor Edgar Erickson on East Indian indentured immigration into the Caribbean.

On August 9, 1950, in my annual report to the Society, I spoke as follows:

'As President, I have set myself two goals: first, to break down particularism in the Caribbean and to emphasise that the history of one part of the area is the history of all; secondly, to combat the danger of the Society becoming an ivory tower organisation divorced from the West Indian people, viewing West Indian history as antiquarianism or a cultural pastime. . . . Arising out of the two goals which I have enumerated, there is a third to which, in my view, the Society should dedicate itself for the future. It is insistence that West Indian history, in its broadest, regional aspect, should be taught in every school, primary and secondary, in the area. The neglect of the subject in most schools, the perfunctory treatment accorded it in a few, are politically unsound, culturally anomalous and pedagogically indefensible.'

The fundamental realities of Trinidad and Tobago knocked all these plans sky-high. The Trinidad and Tobago Historical Society had a name, a meeting place, even a review, everything except members. You could count them on the fingers of one hand. Some people were willing to listen to West Indian history, very few were willing to pay for it. Some disapproved of reminders of slavery; all I could raise from Indians for Erickson's book was $180, and even that with the greatest reluctance – it was explained to me time and time again that the VIP's wished not to be reminded of the days of indenture.

My popular campaign took other forms. I contracted with the *Trinidad Guardian* to do a series of weekly articles; some forty articles appeared in 1950, until the newspaper curtly stopped them when I reached 1898. Through the extra-mural department of the University College of the West Indies I contracted to do a series of lectures and seminars in both Port-of-Spain and San Fernando, using as my textbook a selection of documents from my collection which the department undertook to mimeograph. These lectures and seminars were very successful and were supplemented by individual lectures at the Public Library in Port-of-Spain and at Naparima College in San Fernando.

The high watermark of this campaign was the personal attack made in 1950 on my scholarship and integrity by the then economic adviser of the Trinidad and Tobago Government, a man called Shenfield. He launched it on August 27 on an article of mine on July 6 in the *Trinidad Guardian*, entitling it 'Dr. Williams contradicted'. The popular reaction was unbelievable. People telephoned me and, when they met me, asked me when I would reply. I replied on August 31. I wrote in part:

'1. Mr. Shenfield accuses me of a concern "to assure the Negro race that it has nothing to fear in comparison with other races". I plead guilty. I see nothing reprehensible in this concern. What would be reprehensible would be to assure the Negro race that it has everything to fear in comparison with other races. I do not do this. I tell Negroes, and the world that wishes to listen, that it was Negro slavery which helped to build capitalism in Britain, France and the U.S.A., that it was the Negro who built up the West Indies and the Southern States of the U.S.A. – Freyre in Brazil says he built up Brazil also – and that their claims in the modern world are for justice and not mercy or charity. I spend my life proving this from the historical record which has been ignored or distorted by those who oppose this view. Mr. Shenfield would have it that this is a "morbid" purpose. As they say on the films, "if you say so". But I assure Mr. Shenfield that I would give the same assurance to Indians, Chinese, Indonesians, and to Jews. I feel constrained to ask Mr. Shenfield whether he would consider that such an assurance, to Jews, for example, would indicate a "morbid" purpose.

2. Mr. Shenfield states that I am wasting my time. "No competent anthropologist believes that there is any proof that the Negro race is by nature an inferior one". I am happy to welcome competent anthropology to the cause of humanity and the banner of equality. If Mr. Shenfield is really so ingenuous, such a babe in the woods of race relations, I recommend that he paint his face black and go and preach competent anthropology in the Southern States of the United States, or in the Union of South Africa, or in Kenya. He will know much better than I what would have happened to his competent anthropology from the Jewish angle in Hitler Germany. Nor does competent anthropology explain the improvements in race relations any more adequately than it explains the persistence of oppression. The integration of the Negro into modern United States society is taking place through the labour movement – specifically the C.I.O. Whatever the competence which may serve to explain the recognition in our own generation that Indians, Chinese, Burmese, Indonesians, Filipinos, Singalese, Indochinese are not inferior, it is not competence in the discipline of anthropology.'

14

THE NATIONALIST BACKLASH

The Caribbean Commission's letter of May 22, 1954, was a declaration of war. I accepted the challenge immediately. I wrote a private letter to Manley on June 17, 1954:

'I have, it seems to me only two alternatives: to bow down and worship, which means that the boots are waiting for me – this I could never do; or to leave things as they are, leaving it to them to decide next year, but should REC (Regional Economic Committee) materialise, just get to hell out. There is a third alternative, and this is the one that I am now pursuing: to fight them . . . I was denied a fellowship at Oxford – I have always been convinced it was on racial grounds – and every conceivable pressure was brought to bear on me to leave and return to Trinidad. . . . Taylor did not want me at Mona. Macpherson tried to get me out of the Commission in 1945 because of *The Negro in the Caribbean*. . . . Now de Vriendt does not want me. What am I to do, cut sugar cane? They threatened to fail my doctor's thesis because they did not like my view; the British have never ceased attacking me for *Capitalism and Slavery*, very subtly, of course. Local representatives are always opposing my views. Hammond was distinctly rude about *Education in the British West Indies*. I am determined once and for all to put a stop to this impertinent persecution. They suspend the British Guiana Constitution and now they wish to suspend me. I am sick to death of it all. . . . I may be out of a job in a year's time. There are elections here next year, and already I have been asked to come out and join the Independent Labour Party, and the suggestion has even been made that I should be chairman. I do not rule it out . . . If they do not want to deal with me at the level of an innocuous research worker, perhaps they prefer to deal with me as a legislator. If they insist on my being hewer of wood and drawer of water for a metropolitan boss, perhaps they prefer a colonial-metropolitan relationship at the level of my joining in the demand for complete responsible government and the complete West Indianisation of the Trinidad Civil Service.'

In my fight against the Commission, I decided to make use of three weapons. The first was to complete the autobiography which I had begun the year before in Zurich. I immediately took a month's leave when I received the Commission's letter, went to Mayaro, and began to write. This was planned as the first step in a literary campaign which would be followed by an anthology of Caribbean literature and my history of the Caribbean. As I told Manley: 'I am persecuted because of my writings; I think therefore I ought to write some more.'

My second weapon was an adult education campaign. If I could no longer stay in my administrative headquarters at Kent House in order to earn my daily bread, I would make the Trinidad Public Library my intellectual headquarters. If imperialism attacked from Kent House, nationalism would counter-attack from the Public Library. The Caribbean Commission was determined to do nothing to promote the cause of West Indian nationalism and the education of the West Indian people; then I would dedicate myself to the education of the West Indian people and the cause of West Indian nationalism and, by transmitting to them the fruits of the education I had received at their expense, I would repay their investment in me. The Commission wished a showdown; it would get one.

I have always been a hard worker, but the adult education programme that I undertook, principally at the Public Library, would hardly be credible to me today if I did not have before me copies of all the lectures.

I began in September 1954 with a series of five lectures on important topical matters, all involving the presentation of the considerable research I had done over the years. The first series comprised:

September 3 – The British West Indian Sugar Industry and Imperial Preference
September 6 – The Historical Development of Small Scale Farming in the Caribbean
September 8 – The Educational Problems of the Caribbean in Historical Perspective
September 10 – Is there a Caribbean Literature?

September 28 – Some World Famous Educational Theories and
              Developments relevant to West Indian Conditions

One serious lecture every five days in less than a month was enough
for any audience, if not for the lecturer, and so I took a few weeks off
in order to get ready for the second round. This was played out in the
month of November. The series comprised:

November 5 – What is a West Indian?
November 17 – Some Misconceptions of Aristotle's Philosophy of
              Education
November 25 – An Analysis of Recommendations of Education
              Commissions and Experts in Trinidad, 1869–1954:
              (a) State versus Denominational Control

For the New Year, 1955, I decided on an intensification of the
campaign. I organised four different series of lectures, as follows:

(1) Famous Personalities in Caribbean History
(2) The British West Indian Federation – Lands, Peoples, Problems
(3) The Democratic Tradition in Western Civilisation and its rele-
    vance for the British West Indies
(4) A continuation of my analysis of recommendations of Educa-
    tion Commissions and Experts in Trinidad, 1869–1954, with an
    expansion to cover my own views.

My programme at the Public Library for the months January–May
1955 read, therefore, as follows:

January: Series (1) – Bartolome de Las Casas, January 14
           Series (4) – Teacher Training, January 20
           Series (2) – Dominica, January 27
           Series (3) – John Locke, January 31
February: Series (1) – Jean Baptiste Colbert, February 10
           Series (4) – The Curriculum, February 14
           Series (2) – St. Kitts–Nevis–Anguilla, February 17
           Series (3) – Jean Jacques Rousseau, February 28
March: Series (1) – Toussaint Louverture, March 3
           Series (2) – British Virgin Islands, March 31
April: Series (3) – Thomas Carlyle, April 25
           Series (2) – Barbados, April 28
May: Series (1) – Thomas Clarkson, May 3
           Series (4) – A Curriculum rooted in the Caribbean
                        Environment, May 17

Series (4) – Education for Democratic Citizenship
in the Caribbean, May 19
Series (1) – Victor Schoelcher, May 31

In addition I had odd lectures to trade unions, women, and on federation and wrote a series of four articles in the *Trinidad Guardian* entitled 'Reflections on the Aristotelian Revolution in Trinidad' in reply to extensive criticism of my views on Aristotle and education; they appeared on May 18, 20, 24 and 27.

The lectures, no matter how they varied, were designed as elaboration of certain basic principles which I sought to inculcate. The first was nationalism, the defence of the national interests against colonialism. This was the principal theme of my lectures on the British West Indian sugar industry and Imperial Preference. After a long historical analysis of the relations under colonialism, I reached the following conclusion:

'The reduction or elimination of preferences in the sugar industry will present insoluble social and economic problems as no satisfactory substitute for sugar can be foreseen which would accomodate the increasing population and maintain even existing standards of living. . . .'

The second principle I sought to inculcate was the imperative necessity of federation. Federate, federate, federate: that was my battle-cry. As I said in my lecture on Barbados:

'This Federation, I suggest once more, must involve a well-formulated development plan for the region as a whole, involving freedom of movement between the units, and must include, however high the cost, the mainland territories of British Guiana, and British Honduras: The entire British Caribbean region must federate, or Barbados will perish.'

I went even further in my lectures on Dominica and St. Kitts. I ended my Dominica lecture:

'Dominica symbolises the challenge to the incipient British West Indian Federation – the maximum development of all the resources of the British West Indies in the interest of the people of the British West Indies. . . .

On that plan depends the future of Dominica and therefore the future of the British West Indies.'

On St. Kitts I said:

'Only a Federal Government, working on a precise development plan for attracting outside capital and removing idle labour in various parts of the West Indies to the undeveloped resources of other parts, could hope to bring to St. Kitts–Nevis that economic and political stability necessarily lacking in a society dependent on a single industry resting on two foundations, a single factory and a single union.'

What was the lesson I drew from my analysis of the vagaries and difficulties of small-scale farming? Federation. What was the principal weakness I detected in the perspectives for Caribbean education? Disregard of Federation. Thus:

'The task of building a West Indian nation is the decisive task of the present and future. . . .
     The school today in the British West Indies is the most potent force dividing up our communities. The school tomorrow in the British West Indies must be the most potent force bringing together our communities. The West Indian school today despises and disparages its environment. . . . The West Indian school of tomorrow must make a positive fetish of the West Indian environment.'

I was careful, however, to warn against the dangers of ultra-nationalism. As I put it in my lecture on Caribbean Literature:

'(1) we must not substitute Caribbean literature for the great literature of the world; what is needed is an extra course in Caribbean literature as an exemplification of or even divergence from world trends; (2) we must not exclude non-West Indian teachers – or other technically trained people – from our pro-gramme; we need their technical help. What we must do is deter-mine the philosophy ourselves, decide for ourselves what weight to give to its attainment and what funds to allocate to its implemen-tation. That done, we need the best technical assistance we can muster.'

And above all, I stressed the importance of education. I put it this way in my lecture on the educational problems of the Caribbean in historical perspective:

> 'What we need in a British West Indian Federation is a British West Indian philosophy of education. That inevitably means British West Indian control . . . we cannot possibly support continued external influence over the new educational system designed to make us not good Englishmen but good West Indians. The alternative is the hopeless paradox of a nationalist government and a colonial mentality. If West Indians cannot run their own educational system, how can they run their own federated government? . . .'

Then I proceeded to put the West Indian educational problem in international perspective. I dealt with the problem against the background of Rabelais and Montaigne, Comenius and Milton, Rousseau and Pestalozzi, Herbert Spencer and Huxley, and, of course, John Dewey. It was in this international context that I examined the special issue of religious schools in the West Indies, and the several reports of experts and commissions of inquiry in West Indian history. I gave the audience confidence in their own capacity to formulate their own solutions by showing the hopeless confusion and contradiction among the experts.

15

COLONIALISM!
THERE'S THE ENEMY

My third weapon was to carry the fight, within the Commission and the Secretariat, to the metropolitan enemy. I sent to the Commission a long memorandum on November 24, 1954, excerpts from which are reproduced below.

1. The Secretariat Organisation

The Secretary-General since his assumption of duty has steadily sought to undermine the organisational pattern laid down by the Commission. In April 1953, I found it necessary formally to protest to him on a number of issues which had arisen in the Secretariat involving the position and status of the Deputy Chairman. I submitted an exhaustive memorandum, which I requested the Secretary-General to submit to the Commission for adjudication. He advised me that in his opinion all the issues could be satisfactorily adjusted internally. I agreed to this.

A year later, on April 22, 1954, I received from the Secretary-General a memorandum in which he attacked my supervision of the Research Branch. I regarded this memorandum as a vote of no-confidence in my administration. In a memorandum of April 28, rejecting his charges and criticisms *in toto*, I once again drew his attention to the duties and functions of the Head of the Research Branch, as defined by the Commission in 1948. I again recommended reference of the problem to the Commission.

In thus twice urging adjudication by the Commission, it did not occur to me that the Co-Chairmen would decline to enter into any detailed discussion of the conflicting views, ignore the specific directives of their predecessors, and impute faction to and impose punishment on the officer who upheld those directives and showed respect for the constitution and constitutional procedures.

2. My record in the Secretariat

What I deplore most in the Co-Chairmen's letter is its implied attack on my reputation. Here it is necessary for me to vindicate myself, and to do so by reference to my record in the Secretariat.

For the Fifth Session of the West Indian Conference held in Jamaica in December, 1952, I prepared the following documents:

1. Survey of the Work of Previous Sessions of the Conference
2. Report of the Secretary-General to Member Governments
3. Survey of Existing Trade in Caribbean Agricultural and Forestry Processed Products
4. Collation of papers by experts on:
   (i) Relation of Agricultural and Forestry Products to Industrialisation in the Caribbean
   (ii) Industrial Legislation in the Caribbean
   (iii) Evaluation of Existing Facilities for Vocational Training in the Caribbean and Proposals for their improvement.

The report of the Conference testifies to the general appreciation of my personal contributions and of the research work of the Secretariat. The Conference's comments are as follows:

(a) On the Survey and Secretary-General's Report

(i) 'The Conference was of the opinion that the Report of the Secretary-General and the survey of the work of previous sessions of the Conference served a very valuable purpose in indicating concisely the achievements of the Commission and the extent to which its recommendations are being implemented in the territories and thus in justifying the necessary appropriations for the continuation of the Commission's activities.'

(b) On the Survey

(ii) 'The Conference commended the Deputy Chairman of the Caribbean Research Council and his colleagues on the Secretariat's staff for the painstaking research involved in the preparation of this full and extremely enlightening report, which is of valuable assistance not only to participants in the Conference but to the Member Governments, the Governments of the countries served by the Commission, and all those interested in the work of the Commission. The Conference further recorded its high appreciation, personally, of Dr. Eric Williams, Deputy Chairman of the Caribbean Research Council, for the elevated standard of the work contained in the appraisal and its general clarity.

Mr. N. W. Manley (Jamaica) described the first general appraisal of the work of the Caribbean Commission as a matter of considerable public importance and stated that if Mr. Charles W. Taussig, the first United States Co-Chairman, were alive, he would be a very happy man to read the appraisal, because it was to his inspiration, foresight, and profound affection for the peoples of the Caribbean Area that the Commission largely owed its origin. He considered that the report firmly answered the question: What is the Caribbean Commission doing? In his opinion the dissemination of information for which it is responsible, the holding of technical and other conferences, the research and investigation work were operating as a stimulus to thought throughout the area . . . if the Commission were given a chance to do all the work they wished it to do, he was certain it would remain a powerful influence for good in the area and for the achievement of the legitimate national aspirations of the countries which it serves.'

(c) On the Secretary-General's Report

(iii) 'The Conference commended the Secretary-General on the high quality of his report, both as to the form in which it was presented and to its conciseness. . . .'

(d) On Research

(iv) In the opinion of Mr. V. Bryan (Trinidad and Tobago) . . . 'It was important to remember that, once the specifically wartime functions of the original Anglo-American Caribbean Commission had disappeared, the Commission was bound to be mainly concerned with work in the fields of research, collection of information, consultation and exchange of views with the governments of the area served by it. He accordingly suggested that the time had come when the organisation might appropriately be redesignated the "Caribbean Research Centre", or something to that effect. Under this label it would have an important role to play in the social, economic and technical life of the various Caribbean countries. . . .'

(v) The Conference recommended the expansion of the research and consulting facilities of the Secretariat with particular reference to (i) market research; (ii) technological intelligence; (iii) trade development and transport research; (iv) assistance to Governments of the area served by the Commission in setting goals for, and making measurements of, economic progress; (v) statistical technical aid; (vi) economic planning on a territorial or area-wide basis, as needed.

I not only collated the report of the Conference, but also was Secretariat spokesman to the Commission on the action to be taken on the Conference's recommendations.

I presented to the appropriate Committee of the Commission a comprehensive proposal for disposing of the recommendations of the Conference. The Committee, in accepting this proposal, agreed that I should repeat the proposal in person to the Commission in plenary session and requested me, to this end, to put the proposal in writing as briefly as possible. The Commission approved the request of the Committee's Chairman that I should explain the proposal in some detail. The Chairman of the Working Committee publicly complimented me on my proposals which he endorsed, and withdrew the Working Committee's suggestion for handling the recommendations. All Sections of the Commission associated themselves with his compliment.

The record of the Commission's action, which followed in broad outline the proposal presented by me, reads as follows:

'19. *Action on Recommendations of West Indian Conference (Fifth Session)*

The Commission had before it a document prepared by the Secretariat containing suggestions with regard to action to be taken on the recommendations of the West Indian Conference (Fifth Session). . . . The Deputy Chairman of the Caribbean Research Council explained the document in detail to the Commission. It was noted that if the suggestions outlined were accepted, the immediate action to be taken on most of the recommendations would not entail new financial implications.

The Commission thanked the Deputy Chairman of the Caribbean Research Council for his valuable and comprehensive study and for his lucid explanation thereof.'

As a result of some concern expressed by the United States and the United Kingdom Co-Chairmen regarding the capacity of the Secretariat to undertake the work programme involved in my proposal, the Secretary-General proposed to the Commission 'that since the greater part of the burden of the work will fall on the shoulders of the Research Branch of the Secretariat, would the Chair allow Dr. Eric Williams to sum up the views of the Secretariat. I think it would be illuminating.' The Commission agreed to this.

After what the Chairman of the Commission Meeting called 'the clear picture' given by me, the Commission proceeded to adopt, without any substantial modification, the specific suggestions advanced by me.

My connection with the Secretariat's Work Programme in 1953 continued despite my absence on furlough. At the request of the Secretary-General, I held discussions in Paris with senior officials of UNESCO relating to the collaboration between the two organisations for the Conference on Education and Small-Scale Farming.

The record of the Commission's discussions on this subject reads as follows:

'The Commission . . . commended the Secretary-General and the Deputy Chairman, Caribbean Research Council, for their good work done in the preparation of the Conference and the able manner in which they had enlisted the full co-operation of UNESCO.'

I am unable to reconcile this record of the successful implementation and execution of a comprehensive work programme, on the basis, at every stage of the exercise by the Deputy Chairman of his independent judgement, with the idea, implicit in the Co-Chairmen's censure under Rule 14, that the head of 'the more important' branch of the Secretariat is expected merely to repeat and echo the views of the Secretary-General.

Prior to the Secretary-General's memorandum to me of April 22, 1954, there was not a hint of any dissatisfaction with my work or my exercise of independent judgement from him or from anyone else.

The Seventeenth Meeting of the Commission thus began in an atmosphere of commendation of me and my work by the West Indian Conference, the Caribbean Research Council and the 'Commission itself, and, at least, of apparent harmony between the Secretary-

General and myself. The Netherlands Co-Chairman, in his opening speech, publicly asserted that 'the Trade Promotion Conference will be in the best possible hands – in those of Dr. Eric Williams whose splendid work for the Commission we all appreciate'. That these were no idle words or merely vulgar praise was confirmed by the action taken by the Commission at that meeting, after the Secretary-General had privately asked me whether I would be prepared to accept a renewal of my contract. The Commission's decision reads:

> 'The Commission noted that the contracts of the Deputy Secretary-General, the Deputy Chairman, Caribbean Research Council, and the Consultant for Industrial Development, would expire in July and September 1954 respectively. It AGREED that these contracts should be extended for a further five years under the same terms and conditions.'

I am therefore frankly at a loss to understand why the Co-Chairmen, five months after their vote of confidence in me and in my research work, should write to me as follows:

> 'The four Co-Chairmen consider that the contemplated revision of the Agreement for the Establishment of the Caribbean Commission is likely also to call for a reappraisal of the Commission's Organisation in so far as its research activities are concerned.
>
> In these circumstances, and bearing in mind the above developments reported by the Secretary-General, the four Co-Chairmen have instructed the Secretary-General that your service contract with the Commission, expiring in June, 1954, shall be renewed for the period of one year.'

This decision in effect (a) converts the asset of December into a liability in May, (b) reduces the status of research which the West Indian Conference recommended should be emphasised even more than in the past, (c) serves notice of dismissal on the West Indian head of 'the more important' branch of the Secretariat at the very moment when the Member Governments are considering a unanimous recommendation of the West Indian Conference regarding increased representation of West Indians on the Commission itself.

3. Concluding Observations

I believe three observations of a more general nature, in the same spirit of restraint, will not be inappropriate at this stage.

The first concerns West Indian participation in the work of the Commission. The Commission was established specifically for the purpose of improving conditions in the West Indies.

The very Article 14 of the Agreement to which my attention has been drawn by the Co-Chairmen emphatically stresses that priority must be given, other things being equal, to West Indian candidates for appointment. It cannot, I believe, do the Commission any good to present to West Indian public opinion a concept of 'partnership' between Metropolitan citizens and West Indians whereby, at the least sign of disagreement or friction, the Co-Chairmen, refusing to enter into points of issue, support the Metropolitan representative against the West Indian.

The second point concerns the scepticism with which the Commission and its work have been, and still are, viewed in the Caribbean. This outlook is becoming more and more noticeable in the British West Indies, and particularly in Trinidad. I have been asked publicly why the Commission does nothing to assist the preparation and promote the use of school textbooks based on the West Indian environment which are so obviously needed; some years ago the British Caribbean Union of Teachers passed by acclamation a resolution calling on me to write a history of the Caribbean area for use in schools, and in recent days, two teachers at Queen's Royal College have approached me as to the prospects of early completion of this book in the light of their criticism to the Cambridge Examinations Syndicate of a new text recently adopted.

The British West Indian case at the Commonwealth Conference to consider the Commonwealth policy to the General Agreement on Tariffs and Trade – which I attended as an adviser to the delegation of the Regional Economic Committee – was considerably handicapped by the absence of important statistical data relative to the position of West Indian products in the world market, and more than once I was asked why the Commission had not compiled that data. When I replied that the Commission had specifically excluded sugar, oil and bauxite from its purview, on the ground that these industries would look after their own interests, I was asked whether the Commission was aware that the difficulties of British West Indian sugar, citrus, etc., had for years been demanding the active intervention of the representatives of the British West Indian people *vis-à-vis* the Colonial Office, and that the absence of data on the world situation with respect to all these and other commodities was a serious weakness for the British West Indies, especially with the prospects of the removal of trade restrictions and discriminations at the GATT Conference at Geneva.

As compared with this positive need for the British West Indies in what is a struggle for survival, the Secretary-General a few months ago emphatically rejected my proposal that, as an immediate follow-up of the Trade Promotion Conference, the Research Branch should develop work already in an advanced stage on British West Indian trade with the United States of America in furtherance of a resolution of the Chamber of Commerce of Trinidad and Tobago that a trade mission be sent to the United States of America in the spirit of the recommendations of the Trade Promotion Conference.

The popular scepticism with the work of the Commission can hardly be counteracted by the action approved by the Co-Chairmen. It is bad enough that fundamental research needed in the area is identified with me personally and not with the Commission, and that the limited research undertaken by the Commission is itself throttled by the rapid bureaucratisation of the Secretariat and its duplication of services by other agencies.

The third general observation concerns the relationship between my public and private service to the people of the Caribbean. Since my return to the West Indies in 1948, and particularly in recent months, I have dedicated myself to the adult education movement. The Governor, the Public Library, the Extra Mural Department of the University College, voluntary groups, all call on me for assistance, to an ever-increasing extent, and invitations have come from Mr. N. W. Manley in Jamaica, Mr. Grantley Adams in Barbados, and Sir Frank McDavid in British Guiana.

The people have come in crowds to listen to the clarification of various topics, whether current, complex or abstruse – federation, education, Caribbean literature, small-scale farming, preferences, and the philosophy of Aristotle. These lectures have involved considerable research, and when published, will make available data on the historical background of the sugar industry and educational system of the West Indies not hitherto accessible. I have become the centre of a lively and encouraging movement for an enlightened democracy (which the Commission can use as a basis, if it so wishes, for the dissemination of its own aims and purposes), and the central figure in an active programme of community education in which the Commission has recently begun to show some interest. I have now found it necessary to take steps to bring together all voluntary organisations, teachers' groups, youth councils, women's organisations, trade unions, friendly and co-operative societies, literary clubs, etc., for the establishment of a non-partisan Committee on Education for Citizenship to rationalise the adult education movement and spread it throughout the islands of Trinidad and Tobago. In various study groups which I have myself promoted and with which I have actively worked over the past year, the Commission's publications have been studied, sold and disseminated more widely than they have been at any other time or by any other individual.

It will not be possible for people to reconcile my role in the adult education movement with the dismissal by an organisation established to promote regional co-operation in the Caribbean of the very person who has made the study of West Indian affairs the exclusive concern of his adult life and who is, in some eyes, 'Mr. Caribbean'. I would necessarily have to defend myself. I do not see how the Commission's prestige would be enhanced thereby or its possibilities of service to the area improved.

*   *   *

I was under no illusions as to what I was doing. I knew that the Commission would support its metropolitan blue-eyed boy if only for two reasons: they dared not, in 1954, accept the inferiority of an expatriate to a nationalist; and they lived in mortal fear that, the more I had to do with the Commission, the greater the danger of its doing something worthwhile for the Caribbean people. What I had done was deliberately to put the facts on record with a view to forcing the Commission to choose between the expatriate and the nationalist. There were only two possible lines of action on my memorandum – I had to be appointed Secretary-General or I must be fired.

There was never at any time in my mind the slightest doubt as to which course the Commission would elect to adopt. If I had, the strange silence among West Indians and Labour Party members in Britain to whom I sent my case spoke more eloquently than words – they would not lift a finger in the fight between expatriate and nationalist.

The Commission, with typical metropolitan diplomacy, proceeded in two stages. In the first, after a discussion with me in Trinidad at the height of my adult education campaign, they wrote me on December 3, 1954, hoping 'that when the question of the renewal of your contract comes up for consideration at its Twentieth Meeting to be held in Puerto Rico the experience of the next six months will justify the conclusion of a further contract with you on a basis satisfactory to all.'

And then, on May 26, 1955, they took the plunge. The Secretary-General wrote me on their behalf:

'Your service contract with the Commission, due to expire on June 21, 1955, will not be renewed. . . .

I have been directed by the Commission to convey to you an expression of its appreciation of the services which you have rendered during your tenure of the post of Deputy Chairman of the Caribbean Research Council.'

And so we parted company, the Commission and I. Not altogether. As head of the government of Trinidad and Tobago less than a year and a half later, all the member governments wanted me to continue association with the Commission. I was to meet the French Co-Chairman in Accra nearly nine years later. On my official visits to England and Holland several years later I was to meet two of the principal Netherlands figures who never lifted a finger to change the verdict. The British Co-Chairman had to deal with me for several years on the British West Indian Federation, its birth, its burial and its offspring. The Deputy Secretary-General became the Secretary-General of a new organisation which emigrated to Puerto Rico and in which Trinidad and Tobago politely declined to participate. The Secretary-General himself, looking like a ghost, passed me one day on the streets a little more than a year later; we each went our several ways, he to his expatriate grave, I to my nationalist cradle.

PART 4
THE PRIME MINISTER

16

I CAST DOWN MY BUCKET

On the very day on which I received notice of dismissal by the Caribbean Commission, I held my first discussion about the formation of a political party in Trinidad and Tobago. The basic strategy, pending the discussions and organisation, was to reach the public. This it was decided I would do by giving a public lecture on my relations with the Caribbean Commission in Woodford Square. I got in touch two days later with two teacher friends of mine with whom I had first been associated on the occasion of the publication in Trinidad of my *Education in the British West Indies*. They agreed to hold the meeting under the auspices of the People's Education Movement of the Teachers Economic and Cultural Association. The date fixed was the night of the day I was to depart from the Commission, June 21, 1955.

Things at once began to move. A West Indian friend of mine connected with the Regional Economic Committee promptly offered me a job in Washington on June 7. I politely declined indicating that I had resigned my job at Howard and would stay in the West Indies.

There were an estimated ten thousand people in Woodford Square. I got straight down to brass tacks. I began my lecture as follows:

'I stand before you tonight, and therefore, before the people of the British West Indies, the representative of a principle, a cause, and a defeat. The principle is the principle of intellectual freedom. The cause is the cause of the West Indian people. The defeat is the defeat of the policy of appointing local men to high office.'

I took them through a lecture of fifty-one printed pages – the whole sordid story of my relations with the Commission, the pressures on me, the efforts to remove me from my job or prevent my appointment to it. I put the story in language that was readily understood in

the Woodford Square of Trinidad in 1955. I was the nationalist victim
of colonial pressures. But I was also the trained national exposed to
insults and pressures from relatively untrained expatriates. It was pure
nationalist protest, and not personal pique. And all Trinidad and
Tobago listened when I drew the inevitable conclusion from the story.

And so I came to the grand finale, after exposing the effort to get me
out of Trinidad. I felt strongly about this. The Commission had tried
to get me out of Washington, being even willing to pay the price they
had hoped to avoid at the outset, getting me back to Trinidad or even
Jamaica. Then they tried to keep me away from Trinidad. Now that
I was back in Trinidad, they tried to get me back to Washington.
What was I, a blasted football of the Commission? Who the bloody
hell were the Commission anyway? I let them have it. I told the
Woodford Square audience:

'I was born here, and here I stay, with the people of Trinidad and
Tobago, who educated me free of charge for nine years at Queen's
Royal College and for five years at Oxford, who have made me
whatever I am, and who have been or might be at any time the
victims of the very pressures which I have been fighting against
for twelve years. . . . I am going to let down my bucket where
I am, right here with you in the British West Indies.'

Woodford Square roared its approval, and the roar was heard in
London and in Washington. I had crossed the Rubicon.

The audience had listened with rapt attention. The speech had
been punctuated with deafening applause. I learned later that a man
who distracted his neighbours by striking a match to light a cigarette
was almost lynched. Two denizens of the Square were heard to say,
on leaving, that the Ministers had better start looking for 'work' and
that no one had better come to the people again with dirty collars
and frayed cuffs. One week later, as I was repeating the lecture to
several thousands at Harris Promenade in San Fernando, the audience
stood in the rain as the lecture continued.

We thereupon decided that, as the party discussions and organisation proceeded, I would give more public lectures and would take
them to different parts of the country. The schedule eventually
developed was as follows:

Lecture 2: Economic Problems of Trinidad and Tobago, July 5
Lecture 3: Constitution Reform in Trinidad and Tobago, July 19

Lecture 4: The Historical Background of Race Relations in the
        Caribbean, August 16
Lecture 5: The Case for Party Politics in Trinidad and Tobago,
        September 13
Lecture 6: The Pros and Cons of Federation, January 5, 1956
Lecture 7: Further Thoughts on Federation, January 17

And so the light was kept burning until the Party was formally and publicly launched on January 24, 1956. The centre of the movement was Woodford Square. My strategy was very simple: if war is a continuation of politics by other means, politics was for me a continuation of education by other means. All hell broke loose in Woodford Square when I began my third lecture on constitution reform as follows:

'Now that I have resigned my position at Howard University in the USA, the only university in which I shall lecture in future is the University of Woodford Square and its several branches throughout the length and breadth of Trinidad and Tobago.'

The University of Woodford Square has for the past twelve years been a centre of free university education for the masses, of political analysis and of training in self-government for parallels of which we must go back to the city state of ancient Athens. The lectures have been university dishes served with political sauce. They have given the people of Trinidad and Tobago a vision and a perspective; they have given them an understanding of their own problems in the context of the larger world of which they form a small part; and they have reinforced their own aspirations by placing them in the context of the world struggle, past and present, for human freedom and for colonial emancipation. They have taught the people, what one French writer of the eighteenth century saw as the greatest danger, that they have a mind.

Education is politics, as Aristotle recognized, and so, appropriately, it was in the University of Woodford Square that the People's National Movement was launched on January 24, 1956, its candidates for all elections presented, its election manifestoes read, its memorials on constitution reform, not only for Trinidad and Tobago, but also for the Federation of the West Indies, submitted for ratification and endorsement by the people, and in which the PNM Government makes periodic reports to the people on its activities and plans. PNM's University lectures will provide for future generations historical evidence of the level of intelligence, the standard of education, and the practice of democracy achieved through PNM in Trinidad and Tobago in the short space of twelve years.

Here are some examples of the education revolution as it developed. In my lecture on economic problems, I contrasted Trinidad and Tobago unfavourably with Puerto Rico. The essence of my constitution reform proposals was the substitution for the one-chamber crown colony legislature comprising elected, official and nominated members of a wholly elected lower chamber and a wholly nominated upper chamber which would include representatives of the major economic and religious interests. I said to the audience:

'That, Ladies and Gentlemen, is the constitution I propose for Trinidad and Tobago. I claim, Ladies and Gentlemen, without fear of being contradicted, that it will eliminate the taint of colonialism and place Trinidad and Tobago in the bosom of the world's democratic family. I claim, further, that it will place Trinidad and Tobago, today the most backward territory in the Caribbean, in the vanguard of constitutional progress in the area. I claim, still further, that in my effort to reconcile all conflicting interests and points of view, I have provided common ground for the widest possible measure of co-operation between all classes, races, colours and religions for the constructive work ahead of us in the field of economic and social development.'

The lecture on the historical background of race relations in the Caribbean was a true university lecture which I later developed into a long essay that was published in a volume of tributes to Fernando Ortiz of Cuba. It began with Greek and medieval conceptions of race and went right through the West Indian record, including Hume and Jefferson, Sepulveda and Las Casas, the planter historians of the British and French West Indies, Clarkson and Abbé Raynal, Froude and Kingsley, Victor Schoelcher and Lord Olivier, Antonio Maceo and José Marti. It ended as follows:

'What would happen today, for example, if one included in one's criteria of racial inferiority such things as adultery applied to the Aborigines? What would be the consequences today if ability to understand geometry or competence in vocal harmony or on a capital instrument like the steel pan were adopted as criteria of racial superiority, as they were applied to the Africans in the eighteenth century? Would anyone dare today to say that it is indecent to see people of colour studying to be lawyers, or that the brown-skinned girl should not copy the latest fashion in hair-styles or clothes? Would it not have been a simple matter to verify whether mulattoes could indeed reproduce their kind? Can you imagine any Negro today who would be content to starve for a month if he could appear as a white man for a day or who would even bother to get angry if he was told that his father and mother had tails like monkeys? Did it not occur to the British Guiana medical authorities a century ago that the Indian who picked up dead animals in trenches did so because he could not get enough food to eat on the wage of 25 cents a day paid to him during his indenture?

The root cause of our difficulties today is as much economic as the difficulties in previous centuries. One group is trying to dominate, everyone is struggling for a greater share of a small cake. The solution is very simple unless our community is to tear itself apart – increase the size of the cake and respect the rights of others. What is needed in Trinidad and Tobago is a climate in which each racial or religious group will feel relatively secure, and on the basis of that security, can proceed to make that contribution to the general well being and community progress which each and every group can make.'

The lecture on party politics, after comparing Trinidad and Tobago unfavourably with Jamaica, ended on this powerful note that brought Pericles to the University of Woodford Square:

'The people of Trinidad and Tobago must either be kept down in the ditch in which they are or they must be pulled out of it. My colleagues and I lack the qualifications to keep you in the ditch. We believe that we can help to pull you out of it, and that the way to do this is by the organisation of a party such as I have described – a democratic party of men and women of honesty and incorruptibility, of all races, colours, classes and creeds, with a coherent and sensible programme of economic, social and political reform aimed at the development of the community as a whole, dedicated to its service, appealing to the intelligence rather than to the emotions of the electorate whose political education it places in the forefront of its activities.

Such a party will hold up to you the ideal of the ancient

democracy of Athens which, limited though it was by slavery and the subordination of women, still represents one of the greatest achievements of man, I leave you tonight with a tribute to this small democratic state handed down to us in one of the simplest and at the same time most profound historical documents, the funeral oration of Pericles. . . .'

Harold Macmillan was later to describe Trinidad and Tobago to me, when he visited Trinidad and heard of our activities in the University of Woodford Square, as 'the Athens of the Caribbean'. Direct democracy was seen in action on the occasion when I proposed the outline of a new constitution, essentially the constitution that the PNM has since introduced. An estimated 40,000 people attended the lecture which I delivered in twelve localities. The memorial which I read out on these occasions was signed by 27,811 persons, approximately one-tenth of the electorate.

I followed up this technique by two others, a resolution and an open letter to the Trinidad and Tobago delegates, which I incorporated into the first of my lectures on Federation; both were accepted by the vast audience by acclamation.* The resolution read:

'BE IT RESOLVED that we, a vast and representative cross-section of the People of Trinidad and Tobago, proclaim to the world that, whatever the Delegation of Trinidad and Tobago may say to the contrary, we uncompromisingly oppose any federal constitution which seeks to restrain our legitimate and inalienable right to self-determination by giving the Governor-General those very reserve powers in financial matters and those very powers of appointment which are the principal features of the colonialism from which we are determined forever to emancipate ourselves.'

The Open Letter read in part as follows:

'The Plan for a British Caribbean Federation agreed . . . in April 1953 is not in consonance with the political aspirations of the British Caribbean people, the objective economic necessities of the area, and the progressive spirit which today pervades all colonial peoples. . . .

* Signatures totalled 19,595.

You have made no effort to consult the People of Trinidad
and Tobago before committing them to the proposals you agreed
to in London in 1953. Now, on the eve of another Federation
Conference, in the face of the resolute determination of the Legislature of Jamaica to seek revision of those proposals, and again
without consulting the People of Trinidad and Tobago, you
declare your determination to support your original proposals.

The People of Trinidad and Tobago resent your methods. They
also repudiate your views.'

I specifically demanded: (a) the deletion of the reserve powers in
respect of finance bills: (b) limitation of the reserve powers in respect
of differential duties, currency, defence and international obligations
to a maximum period of five years; (c) appointment of Senators by
the Governor-in-Executive Council in each territory; (d) determination of the composition of the Cabinet by the Prime Minister with
the removal of all officials; (e) the Prime Minister in his discretion
must decide on prorogation and dissolution.

17

ADVISER TO THE WORKERS

Whilst the preparations for the organisation of the party were in progress and I was carrying on my education campaign, I was called to the assistance of the workers. The call came from my friend in Barbados, Frank Walcott, longtime Chairman of the Barbados Workers Union, chairman of the Caribbean Area Division of the International Confederation of Free Trade Unions, recently appointed Permanent Representative of independent Barbados to the United Nations. He wished me to attend as an adviser a conference of plantation workers called by his organisation on the sugar industry to be held in British Guiana on August 8 and 9. I accepted his invitation to prepare a background paper on economic aspects of the sugar industry.

I dealt with my subject comprehensively. I started out with the problem of world overproduction, giving examples from specific areas. I then turned to the problem of reduction of costs of production: on the one hand mechanisation, on the other hand, efforts to increase consumption. I concluded my discussion thus:

'Obviously, the question of organisation of the workers who are still unorganised remains the principal need of the moment. But in pursuing this goal the workers' movement must understand that the sugar worker who is likely to be unionised today may be displaced from the industry tomorrow by mechanisation, and that the present prospect is that the stevedore will soon be little more than a memory. It is difficult to see how the workers can in their own interests oppose or seek to reverse this trend, on which the competitive position of the industry in world markets depends. But the workers cannot be expected to accept, nor should they accept, this position with an air of resignation. Three principal considerations may be presented for discussion now and in the years to come:

1. Representatives of the sugar workers must be actively associated with all future discussions, national and international, designed to achieve stability in prices and rational allocation of quotas. . . .

2. A special research organisation in the Caribbean needs urgently to be established to devote itself exclusively to the needs of workers, with particular emphasis on sugar workers, and to watch Caribbean questions in the context of relevant developments in other parts of the world. . . .

3. The unions should give active attention to general overall economic problems and should view the present and future of the sugar industry in the context of an economic programme, of a scope and magnitude not hitherto conceived, designed to produce jobs for the population. . . .'

The workers were enthusiastic. The direct contact with workers from all over the Caribbean was of great value to me, and that the meeting should have been held in British Guiana, with its suspended constitution of 1953 and its interim nominated government, only enhanced the value. I had an opportunity to increase my contacts in British Guiana by a lecture on Federation which was well attended and well received.

The ICFTU was delighted with my presentation. The upshot of my address was that it invited me to attend as its consultant a tripartite international conference of plantation workers – governments, employers and unions – convened by the International Labour Organisation in Geneva in October; I was also to attend a preliminary meeting of the ICFTU with the workers. This invitation was based on the understanding that I would thereafter spend two months in Brussels, at ICFTU headquarters, advising ICFTU on plantation problems. The terms and conditions of this assignment were to be negotiated in Brussels.

The highlight of the conference, from my own particular point of view, was the statement I presented to the plenary session on October 20, as the spokesman for the ICFTU. I stressed that the International Confederation of Free Trade Unions embraced 55 million workers and 99% of the organised plantation workers of the world. Impressive though this figure was, it still represented only a fraction of the plantation workers in the world. For this reason, the ICFTU had emphasized three principal activities; organisational campaigns among plantation workers, seminars of trade unionists, regional conferences of plantation unions.

I indicated the profound dissatisfaction with which the ICFTU had received the report on 'Effect Given to the Conclusions of the Previous Sessions' by the governments of Pakistan, St. Lucia, Kenya, Surinam, Southern Rhodesia, Uganda.

This brought me to the *pièce de resistance*, the statement of the Government of Trinidad on sick pay: 'The sugar employers do not consider it possible to provide sick pay to plantation workers.'

I emphasised in some detail the significance of this statement in the light of specific views of the sugar employers of the Caribbean area on social questions and the conditions of the workers expressed over the past fifty years.

Whilst the ICFTU was of the opinion that far more could be done under existing conditions than was being done in the field of social justice for the plantation workers, it appreciated that this could not be divorced from economic considerations of markets, prices and production. The ICFTU took the view that this would involve the following measures:

1. Extension and expansion of international commodity agreements.
2. Greater diversification of the economic structure of the plantation countries.
3. Greater efforts to increase consumption of plantation products in the producing and consuming countries.
4. A special study by the ILO in conjunction with appropriate international agencies of one plantation crop, sugar.
5. Reduction of the costs of production.

The ICFTU wished to make it clear that its support of measures for the reduction of costs of production was subject to the following reservations:

(a) the workers must be actively associated at all stages with all such discussions and proposals;
(b) positive steps must be taken simultaneously to reduce the hardships and cushion the shock of mechanisation.

My statement was enthusiastically received. The ICFTU was thoroughly delighted and the ILO very pleased. The commendation of the workers' delegates was very gratifying. The statement enhanced my status at the conference where, through the ICFTU, I sat with the workers' group and was in fact appointed secretary to the workers' representatives on a conference subcommittee.

All this was too much for Albert Gomes, Trinidad and Tobago's Minister for Industry and Commerce, who was an official delegate. He swore to tear me into small pieces. He made three mistakes – he behaved as if he was addressing a Trinidad bacchanal in the Legislative Council to which he belonged; he attacked the Indian delegate's 'fixation on the colonial question'; he launched a personal attack on me and my obsession with 'fossils of the past' and 'the wastepaper basket of history'. The Conference gave him a good beating.

I left Geneva for Brussels on October 31. I reported for duty at ICFTU headquarters on November 2 and remained in Brussels until December 2 when I left for London.

Brussels was a near calamity. After much haggling with the Secretary-General who was Dutch (it seemed I had jumped from the Dutch frying pan into the Dutch fire – he was dominated by the American member of his staff who smelled of FBI all the way), it was eventually agreed that I would receive by way of salary the princely sum of £86 (about $410 West Indian) per month, plus the following subsistence allowances per day: £5 in Geneva, £3 in Brussels, £4 in London, £3 11s. in Kingston. My Brussels *pension* cost me £1 3s. per day for bed, breakfast and service.

I was literally taken aback at the phenomenal amount of work the ICFTU seemed determined to thrust upon me, as if they wanted to extract so many ounces for every cent of expenditure incurred on my visit. The first assignment was a report to the ICFTU Executive Board on the ICFTU conference in Geneva, with the threat to extend this further to cover the ILO conference itself. I should have thought that this was a more appropriate obligation for a member of the permanent staff. This was followed by a request that I write up a research programme.

We agreed on a certain amount of work which I would be commissioned to do in Trinidad. The first item was an assessment of the various plantation workers' resolutions in the light of ILO provisions and developments in the plantation countries. This was to take the form of a pamphlet entitled *International Standards for Plantation Workers*, a handbook for trade union officials, relating the recommendations of the Plantation Committee to ILO Conventions and Recommendations, against a background of the action reported by governments to the Plantations Session of the ILO. The second study was to be entitled *The I.C.F.T.U. and the Plantation Worker*, covering the historical development of the plantation economy, the plantation economy today, the plantation worker, plantation profits, the ICFTU and the Plantations Trade Union Movement. But the political pressures on my return to Trinidad were too heavy to permit my spending time on a personal interest which would not even pay my keep.

The highlight of my Brussels assignment was a weekend visit to Paris, November 26–27. It originated in a telegram from my old friend, Daniel Guérin, who had been recently in Trinidad collecting data for a valuable book on the West Indies. It arrived on November 17, and read: 'Césaire repudiating assimilation wishes to meet you Paris.'

That *was* news. Aimé Césaire, distinguished West Indian man of letters, poet of note praised by Jean Paul Sartre in *Orphée Noir* as handling the French language better than any Frenchman (his *Cahier d'un retour au pays natal* is one of the greatest documents in West Indian literature and will hold its place in world literature), had been the principal architect of assimilation in 1946 – the erection of the French overseas territories into departments, integral parts of metropolitan France. Mayor of Fort de France in Martinique, deputy in the Parliament in Paris, he was a communist of note who was then on the verge of breaking with the French Communist Party, which he did in his celebrated *Letter to Maurice Thorez* on October 24, 1956.

To meet Césaire I would have gone much further than Paris. There was an air strike on, so I went by train, spending the night with Guérin, and taking in a long discussion with another old friend, Richard Wright, on the Sunday morning to boot. Guérin had arranged for me to meet some West Indian students and others for a general discussion. I quote from my report to my political colleagues in Trinidad on December 1:

> 'I went by invitation to "talk" to a few West Indians, only to find that I had an audience of about 75, which included two Senators and two Deputies from Parliament, students from Haiti, Vietnam and Angola as well as the French West Indies, and that I was expected to give a lecture and answer questions. I spoke in French – a little difficult at first – on "My Faith as a West Indian", and you can judge the success of the occasion by the fact that the meeting lasted three hours and ended after midnight only when the janitor began to shout bloody murder and threw us out.'

The question was mooted, whilst I was in Brussels, of my being sent on an ICFTU mission to the Gold Coast. But the white American was having none of that. Azikiwe also wrote to me asking me to come to Nigeria to advise him on the establishment of a university.

The stone which the British builders had rejected in Jamaica, the same was to be the head of the corner in Nigeria. But it could not be. My first responsibility was to the incipient party in Trinidad; Nigeria and its universities would come later.

From Brussels I proceeded to London, where my principal concern, apart from my routine work for the ICFTU, was to discuss our draft party programme and constitution with George Padmore, C.L.R. James and Arthur Lewis. I addressed a meeting of MPs and others in the House of Commons on federation, with Jennie Lee in the chair, making it clear that our new party would not accept the colonialism of Governor-General's reserve powers and appointment of Senators or British reserve powers in the interest of financial stability. I spoke also to the West Indian students. I also had the privilege of an interview with Madame Pandit, India's High Commissioner in London; we discussed the possibility of a West Indian edition of Nehru's autobiography, with a foreword written specially by Nehru.

From London I went to Jamaica. I was in London from December 2 to 12, and I stayed in Jamaica until December 18, when I returned to Trinidad. In Jamaica I met Manley for discussions and discussed Federation with the Governor, Sir Hugh Foot. I spoke at a Trade Union course on the need for research as an aid in wage negotiations, gave a public lecture on federation, gave an address at the University on the future of the West Indies, and spoke at an open meeting of the National Workers Union at Spanish Town on Plantation Workers.

Back in Trinidad I reported to the party on my mission to Europe in a meeting at Greyfriars Hall, and then on Thursday, December 29, I set a pattern for the future PNM – I reported to the people in the University of Woodford Square.

18

THE BIRTH OF THE P.N.M.

Whilst I continued my public lectures under the auspices of the Teachers Education Movement I was busy working out with a few colleagues the basis of the new political party. We worked steadily on a draft constitution and a draft programme. On January 15, 1956, we convened the Inaugural Conference of the PNM.

The Conference approved the People's Charter, the name we gave to our fundamental principles. This is what we said:

> 'We are not another of the transitory and artificial combinations to which you have grown accustomed in election years, or another bandwagon of dissident and disappointed politicians each out merely to get a seat in the Legislature. We stand or fall by our programme – a comprehensive social security programme for the general welfare of all the people of Trinidad and Tobago and their families. Nor are we an ordinary party in the accepted narrow sense of the word. We are rather a rally, a convention of all and for all, a mobilisation of all the forces in the community, cutting across race and religion, class and colour, with emphasis on united action by all the people in the common cause.'

The People's Charter announced the following objectives: immediate self-government in internal affairs; a British Caribbean Federation with Dominion Status in not more than five years after its establishment; adoption of the international standards worked out for all categories of workers; provision of more and better houses, schools and social services for the population; reorganisation of the economy to make the fullest use of all the resources of Trinidad and Tobago, both physical and human.

We called for a bicameral legislature, revision of the draft Federal Constitution, a Public Service Commission.

In our social and economic programme we pledged ourselves to the encouragement of effective democratic trade unions and the adoption of a comprehensive modern Labour Code, to fair employment practices and the abolition of racial discrimination in employment, to representation of the workers on public bodies. We called for a commission of inquiry to relate the education system more closely to the political, social and economic needs of the country, to achieve the maximum possible integration of the diverse elements which comprised our population, and to ensure the highest possible academic and other standards in all schools. We undertook to provide a steady increase of the number of exhibitions to secondary schools; our goal was stated as 'free secondary education for all children capable of benefiting from it'. We promised to expand and improve the facilities for the training of teachers, and we pledged to reorganise the Board of Education and make it more representative of the principal interests directly or indirectly concerned with education. We planned to encourage Caribbean art and culture.

We looked to the establishment of a National Housing Board, pledged a comprehensive survey of the existing housing situation, and promised a vigorous and comprehensive slum clearance programme with adoption and extension of the aided self-help method and incentives for housing construction. We pledged improvement of the medical services, especially at school level, and promotion and support of a National Health Insurance Scheme.

Our economic programme concentrated on agricultural and industrial development – the maximum utilisation of all arable land, expansion of credit, greater local production of food, government land settlements, encouragement of the search for new sources of oil, encouragement of a chemicals industry based on oil, food-processing industries, reasonable incentives to industrial production, reasonable protection for local products. We pledged also to expand the fishing and forestry industries and to develop adequate hotel facilities and beach amenities, and we promised the necessary infrastructure, roads, and transport. We said that the funds would come from private capital, both local and external. We pledged to set up a Planning Unit and to draw up a comprehensive development plan.

The People's Charter concluded as follows:

'People of Trinidad and Tobago, you have had five years of transition to self-government. What have they brought you? A bogus constitution, a bastard democracy, arrested economic development,

collective social insecurity, increasing frustration, bungling
and indecision by the Ministers which would disgrace even an
imperialist Government. . . .

Do you want a new dispensation, a change for the better? The
People's National Movement promises no paradise, offers no
millennium. It makes no idiotic promise to you that you will not
have to work any more or that pennies will drop from heaven;
it pledges that you will have jobs and decent conditions of labour,
decent wages, a just share of what you produce, and social security
for yourselves and your children. It does not hold out the ridiculous
economics that you will pay no taxes; it pledges that your taxes
will be spent on the social services you need. A vote for the People's
National Movement is a vote for your own education, a vote for
government that is honest and decisive, a vote for the dignity of
labour, social justice, racial fraternity, economic expansion, a sensible constitution, the abolition of colonialism, and a chance for
you to hold your head high and for your children to hold theirs
higher among the peoples of the world.

That is the PEOPLE'S NATIONAL MOVEMENT.

That is THE PEOPLE'S CHARTER.'

Our Party constitution provided that an applicant for membership
must not be a member of any other political party or of any organisation whose principles, policy or programme were inconsistent with
those of the PNM. It made provision for a youth league of those not
less than 14 and not more than 18 years of age. With the experience
of the British Labour Party before us, we were careful not to allow
our Movement to be dominated by the trade union block vote. But
we made provision for affiliation of any democratic trade union,
friendly, co-operative or credit society, professional, technical, cultural
or sports association, or women's or youth group.

We set up specific units of the Movement as follows: Party Group;
Constituency Group; General Council; Central Executive; Legislative
Group; Women's League; Youth League; Annual Convention.

The core of the Movement was the Party Group, consisting of not
less than 20 members and not more than 400, and operating within
the boundaries of polling divisions for Legislative Council elections.
The principal power accorded to the Party Group was the power
'to nominate for consideration by the Constituency Executive
persons for selection as candidates of the Movement' in the various
elections.

The Constituency Group, comprising two representatives from each Party Group in its area, was responsible for supervising the activities of these Party Groups. It was to elect annually a Constituency Executive. Each Constituency Group sent one representative to the General Council. Annual Constituency Conferences were to be held in each constituency, at which two delegates were to be elected to the Annual Convention.

The General Council was the governing body of the Movement. It comprised the officers of the Movement, holding office for a normal term of the Legislative Council (that is to say, five years), 18 members elected by the Inaugural Conference for five years (one-sixth of these were to be women), one representative elected annually by each Annual Constituency Conference, 12 members elected by the Annual Convention to hold office for one year (one-sixth of these were to be women), 8 members from the Legislative Group.

The twelve officers of the Movement, in order of precedence, were: Chairman; Vice Chairman; Second Vice Chairman; Lady Vice Chairman; Political Leader; Education Secretary; Public Relations Secretary; Labour Relations Officer; General Secretary; Assistant General Secretary; Treasurer; Deputy Political Leader. The first seven were elected by the Inaugural Conference, the four following were appointed by the General Council, and the twelfth was elected by the Legislative Group. This arrangement differed from that of other political parties. The Political Leader was not elected by the Parliamentary Group but by the mass movement. The officers of the Movement elected by the Inaugural Conference were elected for a term of five years, thus avoiding either the life presidency or the uncertainties and unsettling character of annual elections. And the administration of the Party was clearly and deliberately taken out of the hands of the Political Leader who was left free to concentrate on his political responsibilities; he ranked fifth in the administrative hierarchy.

The General Council had the responsibility of supervising the functioning of all activities of the Movement, of enforcing the Constitution, and of controlling the funds. It was empowered to set up and supervise committees as necessary. Every unit of the Movement was required to submit annual reports to the Council. The Council was to prepare an annual report and every Election Manifesto for submission to the Annual Convention. It was to establish a Standing Disciplinary Committee to ensure and regulate discipline and investigate complaints, with an ultimate right to appeal to the Annual Convention against the findings.

The Central Executive was a committee of the General Council, with all the powers but responsible thereto. It comprised the officers of the Movement, eight members elected annually by the General Council from its membership, and four members of the Legislative Group elected by the Legislative Group. The Central Executive was empowered where necessary to nominate provisional Constituency Executives and, in collaboration with the Constituency Executives, to approve the Movement's candidates for all elections.

The Legislative Group comprised the Movement's members of and candidates for all legislative bodies in the country – national, municipal, county. It was represented in its own right on the General Council and Central Executive, as well as at Constituency Conferences by the representatives for the constituency or ward, and at the Annual Convention; non-delegates to the Convention had the right to speak but not to vote. This again clearly showed the determination of the founders of the party not to allow the party to be dominated by the Parliamentary Group.

The women and youth were organised on a constituency basis, and provision was made for an Annual Youth Rally and an annual women's conference. The latter elected a Women's League Executive. Both units were represented at the Annual Convention by two delegates each.

The Annual Convention, held between the months of May and September, comprised: one delegate elected by each Party Group; two delegates elected by each Constituency Group; two delegates elected each by the Youth League and the Women's League; the General Council; members of the Legislative Group. Affiliated organisations were entitled to send one delegate for each particular interest represented, provided that such delegate was a member of the Movement.

The Constitution provided for annual audit of the funds of the Movement and included a special section on discipline. The Constitution was to be automatically reviewed by the Annual Convention five years after its ratification by the Inaugural Conference. The emblem of the Movement was to be 'a balisier on a background flag of black, brown, yellow and white, symbolising at one and the same time the Movement's roots in the local environment, its repudiation of external domination, and its interracial solidarity'.

This was the People's Charter, this was the Party Constitution, read out to a mammoth audience of several thousands, in the University of Woodford Square on the night of Tuesday, January 24, 1956, at 8 p.m.

We took the audience by storm. There had never been anything like it in Trinidad.

Trinidad and Tobago in January 1956 was more than ready for a disciplined, national, rational party organisation. To present a party programme, a statement of fundamental principles, a party constitution with defined groupings, powers, responsibilities and obligations from Party Group at the bottom to Annual Convention at the top was unheard of in Trinidad and Tobago. The sections on discipline in the Party Constitution and those on the control of party funds made history. The clear delimitation of responsibility, administrative on one side and political on the other, the avoidance of the undemocratic party leader for life, the fact that the political leader did not and could not preside over the General Council, the Central Executive and the Annual Convention, all this broke new ground not only at home but also abroad. The University of Woodford Square lapped it up.

Between January 24 and June 14, I launched the new movement in fifty-two different meetings all over the country. During this period of nearly five months I placed great emphasis on my appearances in the University of Woodford Square. I appeared there with seven national lectures, which were thereafter taken to sixteen different parts of the country. This University programme covered the Bandung Conference, political trends in 1956, the voter and the vote, a restatement of our fundamental principles.

In addition to launching the party in various districts and my national programme of lectures, I was busy addressing various smaller groups in cottage meetings. One of my favourite topics was 'the place of women in Caribbean Society'. Occasionally I spoke specifically on the place of women in the PNM. Apart from the women, I concentrated on the friendly societies and the trade unions. Sometimes I gave very special lectures, even in the remotest and most isolated districts – 'Europe, America and the Caribbean', 'The Development of a Caribbean Nationalism', 'Caribbean Agriculture in Historical Perspective'. My activities during this period spread to Barbados and Grenada, in both of which islands I was advising the local trade union movement.

Particularly in my lectures at the University of Woodford Square, I made it a point not to talk down to the people. It was straight university stuff, in content and in form as well as in manner, designed to place the problems of Trinidad and Tobago in international perspective. My lecture on 'The Voter and the Vote' was infused with international

experience and laid the foundations of our fundamental PNM reforms
in later years. I dealt with the British attitude to bribery, corruption
and the limitation of election expenses, the problem of non-voting
as tackled in Australia and Belgium, and the voting machines adopted
in Australia and the USA.

The opposition to the PNM mustered all its forces and combined to
deal with this portentous threat to its position in the government.
We were accused of all sorts of things. The full gravamen of the
opposition innuendoes and propaganda was dealt with by our Party
which sent, through me on June 5, a long communication to the
Governor for onward transmission to the Secretary of State for the
Colonies. It reads in part as follows:

'The PNM states categorically that it is neither communist, Fascist,
Poujadist nor Messianic or Jaganist. It is a national Party, deriving
its inspiration from the best in democratic theory, seeking to imitate
the best in democratic practice, applying to the affairs of Trinidad
and Tobago the intelligence, the democratic party discipline and
public morality which in the opinion of the PNM are lacking from
the political life of our community.

Our economic programme, for instance, is modelled consciously
on the experience and achievements of another Caribbean community, Puerto Rico. . . .

Our agricultural programme, with emphasis on the development
of a peasantry, the greater production of local foodstuffs and diversified agriculture, bears the stamp of approval of the Royal Commission of 1897, one of the most powerful Commisions of Inquiry
ever to visit the British Caribbean. . . .

The PNM's political programme is based on modern democratic
thought and practice. . . .

Our labour programme, in its turn, is based on the introduction
into Trinidad and Tobago of the international standards worked
out over the years by the International Labour Organisation. . . .

In its attitude to religion, there is nothing either strange, odd or
subversive in the PNM's programme. . . .

To associate the PNM therefore with subversive activity or
strange or odd doctrines or a programme ahead of its time is thus
to challenge the entire political, economic and social structure of
the modern civilised world. . . .

The PNM takes this opportunity of reaffirming its recent public
pledge to institute legal proceedings against any person or persons

seeking to defame it by alleging that it is a communist inspired movement.'

This communication to the Governor formed the basis of my long lecture in the University on June 14, 'PNM restates its Fundamental Principles'. I was particularly savage on Albert Gomes, leader of the POPPG (Party of Political Progress Groups), the then Minister of Labour, and on his colleague, the Minister of Education and Social Services, who had stated that I would not be able to recite the Lord's Prayer and the Apostle's Creed. In his youth Gomes had distinguished himself, as co-editor with C. L. R. James of *The Beacon*, by his rabid, vitriolic and offensive attacks on religion in general and the Roman Catholic Church in particular. Now he was accusing the PNM of godlessness. I let him have it as powerfully as I could dish it out, to the vast enjoyment of the crowd.

I was also very savage on the Minister of Education and Social Services, a man named Roy Joseph, another self-styled champion of the Roman Catholics. This is what I said about him:

'You cannot use the school to buy votes in 1956 at the expense of educational standards in terms of ability to recite the Lord's Prayer. But the Education Ordinance prescribes other subjects in the curriculum and the Minister of Education must stop condemning what is beyond his capacity. There would not be the slightest point in my reciting the Lord's Prayer to him, for example; he would not understand it because I would recite it in Latin.

I can now restate and amplify the PNM's fundamental principles in the field of education originally stated in our programme, *The People's Charter*.

1. The PNM accepts religious teaching in all schools in the country as a fundamental basis of training of citizenship.

2. The PNM reaffirms its already stated pledge that parents will have the right to send their children to schools of their own choice.

3. The PNM will not permit the prostitution of any school for racial or political ends.

4. The PNM will as soon as it is in a position to do so appoint a commission of inquiry representative of the governing bodies, teachers and parents to recommend a curriculum suited to the needs of our age with particular reference to the maintenance of academic standards and the integration of our cosmopolitan community into a homogeneous unit for the attainment of common

and mutually acceptable, economic, social and political objectives.
5. The PNM, as an integral part of its comprehensive policy of economic development, will give priority to the raising of academic standards in rural schools.
6. The PNM demands the appointment of a Commission of Inquiry to investigate the financial operations of the previous government with special emphasis on the building of schools in the past six years and on the award of contracts.
7. The PNM pledges itself to promote the establishment of a single, representative, democratic union of teachers, free from the government interference, intimidation and downright chicanery which have disgraced the record of the past six years.'

My responsibilities were increased when I was selected, being unemployed, as the editor of the party newspaper, *PNM Weekly*, which made its first appearance on July 14. With one or two brief gaps, this paper still survives after eleven years under the new title of *The Nation* as a weekly party paper.

The scope and tone of the new paper were clearly set out in my first editorial 'A Movement is born'. I wrote in part:

'Every political party must have an organ for the presentation of its views. Every University must have textbooks for its students. Every country must have different points of view presented to its citizens and voters. The People's National Movement, which has given Trinidad and Tobago its own University of Woodford Square, now presents to the people the *PNM Weekly*, and through it a point of view not now available in the country's press. . . .'

I followed this up week by week with editorials of a particular type and quality in which I was concerned at one and the same time with political education and with separating our paper sharply from the daily press.

My editorial on the 'Trinidad Oil Deal' dealt with the reported sale of Trinidad Leaseholds Ltd., a British oil company, the largest in Trinidad, to the American giant, Texaco. In my editorial on 'A Disunited Front' I dealt with the proposition that PNM should form a coalition with other parties to oppose the Government. I opposed this quite firmly – from the start PNM has eschewed all these shady coalition deals. I followed this up with an editorial entitled 'PNM

Bus Ride', in which I made it clear that PNM would not tolerate those applications for enrolment which were being made or proposed in respect of a discordant variety of politicians seeking only to thumb a ride on the PNM bus in order to get elected or re-elected. This is a great danger the PNM has always faced, that of being embarrassed by and saddled with people with dubious political pasts and associations.

In my editorial on 'Civil Liberties and Civil Servants' I dealt with a government circular issued for the guidance of civil servants in the impending elections advising them that, whilst they were free to join political parties and to express opinions in private or the ballot-box, they could not hold office in any party political organisation, could not write on party political matters, could not without the permission of the Secretary of State for the Colonies or the Governor contribute to the press matters of a political or administrative nature, or could not ask questions at political meetings. This extended to part-time officers and officers on contract as well. This is an issue which had dominated the PNM over the years, the political rights of civil servants based on the experience in the United Kingdom, to which we gave expression in our Civil Service Act of 1965. I dealt with it quite firmly.

I began my editorial on 'Democracy and Political Parties' by quoting Ostrogorski's *Democracy and the Organisation of Political Parties* and Michel's *Political Parties, a Sociological Study of the Oligarchical Tendencies of Modern Democracy*. On July 30 I put the PNM's first Annual Convention in the context of conventions of the Labour and Conservative Parties in the United Kingdom. One of my better editorials was on 'Revolution in Intelligence' on August 9. This excerpt is a good indication of my method and perhaps the handiest explanation of the success of the PNM in the September elections.

'The revolution in intelligence has already manifested itself in several ways. The people of the country today have a new attitude to the legislator or the aspirant to Legislative honours; several of the Constituency Executives consulted by the PNM's Executive with respect to the candidates to be nominated for their respective constituencies have, after hearing the candidates questioned, expressed themselves the view that the aspirant or aspirants are unsuitable. The Party Group delegates at PNM's First Annual Convention showed an awareness of political issues which few anticipated, and the Election Manifesto was amended by them in several respects. Molière in one of his plays has a famous passage, in which the Bourgeois Gentilhomme learns, to his surprise, that he has been talking prose for forty years and never knew it. Through PNM the people of Trinidad and Tobago have learned that they have been talking good politics for forty years and never knew it. . . . In an absolute monarchy the political centre of gravity is the Court. In a constitutional monarchy it is the legislature. In a dictatorship it is the army. In Trinidad and Tobago's confused political pattern of mis-government by the people's representatives, the political centre of gravity is the University of Woodford Square. Revolutions in the history of the world have been caused by unrest, stimulated by intrigue, and effected by blood and iron. The revolution in Trinidad and Tobago is unlike any other revolution anywhere in the world. It has been peaceful, bloodless, without bitterness or fury, bringing classes together instead of setting them apart. . . . It is a revolution of intelligence, for intelligence, by intelligence.'

In my editorial on 'Legislator and Constituents' I dealt particularly with the recall. In 'The Intellectual in Politics' I showed the role that Oxford has played in British political life and in the life of the colonies, and the role of the American Universities (Woodrow Wilson) in American political life.

In 'Race and Politics' on August 30 I dealt firmly with the racial situation in Trinidad and Tobago. Basing my editorial on the philosophy of José Marti of Cuba, and illuminating it by the contribution of Phoenicians, Mayans, Egyptians to world civilisation, whilst attacking Gobineau, Acton, apartheid in South Africa, Jim Crow in the USA, the Kaiser's Yellow Peril and the White Australia Policy, I stated PNM's interracial solidarity firmly as follows:

'This is the goal – these the objectives of PNM – a multiracial party with European members, with Chinese Party Group chairmen, with Portuguese Party Group vice-chairmen, with Indian Party Group secretaries, with Negro Party Group treasurers. Recognising and, indeed, welcoming cultural diversity, PNM calls for unity among racial groups on one common platform – agreement on common economic, social and political objectives: utilisation of all resources, human and physical, for the common good, as determined by the general will. In the forthcoming elections, PNM proudly exhibits its banner on which are emblazoned the words revolutionary for

Trinidad and Tobago – POLITICAL LIBERTY, SOCIAL EQUALITY, RACIAL FRATERNITY.'

This was the *PNM Weekly*. It did not seek to compete with the regular newspapers. It was, and was intended to be, rather a review, for discussion of purely political issues, presenting information for the education of voters, and, naturally, disseminating PNM's views. Its initial circulation was 10,000. After the first issue, this was raised to 12,000. The issue of August 9, containing our election manifesto as a supplement, numbered 20,000 copies. This was magnificent for the new journal, born on July 14, of a new party, born on January 24.

And so the stage was set for our important first Annual Convention, held on July 28 and 29. Present were delegates of some eighty Party Groups representing thousands of members all over the country.

The Convention began with a Political Review by me as Political Leader, which was repeated on July 30 in the University of Woodford Square and on July 31 in San Fernando, at what was by then conventionally known as the College of Harris Promenade. My review covered two principal themes – PNM's democracy and PNM's nationalism.

On the first I spoke as follows:

'First PNM democracy. It is rather amusing to read among the many criticisms of PNM that it is a totalitarian party ruled by one man. . . .

I need only draw your attention to the party democracy which you yourselves have been practising in your Party Groups. You admit applicants. You elect your officers and run your own affairs. You are raising funds for election expenses the disbursement of which, through your Constituency Election Committee, you will control. You have nominated a candidate for the General Elections for the approval of the Executive, and in your choice and in your discussion with the Executive you have shown undoubtedly that you want a candidate of integrity and ability whom you help to choose freely, not one who seeks to buy your favours, not a dressed-up crapaud imposed on you from above as happens, I understand, outside of PNM. You have chosen your delegates to this Convention. You have selected your representatives on the Provisional Constituency Executives. As soon as time permits and the Party Groups are divided up according to Polling Divisions you will select your representatives to the Constituency Groups from which

Constituency Executives will be selected. At this Convention you will pass judgment on the activities of the Movement since the launching. You will receive the audited report of the funds you have helped to contribute. You will approve the Election Manifesto which the Movement will present to the electorate. You will debate the resolutions put forward by Party Groups. You will elect 12 representatives to the General Council which is the governing body of the Movement. If this is totalitarianism, then the moon is made of green cheese.'

I then proceeded to deal with the nationalism aspect. The principal battleground in this nationalist struggle was the school, as I noted. I then proceeded to state PNM's attitude to denominational education. I put it this way:

'Trinidad is neither like Britain, predominantly Anglican, nor like India, predominantly Hindu, nor like Puerto Rico and France with their state schools, predominantly Roman Catholic. It is a multi-racial, multi-religious society groping towards nationalism. How can the denominational system be brought into the current of nationalism without sacrificing minority rights, denominational rights, vested rights or the right of the individual to decide his educational system? That is the question which PNM, a multi-racial, multi-religious, nationalist but democratic party, has set itself to answer. The answer, I say it again, is (1) respect for the law of the land, which provides for denominational participation in education with state aid; (2) enforcement of that law with respect to state control of buildings and building standards, curriculum and textbooks, the condition of employment of teachers, and the proper use of state funds; (3) the elimination of racial and political influences; (4) the working out of a curriculum suited to the needs of the expanding economy which PNM will make possible; (5) the integration of the various sections of our community into a single unit where social, economic and political objectives are concerned; (6) most important of all, the raising of standards, especially academic, in all schools. That is PNM nationalist education.'

Two unsolicited tributes to our achievement were paid during this period. The first came from the pen of the distinguished Barbadian novelist, George Lamming, who had already published *In the Castle of My Skin* and *The Emigrants*. It came in the form of an article entitled 'Trinidad and the Revolution in Intelligence' which appeared in *PNM Weekly* on August 30. I quote largely from Lamming's tribute, which began with a description of Trinidad as he knew it in 1946.

'I think this represents quite frankly, in terms of fiction, the kind of social situation which the People's National Movement found and which their initial efforts have managed, beyond all expectation, to survive and reform. Any serious political organising had to start from that point of crisis, and Dr. Eric Williams started in a way which, to my mind, is unique in the history of Caribbean politics. He started with an intensive and quite exhausting campaign of popular education. He turned history, the history of the Caribbean, into gossip, so that the story of a people's predicament seemed no longer the infinite, barren track of documents, dates and texts. Everything became news: slavery, colonisation, the forgiveable deception of metropolitan rule, the sad and inevitable unawareness of the native production. His lectures retained always the character of whisper which everyone was allowed to hear, a rumour which experience had established as the truth. And whatever misgivings we may have about the ultimate value of popular education, this undertaking, it seems to me, has become an achievement of genius on the part of a teacher. Dr. Williams himself is already history, living history. No other British West Indian politician has exposed himself so consistently to that gravest of all political risks; the risk of refusing to talk down to an electorate. He distinguished very early and quite clearly the difference between formal education which is often wasteful, and native intelligence; and having done that, he worked on the native intelligence by demanding at all times an adult attention and response to his lectures. This was an example, probably the first of its kind in our part of the world, of the teacher, in the noblest sense of teacher, turned politician, and of the politician, in the truly moral sense of politician, turned teacher. The result has taken a novel turn, a turn of discovery which is the beginning of action. Today's Trinidadian, who was very much a part of the ugliness I have described above, did not know that he was capable of understanding. And in a sense that is most urgent, and therefore absolutely important, he understands. It is this discovery which explains, I feel, the present character of that square which is today known throughout Trinidad and Tobago as The University of Woodford Square.

I try to recall a picture of Woodford Square in 1946. It was as I remember it, a market for night-food. All transactions were done in the shadows. Women strolled about in search of male friends whom they had not yet known. Men sat on the benches in an attitude of tolerable and even pleasing boredom. And there were always a few lunatics who had either avoided or escaped the attention of the state. Today, this same Woodford Square has become Mr. Everyman's Academy. The same people who used it appropriately, or inappropriately, as you like, in the past, now assemble there to learn.

It is this transformation of Woodford Square which is going to have the most profound effect on the forthcoming elections, and the forthcoming elections will most certainly be the most interesting, the most serious and the most historic Trinidad and Tobago will have experienced so far. This is precisely what I mean by the phrase, Trinidad and the revolution in political intelligence. It is the first time that the meaning of the machine, political party, has taken practical shape among Trinidadians, and it is certainly the first time that many a student of Woodford Square will have come to respect the importance of that powerful little weapon, the vote. It is the first time that many will be using that weapon with intelligence and effectiveness. And this raises the question of moral responsibility and what, to my mind is the real significance of the People's National Movement. The significance which now expresses itself in political terms (and it is right to the circumstances that this should be its most urgent and important significance) is deeper than politics. It has to do with the whole man of which his political reason is only one aspect. The entire West Indies is doomed until the sense, the tradition of the individual's unconditional worth, is firmly established. . . .

So this, then, is my story. I do not know what strange conversion, what magic, if you like, took place in Trinidad between 1950 and 1954. But when I returned to Port-of-Spain in 1955, I did not believe the rumours I was told about this change brought about by the PNM. And I would certainly not have believed if I hadn't seen it myself then and during a later visit in 1956. The tidiness, the order and that consuming sense of serious application which I experienced at the Party's Headquarters; the competence, the precision and the range of the party's manifesto which I studied; the efficiency and the power of the whole Party machinery which has rolled itself into every corner of Trinidad and Tobago, the excellent standard of its newspaper which is easily the best political weekly in the whole British West Indies: these are qualities and achievements which none of us could honestly have associated with Trinidad and Tobago before 1954.

As a result of this experience two things have become clear to me. The first is this: no Trinidadian in his right mind can in future undertake to go into politics without being prepared to work harder than he has ever worked before. The second lesson has to do with the future of the Trinidad Legislative Council. No opponent of the People's National Movement, for whom the words honour and dignity have meaning, can now escape a feeling of shame, regret and humiliation, produced by the terrific achievement of the PNM in so short a time. And after the September elections, the standard of debates in the Legislative Council will reach a stage of excellence and decency with which Trinidadians have never before been blessed. It is the first time the place has ever been offered what can frankly be called a GOLDEN OPPORTUNITY.'

The second tribute came at the Convention itself, from Professor Gordon Lewis of the University of Puerto Rico, husband of a Trinidad girl, as reported in *PNM Weekly* of August 9:

'Professor Lewis emphasised that the PNM is a party in the proper sense of the word, which has not made the usual political mistake of underestimating the intelligence of the average West Indian, which has not held out to the voter the hope of taking him into the promised land only to desert him in the wilderness.

Professor Lewis emphasised also the relationship which PNM has been able to work out between the intellectual and the masses. In this connection he compared PNM's Political Leader, Dr Eric Williams, with Professor Harold Laski who, for so long until his death, has been the chairman of the British Labour Party. He stressed Dr Williams' role in making effective use of the research accumulated on the shelves of the Caribbean Commission at Kent House in Port-of-Spain. He quoted a Democrat politician in New York who, when asked the technique of success in politics replied: "I do not talk Shakespeare in the Fifteenth District; they do not understand it". Professor Lewis retorted: "Dr Williams has proved that this is not so; you can talk Shakespeare in the Fifteenth District. . . ." '

You could indeed! One night at a mass meeting in my own constituency in South-east Port-of-Spain, a man accosted a woman. The woman was overheard to say: 'Are you addressing me, sir? Do you wish to make an appointment? Well, you will have to see me after the lecture.'

19

THE 1956 GENERAL ELECTION

It was a very hard election campaign. From the presentation of candidates in the University of Woodford Square on July 30 to my last two meetings in the University on September 23, I held 157 election meetings all over the country.

During this period I held two major meetings at the University of Woodford Square. At the first, on August 14, I lectured on 'Two Worlds in Conflict'. My second lecture was entitled 'An Evening with Hansard'. It was delivered in the University on September 6. I had the large crowd convulsed with laughter at the antics of the members of the Legislative Council. I quoted liberally from their speeches. One member had threatened another, 'I will meet you shot for shot, fire for fire'. Another, recalling unsolved murder cases, had told a colleague that he wished to fill the House with 'cut-throats and murderers'. A third had threatened, 'I intend to go into the gutter as may be necessary and disembowel them there'. Much fun had been poked at a member whose deficient English had produced 'as far as whey I can see'. The Council had poured scorn on Butler's motion for the recall of legislators; it was said by the Speaker that in all his books on comparative government he knew of no country which had similar legislation, whereupon a nominated member tabled *Gulliver's Travels*. I pointed out that not one member of the Council seemed to know, what every university freshman knew, that the recall was an ancient, honourable and conventional device associated with Switzerland and certain States in the USA and had not led to irresponsible elections.

Our election manifesto was a veritable masterpiece in the Trinidad and Tobago of 1956. We pledged first and foremost constitution reform, a bicameral legislature and the Cabinet system.

We undertook to reduce the cost of the Ministerial system and proposed how the portfolios would be distributed. We laid stress on political education, and specifically pledged to correct the notorious deficiencies of the election machinery.

We undertook to rid the public service of favouritism and nepotism and to give wider powers to local government bodies. We pledged to protect the rights of the citizen against the State by enacting a Crown Proceedings Ordinance, and to ensure equitable protection of both buyer and seller by a Hire Purchase Ordinance. We guaranteed to support constructive proposals for an economically sound Federation with Dominion status in a period of not more than five years after its establishment, and undertook to provide trade and diplomatic representation abroad for the promotion and protection of Caribbean interests in the USA, Venezuela, Australia, India and West Africa. We emphasised our economic and social programme·based on the People's Charter. We stressed the fundamentals of our education programme, as follows:

'* The maintenance of Government schools
* The giving of religious instruction shall be compulsory in all schools maintained or assisted by Government
* The maintenance of the right of the citizen to send his child to a school of his own choice
* The earliest possible enforcement of compulsory education at the primary level
* The granting of assistance to Voluntary schools (including both Church and lay schools).'

We paid attention to the citizen's home and his need of leisure. We worked out a special programme for Tobago based principally on an efficient steamer service and around the island road transport. We concluded with our Code of Public Morality which pledged the conventional human rights, freedom of worship, freedom from political interference in the public service and police force, independence of the judiciary. We gave the pledge that birth control was a private and religious matter and specifically undertook to honour 'all International Obligations, financial, economic and military, with special reference to the Agreement on the United States Bases'.

As the election campaign drew to its close, I spent Sunday, September 23, in a huge motorcade holding spot meetings in Carenage, in St. George West and all the Port-of-Spain constituencies. The enthusiasm was incredible, and had to be seen to be believed. We ended up at six o'clock in the evening with a meeting in the University of Woodford Square.

I thought the campaign was over. Tired out after the enormous strain, I went home and got under the shower, relaxing, getting the tension out of my system. Suddenly the telephone rang, and two calls followed immediately thereafter. The first call was from a resident opposite Woodford Square, the second was from my party colleague Wilfrid Alexander, and the third was from a senior police officer. All indicated that a huge crowd had gathered in the University and was clamouring for a meeting.

It was obvious that, if only for psychological reasons, I had to comply. It was the eve of the election. I don't know where I got the energy from, or what hidden resources I drew on. What I do know is that it was the most successful meeting of the campaign. The power in my voice was something to hear; no one would have guessed that I had over 150 meetings in eight weeks. Wilfrid Alexander urged me to give them a short speech and promised to pull my coat if I was going on too long. He has not yet pulled my coat. My theme was an anonymous centre page article in the *Sunday Guardian* which we attributed to a well-known Roman Catholic priest who had consistently and belligerently opposed us, and which purported to compare me with Hitler. I tore into him, to the satisfaction of the enormous crowd, and pledged that nothing would stop our victory the next day, when I would be returned to deal with him and his ilk. It was a terrific occasion.

But the greatest triumph was to come. There was great tension in the country and all sorts of rumours of violence and confusion. A British frigate had arrived at the call of the Governor and was anchored offshore. I urged my audience to go home right away and stay off the streets on election day after voting. To my complete astonishment, by the time I ended my peroration, the University was almost empty. There they were in their thousands, taking my advice literally, streaming out of the several gates on their way to their homes. The Governor told me afterwards that he had known of many political leaders who had won and retained their power by calling the people on to the streets; I was the first in his experience who had won power by telling the people to keep off the streets. What astonished him even more was that the people complied.

And so the glorious morning came, September 24. I spent the day in my constituency, visiting the polling stations. We just missed a serious riot. A Roman Catholic priest, whose name I forbear to mention, had distinguished himself by going the rounds of the constituency urging the voters to vote for my Roman Catholic opponent. I caught

up with him perilously close to the 100-yard limit in one polling
station within which no canvassing or influencing of the voters was
permitted by law. I left him there and walked leisurely up the street.
A few minutes later someone ran up to me terrified, telling me to
come quickly. The rumour, which spread like wildfire, was that the
priest had slapped a woman who refused to vote as he directed. The
crowd, which appeared like magic, from nowhere, converged on the
priest, who took refuge in a Catholic house near to the corner of
Queen and Duncan Streets. As I got to the house I found thousands of
persons yelling and shouting all kinds of abuse at the priest. With the
enormous pressure, the railings of the house were almost down. I
forced my way forward. As I was recognised, the people's rage subsided, and I picked out a few prominent party members and called on
them to help me disperse the crowd. The police were helpless in the
situation. When the tumult subsided, I brought the priest out of the
house and put him in a police car, which took him to the Cathedral;
he was shipped out of Trinidad a few days later.

It was a narrow escape. I knew that we had won the elections when
an unknown man came up to me. He flashed a police badge and said
to me, 'I am a security officer. I must ask you to leave the scene immediately and not risk your personal safety.' It was then that I was conscious of being followed by a security car. I went to my car at once
and drove away, understanding that the future Chief Minister was
under police protection.

The election results came out the same night. After being declared
the winner in my constituency, by a margin of 6,067 votes against
2,217 for my three opponents, I went over to party headquarters
where the top officers had gathered to hear the results. As they came
in one by one, we realised that we had brought off the greatest coup
in Trinidad's history – a party nine months old had won the elections and gained 13 of the 24 seats. Two of them were by narrow
margins of 109 and 179. Our biggest success was the victory of Ulric
Lee, a young trade unionist, over Albert Gomes by a large majority
of 1,458. Our biggest disappointment was our defeat in Tobago by
an old-school politician by the narrow margin of 245. Two other
Ministers lost their seats – the Minister of Health in Port-of-Spain and
the Minister of Education in San Fernando.

A total of 271,534 votes were cast in a total electorate of 339,028.
PNM's popular vote was 105,153. The PDP got 55,148 votes; Independent candidates 40,523; the Butler Party 31,071; the POPPG
14,019; the Trinidad Labour Party 13,092; the Caribbean National

Labour Party 3,864; the Caribbean People's Democratic Party 627; the left wing West Indian Independence Party 446. The PNM was the only party to contest all 24 seats.

With so many parties and so many independents a splitting up of the vote was inevitable. But PNM easily emerged as the most national of all the parties. We completely dominated the three major towns, Port-of-Spain, San Fernando and Arima. We won all the seats in the most populous county, St. George. In the ten St. George seats 111,800 votes were cast (over 40% of the total in the country), of which PNM polled 63,568 or 57% of the total. We had scored over 38% of the total vote in the country. In eight of the thirteen seats won by us we polled over half the popular vote; in four of the others we polled over 40%. We won in just under half of the total polling divisions in the country; we came out worst of all in St. Patrick, where we won in 12 divisions out of 142, and we came out best of all in Port-of-Spain, where we won in 133 out of 142 polling divisions and in San Fernando where we won in 56 out of 69 polling divisions. Whilst that demonstrated a domination of the urban areas rare in the history of the successful political parties in the West Indies – note the division over Kingston in Jamaica between Manley and Bustamante, Barrow's failure to carry Bridgetown in Barbados, Burnham's control of Georgetown in Jagan's British Guiana – the fact that we carried Ortoire-Mayaro, eminently rural, carried St. George East which, Arima apart, is solidly rural, and lost rural Tobago by only a slender margin, showed that we had great strength in the rural areas on which we could build a truly national party in years to come. Our great weakness was in the oil belt of St. Patrick. For even in Caroni's sugar areas, with their predominantly Indian population, we won in 29 out of 149 polling divisions and polled 8,942 votes against 19,045 for the PDP – we achieved just under half the PDP total.

The world acclaimed our victory and congratulations poured in from everywhere. Manley in Jamaica called our victory an 'outstanding triumph . . . great news for West Indian politics . . . a clear breakthrough for honesty and a new purpose . . . a victory won against all comers by courage and determination'. The *Daily Gleaner* of Jamaica saw our victory as 'a triumph for a man with an ideal', a victory for a 'political campaign based on the lecture rather than the harangue', the 'repudiation of sheer racialism'.

The *Times Educational Supplement* in England saw the election as likely to result in 'a revolution in the colony's educational system'. The *Economist*, whilst lamenting the disappearance of Gomes, saw us as a 'responsibly-officered' party looking leftwards, by which, however, 'oilmen probably need not be too scared'; it saw 'the most hopeful aspect' of our victory in the fact that we were a 'federal-minded party', and predicted that this would 'ensure a more rapid advance towards the Caribbean Dominion'. The *News Chronicle* looked to the PNM to form with Jamaica's PNP 'an alliance which will be a most powerful federal party'. The *Manchester Guardian* stressed that I was 'clearly destined to be a leading figure in the Federation before long'.

The *Courier-Journal* of Louisville, Kentucky, saw the election as 'a political miracle that may have a marked effect on the Caribbean Federation, now in process of formation'. Toronto's *Daily Star*, regarding me as 'an untiring worker for confederation', said that I 'might be called the Sir John A. MacDonald of the West Indies'. *Time's* Latin American edition commented that our written programme was 'limited and sound'; 'an invitation to domestic and foreign capital to help create jobs'. India's *Times* looked upon us as 'the first party in Trinidad ever to place principles and policies above personalities', and looked to me to 'maintain his sensible stand on the racial issue and help to have the Indian population – which numbers 35 per cent of the total – completely and justly absorbed in the Trinidadian nation'.

On September 25, 1956, my forty-fifth birthday, the day after the triumphant election, the Governor sent for me and asked me to form a government. Thus began the first constitutional crisis in the history of the PNM. It took the better part of a month to have the issue resolved.

The issue involved the nominated members of the unicameral Legislative Council, which comprised 24 elected members, plus two official members, plus five nominated members. The Governor pledged at once the full support of the two official members. That, with PNM's 13 elected members, made a total of 15. Against that there were 11 elected opposition members and the 5 nominated members. I at once made out a case for the nomination of two PNM members and for the right to be consulted in the selection of the other three. I based my case on precedents the Colonial Office had already set in Singapore and Malaya. The Governor was adamant; he would promise only to nominate persons not unsympathetic to the PNM. The Party Executive and I accordingly drew up a memorandum which we submitted to the Governor on September 30 for transmission to the Secretary of State for the Colonies, and which concluded:

'. . . the present situation calls for the following modification of the nominated system:

Nominated Members –

(a) must be persons of specialised knowledge and experience;

(b) cannot be rejected because of their identification with the PNM;

(c) must be rejected because of their identification with the well-established Opposition to the PNM.'

The outcome was a complete vindication of our stand. The Secretary of State for the Colonies ruled that we should nominate two PNM members and that the Governor should consult me in his selection of the other three.

The road was then clear for our assumption of power. We were sworn in on Friday, October 26, in an historic ceremony. After the ceremony, our thirteen elected members and two nominated members proceeded to a noon meeting in the University of Woodford Square at which we all made brief speeches and pledged to work in unison for the glory of the PNM and the development of the country. The occasion was unprecedented in the history of the country. After ten years of power you can still hear persons giving their reminiscences of this wonderful gathering.

We thus entered upon our first term in office with Trinidad and Tobago firmly planted on the road towards the achievement of PNM's foremost goal – full internal self-government and the elimination of colonialism.

20

CONSTITUTION REFORM

As Chief Minister I also took the portfolio of Finance, Planning and Development, and I appointed myself Minister of Tobago Affairs, with a Parliamentary Secretary to assist me as Chief Minister and in respect of Tobago. The first five years were years of hard work. We had a series of important issues to tackle and decide. Two of these I shall deal with separately – Federation and Chaguaramas. But there were many others – constitution reform, the organisation of the Ministry of Finance, the first five-year development plan, free secondary education, Tobago affairs, the telephone issue, important legislation implementing the party's election manifesto, reorganisation of the public service. All of this was accomplished in the five-year period.

We immediately set about changing the constitution. The first step was for the Ministers to meet privately before Executive Council, so that we could present a united front; I was normally the spokesman for the Ministers in the Executive Council. We called this meeting of Ministers 'Cabinet'. So from 1956 Trinidad and Tobago had a *de facto* Cabinet. We set out to make it *de jure*.

To this end a motion was introduced by me in the Legislative Council on September 20, 1957. This motion called for the recognition of the conventions of party government in the appointment of a Chief Minister and his ministers, the introduction of the Cabinet system, and the remodelling of the Public Service and Police Service Commissions.

The opposition, led by the daily press, fastened on the civil service reforms which, they claimed, would lead to political interference with the civil service and the police force. In presenting my motion I therefore emphasised the position of the civil service in the United Kingdom and drew parallels from the constitutions of Ceylon, Nigeria and the Malayan Federation.

The opposition was unmoved. They continued with their parrot chant of political interference. In my reply I let them have it. If the United Kingdom traditions, one thousand years old, were too much for us to aspire to, what of Malaya, where the traditions were only three weeks old? I placed particular emphasis on the provision in the existing constitution which allowed any civil servant who disagreed with his Minister to send a statement in writing to the Executive Council which would dispose of it. I tore up the constitution in their faces. It was a symbolic act. Trinidad and Tobago would proceed under my leadership to full internal self-government in a fully independent Federation.

These proposals were accepted by the Colonial office, but before they could be brought into effect, we decided to move forward another few inches. On November 21, 1958, I introduced a motion in the Legislative Council calling for the immediate appointment of a select Committee to make recommendations for a new constitution. I had unsuccessfully in September tried to get a team of outside experts with the following terms of reference:

'Using Trinidad and Tobago as a case study, to consider and make recommendations on the Legislative machinery at all levels appropriate to our present and future needs, bearing in mind (1) the effect of the establishment of the Federal Government on the Legislative competence of unit territories; (2) the relationship of the Central Government to Local Government bodies taking into account also current suggestions for the increase in number, scope and powers of Municipalities and County Councils; (3) the influence that the political and constitutional structure of Trinidad and Tobago may exercise on its smaller neighbours seeking to remove the present disparity in constitutional development; (4) the overall cost of the legislative machine in the light of available financial resources.'

I had written to the following: Professor Vincent Harlow; Professor Kenneth Wheare of Oxford, the well-known authority on federation; Professor Denis Brogan; Professor Gordon Lewis; Dr. T. O. Elias of Nigeria, then associated with the Institute of Commonwealth Studies at Oxford. I had also asked the Indian Government to make available the services of a political scientist of repute in one of the Indian Universities.

I had hoped that the findings of this team of experts would be available to the Select Committee of the Legislative Council. But, alas! I had reckoned without the obligations and commitments of top university men, and it proved impossible to get the team together.

Whilst this larger exercise was in progress, we decided to request from the Secretary of State the permission to appoint a ninth Minister, to whom we would transfer control of the police. Everything was set for the inauguration of the new Legislative Council and the celebration of Cabinet Day on June 26, 1959. We sent the telegram to London one week before. The day before, on June 25, a telegram came back stating that there had been 'misunderstandings' on our part and that the Secretary of Sate was sending his Parliamentary Under Secretary Julian Amery, to discuss things on the spot. We had declared Cabinet Day a public holiday. It was too late to do anything about that. But, after consulting our General Council, we cancelled all the arrangements for the inauguration of the new Legislative Council on June 26.

Amery was as rude as possible. He saw the Chief Minister only after he had seen the Chief Secretary and the Commissioner of Police. We had decided we were not backing down. So I did not spare him. I accused him of using the constitution reform issue as blackmail on the Chaguaramas issue, where we had recently been led to suspect that radiation was involved, and I declined to argue the matter. I stood on my rights. He went around meeting people, including members of the opposition, and eventually capitulated. I promptly went to the University of Woodford Square to report to the people on July 31. I said in part:

> 'There was a crisis, ladies and gentlemen, true enough. The central issue had nothing to do with police, it had nothing to do with elections, it had nothing to do with the Police Force, it had nothing to do with the ninth Minister, it had nothing to do with dictatorship. The central issue in the crisis was Chaguaramas (loud applause).'

It was a great triumph for us. The Party and the population stood firm, shoulder to shoulder with the Government.

I tried to make clear to the population the significance of Cabinet Day in a radio broadcast on July 9. I discussed my new relations with my colleagues, with the Governor, and with the civil service, and indicated that we would proceed to independence for the Federation.

And then the next day, July 10, 1959, our triumph culminated in the first Speech from the Throne written by the Cabinet. In a packed council chamber, with thousands upon thousands listening in Woodford Square and in the streets surrounding, the Governor read the Throne Speech which I handed to his aide-de-camp to pass on to him.

The next big landmark was my announcement to the Legislative Council in November 20, 1959, that, on our nomination, the next Governor was to be a West Indian. We selected Solomon Hochoy, the Chief Secretary, who had worked with us from 1956. He had risen from the lowest rungs of the civil service ladder, had been a popular Commissioner of Labour, had made a most efficient Chief Secretary, and was well liked and respected by all. I had grown to like and respect him myself when he accompanied me to Jamaica to the Federal Capital Conference in February, 1957; after that I developed a tremendous respect, which I still have, for his 'nose' – he could smell things a mile off. The appointment was universally accepted and Sir Solomon – for we recommended a knighthood for him also – was later to become the first Governor-General of our independent nation.

By the time we announced Hochoy's appointment, constitution reform discussions were in full swing in London. My deputy Solomon was there, in charge. The Select Committee of the Legislative Council had done its work; the PNM had submitted a memorandum based on the report of a committee which it had appointed, with myself as chairman. We were demanding the bicameral legislature to which we stood committed. Solomon kept me informed of progress. Suddenly a telegram came in from him indicating that the negotiations had broken down. I smelt a rat – Chaguaramas again. I summoned him and the delegation back to Trinidad, breaking off negotiations, and promptly announced a meeting on December 10 for the University of Woodford Square. There were two speakers – Solomon on the progress of the constitution discussion, and myself on Chaguaramas and on our relations with the Colonial Office.

I read out in the University the document I had sent as Premier to the Secretary of State for the Colonies. Macleod's alibi was the Opposition's objections to our proposed Senate. I recited the record on the question of the second chamber. I continued:

'You justify your position by two statements: "It would be quite wrong for me to takes sides", and that "I am willing to accept either a bicameral or a unicameral legislature whichever is endorsed by the electorate".

In the first place your statements, in effect, represent an un-willingness to accept the bicameral legislature endorsed by the electorate on September 24, 1956.

In the second place, your statements represent a reversal of the policy pursued by your predecessors. . . .

Your proposition will only strengthen the prevailing impression – nurtured by the "crisis" which attended the inauguration of the Cabinet system – that every effort is being made to force upon us at all costs an election at the earliest possible moment, to give the opposition an election issue, and to set back the movement for self-government to the degree that it is associated with the People's National Movement.

We are unable to accept your proposition. It is inconsistent with good government and incompatible with self-government. It can serve only to maintain the suzerainty of the Colonial Office with all the restrictions therein entailed on colonial emancipation and colonial development, and to hamper our progress towards the full development of democracy.'

I let them have it on Chaguaramas also; but that I deal with separately.

Thereafter there was silence – until May of 1960, after our famous April 22 march for Chaguaramas, the Secretary of State decided that since Mahomet would not come to the mountain, the mountain must perforce come to Mahomet. He decided to visit Trinidad himself in June, 1960. We met, discussed pleasantly, settled all outstanding problems in one or two sittings of a few hours, and Trinidad and Tobago had its full internal self-government with a bicameral legis-lature which came into effect after the General Elections on December 4, 1961.

21

FEDERATION

Federation of the British West Indies was first proposed, in limited form, almost a hundred years ago, coinciding virtually with the establishment of the Canadian Federation in 1867. Up to the time of the inauguration of the Federal Parliament in 1958, the discussions on the subject revealed two dominant characteristics.

The first was that Federation was superimposed on reluctant communities. Federation was a British scheme designed to promote British goals and achieve British ends in the Caribbean. A formal proposal made by the British Government in 1876 was the quintessence of modesty, involving freedom of movement for lunatics and prisoners, and the federation of lepers and policemen in the Windward Islands and Barbados. Barbados would have none of it.

The second dominant characteristic of the federal discussions before 1958 was the paucity and inadequacy of West Indian public opinion. At its most vocal in 1932, a conference of certain West Indian territories was held in Roseau in Dominica, the moving spirit being Cipriani of Trinidad. The conference proposed a very backward constitution whose goal was the Canadian constitution of 1839 as enshrined in the Durham Report, not the Canadian Constitution of 1932.

This was the background to the crucial discussions in Montego Bay, Jamaica, begun in 1947 which ended up by agreeing, at the London Conference in 1956 after much shillyshallying and hemming and hawing in the preceding years, to a weak and anaemic Federation which was restricted for the first five years to a mandatory levy totalling $9,120,000 annually contributed by the territories according to prescribed percentages. The Federation was debarred from the income tax field and had no powers over economic development.

Attention was principally focused on the site of the federal capital. Majority opinion favoured Trinidad, but in 1953 the opinion had been expressed that the smaller island of Grenada should be selected.

The problem led to the appointment in 1956 of an expatriate commission to select a site for the capital. The commission, whose report was published at the end of 1956, suggested three islands in order of precedence – Jamaica, Barbados, Trinidad – where suitable sites might be located. The selection was based on the statements that Trinidad's public life was corrupt, that the Indians were a minority opposed to Federation, and that it was too great a risk to place the Federal capital in Trinidad.

This was the general situation in which PNM came to power on September 14, 1956. We immediately concentrated on three lines of action. The first was to make clear that, minor changes apart, we would operate the disgraceful Federal constitution, colonialist from top to bottom, seeking forthwith to amend it and introduce Dominion Status within five years from its inception.

The second was, in the name of Trinidad and Tobago in general and the Indian minority in particular, to repudiate the allegations against the Indian population made in the report of the Federal Capital Site Commission. I stated the case in the University on the first anniversary of the launching of our Party on January 24, 1957. I repeated the substance of this at the Federal Capital Site Conference in the following month in Jamaica when I asked that my statement be recorded and appended to the official report of the United Kingdom Commission for subsequent widespread distribution. I dealt with the large number of West Indians resident in Trinidad, arguing that to condemn Trinidad was to condemn the West Indies, and I pointed out that the rejected Indian community was making on a *per capita* basis a higher contribution than any of the other territories.

On the other allegation of the Commission, that Trinidad was not a safe place for the Federal Capital, I told the Conference that the PNM dominated Port-of-Spain and there was no safer spot for the Capital.

The third general line of action taken by the PNM in the early days was to announce that we would take no part in the anticipated scramble for seats in the Federal Parliament. I made my own position crystal clear at a meeting in Port-of-Spain on Thursday, October 3, 1957, in support of our PNM candidate for the Municipal Elections: I was not a candidate for the position of Prime Minister. Manley was present at the meeting. He told me afterwards that he was surprised that I had made up my mind so early, and even more surprised that I had made my decision public.

With this background, we proceeded to deal with the key question – what type of federation? This raised two issues in particular – the first, the federal powers over economic development; the second, the amendment of the colonial constitution and the achievement of independence. On both Trinidad and Tobago's position was made impeccably clear by me – we stood for a strong, independent Federation, with the usual powers over the constituent units.

On September 11, 1959, we went to the Legislative Council with our proposals. The motion standing in my name read as follows:

> 'Resolved: That this House endorse the principle of a strong independent Federation, vested with the powers and responsibilities pertaining thereto, and mandate the Trinidad and Tobago delegation to the Intergovernmental Conference preceding the Conference on revision of the Federal Constitution to seek the approval and support of other territorial Governments of the Federation for amendments to the Constitution designed to achieve this goal and enable the West Indies Federation to take its proper place in the Commonwealth and the United Nations.'

Our case was that the future could be 'nothing else than a consolidated Nation, free and independent, a strong Federal Government, an economic development on a national scale'. I surveyed previous attempts at federation, including the British Government's proposals of 1876 and the Dominica Conference of 1932, together with all the committees and commissions which the British Government had sent out in 1921, 1932, and 1938. None of these reports gave any 'idea of why we have federated and why we must federate'. There was in these reports 'the total absence of any clear, elevated, comprehensive conception of what the Federation is designed or expected to do'. Thereupon I proceeded to compare three federal constitutions – Canada, Malaya and Nigeria – and showed the position with respect to the Exclusive List, the Concurrent List, and the Residual List in terms of the relations between the federal government and the unit territories. I concluded: 'This, Mr Speaker, is Federation today. Anything else may be what you like to call it, but it is not Federation.'

After taking a look at the European Common Market and the Central American Common Market, I continued:

> 'Those who are opposed to the particular line that we put forward, I want to ask them on what do they base their views. Sir, I have heard demands from them; I have heard requests from them. But

what principles, what policy, what trend in world affairs they represent, we are yet to be informed. We do not know. But when they
are examined, to the degree that these demands and requests have
already been put forward, they seem to be nothing else but a
modern dressing for the same old policies and programme which
have strangled us for so long, and for so many centuries – nothing
else but the same isolationism, the same inter-territorial jealousies, the
same insularity, the same absence of a comprehensive conception of
Federation, the same lack of clear economic perspectives, the same
pedestrian approach which can produce nothing but the same
bankruptcy, moral and political, which has stultified our en-
deavours for so long and which rapidly threatens to make us the
laughing stock of the entire world. That is to say, Mr Speaker, if
we are not already the laughing stock.'

The only Federal constitution I could find which paralleled the weak
and anaemic West Indian Federation was the Central African Federation, and 'that ought to be enough to consign our Federation and all
who stand for it today to the eternal damnation which is rightly their
due'. I stated our counter proposals boldly, going so far as to envisage
common action in the field of education.

In concrete terms our proposals meant the surrender of considerable
revenue to the Federal Government by the unit territories. I concluded
what was one of my strongest speeches in the Legislative Council with
a peroration to the many thousands listening in in Trinidad as well as
in the other territories, onward to independence. I said:

'There is nothing we have to be afraid of except ourselves. In 1867
Canada was like us in 1959 and it did not have our oil; it did not
have the considerable development of the resources as in Trinidad,
Jamaica, British Guiana and elsewhere. All that we have to do is to
go on to independence, go on in the tradition of all the great
Federations of the past and present, go on in accordance with the
laws of world politics and world economics, go on by our own
resources – mental and material – trying to develop a society which
would satisfy the aspirations of our people – full national independence, nationhood, organisation of our economy in the national
interest . . . independence on April 22, 1960 when, if I may
speak for myself, I would look forward to the Walls of Jericho
come tumbling down to the acclamations of the population.'

We made major studies on the question of Federation. The first of these was entitled *The Economics of Nationhood* and was presented to the Council with my motion. The first part set out the division of powers proposed, with 'the right to impose taxation' on the Exclusive List and industrial development and economic and social planning on the Concurrent List. I wrote:

'These islands have a long history of insularity, even of isolation, rooted in the historical development of their economy and trade and the difficulties of communications for centuries. No amount of subjective, that is to say historical, cultural or other activity of the time can be expected to overcome this heritage. Only a powerful and centrally directed economic co-ordination and interdependence can create the true foundations of a nation. Barbados will not unify with St. Kitts, or Trinidad with British Guiana, or Jamaica with Antigua. They will be knit together only through their common allegiance to a Central Government. Anything else will discredit the conception of Federation, and in the end leave the islands more divided than before.'

Our second study was an elaboration of the case for economic aid and saw the light, officially, in October 1960. It was entitled *Economic Development of the Independent West Indies Federation I – The case for United Kingdom Assistance*. Prepared in the Office of the Premier and Ministry of Finance, it had the *imprimatur* of the Cabinet. We gave priority to the development of greater and improved transport facilities between the Territories, and proposed a West Indian National Air and Sea Transport Service. We emphasised the need of technical assistance for the smaller territories at all levels. And we paid particular attention to planned migration within the area. We dealt with the mechanism of federal economic planning. We analysed the development needs of each territory in relation to the requirements of integration and the availability of funds. And then we proceeded to propose a programme of United Kingdom economic aid for the period 1959–60 to 1968–69.

Summarised, our proposals were that, for the ten-year period, the West Indies should receive the sum of $316·1 million in Development Grants. Of this total $171·1 million would go to the Leewards and Windwards combined, $8·3 million to Barbados, $38·2 million to Trinidad and Tobago, $33 million to Jamaica, $64·9 million to the Federal Government. If British Guiana was included, the total grant for the ten-year period would be $442·1 million. The Federation I proposed was always intended to include British Guiana.

Our third study related to the prospect of Britain joining the European Common Market. Entitled *European Integration and West Indian Trade*, it was closely related to the case for economic aid and was published in September 1960. The thesis of the document was contained in the following paragraph:

'There was a time when the prosperity and wellbeing of the people of Britain depended upon the products of the West Indies. The foundations of Britain's greatness and wealth were laid, in effect, by the efforts of the ancestors of the present peoples of the West Indies. The opportunity is now available to the people of Britain, by a conscious act of policy of Her Majesty's Government, to ensure the future well-being of the West Indies, not only by preserving intact the share of the British market which their products now enjoy, but also by providing them with the means of increasing both the range and the efficiency of their economic activities.'

We commissioned Dr. T. O. Elias of Nigeria and Dr. Gordon Lewis of Puerto Rico to do further studies in the field of a strong Federal Government. These studies were entitled: *Federation vs Confederation and the Nigerian Federation*, and *Puerto Rico: A Case Study in the Problems of Contemporary American Federalism*. Both were published by the Government of Trinidad and Tobago in 1960. Both attacked the Jamaican conception of Federation root and branch.

Our final study related to migration and freedom of movement. Before PNM's 1956 victory it had been agreed that freedom of movement would be deferred for five years. On the occasion of its selection as the federal capital site, Trinidad and Tobago had undertaken to lift its restrictions on workmen coming to Trinidad to build the federal capital. We went further than this, and as a gesture in 1958 we lifted the restrictions. The result was that 10,135 West Indians came to Trinidad and Tobago on temporary permits which 7,794 exceeded. This was clearly unsatisfactory. We had presented the case for our integrated Federation with a Federal Government endowed with wide powers for the development of the national economy. Freedom of movement of persons could not be divorced from freedom of movement of goods and capital.

It was for this reason that, in our case for economic aid, we argued

for planned migration and proposed for Trinidad and Tobago 'a substantial capital grant to meet some of the serious economic and social
problems created by freedom of movement which will result from
independence.'

The situation became more serious as the pressures on West Indian
migrants increased in the United Kingdom. I made this clear to the
Legislative Council on February 3, 1961:

> 'If you close the door in the United Kingdom, Trinidad and
> Tobago has the pressure to open its doors. In the territories that
> now send very few emigrants to Trinidad and Tobago there is a
> fairly large emigration to the United Kingdom; Antigua 353
> against 34; Barbados 1,514 against 295; Dominica 1,116 against 70
> (for every 15 or 16 that go to the United Kingdom one comes to
> Trinidad); Montserrat 455 as against 24 (20 go, to one who comes
> to Trinidad); St. Kitts 705 to 41; St. Lucia 970 to 334. Those are
> close to Trinidad, but can anyone prophesy, Mr. Speaker, that if
> there was difficulty in the Jamaicans going to the United Kingdom,
> the 12,573 Jamaicans who went to the United Kingdom as against
> the 32 who came to Trinidad, the picture will not change and
> Trinidad might provide an avenue for many more Jamaicans than
> it now does? Where you have a little limited emigration to the
> United Kingdom you have a large immigration into Trinidad.
> Grenada 594 to 3,274, almost six to one; St. Vincent 310 to 2,011,
> nearly seven to one. . . .
>
> The position is that today, Mr. Speaker, the emigration from
> Trinidad and Tobago to the United Kingdom is relatively small;
> whatever the void that is left by that emigration, it is filled up many
> times over by the immigration from Grenada and St. Vincent. In
> 1958, 939 Trinidadians went to the United Kingdom and we got
> 4,894 from the rest of the Federation; a net gain to Trinidad and
> Tobago by migration of 3,747. In 1959 where 1,073 went to the
> United Kingdom from Trinidad we got from the rest of the
> Federation 6,360; nearly six to one. For every one who goes, six
> come in. The situation obviously will not be improved if you close
> the British door.'

The Federal Constitution of 1958 was incompatible with the strong
Federal Government propounded by the PNM. It therefore had to be
drastically amended, and PNM concentrated on this from the start.
A Committee of the Legislative Group of the PNM was appointed

with myself as chairman, to make proposals which, based on a clause-by-clause study of the Federal Constitution, were submitted, through the General Council, to a Special Convention held on September 5 and 6, 1959. They were accepted unchanged by the Convention and thereafter became the PNM's guide in the Legislative Council, and in our contacts with our Federal colleagues in the West Indian Federal Party.

We of the PNM fought this issue of Federation alone. We got no help from the Opposition in the Legislative Council. Their principal spokesman on March 1, 1957, in discussing the problems arising out of the selection of Trinidad as the Federal Capital laid great stress on his parochialism – he was 'not willing to sacrifice Trinidadians for the benefit of any small islander, however parochial I may be termed. . . . Trinidad before the West Indies as far as I am concerned.' In the debate on my motion for a strong federation on September 11, 1959, he asked:

'What has the Constitution of Switzerland, New Zealand and all these places got to do with Trinidad? What has it got to do with us? What has the Constitution of Canada, America, Australia and New Zealand got to do with Trinidad and the West Indies?'

He berated me for advocating a Federation 'so powerful that it will have the right to secede at any time from the Commonwealth of Nations'. In woeful ignorance of the problems faced by Canada in Quebec, by Nigeria with its tribalism, and by Malaya with the Chinese, he accused me:

'He has quite conveniently forgotten to tell us that these various Federations are made up of one type of people, one common nationality with the same language, the same aims, the same aspirations, the same hopes, people who by common link, common ties, common nationality are solidly bound to each other. He has forgotten to tell us that the West Indies is the melting pot of races of various cultures, of varying loyalties, of various idiosyncrasies, so that it was not easy to rouse that spirit of nationalism which the Premier regrets so very much. . . .'

He described my proposals as extravagant, and claimed that my case for a strong federation was 'enough to destroy the Federation'. The

Opposition spokesman concluded that they would take no further part in the debate.

And so we moved to the Intergovernmental Conference on the Federal Constitution, convened by the Federal Government at Federal House in Port-of-Spain. The first began on September 28, 1959 and ended on October 8. The second met from May 2 to May 16, 1961. I attended both as head of the Trinidad and Tobago Government and leader of the Trinidad and Tobago delegation.

The Government of Trinidad and Tobago made careful preparations for the Conferences. On January 30, 1959, I appointed a special committee of Government experts to study the problem of Customs Union and on February 20 I appointed a sub-committee of this Committee to study the existing concessions and incentives to industry. This was followed by a careful analysis by the Office of the Premier and the Ministry of Finance of some eight or nine papers prepared by the Federal Government and circulated to all territories on various matters which the Federal Government proposed for inclusion in the agenda of the Conference. We worked out very clear and precise views as to the difference between the Federal proposals and our own thinking, and as to methods of bridging the gap between the two where a gap existed.

Trinidad and Tobago went into the Intergovernmental Conference armed with facts and figures based on historical precedents and economic analysis and with concrete proposals for a fundamental revision of the Federal Constitution.

We had a further advantage. We went to the Conference with concrete proposals for Dominion Status; we had even fixed a date, April 22, 1960, which had been popularised all over the country and which had been found to be generally acceptable. The date was not an arbitrary one pulled out of a hat. It was the date proposed by a Special Convention of our Party as far back as September 1957, a Convention which had considered the Election Manifesto for the Federal Elections. That Convention had decided that Dominion Status should not be envisaged in any vague period like 'within the first five years', or 'at the earliest possible moment'. It preferred to fix a precise date – two years after the inauguration of the First Federal Parliament, in other words, April 22, 1960.

With respect to the economic implications of Dominion Status, we were able to tell our colleagues in and out of the Conference that there was no reason why the West Indies should be in any worse position in respect of existing preferential markets than other Commonwealth

countries like India, Ghana and Malaya. We drew attention to the
International Sugar Agreement which assured a guaranteed market
for West Indies sugar up to 1966, Dominion Status or no Dominion
Status, the price being fixed by negotiation, each year. The Governments concerned, including Trinidad and Tobago, were then studying
proposals for British assistance to the citrus industry until 1964,
no matter what happened on the issue of Dominion Status in the
intervening years.

The question of Development and Welfare grants was very important
for most of the territories, particularly Jamaica, which, up to the end
of March, 1959, had received some $45 million from this source. It had
relatively no importance for Trinidad and Tobago, whose receipts
from this source had been approximately $7 million. Nevertheless,
we drew attention to the fact that the abolition of colonialism and the
substitution of Dominion Status would merely substitute one form
of financial assistance for another. If Development and Welfare grants
were no longer available to the West Indies when it became a Dominion, we could get assistance from Commonwealth as distinct from
colonial sources.

As one example we gave the activities of the Colonial Development
Finance Company. In addition there was a whole series of international and foreign as well as commonwealth institutions and
agencies which gave assistance in one form or another to former
colonies. This was one of the reasons why we urged a strong Federal
Government. Such a Government would be in the best position to
take advantage of these opportunities for international assistance and
to ensure that the best use was made of such assistance in the interest
of the West Indies as a whole.

It was in this atmosphere that the Conference began, proceeded
and adjourned. The first argument that developed was on the agenda
of the Conference. What was the Conference to discuss? From the
start the problem was posed in all its nakedness. The Conference
appointed a Steering Committee to work out a draft agenda. I represented Trinidad and Tobago on the Steering Committee. The Committee ended in complete deadlock after nearly four hours. The
Jamaica representative insisted that the Conference must discuss first
the basis of representation in the House of Representatives. All the
other members of the Committee unanimously disagreed with
Jamaica. They agreed with Trinidad and Tobago, Dominion Status
first. The Jamaica representative insisted, however, on submitting a
minority report.

The argument was therefore transferred to the Conference itself. The Jamaica delegation proposed the adoption of Jamaica's minority report, warning that, if that was not done, Jamaica would not be able to participate in discussion of other items of the agenda. There was general resistance from the Conference. Another deadlock ensued, and this was broken at the end of the morning session of the second day when, on behalf of the Trinidad and Tobago delegation, I pleaded with the Conference to let Jamaica have its way and take the issue of representation whenever it pleased, first, last, or in the middle.

The Conference then got under way and Jamaica presented its case. The case was simplicity itself – recognition of the principle of representation on the basis of population, and adoption of a formula of one seat for every 50,000 of population, on the understanding that no territory was to have fewer seats than it then enjoyed. On the basis of 1957 population figures this would yield a total House of 65 with a Jamaica contingent of 32. The Jamaica delegation added that, if its case was not conceded, it would take no further part in the Conference, and that on this matter Government and Opposition were presenting a united front and expressing public opinion in Jamaica.

Whilst there was a general readiness to concede the principle enunciated by Jamaica, there was a general fear of the consequences of such a dominating position, and Jamaica's truculence did nothing to allay those fears. The Trinidad and Tobago delegation, through me, drew attention to the other factors involved. We emphasised the inequality of the position of Trinidad and Tobago whose higher *per capita* contribution paralleled Jamaica's greater population resources. We stressed the nature of the compromise between population, finance and area which had been agreed upon nine years ago. We urged that the question of increased representation could not be divorced from the consideration of the nature and powers of the Federation – whether it was to be a Dominion based on customs union, etc. I therefore moved that the matter of representation be referred to a committee for study 'in the context of the financial, economic, legislative or other factors involved in a West Indies Federation with Dominion Status'.

The Jamaica delegation resisted this proposal to the end and persisted in their stand. We then proceeded to demolish the Jamaican formula, in itself, on the basis of Australian precedents, and on the inconsistency of a principle which involved exceptions for seven out of ten territories. On the fifth day of weary wrangling, after I had rejected a private United Kingdom suggestion that we should abandon the Conference and proceed to refer the agenda items to study by

Committees, I put forward a peace formula to the Conference. The formula involved the increase of the number of the House from 45 to 73 based on two principles – the allocation of one basic seat to each territory and thereafter the adoption of the Jamaica ratio of one seat to 50,000 persons or any part of 50,000 above one-half. This formula gave Jamaica 34 seats out of 73, a percentage of 46·6 as compared with the percentage of 49·2 claimed by them.

Jamaica accepted our proposal subject to the elimination of the fractions – one seat for 50,000 exactly and for no part whatever thereafter. The result was to give Jamaica 34 out of 69 seats, the exact percentage it had claimed in the first instance. After one week we were back where we had started. Trinidad and Tobago withdrew its offer and moved that the Conference proceed with the rest of the Agenda. I told the Conference that I could think of only one historical parallel – several centuries ago when someone had thrown the whole world into a turmoil over a diphthong; now Jamaica threatened to throw the whole West Indies into a turmoil over a fraction. They had come to the Conference with 17 seats out of 45. They came to demand 32 out of 65. We offered them 34 out of 73. They retaliated with a demand for 34 out of 69.

The Prime Minister of the Federation proposed at the beginning of our second week that we should refer everything to various committees, and that the Federal Government should be requested to prepare terms of reference for those committees; he expressed the hope that these terms of reference would be accepted without discussion or with a minimum of discussion. Jamaica agreed. Trinidad and Tobago disagreed. Five territories voted for the Prime Minister's proposal; the others including Trinidad and Tobago, Jamaica and Barbados abstained. The Jamaica delegation indicated that there was no reason for more than one of its advisers to remain for this stage of the Conference and left for home.

Every effort was made to avoid or evade basic discussions. Students of Church history will understand my reference to the turmoil over a diphthong. Behind that turmoil lay the uncompromising assertion by Athanasius the Great of the two fundamental Christian truths of the unity of God and the divinity of Christ as against the heresy of Arianism that Jesus Christ was neither truly God nor truly man. Behind the turmoil over the fraction lay the uncompromising assertion of Trinidad and Tobago of the two fundamental West Indian truths of economic integration and Dominion Status as against the position of Jamaica that was neither truly Federation nor truly Confederation.

And so the Conference petered out, dragging, like Pope's Alexandrine, its weary length along until the end of its ninth working day.

The Conference was a failure, a dismal failure, a failure of the Territories to prepare for grappling with the issues. There were, however, important lessons to be drawn from it.

For one thing it revealed the powerful cross currents of two diametrically opposed conceptions of Federation. The conflict between those two conceptions had to come into the open next time. The Committees had been given specific terms of reference which must bring them into the open. The proposals of the Trinidad and Tobago Government, accepted or not, would form the basis of subsequent discussions. People would be for or against. They could not evade, by-pass or ignore them; they could not remain neutral. The figures put forward by us were not a blueprint. They were tentative, but we insisted upon them to prevent the very vagueness and abstractness and even refusal to discuss which characterised this Conference.

We were not raising the question of independence and a strong Federal Government for abstract reasons either of pride in the first place or limitation of previous Federations in the second place. For us it was the very life of the Federation which was at stake. Independence meant the turning of the minds and ideas of the West Indies from London and the Colonial Office, which had hitherto been our centre, to the Federal Capital, where the politics and economics of the West Indies would be decided. It was through such a political medium also that we of the West Indies would be able to unite ourselves.

The Government of Trinidad and Tobago independently initiated its studies of its own during the period after the inconclusive conference in 1959. We also made three special studies: the first of Jamaica's economic viability; the second comparing Tobago with the smaller Units of the Federation; and the third estimating the total cost of Government at all levels in the West Indies. Some of this information was made public in my Budget speech of April 12, 1961 and in the ensuing Budget Debate.

Thus the Intergovernmental Conference of 1961 was vastly better prepared, politically and intellectually, than its predecessor in 1959. It had a vast mass of documents before it, the result of studies, collective or individual, by people who were themselves West Indians, by birth or by adoption. The 1961 Conference was also better prepared, psychologically. The eighteen months which had elapsed between the two conferences had seen the excesses of Cuba on the one hand, the extravagances of the Congo on the other. Sitting around the conference table as equals of the United Kingdom and the United States of America, we had worked out a new agreement on Chaguaramas and other leased areas. The Secretary of State for the Colonies, Mr. Macleod, had come in June 1960, and the Prime Minister of the United Kingdom, Mr. Macmillan had followed him in March 1961; both had brought us the same message, hurry to independence. During the conference itself the United States Government announced the establishment of a diplomatic mission in the Federal Capital with the head of the mission holding the rank of Ambassador.

The Intergovernmental Conference resumed under the best possible auspices. It resumed too late rather than too soon. The Committees of the Conference were instructed to report by March 31, 1960. For various reasons they did not do so, and it was only in November of 1960 that the Working Party was appointed. The Government of Trinidad and Tobago was unsuccessful in its efforts to achieve resumption of the Conference earlier in 1961. Eventually it was only at a meeting held in Port-of-Spain on February 11 under the chairmanship of the Parliamentary Under Secretary of State for the Colonies in the United Kingdom, Mr. Hugh Fraser, who was in Trinidad in connection with the signing of the new Leased Bases Agreement, that agreement was reached on the Trinidad and Tobago proposal – resumption of the Intergovernmental Conference on May 2; commencement of the Independence Conference on May 31 in London.

The 1959 Intergovernmental Conference had, by its very failure, made one fundamental point stand out starkly – if there was to be a Federation, there had to be an accommodation between the divergent views of Trinidad and Tobago and Jamaica. If no such accommodation was possible, there would be no Federation. For Jamaica, referendum or no referendum, would walk out of the Federation if it failed to secure some of the safeguards which, rightly or wrongly, it demanded; and if Jamaica left, Trinidad and Tobaco had made it clear that it would not undertake to carry the rest of the Federation.

Now the only way to find out if an accommodation is possible is by discussion. As Premier of Trinidad and Tobago, with the foreknowledge of a few of my colleagues, I initiated these discussions privately and informally with Mr. Manley, Premier of Jamaica, as early as February 1960 in Port-of-Spain. We continued them at another meeting in Port-of-Spain in May. The top official advisers to both Premiers met over a weekend in Jamaica later in that month. Mr. Manley and I met again in Port-of-Spain in June 1960, this time with

Mr. Macleod. And then, by mutual agreement, after some study had been given to the ideas which emerged from these informal discussions, I met Mr. Manley in Antigua in September; two of my top civil service advisers were present and one of his.

Let me summarise the divergent positions of Trinidad and Tobago and Jamaica so that the problem involved in finding a compromise formula which would preserve the Federation can be seen.

The Trinidad and Tobago position was that, taking into account the urgent need of economic development in the area and the long tradition of insularity, the Federal Government should be endowed with sufficient powers and adequate revenues to promote the integration and co-ordinations of the several insular economies. This philosophy involved, in our view, the placing on the Exclusive List, on which the Federal Government could alone legislate, such matters as (1) the right to impose taxation, subject to a Financial Agreement with the Territories, (2) customs, (3) external loans for the Territories, (4) external and internal loans for the Federation (5) external debts of the Territories, (6) external and internal trade, (7) postal services, (8) civil aviation, (9) television and radio broadcasting, (10) education, (11) a common system of law for the Territories, (12) aliens. On the Concurrent List, on which both the Federal and Territorial Governments could legislate, with Federal Law superseding Territorial Law in case of conflict, Trinidad and Tobago placed such matters as (1) industrial development, (2) economic and social planning, (3) social security, (4) price control and production controls, (5) trade unions, (6) labour legislation, (7) savings banks and development banks, (8) the raising of internal loans by the Territories. The effect of this assumption of Territorial services by the Federation and the corresponding transfer of the revenues involved in our proposals an annual Federal revenue of some $143 million in the first instance of which Trinidad and Tobago would provide $59 million – or 41 per cent of the total – and Jamaica $64 million – or 46 per cent of the total.

As against Trinidad and Tobago's conception of a Federal Government playing an active and positive role in the integration of the national economy, Jamaica presented its conception of a Federal Government shorn of all powers in this field. Jamaica advanced the view that 'the stability of the Federal future and the ability of the Federal Government to make a reasonable contribution to the development of the economies of the smaller Units and to the expansion of the services which they require depends upon maintaining and expanding the economic development programme of the two main islands.

Jamaica and Trinidad, which together contribute over 80% of all the resources of the Federation.'

These were the two opposing conceptions of Federation, and students of Federal systems of Government will find nothing unique about them. Similar problems have existed elsewhere. An obvious opportunity for compromise immediately presented itself. Jamaica was insistent that the Federation should start off with limited powers and assume more as it developed competence, familarity and expertise. Trinidad and Tobago, on its side, had not attempted to date its proposals; it had not said now for now, ten years or twenty years. The formula agreed to as a possible basis of reconciliation between Mr. Manley and myself was this; accept Trinidad and Tobago philosophy in principle but delay the exercise of the Federal powers. Mr. Manley coined the phrase 'Reserve List'. The Reserve List, however, involved further agreement on two points – (a) the period of delay, (b) the procedure for transferring matters from the inactive to the active Federal List.

In this general context of a Reserve List, on which would be placed the two items of greatest concern to Jamaica – industrial development and income tax – there were two further safeguards Jamaica insisted upon: (a) representation on the basis of population, (b) the Council of Ministers. The first was simplicity itself, and Trinidad and Tobago had little difficulty in accepting what in fact is a fundamental principle of the representative system. We made only one reservation – representation must be on the basis of the 1960 population figures and not on the basis of the 1958 estimates which Jamaica had originally used. On this basis, which the Conference accepted, Jamaica, which then had 17 seats, would obtain 30 seats out of a House of 64; and Trinidad and Tobago, which then had 10 seats, would have 16 seats.

It was also easy for Trinidad and Tobago to accept the Council of Ministers. Its principal justification was the traditions of insularity and provincialism which strangled us at every step. We had no traditions of political co-operation and consultation in the West Indies. Our whole history was against us, three centuries of history.

Once the Intergovernmental Conference had taken the basic decision to leave economic development in the hands of the Unit Territories, then it became almost mandatory to ensure in the Constitution protection of the Territorial interests recognised by the Constitution. In respect of such matters as radio broadcasting, television, telephone services, and civil aviation, the Conference specifically agreed that Unit Territories should have the right to operate such services under

the overall Federal regulatory umbrella. The question then arose as
to the protection of these Territorial prerogatives against Federal
encroachment. That was why Trinidad and Tobago supported the
proposition that it should be specially stipulated that whenever the
Federal Government proposed to assume responsibility in whole or
in part for any subject or service on the Concurrent Legislative List
which had hitherto been within the jurisdiction of a Unit or Units,
the matter must first be discussed in the Council of Ministers. This was
all part and parcel of the recognition of the rights and interests of the
Territories which led Trinidad and Tobago to propose successfully to
the Conference that Senators must be selected by the Cabinets of the
Territories and that Montserrat, notwithstanding its size, must have
equal representation in the Senate.

What really happened at the Conference was this. Trinidad and
Tobago had from the start proposed a Federation in which economic
development was primarily the responsibility of the Federal Government. Jamaica had from the start proposed a Federation in which
economic development was primarily the responsibility of the Territorial Governments. When the Conference accepted the Jamaica
proposal for the transfer of industrial development and income tax to
the reserve list, it in effect stated that the Jamaica conception of gradual
growth would prevail. We of the Trinidad and Tobago Government
mandated by the Cabinet, at once pointed out that this decision on
industrial development and income tax could not be considered in
isolation, and must be applied to the whole wide field of economic
development. I specifically warned the Conference that they were
creating a patchwork Federation, and that we would not allow them
to take out of Trinidad and Tobago's proposals what they liked while
rejecting the rest. I told them unambiguously: 'If you are patching,
patch; Trinidad and Tobago will add a few patches of its own.'

We adopted this stand, because we could see no other way of saving
the Federation, because we were convinced that to insist on our conception would break up the Federation. We disagreed with Jamaica's
thinking on the subject. We believed Jamaica's fears exaggerated. But,
if to save the Federation it was necessary for us to respect those fears,
to respect apprehensions which would, at worst, drive Jamaica out of
the Federation, or might, at best, jeopardise Jamaica's stability and
thus endanger Jamaica's capacity to contribute, jointly with Trinidad
and Tobago, over 80 per cent of Federal revenues, by whatever formula you derived those revenues, then we of Trinidad and Tobago
decided that Jamaica was not to be pushed to the wall, Jamaica was to

be saved for the Federation, and the growth of the Federal power would be more gradual than in our hearts we had originally anticipated.

We of the Trinidad and Tobago delegation urged the Conference to appreciate Jamaica's difficulties and understand, if even it did not accept, Jamaica's fear that these difficulties might be aggravated by Federal lack of expertise. We stated publicly that it was because we recognised these difficulties that we would accept Jamaica's stand on representation, the Council of Ministers, the Reserve List, the phasing of Customs Union over nine years. But we indicated to Jamaica that, in our opinion, it did not sufficiently emphasise the advantages Jamaica would gain from Federation. One such advantage was the economies in respect of defence and diplomatic representation. Another was the advantage in trade negotiations conducted by an independent West Indies. A third was that internal free trade, by exposing Jamaica's industry to the gentle breeze of competition from Trinidad, would prepare it for the ruder shock of world competition from which it could not indefinitely hope to insulate itself. And finally we pointed to the Postal Services as a concrete gain to Jamaica from Federation – transfer of the Postal Services to the Federal Government meant the transfer by Jamaica of an annual deficit of $2\frac{3}{4}$ million as against a transfer by Trinidad and Tobago of an annual surplus of $\frac{1}{3}$ million. We therefore asked the Jamaica delegation to the Conference to reconsider their stand on the method of transfer from the Reserve List – in other words we asked Jamaica, in return for our recognition of her present difficulties and our readiness to agree to a ten-year moratorium on the subjects on the Reserve List, not to subject the Federation after ten years to a veto of a single Territory in circumstances that could conceivably be quite different and not as favourable to Jamaica as they then were. Mr. Manley agreed to this, and we awaited a new Jamaican formula at the London Conference.

From this basic decision of the Conference everything else flowed, at least as far as Trinidad and Tobago was concerned. The Conference had decided to leave economic development, at that stage, in the hands of the Territories. This, as far as Trinidad and Tobago was concerned, applied to economic development in general, especially to freedom of movement.

There were those who, like Manley, argued that Trinidad and Tobago sought unreasonably to attach freedom of movement to other issues, particularly customs union. There was nothing the least bit unreasonable about the attachment, which was explicit in the preamble to the existing Federal Constitution, and implicit in the article of that Constitution providing for constitutional review after five years. The Conference, without any controversy, adopted the report of its Committee which recommended that Customs Union should be phased over a period of nine years, at the end of which certain basic commodities would still be excluded which involved contractual obligations on the part of the Territories whose peculiar circumstances warranted special treatment. Such exemptions were the cement, meat and milk of Jamaica, the rum of Dominica, and the crude oil imports of Trinidad and Tobago. If such was the decision on the freedom of movement of goods, a similar line of reasoning necessarily must be applied to the freedom of movement of persons, especially as it was quite certain that the significant effects of customs union were not likely to be felt by Trinidad's industries until after the end of the transitional period of nine years.

The Trinidad and Tobago Delegation advanced four principal arguments on the question of freedom of movement. The first was that, since the Conference had agreed with Jamaica to place industrial development and income tax on a Reserve List, to phase customs union over the nine years, and to take economic and social planning off the Concurrent List, it was therefore illogical to give the Federal Government an exclusive power over freedom of movement between Territories which had the exclusive power to determine their own economic development. People could not be allowed freely to come to a Territory to find a job in factories whose products could not be freely sold in the Territory from which they came. We therefore proposed, on instructions from the Cabinet, that, whilst Freedom of Movement should be placed on the Exclusive Legislative List, the Federal Government should be debarred from exercising its powers in this field until such time as it assumed jurisdiction over the subjects on the Reserve List.

Our second principal argument was that freedom of movement, originating as it does in lack of employment opportunities in the exporting country, could conceivably inflict an injury on the smaller exporting countries. After all, large-scale migration from Jamaica with 1½ million people was something vastly different from large-scale migration from Grenada with 88,000 people, or Tobago with 33,000, or Montserrat with 12,000. We put the argument this way, with particular reference to Grenada. Grenada legitimately was concerned with its economic development. That meant jobs for its people. Where were the people to find these jobs – in Grenada or in other countries? To put the question differently – was capital to be brought to the available workers in Grenada, or were the available workers in Grenada to be taken to the capital in other countries?

The third principal argument advanced by Trinidad and Tobago on the question of freedom of movement had to do with the cost for Trinidad and Tobago. We had studied this very carefully. We had assumed an average of the migration over the years 1958 and 1959, taking as the annual minimum the 5,000 migrants of 1958, and as a maximum the figure of 12,000 based on the arrivals for the peak months of January, February and April 1959. We worked out the average at 7,500 a year. On this basis we put the following facts before the Conference:

1. This migration would add at least 1 per cent annually to our population but would represent between 22 and 54 per cent of the annual increment to our population from natural increase, which was already the highest in the West Indies.

2. This annual migration would represent between 2 and 4 per cent of the labour force; but, assuming that 75 per cent of the migrants were job seekers, this would represent two-thirds of the annual net increment to our labour force from natural increase, in a society with large-scale unemployment and underemployment.

3. The cost of placing these migrants in jobs in secondary industries, allowing for a capital investment in manufacturing industry of $7,500 per worker per annum, would be $422 millions in ten years.

4. The cost of placing these migrants in decent houses, allowing for 2-bedroom family units of $7,000 each at 1960 prices, would mean a Government investment over 10 years of $70 millions to take care of two-thirds of the migrating families.

5. The cost of providing school places for the children of these migrants, at 1960 prices, would be $1·3 million in capital expenditure and $5·5 million in recurrent expenditure over 10 years, exclusive of the $8·3 million in capital expenditure needed for the existing backlog of 50,000 children, and exclusive also of the $10·2 million in capital expenditure which we estimated would be needed to satisfy the annual new demand in the decade for school places resulting from the natural increase in population.

6. The cost of providing an adequate water supply for these migrants over ten years we estimated at $11 million.

The fourth principal argument was the historical. Our opponents claimed that there can be no Federation, no West Indian citizenship, without freedom of movement. But the opposition went further and claimed that freedom of movement was included specifically in the

constitutions of Nigeria and Malaya. We had to point out that the
Nigerian and Malayan Constitutions gave the Federal Government
exclusive or concurrent power over the very subjects which the West
Indies Federal Government would not control.

But the historical argument adduced by our opponents was a fallacy.
The Nigerian Constitution permitted the Regional Governments to
impose restrictions on freedom of movement on grounds of defence,
public safety, public order, public morality or public health – very
wide powers, indeed. The Treaty establishing the European Economic
Community specifically links freedom of movement of workers to
freedom of movement of goods and capital, and spreads it over a
transitional period of twelve years which can, in certain circumstances, be extended to a maximum of fifteen years.

The Treaty goes on to exclude from this phased and restricted
freedom of movement the right to employment in the public administration, and prescribes that freedom of movement shall be worked out
on the basis of a carefully prepared plan which must ensure close
collaboration between national labour administrations, and which
would involve 'setting up appropriate machinery for connecting
offers of employment and requests for employment, with a view to
equilibrating them in such a way as to avoid serious threats to the
standard of living and employment in the various regions and
industries'.

There was no passion in our arguments, only logic, reason, objective
economic analysis, and historical precedents. No one therefore could
take seriously the opposing delegation which stated that it was not
interested in our statistics – how can one initiate Federal economic
planning if one is not interested in statistics of employment and costs
of development? No one could take seriously the argument that
another Government would be only too glad to pay pauper allowances to any of its migrants who might become public charges in
Trinidad; if pauper allowances must be paid they are better paid in
the home Territory. No one could take seriously the argument that
there was much potential in Trinidad for agricultural development to
produce some of the food that is now imported; the food can be produced in the Territory that sends the migrants and can then be
exported to Trinidad, while Trinidad is now steadily improving its
local food supply with local labour. No one could take seriously the
argument that restrictions of freedom of movement to Trinidad could
encourage restrictions on West Indian freedom of movement in the
United Kingdom. We contrasted for the Conference the situation

in the United Kingdom, where during the third quarter of 1960 there were 244,376 adult outstanding vacancies and 17,684 West Indian migrant arrivals, and in Trinidad and Tobago where in May 1960 there were 38,300 unemployed and 20,200 underemployed, with over 6,000 migrants arriving in 1959.

Apart from the question of freedom of movement, the other great issues at the Conference involved the questions of the powers of the Federal Government, the sources of Federal revenue, and the Federal Budget.

The question of powers of the Federal Government could not be considered in the abstract, divorced from the basic decision on economic development. It was therefore logical for Trinidad and Tobago to insist on Unit participation in the field of foreign affairs especially when a Federal Government as such would necessarily have no previous experience in such matters as Venezuela relations, and especially when the compromise arrangements on the Chaguaramas question had recently yielded such satisfactory results. Briefly, our position was that a Unit Territory should have the right to negotiate on matters within its legislate competence with a foreign government, subject to keeping the Federal Government informed at all stages of the negotiations, and subject to Federal ratification of any agreement reached.

The Conference decision on sources of revenue stemmed logically from its decision to leave economic development within the jurisdiction of the Territories and to phase customs union over a period of years. An earlier proposal had suggested three sources of Federal revenue: consumption duties on five selected commodities (gasoline, rum, beer, other spirits, cigarettes), plus a percentage of income tax revenue plus a percentage of revenue from import duties. The argument was that the Federal Government would, through the consumption duties, have an independent taxing power, whilst, through a percentage of income tax revenue, it would be taxing the rich. These arguments, fallacious in themselves, missed the entire point. If economic development was to remain the prerogative of the Territories, no one could possibly expect the Territories to subject themselves to an arbitrary Federal power over select commodities which would, in the case of Trinidad and Tobago, be certain to affect not only our large revenue from these sources but also the local consumption of these commodities.

The same held true of income tax. The Conference could not agree in one breath to put income tax on the reserve list, and in the other, before even we had agreed on the method of taking it off the reserve list, give the Federal Government the constitutional right to a fixed percentage of income tax revenue. In other words, the Conference could not have its cake and eat it. Thus, when Jamaica proposed that the main source of Federal revenue should be the revenue from import duties on the items on which tariffs were to be harmonised in Stage I of the Customs Union Plan, this revenue being estimated at over $28 million, the Trinidad and Tobago Delegation immediately supported the Jamaica proposal; this, in fact, was a specific directive from the Cabinet. Jamaica went on to propose two measures to increase Federal revenue: (a) the Federal Government in its discretion should have the right at the end of the first three years to levy a surcharge on all import duties on items not yet under its control, limited to such charge as would produce an overall five per cent increase of the total yield on such terms; (b) the Federal Government should have the right to raise the import duties on the items on which the tariff was to be harmonised in the first three years.

The Trinidad and Tobago delegation was unable to accept either of these proposals. It proposed instead, and the Conference agreed, that any additional revenue over the $28 million that the Federal Government might need after the first three years should be provided by a contribution by the Territorial Governments of not more than five per cent of the revenue from import duties on the items not to be harmonised in the first stage of the Customs Union Plan.

The argument over sources of revenue was purely academic. Six different combinations were considered by one of the Intergovernmental Committees designed to provide the Federal Government with a revenue of either $25 million or $30 million. All the proposals had two points in common. First, Jamaica and Trinidad and Tobago combined, which then provided 82 per cent of the Mandatory Levy, would continue to provide over 80 per cent of the proposed Federal Revenue. The second point which all the proposals had in common was that Trinidad and Tobago's *per capita* contribution was higher than any other.

Time did not allow the Conference to proceed adequately with any of the fundamental and vital issues which, at the insistence of the Government of Trinidad and Tobago, were included on the Conference Agenda. These were: (a) United Kingdom defence assistance, (b) the European Common Market, (c) United Kingdom economic aid, (d) Migration to the United Kingdom. All these were reserved for London, with Trinidad and Tobago leading the way.

The other vital question facing us in London was the date of independence. As instructed by our Cabinet, we proposed at the Conference that April 22, 1962, be designated Independence Day and be declared an annual public holiday throughout the West Indies.

And so we proceeded to the Lancaster House Conference, determined on independence, even though the Federation would be far weaker than we had anticipated. What it all meant was getting the Colonial Office out of our hair. I enlarged on this in my address to the Fourth Annual Convention, when I made it clear: 'Let me state the alternatives bluntly – either a strong independent Federation with all of us, or a weak Federation without Trinidad and Tobago.'

And, lo and behold, Macleod came to the West Indies, Mr. Colonial Office himself, and said I was right and my opponents wrong. Hurry to independence, was Macleod's message. *The Nation*, our party weekly, had a field day. It wrote an 'Open Letter to Dr Williams' on June 24, 1960, in which it stated:

'On the question of independence you have been vilified, abused and ridiculed from end to end of the West Indies. You have been represented as a crazy fanatic, as a man with a chip on his shoulder, as anti-British, as ignorant of reality – there was no term too opprobious to apply to you, simply because of your insistence upon the fact that today the primary necessity of politics, of economic development and of social life in the West Indies, was the attainment of independence. We have lived to hear from a Secretary of State for the Colonies, and a Conservative Government to boot, that for two years they have had on their list as a first priority a Bill for West Indian independence. This means that they were expecting that as soon as possible after April 22, 1958, the West Indies would present such a bill. Not only the delay in presenting it, but the shameful denigration to which you have been subjected will ever remain one of the most scandalous pages in the history of the passing of colonialism. If some shreds of honour and reputation have been saved for us, it is because you and your Party and you alone held the line straight and clear.'

As I told the University at the mass meeting to celebrate the first anniversary of our April 22, 1960, demonstration, 'I can forecast this April 22, 1962, the West Indies Federation will either be independent or there will be no West Indies Federation'. As events proved, it was to be the second of these alternatives – through no fault of ours.

I did not tell the story of the Lancaster House Conference until after the Jamaica referendum. As soon as I returned from the United Kingdom, as head of the delegation, I prepared a report to the community through the then Legislative Council of what transpired. After consulting my colleages it was decided that we would not present that report to the community at that time, we would suppress the report which was approved by all the Trinidad and Tobago delegates to the Lancaster House Conference and was based on extensive notes that I, as head of the delegation, used for my submissions, notes which were expressed publicly, on the basis of the approval of the entire Trinidad and Tobago delegation. I released the report in the Legislative Council on January 12, 1962, when moving the approval of the Governor-General's address which anticipated independence for Trinidad and Tobago. The story reads:

'The first major obstacle at the Lancaster House Conference concerned the question of the Reserve List, that is to say, the power of the Federal Government over industrial development and income tax. . . .

From this emerged the crucial question as to how matters placed on the Reserve List were to be transferred to one of the active Federal Lists. Jamaica proposed that this should take the form of approval by a majority of the Territorial Legislatures representing two-thirds of the population. Trinidad and Tobago made it clear that this attempt to give Jamaica a permanent veto on the normal course of Federal development was offensive in theory and untenable in practice. . . .

Before the Trinidad and Tobago Delegation left for London, however, we were advised by the Jamaica Government that as a result of certain local events at the level of both Government and Party, the Jamaica Delegation was unable to alter the stand proposed in Trinidad and had no room to manœuvre in this matter. In fact, this was the formal position adopted in London by the Jamaica Delegation.

The Trinidad and Tobago Delegation unanimously rejected the Jamaica proposal. We put forward an alternative procedure which, including as it did all the safeguards which Jamaica had at one time or another insisted upon, we felt had a reasonable chance of commending itself not only to our colleagues but also to Jamaica.

The proposal was as follows:

"There should be a moratorium of nine years during which the

items of income tax and industrial development shall remain
on the Reserve List unless the Council of Ministers is unanimous
on the desirability of the transfer of industrial development to
the Concurrent List and income tax to the Exclusive List (subject to a financial agreement between Units and Federal Governments). In this event, the matter would be dealt with by a
simple resolution in both houses of the Federal Parliament. If
there is no unanimous view in the Council of Ministers, the
matter shall be reviewed in the tenth year after Independence
in the manner set out below:

If on the review referred to above there is a majority in the
Council of Ministers in favour of transfer of the items from the
Reserve List, the matter is to be referred to the Legislatures of
the individual territories. If a majority of the Legislatures
representing two-thirds of the population of the Federation
agree to the transfer, the transfer shall take place in the eleventh
year of Independence. If there is no such majority of Territorial
Legislatures, a referendum on the question of transfer shall be
held after a further two years, that is, in the thirteenth year of
Independence, and the matter shall be decided by an absolute
majority of the voting population. If the result of this referendum
is against transfer, the matter cannot be referred for referendum
again for a further period of five years, and the matter can at
that stage be decided only by way of referendum procedure."

As an alternative to this procedure, the Secretary of State for the
Colonies produced an entirely new formula which, to put it as
mildly as possible, took the Trinidad and Tobago Delegation
completely by surprise. The formula was as follows:

"No provision shall be made in the Federal Constitution for the
establishment of a Reserve List. The items of income tax and
industrial development which have hitherto figured in the
Reserve List proposals shall be placed on the Concurrent List.
The Constitution will however provide that the Federal Legislature may not make laws on either of these items on the Concurrent List until a proposal that they should assume these powers
has been approved by a two-thirds majority of each House of
the Federal Legislature and by an absolute majority of the representative House of each Unit Legislature.

There shall be a review at the end of nine years at which, if no
earlier decision has been taken to allow the Federal Legislature to
exercise its powers in this matter, the Federal and Unit Govern-

ments shall consider together whether any change should be made in existing arrangements; provided that in the absence of agreement by all Governments these arrangements shall continue. Further reviews would take place under arrangements to be agreed."

Not a single delegation at the Lancaster House Conference supported the Trinidad and Tobago proposition. On the other hand, Barbados and the Federal Government supported the Secretary of State's formula which was adopted by the Conference with Trinidad and Tobago recording its dissent.

Hon. Members will no doubt appreciate the full significance of the Conference decision. In the first place it transferred the veto power from Jamaica, which Trinidad and Tobago considered offensive, to any single Territory, thereby compounding the offence. It effectively suppressed any prospect of emergence of a movement in Jamaica itself to bring Jamaica more in line with the thinking in other parts of the Federal area. What is much worse, it effectively blocks any hope of effective action on the basis of population by the accession of British Guiana, which would immediately upset the population balance which Jamaica has sought throughout to maintain in its favour. And worst of all, it showed the power of the Colonial Office. As we said privately to the Colonial Office representatives, the power and influence of colonialism were never greater than on its death bed. The Colonial Office had merely to crack the whip and all the Territories fell in line – all the Territories except Trinidad and Tobago.

I turn now to the question of freedom of movement. . . .

The demand was raised for full and immediate freedom of movement, modified by a proposal from the St. Kitts' delegation.

Our first submission was as follows:

(1) Trinidad and Tobago had originally proposed that freedom of movement should be guaranteed by the Constitution. . . .

But this was in the context of a strong Federal Centre adequately equipped, both constitutionally and financially, with the means of integrating the territorial economies.

(2) Contrary to the specific proposals of Trinidad and Tobago in respect of the powers of the Federal Government, the Conference had decided to limit the powers of the Federal Government over the national economy and to leave the important subjects of industrial development and income tax within the sphere of States' rights.

(3) Following on this basic decision by the Conference, the Trinidad and Tobago Delegation has inevitably been forced to make the necessary consequential amendments to its original proposals. We were careful to itemise these for the Conference. . . .

(4) Indiscriminate migration would damage the economy of Trinidad and Tobago where there was already an insufficiency of jobs and an inadequacy of social services.

(5) Frequent references had been made by other Territories to mandates from their population and to the state of public opinion. One Territory had suggested that it would be for Trinidad and Tobago to make out a case. The Trinidad and Tobago Delegation agreed that it would indeed have to make out a case, but that case would be to the people of Trinidad and Tobago and not to the delegates in the Conference Room. I had received a number of telegrams while I was in London which together constituted the unanimous view of the people of Trinidad and Tobago. . . .

(6) The Trinidad and Tobago Delegation had initiated a study of the comparative cost to the Territory of remaining in the Federation and seeking Independence alone, as Independence was top priority for the people of Trinidad and Tobago. We were satisfied that the $10·8 million, which by present estimates Trinidad and Tobago will have to contribute to the $28·3 million decided upon for the Federation, would be more than adequate to meet the cost, if Trinidad and Tobago went it alone, of external representation, defence, and University education. . . .

There was widespread opposition to the new formula proposed by Trinidad and Tobago. The smaller Territories persisted in their claim for immediate freedom of movement. The Premier of Jamaica expressed the view that the new Trinidad formula would vary the commitments he had given to the people of Jamaica and therefore he could not accept it.

The Trinidad and Tobago Delegation reiterated its basic stand. . . .

On proposition after proposition the Conference had recognised the primacy of the Unit Territory over the Federation, contrary to the formal and carefully worked-out proposals of Trinidad and Tobago. On freedom of movement, and on freedom of movement alone, the Conference wished to reverse the procedure and submit the rights of the Territory of Trinidad and Tobago to control its own economic development, agreed to in principle by the Conference, to the arbitrary exercise of the power of the Federal

Government which had been denied in every other respect. Trinidad and Tobago took its stand firmly on economic logic and political consistency. . . . I personally would return to Trinidad to put my position and the Delegation's position before the people of the country. No amount of misrepresentation in London or elsewhere would deter our Delegation from what it regarded as its duty. We wished to say nothing whatsoever which would detract from the dignity of the conference. The matter would be decided not in Lancaster House but elsewhere and would not be restricted to the question of freedom of movement alone. The arbiters in the matter would be the people of Trinidad and Tobago.

My position I made clear, that if there was to be any jeopardising of Trinidad and Tobago's economic viability and political stability by indiscriminate freedom of movement and a totally untenable adherence to one essential principle of Federation by the very people who were prepared to consign all other essential principles to the wastepaper basket, I personally would put the issue before the people of Trinidad and Tobago with a recommendation that they should reject the sort of structure which emerged from the Lancaster House Conference. If the people wished to go into that type of structure, that was their business. They would have to do so by repudiating me and I would then retire into private obscurity. . . . The Conference rejected the new formula proposed by Trinidad and Tobago. Only one vote was cast in its favour, the vote of Trinidad and Tobago. The majority of the Territories voted in favour of the compromise formula reached in Trinidad. The others dissented and expressed the view that they would have to consult their Legislative Councils. . . .

That, Mr Speaker, is the story of the bastard Federation which died at Lancaster House and which was buried in Jamaica in September 1961.'

It was the Jamaica people who took matters into their own hands, not the people of Trinidad and Tobago. By a majority vote, with one-third of the population abstaining, they decided in the referendum Manley called to secede from the Federation. Public feeling in Trinidad about Jamaica's vote was summed up, as so often, by Sparrow in his calypso on Federation. The Chorus reads:

'But if they know they didn't want Federation
And if they know they didn't want to unite as one

Independence was at their door, why didn't they speak before
This is no time to say you ain't Federating no more.'

One of the principal difficulties that faced the Federation was the
absence of a properly functioning party organisation. The West Indian
Federal Labour Party was a party in name only. It was a loose association of ruling parties in the different territories, with a socialist label,
open to socialist parties. As such the PNM was not free to join, as we
were not a socialist party. I had therefore to prepare the ground for
our possible participation in a socialist party. I did this in the University on January 24, 1957, before leaving for Jamaica, in a prepared
statement authorised by PNM's Central Executive. After discussing
the socialism of the Utopian Socialists, I showed that the 'socialism'
of Manley and Adams was nothing but good trade unionism.

On May 15, 1957, our Central Executive decided to join the West
Indies Federal Labour Party as an affiliate member. I represented the
PNM on the WIFLP Executive.

Our relations with the Federal Labour Party reflected the differences
between us and other territories in respect of Federal matters. The
question of the date of independence bedevilled PNM's relations with
WIFLP. As the Chaguaramas issue developed, relations became so
strained that in 1959 PNM's General Council convened a special meeting on May 24 to consider PNM's relations with the WIFLP. The
General Council appointed a Select Committee, with myself as chairman, to go thoroughly into the entire question and report back
within a fortnight. We decided on a more active role by the PNM
in the leadership of the WIFLP, and proposed that, to this end, PNM
should demand the convening of the WIFLP Annual Conference.

The WIFLP were virtually driven into their Annual Conference,
which was held on September 26 and 27, 1959. The Conference discussed revision of the Federal Constitution, revision of the 1941 Bases
Treaty between Britain and the USA, and the Constitution of the
WIFLP. PNM was represented by myself and four other members of
the Central Executive. The Conference was inconclusive and no
decisions were taken on the two key questions – the date of independence and Chaguaramas. This was September 1959. The Federation thereafter proceeded to its date with disaster almost as if the
WIFLP did not exist.

There can be only one explanation of the whole mess. Everybody,
beginning with the Jamaicans, wanted Jamaica out of the Federation
and Trinidad and Tobago to lead the rump. The smaller islands

repeatedly expressed disinterest in Jamaica's antics; all they were concerned about was freedom of movement to Trinidad and Tobago.
This was British policy to let Jamaica out of the net. I received my
first hint of it when Amery came to Trinidad in 1959. It was openly
confirmed by Macmillan, who told me that Manley was not the man
for Federal Prime Minister (as I indicated), Manley had too many
problems on his hands, I was the man. I told him politely, nothing
doing; a Federation with Jamaica or no Federation. I dealt with the
matter publicly after the referendum: 1 from 10 leaves 0. It was good
mathematics and better politics. We refused to discuss the matter and
the future attitude of PNM at the height of the 1961 General Elections.

The relations within the Federation before the Jamaica referendum
had deteriorated to the point where I was able to say to the Legislative
Council on April 28, 1961, in the course of my reply to the Budget
Debate:

'For months and months and months the Federal Government, in
one form or another, has been associated with only one activity in
the West Indies, and that is an attack, direct or indirect, consciously or unconsciously, open or concealed, on the Government
and the representatives of Trinidad and Tobago.'

The key to the bad relations was Chaguaramas.

22

CHAGUARAMAS

(i) The Federal Capital Site

The voting for the Federal Capital site at the Jamaica Conference resulted as follows:

First ballot: Barbados 5 votes; Jamaica 4 votes; Trinidad 7 votes

Second ballot: Barbados 5 votes; Trinidad 11 votes.

There remained the choice of the capital site. The Standing Federation Committee appointed a Sub-Committee to work with the Government of Trinidad and Tobago in this matter, examine possible sites, and make recommendations.

The Sub-Committee met in Trinidad in March 1957. It had before it the recommendations of a Federal Capital Site Committee appointed by the Government of Trinidad and Tobago, representatives of persons eminent in the field of shipping, electricity, town planning, commerce, bus transport, engineering, public works and journalism. The Committee opted for the North-West peninsula, the site of an American naval base at Chaguaramas.

The Sub-Committee of the Standing Federation Committee, with this report of the Trinidad Committee, reached the following conclusion:

> 'On a division, it was *decided* by a majority that it be conveyed to the Standing Federation Committee, that the Sub-Committee considered the North-West Peninsula, on grounds purely of its location by the sea, scenic beauty and its existing facilities, to be the most suitable site for the Federal Capital . . . but having regard to the position explained by Hon. Dr. Solomon the Sub-Committee leaves it entirely to the Standing Federation Committee to decide whether the matter will be pursued. . . .'

The Sub-Committee's recommendations were considered by the Standing Federation Committee at a meeting in Trinidad from May 6-17, 1957.

The Standing Federation Committee decided by majority vote as follows:

'Being conscious that an early decision on the actual site of the capital is of paramount importance to the Federation, especially in its financial aspect;

Recognising that the most desirable site is under occupation by a friendly power whose tenancy is covered by an agreement with Her Majesty's Government at Westminster;

Being assured that the foreign power in question is anxious to extend the hand of friendship to, and to preserve the closest possible link with, our nation now in embryo; BE IT RESOLVED

(a) that this Committee agrees upon the North West Peninsula as the site of the Federal Capital;

(b) that Her Majesty's Government be immediately apprised of our decision and requested to support it and arrange for a delegation from this Committee to be received by the United States Authorities, including the President, for the following purposes:

(1) the handing over to the West Indies Federal Government of the US base at the North-West Peninsula on such terms as may be agreed on; and

(2) arriving at agreements between the United States of America, the United Kingdom and the West Indies Federal Government for the security of the West Indies.'

For this purpose the following delegation was appointed: Premier of Barbados; Hon F. A. Baron of Dominica; Chief Minister of Jamaica; Hon R. A. Bradshaw of St. Kitts–Nevis–Anguilla; Chief Minister of Trinidad and Tobago.

As a result of this decision the Government of Trinidad and Tobago found itself in a quandary. On the one hand, the party in power was bound by its 1956 election pledge which included in its Code of Public Morality a specific guarantee to respect international obligations with particular reference to the 1941 Agreement on the Leased Bases; on the other hand it could not resist its Federal colleagues or inflict on the Federation a capital site of its own choice.

It proposed therefore that it should have observer status only at the Conference, but the Standing Federation Committee urged it to reconsider this decision. The Government of Trinidad and Tobago thereafter took pains to explain its position to the Governments of the United Kingdom and United States of America and sought to ascertain whether, in the circumstances, its full participation in the Federal Delegation would be regarded as a breach of its international pledges. It was assured by both Governments that it would not. On this basis the Government of Trinidad and Tobago sent a delegation comprising me as Chief Minister and the Attorney-General to the London Conference, making it clear that it was doing so in two senses: (a) as a full member of the SFC delegation; (b) in its own right, as an interested party to the 1941 Agreement.

(ii) The London Conference

The Conference convened at the Foreign Office, London, from July 17–23, 1957. The West Indian case was very precisely stated by Mr. Manley who urged the USA to consider the need to preserve and enhance its good relations with the West Indies in the future.

The United States Government had submitted a memorandum setting out the reasons why it was impossible to cede Chaguaramas either in whole or in part, but promising to give sympathetic consideration to any request for the release of a part of another base at Waller Field. The United States Ambassador summed up the conflict between the West Indian and United States points of view as 'a conflict between our mutual defence interests and our mutual political interests'.

As Chief Minister of Trinidad and Tobago I made a separate statement on behalf of Trinidad and Tobago wholeheartedly endorsing the West Indian request on the basis of new information that had reached me since the May meeting of the SFC. That new information from our files indicated that there had been powerful opposition in Trinidad in 1941 to the cession of Chaguaramas, that the United Kingdom had bowed to pressure from the United States, that Chaguaramas had been selected without any competent survey to determine the best suitable site for a naval base taking into account political, economic and related factors, and that the Trinidad and Tobago Government and People had not been consulted on the 1941 Agreement. The Governor of the day suggested instead the reclamation of the Caroni Swamp and proposed the appointment of a Joint Commission to go into the entire matter.

Accordingly I formally proposed in the name of the Government of Trinidad and Tobago:

(a) the evacuation of Chaguaramas by the USA;

(*b*) establishment of a Joint Commission of the four interested parties – Trinidad and Tobago, West Indies, United Kingdom, United States of America – to select a new site for a combined base (naval, military, air);

(*c*) revision of the 1941 Agreement under Article 28.

The Conference ultimately agreed, after telephone contact between President Eisenhower and Prime Minister Macmillan, to the appointment of a Joint Commission, to investigate all aspects of the British West Indies request to make Chaguaramas available, taking into full account military and economic considerations, and to report to the parties concerned as early as possible.

(iii) The Chaguaramas Joint Commission

The decision to appoint the Chaguaramas Joint Commission posed three immediate difficulties for the West Indies.

The first was the hostility of a section of the press and of political opinion, both in the West Indies and the United States, on the ground that the request for the release of Chaguaramas would antagonise the USA and scare away US capital, and was detrimental to the defence interests of both the USA and the West Indies.

The second difficulty was the decision of the USA to proceed with the enlargement of facilities at Chaguaramas whilst the issue of Chaguaramas was *sub judice*. This consisted principally of the construction of a missile tracking station at Tucker Valley. The Trinidad and Tobago Government protested, to no avail, that this unilateral decision constituted:

(1) a complete disregard of all that is implied in the agreement to appoint the Joint Commission;

(2) substantial prejudice to the efforts of the Commission to find a fair and just solution of the problem referred to it;

(3) in the minds of the public, an indication of a thorough lack of sympathetic understanding on the part of the US Government of the West Indian request for the release of Chaguaramas as the capital of the West Indies;

(4) reasonable ground for public resentment at what was generally interpreted as an attitude of domination to a small, friendly neighbour.

The third difficulty encountered by the West Indies with respect to the Joint Commission was the difficulty of securing expert naval and engineering advice. The Government of Trinidad and Tobago turned to India, whilst the West Indian representatives contemplated recourse to Canada and the Netherlands. The Government of Trinidad and Tobago was, however, discouraged by the United Kingdom from an appeal to India on the ground that the United States of America would not be agreeable to sharing its defence secrets with a non-Western Hemisphere power; and considerations of a similar nature applied to the countries contemplated by the West Indies.

It was in these inauspicious circumstances that the Chaguaramas Joint Commission began its task. Its Chairman was Sir Charles Arden-Clarke, former Governor of the Gold Coast Colony and first Governor-General of the Dominion of Ghana. With two representatives each from Trinidad and Tobago and the West Indies, the Joint Commission was inevitably dominated by the Admirals representing the US Navy and the Royal Navy.

The Commission, whilst locating five possible alternative sites for the Base, found that Chaguaramas was the most suitable site and that its partition was impracticable. The Governments of the United Kingdom and United States of America regarded this as the end of the matter. The Governments of the West Indies and of Trinidad and Tobago protested vigorously against this conclusion, on two grounds – (a) it was issued unilaterally by two of the parties to the Commission; (b) it contravened the distinct understanding of the 1957 London Conference, as well as common sense, that the report of the Joint Commission would be referred to a political conference of the four parties.

The Federal Government's request for a conference was endorsed by the Legislative Council of Trinidad and Tobago which, on June 6, 1958, debated a motion moved by me as Chief Minister. I protested against the unilateral statements of the British and American Governments. I then proceeded to analyse the Report of the Joint Commission and to draw from its conclusions the exact opposite of those drawn by the Governments of the United States and the United Kingdom. I emphasised that the report was incomplete in that it consciously omitted the economic aspects of the Base where Trinidad was concerned. I stressed that the very importance of the total amount of the trade protected by the Base contradicted the two Governments' statement that it was too costly to remove the Base.

I repudiated the statement of the two Governments that, according to the Joint Commission's report, Chaguaramas was the only site for the Base. I stated:

'The Commission found five alternate sites. . . . How can you, in spite of these five alternative sites taking different periods of time to develop, costing different sums of money – how can you sit down at somebody's desk and say, "We accept the Report"! What do you accept in the Report? The Report said that you have certain requirements for a base. The Report said that Chaguaramas can meet those requirements. The Report said that there were five alternative sites which fulfilled or could be made to fulfil these requirements. . . . I am absolutely convinced that the Chaguaramas Joint Commission and in particular the United States Naval Representatives left themselves a line of retreat from Chaguaramas to Irois Bay should it be found necessary for them to vacate Chaguaramas . . . the Government of Trinidad and Tobago says today it is quite possible to accommodate the Base at Irois Bay and the Capital at Chaguaramas – far more than to accommodate the Base at Chaguaramas and the Capital at Irois Bay.'

Thereupon the United States Government, with the approval of the United Kingdom Government made public two assurances which the Prime Minister of the West Indies accepted in an announcement made in the House of Representatives on June 16, 1958, that it would be prepared to review the situation in 'say ten years' time' and that it was prepared to give sympathetic consideration to the revision of the agreement of 1941.

I, in my turn, speaking on behalf of the Executive Council of Trinidad and Tobago, announced on June 20, 1958, the appointment of a Commission of legal experts to inquire into and report upon the legal basis of (a) the occupation by the United States of areas of Trinidad and Tobago from 1941 to the present day, and (b) the terms and conditions relevant thereto.

(iv) The 1941 Agreement

Without consulting the people of Trinidad and Tobago and the West Indies, the United Kingdom Government agreed to lease certain areas to the USA for bases in return for 50 over-age destroyers. The deal was thus described by me in my statement to the Legislative Council on June 6, 1958, quoting from a biography of Roosevelt and the opinion of the American Attorney-General of the day:

'Sir, all this was done in return for 50 vessels which, had they been sold in 1930, ten years before, would have fetched a price varying between $263,000 and $340,000, an average of $300,000. It was commonly said at the time that Trinidad represented 40 of these 50 destroyers, so that a sizeable portion of Trinidad was leased in exchange for destroyers which, if sold in 1930, would have fetched $240,000. No Trinidad representative would ever have accepted any such arrangement. . . . We never consented to be sold for scrap. Knowing Trinidadians, as I do, if we had had any say in the matter we might have insisted on being sold for aircraft carriers (*laughter*).'

If the people of Trinidad and Tobago were not consulted in the surrender of their land in return for fifty destroyers, their views were ignored with respect to the particular areas to be ceded. Within ten days it was all over, and the US military mission had made up its mind. The Governor and Executive Council of Trinidad and Tobago of that day led the fight against the decision to take over Chaguaramas. The United States, however, was inclined to pooh-pooh any suggestions of political difficulties if US soldiers and sailors were dotted all over the island. The Governor complained that the American attitude was all take and no give.

The Governor was of the opinion that the United States was seeking not a naval and air base for the United States in a part of the British Empire, for the security of which the British Empire was and would remain responsible, so much as a naval, military and air base in an outlying island of the South American continent, for the defence of which the United States Government would assume responsibility, and which was to serve if necessary as a jumping-off ground for operations by the United States Army in South America. It was practically impossible for the United States to get any equivalent facilities in Venezuela or other parts of the north of South America because of the sensitiveness of all South American Republics about giving the United States permanent facilities on their own territory.

The Governor's views were fully endorsed by his Executive Council, which advocated a combined base, opposed the cession of Chaguaramas or at least for 99 years, and supported the view that the siting of permanent facilities should be carefully considered before a decision was reached. The Governor expressly warned of the constitutional aspect of the problem. He made it clear in Washington that the British Government was even then considering constitution reform proposals recommended by the Moyne Commission, and accordingly expressed the view that in making arrangements which were to hold good for a century it would be prudent to bear in mind the degree of self-government which might be attained by the people of the Colony before the end of that long period. The Governor added that it was essential that any agreement between the British Government and the US Government affecting Trinidad must command the consent not only of the then Legislature but so far as could reasonably be foreseen of future Legislatures throughout the 99-year period.

But the US Government was prepared to exert pressure on the West Indian Governments as well as on the British Government. Their attitude indicated that American Service interests were put first, second and last with disregard of West Indian political conditions, constitutions and outlook.

Thus was the stage set for future difficulties, as I made clear in my report on the London Conference of 1957 to the Legislative Council on August 7, 1957:

'On every point the Governor of Trinidad and Tobago was overruled, and, no doubt as a result of the exigencies of the war situation in 1940 the United Kingdom Government acceded *in toto* to the wishes of the United States Government.

I reminded the Conference of Sir Winston Churchill's reference in his war memoirs to certain things done by the United States Government which were "harsh and painful" and I stated that these are the precise words to be applied to the 1941 Agreement. . . .'

(v) The Legal Aspect of the Agreement

Under the 1941 Agreement, certain areas were ceded to the USA for 99 years, but under Articles XXI and XXVII the original leased Areas were revised. In the absence of duly executed leases, the position with respect to many of these arrangements was very obscure.

The 1941 Agreement itself called for substantial amendment or modification of the laws of Trinidad and Tobago, under Article XXIX. In the spirit of this Article the Government of Trinidad and Tobago passed, in 1941, two Ordinances. These, one of them temporary, and the inconsequential Regulations made thereunder left untouched the central feature of Article XXIX – legislation by the Trinidad and Tobago Government to give effect to the major concessions to the

US enshrined in the Agreement. The scope of this legislation included jurisdiction over US Forces and Trinidad and Tobago nationals employed on the Bases; security legislation; arrest and service of process; right to use the public services of Trinidad and Tobago; right to make surveys even on private property; exemption of US public vessels from compulsory pilotage or light or harbour dues; right of US left-hand drive vehicles to use the roads; exemption from licensing and registration fees; exemption from the Immigration Ordinance; exemption from import, excise, consumption and export taxes; right to establish postal facilities in the Leased Areas; exemption of US forces and nationals employed on the Base from income tax; right of the US to take any necessary measures in the vicinity of the Leased Areas to improve sanitation and protect health.

To this end, legislation to implement the US Bases Agreement, the Government of Trinidad and Tobago took as its first step appointment of a legal Committee on June 17, 1941. The Committee, working expeditiously, completed a draft ordinance which was submitted to the Colonial Office in October 1941.

It was thought desirable and found necessary to achieve some uniformity in the implementing legislation of the Bases Territories – Bermuda, Bahamas, Jamaica, Antigua, St. Lucia, British Guiana as well as Trinidad. Accordingly in 1944 a conference was convened in Trinidad of the legal officials of these territories under the chairmanship of the Legal Adviser to the Secretary of State for the Colonies, Mr. K. Roberts-Wray.

The 1944 Conference, which took as its model the draft prepared by the Trinidad Legal Committee, produced a draft ordinance which was then sent to all the Territories for further study and comment. By that time every one was fully aware of the urgency of the legislation. The Agreement was being enforced by administrative action which in many respects had no background in law. In the absence of the required legislation, the legal rights of both parties, the people of Trinidad and Tobago and the Government of the USA, were indeterminate, and in Trinidad one had constantly to ignore the law in order to avoid what might have turned out to be serious incidents.

I then continued in the Legislative Council on June 20, 1958:

'To this day, however, Mr Speaker, the necessary legislation has not been passed. No Government dared to introduce such legislation into the Legislative Council. . . . The Government of 1950–1956 did not introduce the legislation. Was it that it considered it too controversial? Was it that it considered the time in-opportune? Let us assume that, in its first year in office, in 1951, it was too busy finding its feet and feeling its way.

Why not then introduce it in 1952, the year when certain areas were deactivated and released? Was that year inopportune? Was it inopportune because opposition had begun to develop in British Guiana and because Bermuda appeared to be hostile to the idea of similar legislation? The Government had survived a vote of no-confidence early in 1954. Could it not have introduced the legislation then? Was it that it feared that local politicians would precipitate an acrimonious debate which might alienate or antagonise the US, and give the impression of a vendetta against the US? Why did it suggest to the US authorities in 1955 indefinite postponement? Was it afraid of the elections which should have been held in that year? Did it consider it inopportune and impolitic to raise the issue in the election year of 1956? Could it be that our predecessors wanted to consult their constituents first? Were they perhaps apprehensive that the Trinidad concessions exceeded those made elsewhere, in Newfoundland, in Iceland, and in fact went far in excess of the 1941 Agreement itself? Was it afraid that the legislation would give rise to further demands from the Americans – for example, that they would once more propose the amendment of the Trinidad law in respect of marriages to conform with the US military ban on inter racial marriages? Or was it that they preferred to have the matter dealt with by other means besides local legislation, by Order in Council, or by Act of Parliament?

May I now, Mr Speaker, summarise the position for the benefit of Hon. Members? The United States of America is in occupation of extensive areas in Trinidad. Its legal title is based on leases which in one respect or another appear to be unsatisfactory. These leases derive from an Agreement, a Treaty, which places on the shoulders of the Government of Trinidad and Tobago the onus of introducing new legislation or amending existing legislation utterly at variance with the laws of Trinidad and Tobago. Such legislation has not been implemented out of fear of the wrath of the population of Trinidad and Tobago.'

(vi) The Public Campaign

I used every possible artifice to keep the Chaguaramas issue alive and before the public and embarked on a relentless campaign to this end.

The public campaign began in 1957 on the occasion of PNM's Second Annual Convention. Our 1956 election pledge could not be sustained in the light of the new knowledge that had emerged, and the Party's General Council therefore put the issue squarely before the Convention. The following resolution was passed decisively, by a vote of 164 to 1:

> 'BE IT RESOLVED that this Second Annual Convention of the PNM meeting on September 29, 1957, while reaffirming the pledge to honour all international obligations, financial, economic and military, with special reference to the Agreement on the United States Bases, go on record as endorsing a review of the Agreement under Article XXVIII to provide for (a) the transfer of the Naval Base to an alternative site, and (b) the formal association of the Government of Trinidad and Tobago with the signatories of the Agreement.'

Thus inspired, I jumped into the fray, fortifying myself with a thorough study of the voluminous files we had on the subject, and particularly the record of the 1941 Conference in London. I kept the issue alive, first and foremost, through the Legislative Council. My speeches were a forthright defence of the rights and interests of Trinidad and Tobago. My tone and my line were laid down in my speech on August 7, 1957, reporting on the Chaguaramas Conference in London. I said:

> 'This matter of the Federal Capital is settled. The capital of the Federation is in Trinidad and the Trinidad Government has accepted the consequence involved, that if the Federation wants Chaguaramas to be the Federal capital then the capital will be Chaguaramas.'

In replying to a no-confidence motion of February 21, 1958, I attacked the Leader of the Opposition for betraying the interests of Trinidad and Tobago. I said:

> 'I did not have the honour of becoming the Queen's first Chief Minister of Trinidad and Tobago to preside over the perpetuation of Colonialism.'

In any conflict between USA and Trinidad over the Base, the USA must give way. It seemed to me on June 6, 1958, that if Irois Bay was a little too far from the mouth of the Gulf of Paria, that was too bad: 'I am not going to put two hours of steaming time in the balance against the fundamental responsibilities of a Trinidad Minister to the Trinidad people.' In any such conflict between Base and Capital, we had to recognise that 'an emerging nation is coming up, symbolised by the cradle – the cradle of the new capital – as against the grave symbolising the base down at Chaguaramas.'

I laid down as an axiom that 'we were not accepting any further division of Trinidad by two Governments sitting down in London or Washington'. When it came to brass tacks, 'on what terms will they stay or go? Will it be 99 years? Since 1940 a lot of water has flowed under the bridge.' NATO was for 20 years, the US treaty with Spain for 10 years. I went on to inquire:

> 'Why should they pay rent in Morocco? Why should they pay rent in Libya? Why should they have Point Four Economic Assistance in Libya? What sort of international agreement is this that can be one thing for Trinidad and something totally different for other parts of the world?'

I was emphatic that 'I did not take any oath of allegiance to defend a 1940 Agreement'. We were a society as well as a base, and if the Opposition wished to be 'mouthpieces of a foreign power', as far as I was concerned 'nobody is going to play fast and loose with Trinidad's property, with Trinidad's resources, with Trinidad's soil, except with the consent of Trinidad's Ministers.'

On Chaguaramas the Opposition had the time of their lives. One inquired when I first raised the issue, on August 7, 1957, whether I thought it wise to resurrect those matters, who would pay compensation if the Americans had to leave? Another, later transferred to the Federal superstructure, indicated that the Opposition would not support any demand for the evacuation of Chaguaramas. The leader of the Opposition went to town in accusing me of a vendetta and complaining of my 'bombastic attitude'. A fourth member, who later also went federal, argued that the masses were in favour of American retention of the base. Another one complained that I had created ill-will and bitterness with my 'political band-waggon', with my 'Chaguaramas morning, Chaguaramas noon, Chaguaramas night'. Yet another Opposition member accused me of pin-pricking in Hitlerite fashion, as Hitler had done with the Treaty of Versailles. He claimed that I had gone back on the country's solemn word. He accused me of 'international rape of an agreement entered with the United Kingdom'. He claimed that I was following the 'path of barbarism'.

He accused me of organising 3½ years of fighting, bitterness, acrimony, pin-pricking, and vindictiveness.

How long would the agitation continue? I was asked. Was I going to carry on a political campaign against Washington, or was I going to march on Chaguaramas? The member accused me of 'using the language of Nehru without the economic resources of Nehru . . . using the language of the Prime Minister of Ceylon without the resources of Ceylon'.

Another member attacked what he called 'the continuing buffoonery of this Government'. In his view Downing Street was 'the only one competent body to speak' for us; we were 'miles and miles away from responsibility'. Had we become 'highway robbers to want the valuables of other people just because they have been in occupation of a piece of country belonging to us?'

In taking the fight against the enemies to the public my second weapon was my Saturday morning Press Conference. Week in, week out, I dealt with Chaguaramas. I gave the enemy no peace. Here is a sample from my press conference of September 20, 1958, on the question of agricultural production on the Base. This raised the questions of income tax, customs exemption on agricultural equipment, the operation of the Wages Council for Agricultural Workers. I poured scorn on all these commercial and other activities at the so-called military base which the Joint Commission had stated was too important to be given up. I said:

'Suppose we accept the statement that the whole Base represents the defence against submarines, this whole area. But part of this area is a disused hospital, part of it is a beach club. I have heard people myself, in the United States of America, refer to Chaguaramas Base as the "Honeymoon Base". It is one of the biggest bingo centres in Trinidad. And now you find that the place that they can't release, because it is essential to the functioning of the Base, 2,000 acres of this land is used for plantation activity competing with Trinidad farmers. The more I think of this question, the more I believe that we misunderstand this Base. Chaguaramas is not an American Base for the defence of Trinidad. Chaguaramas is a base where in numbers of ways – the total cost I have not yet figured out – Trinidad has been making a military and financial contribution to the defence of the United States of America which puts it on a totally different footing.'

So I demanded partition of the base, which the Joint Commission had specifically opposed, and which Manley had proposed at the 1957 London Conference.

The following Saturday I was back at the theme with variations – the Americans were rearing pigs, had previously sold grass, had once applied for permission to export coconuts to Puerto Rico, payment for their citrus was to be made to the Treasurer of the United States. The *Trinidad Chronicle* had attacked me and my policy. I counter-attacked in a statement which, like all the Press Conferences, was subsequently broadcast: 'am I to be crucified for respecting the laws of Trinidad and Tobago?'

This was the atmosphere in the country when the United States, forced to give ground, sought to placate us by agreeing to a conference to discuss what it called the day-to-day difficulties arising out of the occupation of the base. Making it clear that this was without prejudice to our demand for a four-power conference to discuss revision of the 1941 Agreement, at which Trinidad and Tobago would be separately and directly represented as of right with equal status, we agreed to the conference which began on May 14, 1959. Eight meetings were held, by which time it was clear that on every issue the Agreement itself was involved, in addition to which the Americans had to refer every-thing to Washington for instructions. So we considered that the Con-ference served no useful purpose and abandoned further discussion.

I gave the Americans a preview of the ultimate four-power con-ference.

(1) On the general subject of commercial activities on a military base I put into the record the objections and fears voiced by Trinidad and Tobago as far back as 1941, that such activities should not be per-mitted or at least would be subject to local taxes.

The US Consul-General argued that Macqueripe Plantations was an administrative sub-division of the United States Naval Station at Chaguaramas. The plantation was a military facility, its operation was a military activity, and its losses were made up out of appropri-ated funds.

(2) On the subject of the Macqueripe Club, a service club operat-ing on the basis of restricted local membership, I stressed that the Trinidad and Tobago public regarded the Club as 'one of the remaining strongholds of racial discrimination'. I raised the question of local purchases by the Club. I observed that West Indian earnings went to finance, at least partially, the operations of the Service Club. I quoted from the United States Bases Agreement with Libya to indicate the

United States Government's attitude in 1954 on the question of utilising local produce to the maximum extent possible.

Two problems were involved in this issue – (a) was the Club a profit-making organisation, subject to income tax?; (b) had the Trinidad members violated the exchange controls by paying membership dues of $60 per individual and $100 per family unit?

(3) The hardest nut for the Americans to crack concerned the evasion of customs duties involved in the purchase by local residents of goods imported into the base duty-free under the Agreement, but for military purposes or for use by military and associated personnel.

I cited the instance of a jeep seized recently as well as cigarettes and indicated there were other instances. I quoted from the Agreement on Bases with both Libya and Iceland to show that later on much more stringent arrangements were accepted by the United States with regard to Customs than were possible under the 1941 Agreement. On this matter I quoted the view of the Trinidad and Tobago Comptroller of Customs in 1942 on the question of the provision of customs posts at the points of exit from the leased areas. This view was as follows:

'I have given this matter very careful consideration and cannot but feel that the establishment of control gates to the Naval Base at Chaguaramas would be an irritating step which would be strongly resented by the US Naval authorities . . . I fear that these will be a source of continual friction since objection will be taken by US personnel to having their cars, etc., stopped and searched by Negroes and I tremble to contemplate possibilities where US citizens are armed – and particularly while under the influence of liquor.'

The American Consul-General, all hot and bothered, fell into the trap. He accused the Comptroller of not really knowing Americans; he pointed out that thousands of American tourists visit the Caribbean each year without raising any such issue. I replied that this view had been the view not only of the Trinidad Comptroller of Customs but also of President Roosevelt himself. The Governor of the Leeward Islands, Sir Gordon Lethem, had reported on January 23, 1941, on a conversation with the President, at which a representative of the British Embassy was present, as follows:

'The President said that he had no doubt at all there was a considerable psychological element involved, and that this should and could be easily and properly met. He went into certain matters of detail, such as disciplinary action which might be necessary *vis-à-vis* United States enlisted men, the undesirability of their having to go before courts on which sat coloured Magistrates or Judges, and of arrests being made by Negro police. This could be met better by the use of United States military police, and disciplinary action being taken in United States military courts.'

(4) I dealt effectively with the unauthorised landings of American military aircraft at Piarco. I quoted from an official report to show how persons and goods arriving in and departing from the country by the Military Air Transport Service were absolutely free to contravene any of the territory's laws and how impossible it was to be even aware of it. In one case cited, non-military personnel, i.e., the local wife of a serviceman, arriving by MATS, who should have gone through Customs and Immigration, was only detected because of the commotion caused by the welcoming party of relatives and friends. In another case there had been a tubercular passenger on the aircraft. Without any health inspection fellow passengers had landed and gone off to visit friends, relatives and a nearby airport hotel.

If the planes did not land at Piarco, there would not be these difficulties, but the planes did land, and in astonishing numbers. Trinidad revenue suffered considerably by loss of landing and parking fees; Trinidad expenditure on airport maintenance was increased considerably by reason of damage to runways from the tremendously heavy military planes, the weights of which were far in excess of those of commercial planes. All this affected the personal relationships between Trinidad Government officials and American military and civilian representatives.

(5) The United States sent armed escorts to Piarco with its airmail. After some discussion as to whether the security arrangements provided by the Trinidad Government for its mail were inadequate for the Naval Station's mail, I asked by what authority did the United States Naval Authorities implement their own procedures which involved the presence of armed personnel at a civilian airport. This was assuming that the Trinidad Government's measures were inadequate and I was not accepting that.

(6) A perennial source of friction was the transfer of military personnel who were summoned to attend Court on one charge or another out of Trinidad. My official information was that over a period of 16 years up to February 12, 1958, United States personnel had been

involved in 1,127 incidents of offences including accidents, assault, disorderly behaviour, breaches of the Motor Vehicles and Road Traffic Regulations, malicious damage, larceny, found on premises, obscene exposure, discharging firearms, throwing missiles, refusing to pay taxi, wounding and robbery. This did not include incidents of murder or shooting with intent.

I decided that the time had come to go outside the Legislative Council and beyond the Press Conference. I would go to the people. So I arranged to speak at a mass party meeting in Arima on July 17, 1959. My subject was 'From Slavery to Chaguaramas'. It was one of my best and most effective speeches, rooted in the history of the West Indies. Beginning with the division of the world by the Pope between Spain and Portugal towards the end of the fifteenth century, I proceeded to a long analysis of competing imperialisms ending with American supremacy in the Caribbean. I emphasised that we were no longer colonial in outlook, that Whitehall, Port-of-Spain (the Premier's Office), had replaced Whitehall, London, and publicly repudiated the American assurance which the Federal Government had accepted. Trinidad and Tobago was no longer a colony. It was governed by a Cabinet. That was the essential difference between 1959 and 1941.

> 'There was no Cabinet in 1941. They slapped the Governor of Trinidad and Tobago down, they moved him, and they put somebody that they thought would work better with the Americans. . . . They can't move a Chief Minister or Premier today. (Applause)'.

We had stated our case to the Americans. It was for them to reply. Time was on our side, and we would win our Independence.

> 'Mark my words, the Trinidad flag will fly over Chaguaramas before many of us are many days older. (*Thunderous applause*.) Don't be under any illusion as to that. . . . We in the PNM did not form a political party in order to substitute American colonialism for the British colonialism we pledged to the country that we would fight.'

'From Slavery to Chaguaramas' set the tone of my public campaign. I never ceased to enlighten the Trinidad and Tobago population on the issues involved. I had already publicly attacked the Opposition by

putting eight questions to them during my speech on January 24, 1958
in the University on the principal issues at stake in the Federal Elections.
These questions read as follows:

'1. Will the Opposition state whether it is or is not true that
when a state becomes a member of a Federal state, all its former
treaties of alliance are *ipso facto* cancelled, as the US Constitution
itself expressly forbids any state of the Union "without the consent
of Congress . . . (to) enter into any agreement or compact with
another State, or foreign power"?

2. Will the Opposition confirm that the former French colony of
Morocco, which achieved sovereign status in 1956, has entirely
reserved its position in respect of the secret agreement of 1950
between France and the USA regarding bases in Morocco, and that
the US Government, notwithstanding this, provided US $20
million in economic aid to Morocco?

3. Will the Opposition confirm that the former Danish colony
of Iceland, in which the US obtained base rights in 1941, which
became a republic in 1944, has officially requested a revision of the
1951 airbase agreement with the US? Will it confirm that the
Opposition party which advocated the maintenance of the base,
lost seats in the general election of 1956, which was fought principally on the issues of the base? Will it further confirm that the
Iceland and US Governments have reached an amicable agreement
which among other things, provides for the appointment of a
Standing Group consisting of three senior representatives of each
Government to study problems arising out of the 1951 agreement
and specifically "to prepare plans for employing Icelandic nationals
at the US airbase in so far as qualified personnel are available, and
to begin training programmes to qualify them for such work?"

4. Will the Opposition confirm that the US Government has
been negotiating a revision of its airbases agreement with the former
American colony of the Philippines, and that negotiations have
recently broken down on Philippine insistence on the right to
control the use of bases in the event of war and on the question of
legal jurisdiction over US military personnel for offences committed against Philippine nationals within the base areas?

5. Will the Opposition confirm that, by agreement reached
between the USA and Brazil on January 21, 1957, regarding the
construction of a guided missile tracking station, construction and
operation are jointly the responsibility of both countries, with a

Brazilian officer in command of the station and the Brazilian flag flown at the station, while Brazilian technicians will gradually replace US technicians and the buildings and fixed structures erected will become Brazilian property without payment on the termination of the 5-year agreement?

6. Will the Opposition confirm that at hearings in 1957 before a sub-committee of the Committee on Appropriations of the House of Representatives of the US Congress in respect of the Appropriations for 1958 for the Department of Defence, top representatives of the US armed forces made it quite clear that the aircraft carrier is a less vulnerable target than an airbase, especially in these days of ballistic missiles, and that US defence planning is predicated on the possible loss of bases, if only for the reasons stated by the US Secretary of Defence:

"I think the basic thing is this. We will occupy the bases in any one of these places where we have a base as long as those people like us and are good neighbours, and recognise that the base gives them protection and if they do not like you and want you out, no matter what the previous agreement is, you are in trouble."

7. To avoid further misconception as to Trinidad and Tobago's contribution to the maintenance of the US bases, will the Opposition confirm that by the leases Trinidad surrendered for 99 years a total of 36,772 acres for which no rent was charged; that between 1942 and 1957 the Government of Trinidad and Tobago lost $1½ million in revenue from excise duties through the delivery at the Base of 10½ million gallons of gasolene and 1⅛ million gallons of kerosene free of duty; that between 1941 and 1951 the Government of Trinidad and Tobago refunded to authorised personnel at the Base nearly $900,000 in customs duties; that the Government of Trinidad and Tobago lost an undisclosed sum in customs duties on articles illegally imported from the Base on a scale represented by the seizure on various occasions of bicycles, a cash register, a jeep and two automobiles; and finally that the Government of Trinidad and Tobago has incurred expenditure which cannot be precisely determined on the maintenance and upkeep of roads used freely by official vehicles stationed at the Bases which, by the 1941 Agreement, are exempt from licence and registration fees?

8. Will the Opposition confirm that in demanding Waller Field

as the Federal Capital they are in effect trying to drive the capital
from Trinidad and thus to break up the Federation?'

I continued thereafter my campaign with Party and People. In my
Fourth Convention address on the approach of independence I had
this to say:

> 'The war of Independence is on. The opposing divisions are at the
> crossroads – one leading back to the Colonial dirt track, the other
> leading on to Independence Highway. The army of reaction has
> military power on its side – jet planes, radiation, cruisers, nuclear
> missile-launching submarines. Its base is Chaguaramas. The army
> of progress has political power on its side – mass meetings, popular
> alertness, development programme, constitutional ambitions. Its
> base is the University of Woodford Square. It is a war of weapons
> against principles, of military discipline against political discipline,
> of armies and navies versus people – or, more simply, of might
> versus right.
>   The world history of the last ten years is there to tell us the out-
> come of this struggle.'

I made the position even clearer in my San Fernando speech of May
30, 1960, 'Perspectives for the West Indies'.

> 'Independence means, first and foremost, external relations, foreign
> policy. The broad outlines are already clear. The world is divided
> into two camps; the hot war will follow the cold. Where do we, a
> new nation of three million people stand? If the Iron Curtain is the
> great divide separating the two camps, then it is axiomatic that we
> are West of the Curtain and not East of it. There can be no argu-
> ment about that.
>   That is the anchor of our foreign policy as we emerge into inde-
> pendence in 1960.
>   But it must be just as clearly understood that within that frame-
> work we enjoy political, constitutional and moral equality. Within
> that framework we re-examine the colonial antecedents designed
> to suit the metropolitan country and establish new forms designed
> to suit our own needs. . . .'

I never swerved from the central issue – 'if the site of our Federal
Capital were London, Washington or Tierra del Fuego, Chaguaramas
would still remain the crux of West Indian nationalism, the symbol of

West Indian independence'. In a special supplement in *The Nation* on
March 11, 1960, in connection with our Fourth Annual Convention,
I rammed the message home. I wrote:

'Thus it was left to the PNM to raise the crucial issue of independence – Chaguaramas. Chaguaramas means the reversal of a deal
imposed on us by colonialism. Chaguaramas means reversion of
our soil and resources. Chaguaramas means vindication of our
governmental rights and prerogatives. Chaguaramas means independence in the sphere of foreign policy. Chaguaramas means
capital before base. Chaguaramas represents for us an acid choice
between the alternatives – an independent nation with a will of its
own or a banana republic the satellite of a foreign power.
Chaguaramas and Independence go hand in hand; the road to
independence leads through Chaguaramas.'

All this was the background to the broadcast row I had with Adams,
Federal Prime Minister, in the middle of March, 1960. The central
issue was Chaguaramas. As I made clear to the population:

'What is the position of the Federal Government on Chaguaramas?
We have more or less an idea of where the British Government
stands. The United States Government has made it clear by now
where it stands. Where does the Federal Government stand?
Chaguaramas is not a new problem . . . Not only does the United
States Government allow its legislative representatives and other
officials to maintain a constant propaganda on what they assert
are American interests in this matter. A representative of the
American Legislature, a man of certain standing in American
politics, has stated unequivocally that he has visited Trinidad, that
he has held discussions with the Prime Minister and other members of the Federal Government, that they have declared to him
that they are in sympathy with the aims of the American Government, that they are opposed to the policy of my Government on
Chaguaramas. He went so far as to say that the Federal Government recognised a moral obligation to maintain the conditions of
the 1941 Agreement. All this, of course, is made much of by the
daily press.
    The question that immediately arises is: where does the Federal
Government stand? First of all, there is this long silence on the
fundamental issue of Chaguaramas, an issue on which, in our

opinion, no West Indian should hesitate to express an opinion. But, in addition to this, which is a matter of deep concern to my Government and my Party, this statement by the United States legislator, committing the Federal Government to the American point of view on this issue, passes unchallenged by them. It would be the simplest matter to deny this allegation that has been trumpeted throughout the West Indies and the United States – this allegation that the West Indies are aligned with the United States on Chaguaramas. Is it in any way strange, Ladies and Gentlemen, that there has grown up in the minds of all of us in Trinidad and Tobago a distrust and a suspicion of what the Federal Government thinks and of what it will do in any tripartite talks in which the Government of Trinidad and Tobago does not occupy an independent position?'

I went my way. I discussed the whole issue privately and effectively with Adlai Stevenson who paid us an unexpected visit early in April 1960. *The Nation*'s open letter to me of June 24, 1960, testified to the personal part I played in the Chaguaramas problem. *The Nation* wrote:

'On the question of the return of Chaguaramas there is the same miserable story to tell. By means of immense labours, tireless vigilance, inflexible determination and at the same time the utmost flexibility in approach, you have educated the people of this country (and people of larger countries as well) in the needs and rights of an emergent nationalism. Here again the record shows that in the days when, practically singlehanded, you undertook this stupendous task you were surrounded by misrepresentation, lies, attribution of your struggle to motives the meanest and most personal, or plain indifference. Where on the one side we have had your herculean efforts, on the other it would be difficult to find sufficient material to fill one page of this paper with unequivocal pronouncements by people who stood on your side, especially in the days when it was needed.'

(vii) April 22, 1960

The first major result of this public pressure was the appointment of a new American Consul-General. They chose Edwin Moline, a personable young man, to whom one could talk as an equal. We got on splendidly, and at our very first meeting, I knew we could do business. In the course of discussion with him on August 12, 1959, I put forward the following concrete proposals for the settlement of the Chaguaramas issue. The proposals were as follows:

'(i) The base is to be a Joint United States–West Indies Base, the United States to provide full training facilities for West Indians at all levels, and allowing for the participation of the West India Regiment and association of Trinidad Special Branch with security duties.

(ii) The Government to agree in principle that the United States must evacuate the Base not later than a prescribed date (which in my opinion should not involve too long a period, certainly less than ten years, dating back from 1957 when I first raised the issue of revision).

Provided, however, that the Government shall undertake to keep under constant review the state of world tension in the context of the date of final evacuation stipulated.

(iii) In the general framework of (ii) above –

(a) The United States should immediately release all areas that are not now being used – Waller Field,˙ Carlsen Field, Macqueripe, Tucker Valley;

(b) the remainder of the Base to be utilised on the joint basis and for the period of time stated above;

(c) the Tracking Station to be a separate military reservation not included in (a) above, special access being the responsibility of the United States;

(d) The Trinidad Government's offer of an alternative site at Irois Bay to stand on the record, the United States being urged to reconsider its decision in this respect at least with a view to constructing a small runway and facilities for a small establishment as the solution of the problem of Piarco and to relieve the United States planes of the necessity of fulfilling the administrative requirements of the Trinidad Government;

(e) the United States to extend all reasonable facilities to Town Planners of the West Indies and Trinidad in respect of (b) to facilitate the preparation of a comprehensive plan for the Federal Capital.

(iv) In this general context, the 1941 Agreement to be revised Clause by Clause'.

In a subsequent discussion five days later we clarified the proposals. It was clear that the Joint Base had changed the whole picture. But Washington moved slowly, and there were persistent rumours of divergence of views between the State and Navy Departments. When months went by without decisive action, without even a word, we decided to step up the public campaign.

The climax was the huge demonstration we organised on April 22, 1960 – appropriately, in the University of Woodford Square. Preparations for the demonstration lifted party and public morale to unprecedented heights, and there was talk of marching on Chaguaramas itself. We in the PNM kept our counsel in this; the final decision was left for our General Council meeting which would consider the recommendations of the April 22 Committee we had set up. The General Council was scheduled to meet on April 19.

The tension was mounting and the Americans became very apprehensive. The Consul-General wrote to the Governor on April 8, 1960, asking for an assurance that the demonstration would be so controlled that the danger of incidents affecting United States personnel would be avoided.

The Governor, Sir Edward Beetham, in turn wrote to me the next day. He and i had worked reasonably well together for over three years. But I was fed up to the teeth with the shilly-shallying and the bad faith that had been demonstrated for many weary months. The blame rested principally, in my view, with the Colonial Office, and the Governor, in the final analysis, took orders from the Colonial Office and not from the Premier. I resented beyond belief his attempt to interfere in party decisions. We had known how to start and organise our campaign. We would know how to carry it out. I had not the slightest intention of proposing any march on Chaguaramas, and the PNM would never have agreed to that; but we saw no reason why we should broadcast that fundamental decision all over the place long before the appointed day. So I let the Governor have it. I wrote on April 13:

'The record is one of total and contemptuous disregard by the United Kingdom and United States Governments of the position repeatedly stated without any ambiguity by the Ministers of Government and the Party to which we belong. My colleagues, Governmental and Party, have now drawn and will continue to draw the inescapable conclusions therefrom: that . . . on this matter of Chaguaramas you and I, Governor and Premier, are on opposite sides.

It is against this background that I view your letter of April 9. I wish to state clearly. . . .

(b) I regard the demonstration on April 22 as within the legal and constitutional rights of my Party and its members.

(c) I cannot understand your suggestions that the demonstration may lead to a breach of the peace or to injury to persons or property. The only suggestions I have heard of possible breaches of the peace come from Chaguaramas – reports of special training in fire-fighting equipment, use of gas masks, and importation of hand grenades.

(d) The decision as to the theme and the route of the demonstration is a matter for the General Council, the Governing Body of our Movement. . . .

(e) I must remind you that the People's National Movement, after four years, stands out as the symbol of order and discipline in the country, the enemy of lawlessness and disorder in the highest places both at home and abroad.

(f) For the same reason I cannot accept your statements that (i) "any disorderly conduct directed at the United States Government must have the effect of nullifying to a great extent the efforts being made to settle amicably the problems which confront us vis-à-vis the United States"; and (ii) that "an unfriendly demonstration directed against them" will be "calculated to make them stick their toes in", and "would make our task of reaching agreement on our outstanding problems a hundredfold more difficult".

The only efforts that I know of to settle the problems amicably have been made by the elected representatives of Trinidad and Tobago. The efforts made by others have been designed, and clumsily designed, to defeat our aims. We have had for nearly three years to fight tooth and nail, every inch of the way, against American intransigence, British hostility, and Trinidadian treachery – to achieve what? a conference to discuss our proposals with separate and independent representation for Trinidad and Tobago in that conference.

We have failed. Knowing the situation as you, Trinidad's Governor, must know it, you will appreciate the distaste of myself as Premier for a communication in which you suggest that our demonstration for independence, long announced, will make more difficult in April 1960 the democratic, reasonable, equitable solution we have vainly struggled for since June 1957. The demonstration is not an isolated act. It is but one stage in a long series of mounting manœuvres, intrigues and brutalities directed against the Government of Trinidad and Tobago, the People's National Movement and myself. The blame will lie at the door of others, not at mine.

As you know, I am fully conversant with the long history of the West Indies in the period of imperialism. I can assure you that I know of no more sordid chapter than the chapter on Chaguaramas. That, I am confident, will also be the verdict of the people when the full facts are made known to them . . . my view will have the support of tens of thousands of decent-minded Trinidadians who are determined to assert, at long last, their rightful claims to a place in the comity of nations and to living their lives, however incomplete, in peace, free from the interminable demands and never-ending tyranny of those who for so long have held them in thrall, stifled their initiative, and dismissed their rights and aspirations with arrogant disdain.

Your Excellency has reiterated that your letter is a personal one. Nevertheless the opinions are personal only in the sense that they do not emanate officially from Your Excellency but are personal on a public matter of grave importance to the parties concerned. It is impossible entirely to separate Your Excellency's position as Governor from the opinions expressed. . . .

Your Excellency is no doubt familiar with the position of Dr. Nkrumah in relation to Sir Charles Arden-Clarke, whom, as you know, I had at one time considered as a suitable person for the position of Governor-General of the Federation and welcomed as Chairman of the Chaguaramas Joint Commission. I was able to appreciate fully Dr. Nkrumah's position when Sir Charles Arden-Clarke told me privately two years ago that it was pointless to continue pressing for Chaguaramas and that his advice to me was that I should endeavour to get financial aid from the United States for the construction of the Federal Capital on another site.

Finally I would bring to Your Excellency's notice what is to me the most painful and depressing aspect of this matter in so far as it relates to Your Excellency's tenure of the governorship. My colleagues, both in the Government and the Party, and I have in the past been happy to think that in you we had a representative of Her Majesty who was a signal example of the relation that we are anxious should exist between us and the metropolitan power in the period immediately preceding and following the attainment of independence. . . .

For reasons which are still inexplicable to us, Your Excellency

now appears as being ranged against the Government and Peopl
of Trinidad and Tobago on issues on which we expected that you
above all were in a position to understand and appreciate our
policy. Nothing would have so smoothed the passing of colonialism
in the West Indies, nothing would have so established the metropolitan and Commonwealth interests which Your Excellency no
doubt has most at heart, as a clear indication on your part that,
while you were mindful of your original responsibilities you
sympathised with the legitimate aspirations and demands of a
people striving to establish themselves and their rights. It is the
considered opinion of my colleagues and myself that a great opportunity has been missed, that no official disapprobation which Your
Excellency might fear on the eve of retirement could possibly be
weighed in the scale against the world-wide approval and enthusiasm for the ideals of the Commonwealth which Your Excellency's stand would have elicited. It is the consciousness of this
failure to do what is crying to be done that has directed the matter
and manner of this reply to your communications. At this stage
of our history, I, as Premier of Trinidad and Tobago and Political
Leader of the People's National Movement, recognise no other
categories, official or unofficial, except two: that which helps, or,
that which hinders, our people in their attainment of our legitimate
aims.'

Our General Council decided to confine the march to Port-of-
Spain and principally the Queen's Park Savannah, and to send small
delegations of carefully hand-picked persons to present a memorial
at the Governor's Residence and the American Consulate.

So the great day came, and thousands assembled at the University
of Woodford Square. I was scheduled to make a major but short
speech, which I have always considered one of the best I have ever
made in my life. It reads in part:

'Two years and eight months ago the Second Annual Convention
of the People's National Movement fixed April 22, 1960, as West
Indian Independence Day and called for a four-party conference
to revise the 1941 Anglo-American Agreement on Chaguaramas.
One year and six months ago I announced publicly in the Municipal Elections of 1958 the hour and destiny – April 22, 1960, at
eleven o'clock in the morning.

For two years and eight months we have beaten our heads in

vain against the forces and agents of colonialism – against the unswerving and often discourteous hostility of the British and American governments, on the one hand, and on the other, against the servile mentality and inferiority complex bred among some West Indians by centuries of colonial rule.

Thus it is that we find ourselves today, on what should have been our historic Independence Day, cheated of our rights and frustrated in our aspirations. By the flimsiest legal quibble and constitutional technicality, which will not bear examination, the British and American Governments, forced every step to retreat from their untenable positions on Chaguaramas, have agreed to discuss revision of the 1941 Agreement, on one condition – that they will not discuss with Trinidad and Tobago.

On the most specious political grounds the British Government has sought to restrain our onward march to full internal self-government, and has expressed itself against the very constitutional check and balance which in circumstances such as ours we would normally expect it to be foremost in advocating – a nominated Second Chamber.

The British and American Governments have, it is common knowledge, intrigued in West Indian politics and today they find themselves still desperately seeking to carry out the classic political manœuvre of colonialism – to divide in order to rule. It is at their door, and at no other, that the blame rests for the present divisions in the West Indies over independence and Chaguaramas. It is at their door, and no other, that the blame rests for the spectre of racialism which has recently reared its ugly head in our midst.

All around us the struggle for national independence continues successfully. Each month new independent countries are added to the comity of nations. . . .

Thus we of the People's National Movement have issued this call to the nation, to all sections and interests, irrespective of race, colour, class, creed, national origin or previous condition of servitude, to this historic national demonstration for Independence on the day and at the hour of destiny long proclaimed – April 22, 1960, at eleven o'clock in the morning.

You have responded magnificently – the Trade Unions, the economic associations, the citizenry generally, and the members of the People's National Movement, men, women, and children, from all over Trinidad and Tobago. We march in our thousands, we march for freedom. We march not only in Port-of-Spain. Our

march in Port-of-Spain is the symbol of our march throughout
the West Indies. We march legally and constitutionally in a grand
political demonstration – without liquor, without jumping up,
without calypsos, without disturbances, without molestation of
onlookers or spectators, without injury to private property of any
sort, peacefully and without missiles, on the route prescribed by
our Party.

With the eyes of the country, the West Indies and the world
upon us, we march with discipline, dignity and decorum, as befit
the citizens of a country who have publicly declared our intention
of Independence. We march to show and tell the world that if we
are not yet independent in law, we today and after today are
independent in fact. . . .

Our enemies said we would never be free. They said we would
never be fit for freedom. They said we could never govern ourselves. They said that we were a lazy, servile race, desirous only of
sitting in the sun and eating yams and pumpkins, capable only of
aping the graces of our European masters. They said we could
never operate democratic institutions, we could never be governed
along European lines.

Our magnificent demonstration today gives the lie to this imperialist indictment of the West Indian people. We today fill with
distinction all the occupations which we were supposed never to
be capable of filling. Our elected representatives with their Cabinets have proved their competence to assume the full panoply of
autonomy and Independence. Our economic development repudi-
ates all the arrogant inhibitions of colonialism restricting us to
certain lines only and restraining competition with our masters. We
have the spirit of independence, the capacity for independence,
the readiness for independence. Only the form is lacking. Our
demonstration today serves public notice that we are not prepared
to wait longer for the gift as of grace of what is ours as of right.

From today, April 22, 1960, 11 a.m. we are a different people.
We are not what we were on April 21. We are here today as West
Indians – the new nation born out of the amalgam of disparate
cultures and different racial stocks. Our demonstration today
demonstrates national unity. Let us go forward in national unity,
the country of all and for all, with a career open to talent, without
the racial discrimination of the past and the social sycophancy
nurtured thereby. Let us march united, resolved to recognise the
equality of all West Indians, moral, religious, political and legal,

resolved to expunge from the West Indian vocabulary the nomen-
clature of colonialism – niggers and coolies, chinks and limeys.
   A demonstration such as this is not only a political leap forward.
It is also a spiritual purification. As we surge forward confidently
to meet the future, we bury the past. And so symbolically, as we
ready ourselves for the demonstration of a people determined to
be free, let us consign to the bonfire the seven deadly sins with
which we have been afflicted.'

And so I consigned to the flames the existing constitutions of Trinidad
and Tobago and the West Indies, the 1941 Agreement, the expatriate
report of the Capital Site, the Telephone Ordinance, the Democratic Labour Party's racial statement, and the *Trinidad Guardian*. I concluded:

   'And so, fellow countrymen, politically resolute and spiritually
   purified, we march, Onward to Freedom! Onward to Independence!
      To me has been assigned the honour of breaking the flags of the
   new Trinidad and Tobago and the West Indies. As they flutter
   in the breeze, let us, each and every one of us, dedicate ourselves,
   in body and in mind, in heart and in spirit, to the service of self-
   government and Independence.
      Long live self-governing Trinidad and Tobago! Long live the
   Independent West Indies!'

My deputy, Dr. Solomon, read a memorial which I had drafted
for the approval of the General Council. The memorial read in
part:

   'WE, THE PEOPLE OF TRINIDAD AND TOBAGO, of all
   colours, races and faiths, assembled in our tens of thousands in
   what has come to be known as our University of Woodford
   Square, on the occasion of this our historic Independence Demonstration on the day long proclaimed, April 22, 1960, at eleven
   o'clock in the morning, we hereby proclaim to the world that in
   the course of human events it becomes necessary for our people
   to dissolve the political bands which have connected us with others,
   and to assume among the powers of the earth the separate and
   equal station to which the Laws of Nature and of Nature's God
   entitle us.

We stand here this morning as the last victims of the colonialism unleashed in the modern world of 1942. . . . In the world of 1960 colonialism has no place. . . . The British Colonies in the West Indies, now federated, constitute today the last remnants and tatters of the colonialism from which the world has steadily liberated itself. The first to be enslaved, we are among the last to be emancipated. The United Kingdom still haggles over self-government. The West Indies Federation is a glorified Crown Colony, a nineteenth-century anachronism. The United States of America claims, by agreement with the United Kingdom, the right to station troops and the most deadly military installations on our soil for the remaining 80 years of a 99-year lease. This is the most deadly menace that has yet appeared to our material interests and our social and political aspirations. . . .

We demand an independent Federation. We demand full internal self-government for Trinidad and Tobago. We demand the revision of the 1941 Agreement between the United Kingdom and the United States of America in a conference in which Trinidad and Tobago enjoys direct, separate, equal and independent representation. We demand the return of Chaguaramas ceded without our consent and against our will. We demand the right, the inalienable and imprescriptible right, to decide our own destiny.

We, therefore, the People of Trinidad and Tobago, in the University of Woodford Square, assembled, do, in the name of the good people of these West Indian Colonies, solemnly publish and declare, that the West Indian Colonies are, and of Right ought to be Free and Independent States, that all colonial connection between them and the State of Great Britain ought to be dissolved; and that as Free and Independent States, they have full power to levy war, conclude peace, contract alliances, establish commerce, and do all other acts and things which Independent States may of right do. And for the support of this Declaration, with a firm reliance on the protection of Divine Providence, we mutually pledge to each other our Lives, our Fortunes and our Sacred Honour.

Long live the Independence of the West Indies!'

And so at eleven o'clock in the morning we ran the West Indian and Trinidad flags up in the University in a simple but extraordinarily moving ceremony. Then our long march began. And as it began, the rains came and continued throughout the march, drenching us to the skin, but keeping the heat down and easing the fatigue. When it was over, with the laying of a wreath on the statue of Cipriani in the area we had rechristened Independence Square, and I left early next morning for a conference in Venezuela, everyone in Trinidad and Tobago knew that we had passed a decisive landmark in our history and that the Chaguaramas victory could not be much longer delayed.

(viii) *The Tobago Conference*

At PNM's Special Convention on September 6, 1959, I reported on Chaguaramas as follows:

'The record will show that, whether in our proposals for partition or removal of the Base to an alternative site, never at any time has there been the slightest hint by myself or any member of the Government of Trinidad and Tobago of any request for the immediate and unconditional evacuation of Chaguaramas.

Today I am glad to report that the Americans understand that our position has always been based on principle and necessity and not on any anti-Americanism.

These are the goals towards which we have been steadily working, and now with some prospects of success.'

My report was based on discussions which had been going on with the other parties to the issue. These discussions covered three points in particular – (1) separate representation for Trinidad and Tobago at the conference I had proposed; (2) the agenda for the conference; (3) proposals I put forward as the basis of a settlement.

On the first point, separate representation for Trinidad and Tobago at the proposed conference, we insisted on this for eight reasons:

1. Chaguaramas is the site chosen for the Federal Capital.
2. Chaguaramas is the only substantial area in the West Indies actually occupied as a base.
3. The day-to-day difficulties arising out of the lease of Chaguaramas were then being discussed by the Governments of the USA and Trinidad and Tobago.
4. The extent and number of areas leased to the USA.
5. The absence of Trinidad and Tobago legislation to give effect to the 1941 Agreement.
6. The problem of Piarco.

7. The Tucker Valley Tracking Station.
8. Trinidad and Tobago has insisted on, and been accorded, separate representation since 1941.

For these eight reasons we insisted that the conference must be held in Trinidad.

On the second point, the agenda for the proposed conference, we held discussions with Mr. Amery and two Colonial Office officials on July 4, when he was in Trinidad, and later sent O'Halloran to advise the Secretary of State for the Colonies directly of my proposals and to inform the Governor who was on holiday in England. Mr. O'Halloran, on instructions, made it clear that Trinidad and Tobago would be prepared to form part of a Federal delegation in a tripartite conference, on two conditions only – (a) that the conference would be preceded by bilateral discussions between the USA and Trinidad and Tobago; (b) that the document which emerged from the bilateral talks should form the basis of discussion at the conference as far as Trinidad and Tobago was concerned. The Secretary of State insisted that the Premier of Trinidad and Tobago must form part of the Federal delegation, expressed sympathy with our views, and thanked us warmly for authorising Mr. O'Halloran's mission.

That was why I spoke in September about 'some prospects of success'. We discussed with Mr. Amery on July 4. We sent our views to the Colonial Office on separate representation on July 31. I put my informal proposals to the United States Consul-General on August 12. Mr. O'Halloran spoke with the Secretary of State on September 15.

I then proceeded to the University. I said:

'It is now December 10. To this day I have waited in vain for any response to the proposals that I have made. They have kept me hanging in the air.

My Party, my Government, the People of Trinidad and Tobago, and above all myself, have been exposed for years to the *Guardian*'s and the DLP's slander, abuse and charges of anti-Americanism. The Colonial Office put us in this mess eighteen years ago. We have been struggling for two and a half years to get out. They have wasted four weeks of our valuable time creating constitutional disorder where there was none, finicking with bicameral or unicameral, further inflating Gomes, building up the DLP. But on Chaguaramas, four or five months after our positive proposals, not one mumbling word. They will sell their souls and ours too if

they could get hold of them, to deprive us of the political credit
of settling the Chaguaramas issue. . . .

In these four or five months the United States has reached a
settlement on the bases in the Philippines. The United States has
reached a settlement on the bases in Morocco. The United States
is reported to be favourably disposed to Panamanian representations on the Panama Canal Zone. On Chaguaramas, nothing
except arguments here, there and everywhere, from Britain, USA
and the Federal Government about PNM's stand, about PNM's
representation, about who would sign, and matters of this kind.
But nothing about the fundamental issues that we have raised.

Now tonight the People of Trinidad and Tobago, the Federal
Government and the whole world know where we stand and what
we are fighting for. My Party is convinced that these proposals
represent the basis of a settlement which is just to all the interests
involved and will bring to a close the sordid chapter in our history.
I want to assure you here tonight that as long as I am Premier of
this country, elected by the people, and the Political Leader of
my Party, I shall fight for this settlement with the last ounce
of strength in my body.'

The break came during Macleod's visit to Trinidad six months later.

On June 8, in a note to the PNM Cabinet, he set out his broad ideas as
to procedure. He proposed a meeting in three stages: (a) London,
between the United Kingdom and the United States, with the Federation as observers; (b) Trinidad, between the United States and Trinidad, with the United Kingdom and the Federation as observers;
(a) Trinidad, for the signing of the new agreement between the United
States and the Federation.

The matter was discussed at a meeting between the Secretary of
State, the Governor-General, the Prime Minister, Premiers and Chief
Ministers of the Territories held in Port-of-Spain on June 17. The
meeting agreed to Macleod's three-stage talks.

We took a powerful delegation to London which included two
members of the Opposition. In caucus discussions we discussed a
draft prepared by me of an opening statement at the Conference. The
document as finally approved by the caucus and read by me reads in
part as follows:

'The Trinidad and Tobago position in 1960 involves the following
propositions:

1. The Anglo-American Agreement of the colonial era of 1941 cannot continue in the era of West Indian independence and self-determination.

2. The unilateral freedom of the United States to use any base or bases for purposes, military or political, that may run counter to West Indian external interests, aggravate the danger from modern war to the West Indian people, and imperil the very existence of the population of Trinidad and Tobago, cannot be accepted.

3. Any new agreement must recognise the fundamental economic interests of Trinidad and Tobago, as those interests are understood by the elected representatives of the people of Trinidad and Tobago in their efforts to utilise their limited resources, particularly their land, for the benefit of the population.

4. Any new agreement must be freely entered into by the representatives of the West Indian people themselves.

5. Any alternative arrangement that may be agreed to in 1960 must, whether in the military or political sense or in the field of economic aid, be patterned on the more recent agreements entered into by the United States of America over the past decade with countries which, like the West Indies, have emerged from the tutelage of colonialism.'

The London stage of the talks was eminently successful. The Secretary of State, Mr. Macleod, presided. The representatives of the United States declared their readiness to release unconditionally the major part of the areas which they then held under the 1941 Agreement, seeking to retain only those which were essential to the discharge of their responsibilities in the field of world-wide and hemispheric defence.

And so we proceeded to the Tobago stage of the Conference, with Sir Solomon Hochoy, in the chair. The conference was held from November 28 to December 9. Representatives from the Federal Government and the United Kingdom attended as observers.

I did my homework for the Conference. I prepared a draft agreement which set out new proposals to replace the Agreement of 1941 clause by clause. The new proposals were based on American agreements in other parts of the world, particularly Libya, Iceland and Greenland, and were used as the basic document for discussion. I discussed them in detail with some of my closest colleagues before we proceeded to Tobago. I presented these proposals in general outline to the Conference at the meeting on December 2.

My most important contribution to the Conference, however, was my statement in respect of economic aid for four major projects – improvements to the road to Chaguaramas, the port, the railway, and a college of arts and sciences at the St. Augustine campus of the University of the West Indies. I also raised the question of a sugar quota in the United States.

The Conference, our first real venture in external affairs, was conspicuous for its harmony and goodwill. In my final speech at the Conference I said:

> 'Our deliberations themselves have been eminently satisfactory and when the history of West Indian Independence comes to be written this Tobago Conference will have its rightful and enduring place. We have substituted, Sir, an Agreement made by us for an Agreement made for us, and the recognition by the USA as well as by the UK of our new status, in fact even before we have achieved it in law, enhances our dignity and fortifies us as we approach the road to national independence. . . .
>
> On behalf of our delegation, Sir, and the people of Trinidad and Tobago, I give the unequivocal pledge, that, as long as I have on Governmental and other levels the responsibility for the conduct of the affairs of Trinidad and Tobago, this Agreement will be carried out not merely in the letter but also in that spirit of friendliness and recognition of mutual needs which has actuated us all in this room.'

The results of the Conference were eminently satisfactory. The United States of America agreed to abandon some 21,000 acres of the land leased under the 1941 Agreement, including unused portions of the Naval Station at Chaguaramas and all the areas outside of the north-west peninsula. In the event of an emergency the US were to reoccupy Scotland Bay and 1,400 acres at Waller Field including the runway. Teteron Bay, which remained under US lease, was to be developed for joint use by the US, the Federation of the West Indies, and the Government of Trinidad and Tobago, for the operation and training of Naval Construction Units, the granting of base facilities to the West Indies Naval Forces, and the resiting of the Trinidad and Tobago Marine Police Launch Station. The US would also provide facilities for vocational training involving the use of the machine shops in the main Chaguaramas area. The US proposed a programme for economic utilisation of areas in the north-west peninsula estimated to cost approximately (US) $1·1 million.

With regard to the duration of the tenure of the areas retained the delegations of the US and Trinidad and Tobago agreed upon the following terms:

1. By the end of 1962 the US would complete the agreed release of areas and the provision of facilities. From the time of signing the agreement until the end of 1962, the Government of Trinidad and Tobago would have the right to utilise the areas involved subject to normal security arrangements.

2. At the end of a further period of five years, i.e., at the beginning of 1968, the parties would undertake a joint review of the operation of the agreement and the need for its continuation in the existing or modified form.

3. Unless they agreed that it should be terminated, the agreement would then continue subject to such modifications as might be agreed upon, for a further period of five years at the end of which time, i.e., at the beginning of 1973, the parties would jointly reconsider the strategic need in the light of the world situation at that time for the defence facilities enjoyed thereunder.

4. If agreement were not reached within a period of one year, i.e., by the end of 1973, on the continued need for these facilities, the US would have a period of four years, i.e., until the end of 1977, in which to complete their withdrawal.

The US delegation strongly recommended US participation in the following high priority projects in Trinidad on a grant basis:

1. improvement of the port facilities in Port-of-Spain;
2. construction of additional road facilities between Port-of-Spain and Chaguaramas, including land reclamation in the Cocorite area;
3. rehabilitation of the Trinidad Government Railway;
4. development of a College of Arts and Sciences of the Branch of the University College of the West Indies in Trinidad.

The population of Tobago gave our delegation a tremendous send-off, and we returned to Trinidad to meet an enormous welcome. The population of Trinidad and Tobago was proud of us and the the PNM for the convincing victory we had won after years of patient and unremitting work.

The results of the Tobago Conference were immediately made available by me to St. Lucia, Antigua and Jamaica, whom I kept advised throughout the Conference, and served as the pattern for similar agreements in respect of those territories. By February 1961, therefore, we were ready for stage three of the talks which consisted principally of the signing of the agreement by the British and American Governments and by the Federal Government and representatives of the Territories. I signed on behalf of Trinidad and Tobago.

February 10, 1961, was a historic day for Trinidad and Tobago. In an impressive and deeply-moving ceremony the Trinidad and Tobago flag, together with the West Indian flag, went up side by side with the American at Chaguaramas.

The next step was to take the Agreement to the Legislative Council for approval which no one had ever dared in twenty years to seek for the 1941 Agreement. We went first on December 16, 1960, with the results of the Tobago Conference, seeking approval. Then, on April 21, 1961, within one year of our April 22, 1960, march for independence and Chaguaramas, I moved the second reading of an Ordinance to implement the Agreement of February 10, 1961.

This left only one issue outstanding – the quantum of United States aid for the projects proposed by me in Tobago. There was much haggling over this. It began at the Conference itself. I told the House in the debate on the Speech from the Throne on January 12, 1962, of the disputes in Committee which resulted in a meeting at the Governor's residence one night at which there was an open split in the American delegation, the Ambassador siding with Trinidad and Tobago.

Discussions then began between the two Governments. I indicated the nature and scope of these discussions in the debate. I said:

'In the course of these discussions, the United States Mission in Trinidad sent me a memorandum dated the 24th October, 1961. . . .
   "While the United States delegation strongly recommended United States participation on a grant basis in projects relating to the port, road, Cocorite reclamation, railroad and University College, at no point did the United States agree to provide the entire costs of these projects. . . ."
The United States remains prepared to work out a reasonable level of participation in the Tobago projects, taking into account (a) the availability of United States funds, (b) the feasibility of the project in question, and (c) the requirements of present United States legislation. . . . The United States believes that, given the level of national income in Trinidad, its participation should be in the form of goods and services of United States origin and that the Government of Trinidad and Tobago should meet the local currency costs'.

A totally new situation, Mr. Speaker. . . . The fact of the matter is, Mr. Speaker, it is obviously untenable to suggest that the Ministers of the Government of Trinidad and Tobago sat down in Tobago to work out a new Defence Agreement to which were related certain fundamental projects which we stated in plenary conference, which we fought over savagely in Committee and in private session at Government House in Tobago, only to find here now that some months later the four fundamental projects that we put forward are to depend upon the feasibility as decided by one of the parties to the conference, or to depend on the availability of United States funds, or worse still, are to depend upon the level of national income in Trinidad.

We did not discuss in Tobago the question of the national income of Trinidad. We discussed in Tobago the question that the United States of America had been in Chaguaramas for 20 years on the basis of an agreement with the United Kingdom, which the Trinidad and Tobago elected Ministers refused to recognise. We insisted on recognising an Agreement reached by us, the representatives of the people. We changed the 1941 Agreement; we wiped it out and substituted a new Agreement. And that new Agreement, an integral part of it was the question of economic assistance; (a) general; and (b) in relation to four specific projects, three of which had some military significance or were directly related to the military facilities, and one which was clearly presented as compensation to Trinidad and Tobago, taking the form of assistance in the defence of the Trinidad and Tobago way of life in return for the contribution that Chaguaramas had made to the defence of the American way of life.

There was not a single reference to national income; there was not a single reference to the availability of funds; there was not a single reference to the feasibility of the projects, not a single reference. . . .

So the memorandum of October 24 proceeded to spell out that Trinidad and Tobago would have – I understand it is there waiting for us now – the sum of $6·6 million US of grants for certain specific projects; first, $1·6 million, a free grant for the total cost of the Library at the University College; secondly, the sum of $1 million US for Port development; thirdly, the sum of $1 million for a road from Port-of-Spain to Chaguaramas; and fourthly, the sum of $3 million US, to be used either for the University College or for any of the other projects.

But on this basis, Mr. Speaker, the United States Government has proposed that the sum of money for the construction of the University College, including the library, would involve the contribution of 60 per cent of the construction costs, and Trinidad and Tobago would have to find the other 40 per cent. And as indicated in the memorandum, the sum of $1 million US for the road is based on a later presentation that that sum of money in United States currency would be available for the foreign exchange aspect of the road, the foreign cost, presumably, Sir, machinery and equipment. Now, Mr. Speaker, I think the problem at once emerges. We did not sit down in Tobago to ask for 60 per cent of a College. We asked them for a College. That College was to defend our way of life as Chaguaramas had defended their way of life. There was no suggestion that there should be a percentage contribution, that, for example, one might build the shell of the rooms and leave the place without a roof – an entirely new type of University. It was to be entirely 100 per cent construction cost of the University, subject, of course, to the working out of the details of the total cost.

When you take the road, Mr. Speaker, what is the cost of the road to Chaguaramas? The cost of the road to Chaguaramas is local labour. The cost of the road to Chaguaramas is local building material. Very little cost might be involved in terms of equipment. We may have the necessary equipment here and, in that case, it would be less than a 60 per cent contribution in terms of the road to Chaguaramas.

As a matter of fact, the argument now stated would permit, if one wanted to be facetious, a statement that one per cent contribution to the cost of any project would involve United States participation on a grant basis. So that, Mr. Speaker, on the 27th October, I wrote to the United States Mission, and I think the first part of the submission ought to be stated here for the information of the House of Representatives and the country. Acknowledging the memorandum of $6·6 million, and so on, I proceeded to set out as follows:

"This Government proposes to request United States economic aid to this Territory in three forms and under three heads:

(1) The four fundamental projects agreed to at the Leased Bases Revision Conference;

(ii) Development loans to this Government under the new Alliance for Progress Programme; and

(iii) Technical assistance. . . .

This Government considers that the four fundamental projects form a distinct category and should be clearly separated from the other Aid projects. . . .

Our Government considers this to be a matter of fundamental principle, on which it will not be possible to compromise, and the population of Trinidad and Tobago would find it difficult to understand such an interpretation of the Tobago Agreement".'

Eventually the Cuban missile crisis intervened and the problem had not been solved. I was in London at the time, and I made it clear in a press conference that the Chaguaramas question was a domestic issue which I did not wish to get embroiled in extraneous considerations. Shortly after President Kennedy sent a special emissary to me in London to make an offer of US $30 million – $51 million of our currency. I accepted. The assistance to the Port has already been provided. A road from Chaguanas to San Fernando is under construction as a substitute for assistance to the railway, and widening of the Western Main Road out of Port-of-Spain to Chaguaramas has been completed. A new $7·5 million College of Arts and Science will be completed at the St Augustine campus of the University of the West Indies in September 1968.

It became fashionable in certain quarters – particularly by James, former editor of our party weekly – to criticise me and our delegation for agreeing to the continued tenure of Chaguaramas for seventeen years. I acted on the instinct that the Americans did not want Chaguaramas at all, not even for seventeen months; what they were concerned with, in my opinion, was in not supplying ammunition for the Panama Canal and the Cubans in Guantanamo Bay. My instinct proved to be sound. Before even the first period of review arrived in 1968, the Americans decided to leave the greater part of Chaguaramas, retaining only the Missile Tracking Station and a new navigational station. The evacuation began on July 1, 1966, and a large area was returned to us in a simple ceremony on June 9, 1967.

The greatest tribute came from the General Council of the PNM, as reported in *The Nation* of February 24, 1961:

'At its regular meeting on Sunday, February 19, 1961, the General Council of the People's National Movement paid glowing tribute to its Political Leader, Dr. Eric Williams, for the oustanding part he played in the achievement of the new US–West Indies Leased Areas Agreement.

Mr. Wilfrid Alexander, 2nd Vice-Chairman of the Party, who took the chair at the meeting, was called upon to deliver the speech in tribute. . . .

Everyone knew the battle that has been won was primarily the battle of the Political Leader. He at all times unswervingly and undeviatingly kept up the fight even in the darkest hour.

He went on to say that the Political Leader should be admired for the tremendous courage and ability he had displayed throughout the struggle for a revision of the 1941 Treaty. The successful negotiation of a new agreement was in a sense the first signal achievement towards the Independence of the West Indies Federation and for this Dr. Williams was more than anyone else responsible. . . .

Mr. Alexander said it was a pleasant duty to thank the Political Leader on behalf of the General Council and particularly so as from his close association with Dr. Williams he knew all the emotional strains and stresses that the Premier went through over the past three years.

The General Council rose in ovation in honour of Dr. Williams.

The General Council gave unanimous approval to a proposal to place at Party Headquarters a plaque suitably inscribed in commemoration of Dr. Williams' part in the achievement by the Government and the Party.'

23

MEMBER OF THE
LEGISLATIVE COUNCIL

As Chief Minister (later Premier) and Minister of Finance, Planning and Development, I necessarily had to carry a heavy burden in the Legislative Council. The head of the government spoke with an authority that his cabinet colleagues obviously lacked. The ministry of finance was an innovation in the 1956 constitution, and it had to be built up bit by bit. The annual budget was my responsibility, and the whole field of taxation and expenditure necessarily devolved upon me. There were the inevitable developments in the five years – exchequer and audit ordinance, public accounts committee, relation with statutory bodies, tenders, treasury bills and foreign loans. But the public service also came within my scope, and the public utilities, especially where the question of public ownership was involved – in the five-year period, 1956–1961, this meant telephones and buses.

The PNM had also introduced the country to planning and had popularised the concept of the development programme. Within a year of taking office we had our development plan ready, having brought in to assist us Arthur Lewis and Teodoro Moscoso of Puerto Rico as we had pledged to do in our election manifesto. So that in the 1958 budget, presented to the Council on December 30, 1957, I introduced the Five Year Development Programme 1958–1962, which we called, to the great wrath of the opposition, The People's Charter for Economic Development.

There were other matters which required my intervention in parliamentary debates. I had a special interest in education, which, when we made it free in the 1960 budget at secondary level, was obviously very much of a finance matter. Immigration came within my portfolio as Chief Minister until we developed the Ministry of Home Affairs in 1960; even then, the whole question of federation was involved and so the Premier was brought in. Town and Country Planning we saw as an integral part of economic planning, and so it came within my portfolio also.

No subject in these five years gave rise to greater acrimony or longer debates than the reform of the electoral procedure for the 1961 election. The debates went on far into the night. It was unthinkable that the head of the government would not intervene; and in any case much historical research was involved.

It was only natural and proper that the head of the government should move a resolution relating to the right of the British Guiana people to self-government. Our agricultural small holdings ordinance, providing for security of tenure, necessarily raised the whole question of landownership and land use in the Caribbean over previous centuries, which was peculiarly my forte. Long years of study and historical scholarship bore fruit in the Legislative Council.

The longest and perhaps the most important speech I have ever made in Parliament was the 1958 budget speech which lasted over six hours. I was particularly concerned in that speech with two major questions – the oil industry and the Development Programme. This was the first really PNM budget, so I was concerned with the education of the population, the elucidation of the complexities that faced our economy, and with putting our small country in the international context.

In dealing with oil, therefore, I paid special attention to developments in Venezuela and Alberta, with particular reference to oil depletion allowances and to the sale of concessions. Our predecessors had given away our valuable marine areas in the Gulf of Paria; it was freedom on our side of the boundary, while Venezuela on its side sold concessions to the highest bidders.

On our $191 million dollar development programme I went to town. Our figure compared with Barbados' $50 million for five years and Jamaica's $480 million for ten years. On a *per capita* basis our expenditures averaged $51 per year as compared with $40 for Barbados and $32 for Jamaica. The principal problem that I tackled was jobs.

The opposition attacked bitterly my budget speech on the basis of the taxation proposals it contained. Opposition economics was dominated by the view that one should not tax the population, one should borrow instead. On this basis they opposed the Pay As You Earn system which I introduced on November 29, 1957, to deal with the large number of taxpayers in arrears, to take care of evaders, and to correct the situation which the English economist, Prest, had described in the Caribbean generally – that there were more owners of private cars than income taxpayers. The newspapers gave the lead to the opposition. They said that PAYE was more suited to industrialised and developed economies. The *Trinidad Chronicle* described the bill as 'an infernal piece of legislation', and called on the Governor to refuse his assent – the very Governor who had presided over the Executive Council which had approved the bill. Yet all that the bill did was to introduce a new method of collection; as I put it, 'we have been having here a system of Pay As You Want, but now we shall have Pay As You Earn'. The opposition, quoting of all people Adam Smith, wanted to delay the bill for six months, which I described as 'obstructionist tactics, the policy of Fabius Cunctator in the age of Sputnik'.

The public reaction to PAYE was quite different. It gave rise to one of the best calypsos in Trinidad's history, the work, as always, of Sparrow. I can still recall the 1958 Carnival when all over the place people were singing:

'The Doctor say, to pay as you earn,
But Sparrow say you paying to learn,
And me father say he sharpening the axe,
For when the collector come to pay off the income tax.'

It was not only that the opposition differed on the mechanics of development; they disagreed with us also on priorities. On May 3, 1957, for example, they wanted us to reintroduce the subsidies on flour and condensed milk which had been abandoned by our predecessors; they alleged the increased cost of living. I had to deal with this argument severely. I emphasised that we could spend the money instead on schools and houses.

Another favourite argument of the opposition was that old age pensions should be increased. It looked different from the vantage point of the Minister of Finance. I preferred to spend the money on development of the depressed areas of Laventille, on development of the sugar areas, on development of isolated Tobago.

For Tobago as for the sugar areas, we sought in 1957 to introduce an interim development programme even before we finalised the five-year programme. As Minister for Tobago Affairs, I presented the problem of Tobago with its 35,000 people on June 7, 1959 as a 'test of the sincerity of the Trinidad Government's pronouncement with respect to the development of the smaller islands'.

It was in this context of the increased and practical recognition of Government's responsibility for Tobago that the Tobago Independence

Movement issued in 1960 a Manifesto entitled 'Calling all Tobago-
nians'. With typical confusion, the Manifesto suggested three alternative ways in which Tobago could become 'an independent unit'.
These ways were: (1) become a Federal area with no individual
financial responsibility; (2) become an Independent Unit as the other
islands with individual responsibility including Finance; (3) revert to a
Colony outside the Federation, such as British Guiana.

I therefore proceeded in my Budget Speech on April 12, 1961, to
analyse this confused thinking on the subject, by comparing Tobago
in its association with Trinidad with three of the Federal territories –
Dominica, St. Vincent, St. Lucia; Tobago had 32,900 people by the
1960 Census as compared with 59,500 for Dominica, 80,000 for St.
Vincent, 86,200 for St. Lucia.

The Tobago Independence Movement was resoundingly defeated
in the 1961 General Election, in which Tobago, with two seats, voted
solidly PNM. The voters of Tobago recognised the Tobago Independence Movement for what it really was: behind all the façade of
Ministers, a Legislative Council of its own and a referendum to decide
the future of the island, it was, as I said in replying to the Budget
Debate on April 28, 1961: '. . . nothing but an attempt to perpetuate
the 18th century plantation in the 20th century . . . an attempt to
maintain a racial discrimination in Tobago'.

But development required money. We drew on our surplus balances
and increased taxation pending foreign aid and going to the market for
foreign loans. We soon had our first taste of foreign aid, British style.
On my visit to London in July 1957 I sought Colonial Development
and Welfare Funds – which Trinidad had never got in any quantity –
for the implementation of the first instalment of our Tobago plan. As
I reported to the Council on August 7, 1957, 'the Colonial Office was
emphatic that Trinidad and Tobago must rely for its development on
its own resources'. Towards the end of our first five-year term we
were successful in getting a loan from the International Bank for
Reconstruction and Development. We sought and obtained the
sanction of the Council to issue Treasury Bills. And we sought to
issue sanitation bonds in the USA for a large sewerage scheme. The
opposition refused to go along with the sewerage scheme and said
we would have to go it alone.

The fly in the ointment was the European Common Market. We
tried without success to alert our Federal colleagues to the danger;
when we did succeed in virtually forcing the United Kingdom to discuss the matter, we took the initiative with Lord Perth and the rest

of the West Indies listened. I reported to the Legislative Council on July 14, 1961, on the questions I had put to the British Government:

'(i) Would it be possible for the West Indies on the threshold of independence to seek an association with the European Economic Community similar to that enjoyed by the Associated Overseas Territories in Africa?

(ii) Would it be possible for the West Indies to seek to form an association with the European Economic Community on the Greek pattern, with provisions which would avoid the political involvement of the West Indies in Europe?

(iii) If the West Indies were to associate with the Six, would it be possible to give protection to her infant industries, as the Press has reported the Irish Republic would insist upon if they joined the European Economic Community?

(iv) Would the Federal Government, and those Unit Governments in the West Indies directly involved, be able to take part in any conference which might be held as part of the process of United Kingdom consultation with the Commonwealth?

(v) Could Mr. Heath give an assurance that the West Indian trading position in the United Kingdom market would not be affected by any United Kingdom association with the European Economic Community?

(vi) What would be the position of petrol and petroleum products from the West Indies?'

As Minister of Finance I was very much concerned with the decision to introduce a Central Tenders Board and take away the power to award tenders from elected representatives of local government bodies who enjoyed the privilege under existing legislation. This unsound arrangement, bad in principle, was further vitiated by the tendency of local government councillors not to award tenders to the lowest bidder. The opposition saw in this an attempt to emasculate local government bodies, deprive them of their rights in law, and introduce the principle of centralisation.

One of the most important issues to come before the Legislative Council was the question of the telephone company. The company operated under an ordinance which, it alleged, made it mandatory on the Government to raise its rates every time its profits fell below 8%. As Minister of Finance, I objected. I wanted facts and figures about their investments, earnings, development programme and so on.

After long and arduous negotiations and cross talk with the telephone company, we decided on a public investigation. On July 24, 1958, I introduced an appropriate motion in the Council.

The company had the day before sought to restrain the Government from taking this action and applied to the courts. The opposition, in turn, sought to prevent discussion of my motion on the ground that the matter was *sub judice*. The Speaker, however, ruled that the action of the company did not interfere with the power, the undoubted power of the Legislative Council. The opposition, including nominated members, thereupon walked out and I was able to proceed with my motion. We appointed our committee, brought in experts from the USA under the International Co-operation Administration, and eventually bought out the British Company for over $12 million in cash. The bill for the acquisition was moved by me on November 25, 1960.

Another major issue which faced me as Minister of Finance was the reorganisation of the public service which I presented to the Legislative Council on November 20, 1959. After the failure of an expatriate commission to deal effectively with the subject, I appointed my Parliamentary Secretary to go through the whole service and make recommendations. It was the whole Cabinet's decision on those recommendations that I presented.

Free secondary education was the highlight of my 1960 budget. But the active association of the religious bodies with education necessarily involved, in the age of the Exchequer and Audit Ordinance and the Public Accounts Committee, careful insistence on proper accounting for government funds entrusted to the denominational authorities. Our opponents saw in this an attack by PNM on the denominational system of education.

On the question of town and country planning we received expert advice from a top United Kingdom authority actively connected with the City of London. On July 29, 1960, I moved an ordinance to make provision for the orderly and progressive development of land in both urban and rural areas, for the grant of permission to develop land and for other power of control over the use of land. I set out the principal considerations in moving the second reading: a stop to the divorce between economic and physical planning, the indiscriminate building on the hills giving rise to floods in the plains, the inordinate number of gasoline stations and drive-in cinemas, the multiplicity of local authorities.

One of the most difficult questions that faced us was the problem of bus concessions. The former Government had divided up the country into seven uneconomic concessions. By 1961 we were faced with the total breakdown of the system. The Tobago concessionaire simply pulled out. The Port-of-Spain concessionaire served notice that he would discontinue his service as from January 16, but we managed to persuade him to continue and even to take over the Tobago concession on the undertaking that the Government would take drastic new proposals to the Legislative Council. This we did on September 5, 1961 – the new arrangement involving, on the basis of recommendations put up by an American expert, a service-at-cost procedure, under which the government guaranteed 14% of the revenue earned by way of profit. I, as Minister of Finance, had called in all the concessionaires and invited them to pool their resources and form one single concession. They bluntly refused, and the Government proposed, as a result, to reorganise the bus service into two concessions only: North including Tobago, and South; the concessions would be awarded on the basis of public tender. This however did not work, and ultimately we decided on public ownership of bus transport.

One of our first excursions into the field of external affairs, apart from Chaguaramas, related to British Guiana. On April 8, 1960, I moved the following motion: 'That this House record its unqualified support of the claim of British Guiana for full internal self-government'. It was a simple motion, directly relevant to our own progress to full internal self-government; as I put it, 'in saying Trinidad and Tobago we automatically say British Guiana as well'. This fitted into our historical position on British Guiana: the PNM was the first political organisation in the West Indies to protest unambiguously against the suspension of the British Guiana constitution in 1953. We expected, and considered ourselves entitled to, the full and unanimous support of the Legislative Council.

To our complete astonishment, one of the opposition members read out a statement on behalf of the Democratic Labour Party which was written by the leader of that party who was then not a member of the Council, Dr. Rudranath Capildeo. The statement opposed our motion on the ground that it would mean majority rule of Indian over Negro.

I tore into the statement which gave rise to a long debate. I said in reply:

'It stinks of racialism. It is the most offensive document ever presented to the Trinidad Legislative Council. It is the most vicious attitude ever expressed opposite . . . what this document is designed to do is to oppose Trinidad and Tobago's demands for full internal self-government. . . . All that it means, Mr Speaker, is that they want the continued intervention of the Colonial Office in Trinidad and Tobago's affairs. . . . This document is not only racial, Mr Speaker, this document stinks of colonialism. . . .'

The reform of the electoral procedure involved three drastic innovations: (1) permanent personal registration, (2) an identification card with photograph and signature (a thumbprint for illiterates), (3) the use of voting machines. The Opposition was furious. Day after day, night after night, it went at us, hammer and tongs. On the system of registration, they claimed that we followed the precedents of the Southern States of America in our design to keep voters away from the polls. I found it necessary to intervene in the debate on the Registration (Amendment) Rules on January 20, 1961. I had made a study of the American system and I was prepared for them. As I put it, forty-six states in the United States had the system of permanent personal registration in one form or another, and one member of the Opposition called it undemocratic. Literacy tests historically, I showed, had nothing to do with the South or with Negroes. I quoted from the latest available American studies of the system, and showed that it was 'an integral part of American democracy'. The Opposition made a great fuss of the cost of the voting machines – about $1,000 US each. Against that was to be set the long life of the machines.

We were back at the issue of elections a week later, the report of the Boundaries Commission. The Opposition accused us of gerrymandering. They claimed that we had given the rural constituencies more voters than the urban, and that we had interpreted the terms of reference of the Boundaries Commission, to pay special attention to sparsely populated areas and to concentrate on natural boundaries such as highways, in a way that would benefit PNM strongholds.

I had made a special study of the 1956 boundaries in the context of the 1956 election report. So I intervened in the debate, which was the responsibility of my deputy, the Minister of Home Affairs. I showed how in 1956 the average Port-of-Spain constituency, emphatically urban, was 18% below the national average, while six seats in St. George, very much urban, were 17% above the national average. The largest constituency, Laventille in St. George, was 188% of the smallest, Caroni South, in terms of voters; or to put it a little differently, the smallest was 53% of the largest. Laventille was 35% above the national average in terms of voters, Caroni South was 28% below. That, I emphasized, was gerrymandering, as compared with the 1961 boundaries, where the largest constituency was 124% in terms of the size of the smallest, and the smallest was 82% of the largest.

The Speaker was chairman of the Boundaries Commission, and the Deputy Speaker was one of PNM's two members; the DLP had one. The fifth member was a High Court Judge. This was not our handiwork. It was the work of the Secretary of State for the Colonies, Iain Macleod. The Speaker was savagely attacked by the Opposition in debate, and so was the Judge. The Opposition moved an amendment to the motion for adoption of the report, that the Secretary of State should appoint a neutral Boundaries Commission. I attacked this unmercifully as 'representative of the last refuge of the obscurantist politicians in this country at this late date in our history seeking to hide behind the coat tails of the Secretary of State for the Colonies who has told him a million times, and is likely to tell him again, that he has no use for colonialism, and he is determined to be the last Secretary of State for the Colonies'.

Concern with general social philosophy underlay my intervention in the debates on the agricultural small holdings tenure bill and the cane-farming industry bill. The dominant fact in sugar was not who owned the land but what market could you find for your production. I took the opportunity in the debate to stake out Trinidad's claim to a share of the United States market, in the following terms:

> 'Castro or no Castro, Cuba or no Cuba, whether the Cuban situation is settled by the removal of Castro or by Castro knuckling down, whatever it is, we consider, on this side, that the West Indies have an absolute right, as a part of the Western Hemisphere, to participate in the American sugar quota . . . not as long as I am around, the Americans are not going to come and use that colonialism of 1896 in order to cut our throats in 1961. I think we will get the quota.'

The PNM had come to power partly on its slogan, 'morality in public affairs'. The Opposition made every effort to attack the Government, therefore, on grounds of immorality and corruption. Three specific issues were raised during the first Parliament – car loans, a boat on the Tobago run called the *City of Port-of-Spain*, and the Swiss Bank.

The car loans issue was first raised in May 1957. It involved a loan to a Minister to purchase a car. A citizen in San Fernando, a mattress maker by profession, filed a writ to determine whether the Minister had lost his seat on the ground that the loan was a contract for and on account of the public service. Two Parliamentary Secretaries and a member of the Opposition had also obtained loans for the purchase of cars, and two other members of the Opposition had applied for loans.

This was a subject that had harassed the United Kingdom for a long time, and I did my patient research into the problem. I raised the question as to whether any member of the Council had an account with the Post Office Savings Bank; British MP's in 1931 who had a telephone agreement with the Post Office ran the risk of disqualification. I drew attention to three members of the Opposition who had leased lands from the Government; was a lease a contract which exposed the member to disqualification? Was an agreement, I asked, to repay a debt to the Government a contract involving disqualification? If so, one member of the Opposition was in jeopardy, having signed an agreement to pay off by monthly instalments a debt due to the Government by way of import duties on scrap metals; whilst two others were still indebted in respect of travelling advances outstanding. A member of the Opposition, as a Minister in the former government, had borrowed money from the Agricultural Credit Bank; was he disqualified?

Thus it was that on September 23, 1957, I moved that the whole question of the possible disqualification of members be referred to a Select Committee of the Legislative Council. I drew largely on British experience and debates on this matter, quoting Aneurin Bevan's demand for 'a sort of constitutional scavenging committee' and Mr. Churchill who had appointed a select committee on this matter of 'great legal complexity and obscurity' in which the law might 'strike here or there by accident or caprice without any reference to any principle of logic, or reason or constitutional doctrine'.

The Opposition dealt in personalities and was intent on seeing corruption where I saw what Mr. Churchill, in viewing the difference between appointments to ambassadorships in Russia and Spain, which did not disqualify, and the High Commissionership to Canada, which did, had stated that he 'had never dreamed that . . . it could have been represented that there yawned and gaped this vast, hideous gulf of constitutional principle'.

The car loans case went to the Privy Council which threw it out. We proceeded with our Select Committee, ultimately specifying a

list of offices which did disqualify and passing validating legislation
out of an abundance of caution, in much the same way as the United
Kingdom had acted in similar predicaments.

On October 23, 1959, a member of the Opposition moved a motion
calling for the appointment of a Select Committee 'to enquire into
the whole transaction involving the *City of Port-of-Spain* and to enquire
also into the suitability of this boat for the functions it carries on at
present'.

The motion related to a boat which had been chartered by the
Government for the Tobago service when the two antiquated steamers,
some thirty years old, the SS *Trinidad* and the SS *Tobago*, were with-
drawn on the ground that they were dangerous to life and limb; if one
of them struck a log, we were advised, she would go to the bottom.
This ship, called the *City of Port-of-Spain*, of Martiniquan ownership (?),
appeared on the scene and was chartered. The Opposition shouted
corruption and argued that the charter fees were high and that we
should have decided to buy the boat instead. I replied that we could
not find out who owned the vessel and I emphasised that throughout
the affair we had had the benefit of adequate advice from our technical
officers.

And so I came to the Swiss Bank. Some foreigner arrived on the
scene to say he was starting a bank that he called the Swiss Bank. It
was only three months from the elections, so the Opposition decided
to fight the issue outside of the Council on the ground of corruption.
They asserted that members of the Cabinet were actively associated
in one form or another with the Swiss Bank in its ventures.

My reply was issued in the University of Woodford Square in a
long address which covered all the facts in the case. I categorically
denied that the Swiss Bank was brought to Trinidad by the Government to finance the Sewerage Scheme. I showed how we had consulted the Colonial Office and the Bank of England on the financing
of the sewerage scheme including the purchase of dollars for the redemption of the bonds, how we had checked with the British Ambassador in Caracas the *bona fides* of the Venezuelan firm which had
successfully tendered for the project, how the tender was influenced
by a proposal to construct a pipe factory to provide 250 permanent
jobs and produce a commodity for export.

I went on to show how we had had dealings not with the Swiss
Bank but with a French group of bankers which was supposed to have
the backing of the French Foreign Office and many of the financial
institutions of the countries in the European Common Market; this

group nominated the Swiss Bank as their agent. I showed how, when the Swiss Bank had come into the picture, they offered to assist in financing telephone equipment, bus transport, and the sewerage scheme, electricity, natural gas, shipyards and graving dock, pre-fabricated school buildings; they offered us a loan of $96 million over a period of ten years.

I showed how our consultants on the sewerage scheme, a reputable US firm, had estimated the cost of the project at US $16·2 million, which was accepted by the Export-Import Bank as the basis of a loan, as compared with the figure of US $8–9 million put out surreptitiously in an anonymous pamphlet. Above all I pointed out how the Ministry of Finance experts had advised against acceptance of any of the proposals put up by the French consortium and the Swiss Bank, whose representative thereupon proceeded to put forward additional proposals for the reclamation of the Caroni Swamp, the extension of the Port-of-Spain harbour, the construction of a slipway in Port-of-Spain, the establishment of a deepwater harbour in San Fernando, a natural gas pipeline, lands for housing development, a model resort hotel in Tobago, a free port, funds for industrial development, aid to the railway, development of the cattle and fishing industries. To the vast amusement of the huge audience, I enquired why they had left out the notorious DLP proposal for the construction of a tunnel to Maracas Bay, and the reclamation of the Gulf of Paria. Why, I asked, did they leave out the Madhouse and the Jail?

And so we killed the *mauvaise langue* of the Swiss Bank.

The Opposition were not united. The disunity that had marked their election campaign was carried over into their activities and behaviour in the Council. This was made manifest shortly after we took power. We invited the leader of the largest opposition party, Maraj, to accompany the Federal Capital Site delegation to Jamaica. Shortly after our return, on March 8, 1957, he made a statement in the Council to the effect that he did not enjoy the confidence of his members.

Even when they were all united in the DLP, they remained dis-united. Maraj took ill and there was a fight over the acting leadership. They nominated the member for Tobago, but he was neither respected nor listened to. One of his followers consistently opposed measures that the acting leader announced the Opposition was supporting – for example, the Public Housing Loans Bill and the Exchequer and Audit Ordinance. On the latter occasion, the acting leader was so incensed at the member's opposition that he got up and moved that the question be put. One advocated food subsidies; another opposed subsidies to the people of Canada. One argued for free secondary education; another spoke against it.

The behaviour of the Opposition members was so scandalous that the Speaker called the Council a fish market. One member X told another Y that to call him a rat would be paying him a compliment; Y retaliated by calling X a stooge of the *Guardian*. In jumped a third member, Z, who called Y a hooligan, a man who would lay a fight with a knife; X invited Z outside, to put his hands on his mouth. Z countered that X was like a wounded animal, very dangerous to deal with; he had never thought that he would live to see the day when one man could be so venomous against his own brother. This was the general pattern of behaviour on the other side.

The most scandalous manifestation of this disunity took place in the Council on April 14, 1960, in the course of the Budget Debate. One member openly called another a murderer to his face, qualifying this by saying, 'the man you are murdering is not yet dead'. He continued, 'let the accused member put into issue pethidine, the single drug pethidine, and if I cannot prove that he should go to jail, I will resign my seat the next day.' The Trinidad and Tobago Legislature had achieved the nadir of respectability.

The fight broke into the open with the selection of Dr. Capildeo to replace Maraj as Leader of the Opposition. Dr. Capildeo's brother in the Council could not stomach this, and attacked the whole party and his colleagues.

The Opposition saw totalitarianism everywhere; it was their favourite charge against the Government. To one my 1958 budget was a 'blueprint of creeping totalitarianism', a 'despotism that would make Nero blush and an oriental monarch ashamed', a 'short cut to Communism'. All I had done was increase some taxes and impose some new ones. The bill to amend the powers of the County Councils and take away from them power to award tenders was described by another as 'a wicked attempt to foist a totalitarian system of Government' upon the country; this same member saw in our proposals for constitution reform 'a shameless grasp for unlimited power, a sinister move to stifle the growing body of people who are opposing this Government'.

To a third, Pay As You Earn was un-British, totalitarian. The Exchequer and Audit Ordinance, providing for rigorous controls of public expenditure, appeared in the eyes of one Opposition member as having many aspects that were totalitarian in every detail; too much power was being concentrated in the hands of ruthless people. To this

MEMBER OF THE LEGISLATIVE COUNCIL

member the Registration Rules, prescribing the procedures to be followed for registration for voting, were totalitarian, 'an insolent invasion of the inalienable rights of the people to exercise their votes'; they struck at the illiterate masses, he argued.

They had a field day with my budgets. One opposed the purchase tax on cars as the most vicious feature of my 1958 budget which he called a 'diabolical monstrosity'; another reminded me that the more cars, the more jobs in washing down cars and in repair shops. A third was sure that we could do all that we wanted without taxing the people. A fourth claimed that in the budget speech, which took six hours to deliver, I had told the Council about the entire globe; another argued that we had not told the people in our election campaign that we would increase taxes and called the budget speech a 'vast travelogue'. Yet another characterised the Government on the occasion of another budget speech as 'a conspiracy of rapacious men which continues to extract the last penny of profit from a penurious people. Taxation to cure inflation has long been exploded as a myth'. He later plagiarised the United Kingdom Chancellor's speech to reply to my 1961 Budget.

The walkout was their favourite technique. They walked out on the telephone issue. They walked out on Chaguaramas. They walked out on the Tenders Board Bill debate. They walked out on Constitution reform. They nearly walked out on old age pensions. They absented themselves from the debate on an interim development plan for the sugar areas. They refused to vote on the issue of a strong federation.

They went to town on the new electoral procedure. The acting leader thought it was embarrassing to take around all the time an identification card which could be destroyed by rats or other pests; he would not 'make this country a prison for its citizens'. In similar vein another called the identification card a badge of serfdom, a convict's badge; 'where is the need for a man to identify himself in a little country like this?' He opposed the voting machine, saying that the population could not use the lever; whereupon he was savagely attacked by another member who refused to be any party to such an insult to the people of his constituency by people who 'cannot pull the W.C. chain on their thoughts'. He asked instead why did we not go to the United Kingdom for our inspiration.

Yet another, colonial to the last, wanted a committee of six members, three Government, three Opposition, with the Governor as Chairman, to reconsider the registration rules.

24

THE PARTY ORGANISATION

Behind the Government's stand on independence, Federation, Chagua-ramas, and in the parliamentary fight over the five-year period, lay one portentous fact – behind us was our Party. As Party Leader, I made it my conscious duty to seek to develop the Party Organisation and to encourage it to live a life of its own.

I set out the perspectives for our Party in my speech to the Third Annual Convention on October 17, 1958. I looked to our organisation and to our education programme to produce an ideal Party member whom I identified as follows:

(a) Every Party Member must feel himself and be seen and recog-nised as the centre of a periphery of citizens or the members of any organisation in which he finds himself.

(b) The party Member must be looked upon as the active leader in all local progressive causes and nationalist aspirations. This does not necessarily mean being in the leadership although that is not excluded.

(c) The public must in time get to recognise the Party Member as the person most likely to be well informed on all the multitudinous international, social and political questions which are pressing on the West Indian population from every side and to which they want answers.

I had boldly called on the Party to take Athens as its guide and inspiration the previous year, in my address to the Second Annual Convention on September 28, 1957:

'The problem of modern democracy is to find meaningful activities for the rank and file party members and to prevent the party from being encrusted in red tape, dominated by party bureaucrats, and overshadowed by party Government.

The more we do this, the more will we in Trinidad and Tobago, through the PNM, approach the decisive advantage of Greek society over all others the world has known – that the body of citizens who formed the public assembly consisted of men who were personally familiar with the business of Government.'

The Party I envisaged I outlined to the Third Annual Convention. I put it this way. The ultimate aim must be:

'To create an organisation which will develop and proliferate in such a manner that in three years' time the island will be aware that its future lies with the Party and the functioning of the Party. On such a basis, legislators can introduce the boldest and most far-seeing legislation, confident that there can be no serious resistance because all reactionary and disruptive elements will be aware of the strength of the Party in the population surrounding them.

(b) Such an organisation from the very start will relieve the legislators to carry out the business of Government. Until they are thus supported, legislators will not know the real possibilities of shaping the destinies of the country. . . .

(c) This building of the Party cannot be carried out by legislators. . . .'

From there I proceeded to the responsibilities of the Party member at election time. Our Party was not just an electoral machine, it must have an independent vitality of its own, it must be principally an educational force. But all would be lost if the Party did not win elections. However, election victories were assured with the right Party.

As far as the Party itself was concerned. I outlined at the Third Annual Convention a Development Programme of $100,000 and called on the members to raise that sum. My priorities were: (1) a Party Headquarters, which we purchased shortly after 1961; (2) a Party Library, which has since been provided; (3) a properly functioning Secretariat; (4) a linotype machine for our Party organ. I called on the Party to carry out its educational mission partly through week-end schools, and several of these were organised, at many of which I was the principal speaker. One of the most important and successful was a week-end school in San Fernando on the Indians in Trinidad. We also organised a number of one-day schools, especially in the constituencies where the Party was less developed; for example, two day-schools were organised in May 1960, the themes being, respectively, 'Officer Responsibility and Party Development' and

'Education for Nationhood'. We organised a special week-end school for PNM candidates in the County Council Elections in 1959.

We had from the start, in organising our Party, made provisions for a Policy Advisory Committee. This comprised the Ministers and Parliamentary Secretaries and Party members appointed by the General Council, with the Political Leader as chairman. It was my practice to refer to this Committee many important issues for advice and consideration before action was taken by the Government. This constituted the most important form of liaison between Government and Party which we sought to develop. The Policy Advisory Committee did very valuable work on development and taxation, the telephone issue, hire purchase, revision of the Elections Ordinance, bus transport, the highway code, radio broadcasting, reorganisation of the public service.

Necessarily, the University of Woodford Square occupied a dominant position in PNM's activities between 1956 and 1961. The thousands in the University roared their approval of the following passage from my address to the Special Convention on September 23, 1961:

'Fellow Party Members, allow me to end on a purely personal note. It has been my privilege to serve you, as Political Leader for six years and as Premier for five. I have sought always to keep faith with the Party and the People. I have placed all my knowledge, acquired at public expense, at your disposal. I have not spared myself in the performance of my duty to you, neither my time, nor my energy, nor my health. You, in turn, have helped and inspired me more than many of you will ever understand . . . the most important contribution that you have made to me personally, one that I can never hope to replay, is that you have given life and meaning and vitality to a long period of training which would otherwise have been an academic exercise and mere intellectual decoration. . . .

Please allow me, fellow Party Members, the privilege of the proud boast that, whatever personal success may be associated with my name, I shall go down to our posterity as the architect of the University of Woodford Square.'

My principal theme in the University, apart from independence and Chaguaramas with which I have dealt separately, was West Indian history. My speech in San Fernando on May 30, 1960, which I entitled 'Perspectives for the West Indies', deliberately dealt with past history.

My speech to the Fourth Annual Convention in March 1960 which I entitled 'The Approach of Independence' sought, in my campaign for an independent Federation, to explain historically the political backwardness of the West Indies. I showed how the metropolitan countries deliberately excluded the West Indies from their policy and ideas, treated them as pawns on the international chessboard, while their university sages justified their political domination and economic stranglehold.

I sought always to instil pride, to give a new sense of dignity to the people. Our history was the politics of the past, made for us by others. It was a necessary guide to the politics of the future, made for us by ourselves.

My opponents were always playing into my hands, giving me opportunity after opportunity to develop my speciality. One such opportunity came my way when Sir Gerald Wight, a respected and quite liberal-minded white businessman, wrote a letter to me on January 6, 1961, which he also sent to the *Trinidad Guardian*. If his forum was the monopolistic daily newspaper, mine was the University of Woodford Square, from which I sent him an open letter on January 24, 1961, the fifth anniversary of the public launching of our party.

In the course of his letter Wight, who had joined the DLP, claimed to see in Trinidad and Tobago the beginning of a trend which might grow into a real threat to democracy. I treated this allegation as it deserved, to the vast delight and edification of the mammoth audience. I replied:

'Let us begin, as so many things necessarily begin, with Aristotle. You are perhaps familiar with his famous defence of democracy. . . .

I ask you now, Sir Gerald – in the light of Aristotle's justification of democracy, do you see the PNM as a threat to democracy? If so, where is the threat? In our policy of free secondary education, designed to educate the many where the former policy was to educate the few? Or do you see a threat to democracy in our programme of political education, in this University of Woodford Square, where we educate the people, report to them on our stewardship? I ask you categorically, is this a threat to democracy, or does it promote democracy? Do you see any threat to democracy in our party structure and organisation? . . .

I skip twenty centuries and go from Aristotle, the Greek philosopher, to Thomas Jefferson, second President of the USA. Are you familiar with his Inaugural Address of 1801? . . . I ask you, Sir Gerald, do you see anything in Trinidad and Tobago subversive of the Jeffersonian principles, which can be construed as a threat to democracy? Is there not equal and exact justice to all men under an independent judiciary, now selected by an executive Judicial and Legal Service Commission? Is there not freedom of religion and is not that freedom of religion extended under the recent Concordat between State and Church to denominational schools, and is not that freedom of religion extended to the freedom to teach religion to pupils of all faiths in all schools in the country? Does not the *Trinidad Guardian* enjoy freedom of the press to the point of daily abusing and prostituting it? Is there not in Trinidad and Tobago freedom of person under the protection of *habeas corpus*? Is there not trial by juries impartially selected with the obligation and privilege of jury service extended by PNM's Government to women who were formerly excluded? . . .

This then is where we stand – our Movement, The People's National Movement, is in the historical stream which runs from Aristotle to Franklin D. Roosevelt.'

In the course of my letter to Wight I had told him and the *Guardian* 'Massa Day Done'. The scribes and pharisees had a field day, saying what a nice person Wight was, ever since the age of eight, thanking Wight for getting so-and-so a job and so on. The DLP thereupon called on me to withdraw 'Massa Day Done' as a wicked statement and to make an unqualified apology for introducing it. I went to the University on March 22, 1961, and gave the massive crowd one of the largest doses of West Indian history ever publicly dispensed in Trinidad. This is what, among other things, I said:

'I categorically refuse to withdraw my statement or to make any apology for it, qualified or unqualified. I repeat, more emphatically than when I said it the first time, Massa Day Done. I accuse the DLP of being the stooge of the Massas who still exist in our society. I accuse the DLP of deliberately trying to keep back social progress. I accuse the DLP of wanting to bring back Massa Day. . . . All that they can see in the slogan, Massa Day Done, is racial antagonism. This is characteristically stupid. Massa is not a racial term. Massa is the symbol of a bygone age. Massa Day is a social phenomenon: Massa Day Done connotes a political awakening and a social revolution. . . .

Massa was more often than not an absentee European planter exploiting West Indian resources, both human and economic. . . . On his West Indian sugar plantation Massa employed unfree labour. . . .

Massa's economic programme was to grow sugar and nothing but sugar. . . . Massa's economic programme represented the artificial stunting of West Indian society. . . . Massa's economy was distinguished by perhaps the most scandalous waste of labour the history of the world has ever known. . . .

Massa was able to do all this because he controlled political power in the West Indies and could use state funds for his private gain. . . . He had no sense of loyalty to the community which he dominated or even to the community from which he had originally sprung . . . Massa was always opposed to independence. . . . Our whole struggle for self-government and independence, therefore, is a struggle for emancipation from Massa.

That was the West Indian Massa. . . . But not every white man was a Massa. . . .

If Massa was generally white, but not all whites were Massa, at the same time not all Massas were white.'

That was the theme I constantly harped on – interracial solidarity, the national community. I never missed an opportunity of emphasising what was one of the principal goals and objectives of the PNM, one of the guiding principles which had led to the birth of the Party. The fourth responsibility that I imposed on the Party member in my address to the Fifth Annual Convention was to remember always that 'he is a member of a nationalist party, consciously dedicated to the promotion of the national community, with emphasis on inter-racial solidarity'. I continued:

'That is what you, the PNM party member, represent. . . . I call upon all party members to stop once and for all this infuriating nonsense that every Indian is anti-PNM. Every Indian is not anti-PNM, nor is every white. Some of the worst enemies of PNM are as black as the ace of spades. Reaction knows no colour. What is the colour of the opposition in Ghana? Or in India? . . . I will say it to you as often as may be necessary, a PNM Indian, trustworthy, loyal, devoted to PNM is a thousand times better citizen than an anti-PNM African. Indians and Africans are fighting together in South Africa against *apartheid*. We do not segregate the Indians in Trinidad at lunch counters or prevent them from living in St James or deny them the vote or make them show passes when away from the estate. . . . We were slaves and indentured workers together

in the age of colonialism, equal in our oppression, equal in the dis-
abilities inflicted upon us. We are citizens together in the days of
independence, equal in our rights, privileges, responsibilities and
obligations to the national community.'

Apart from the University of Woodford Square, where I gave priority
to West Indian history and the national community, my second agency
for the education of the community and the Party was the Premier's
Press Conference. These press conferences were broadcast because of
the hostility of the daily press, and eventually the *Guardian* refused to
attend them for this reason, which meant they continued in the
absence of the *Guardian*. They were very popular, not only in Trinidad
and Tobago but also in the West Indies generally; and we had information to the effect that they were listened to regularly in Venezuela
and were even heard as far afield as Sweden.

We lived with the hostility of the daily press. The *Guardian* never
forgave me for winning the election of 1956 and never allowed the
country to forget that it had advised against voting for a party in that
election. They were obsessed by the old individualism and wished to
see a return to the pre-1956 pattern, where discordant individuals
would seek to form a coalition government.

The *Guardian*, however, went further than this. It complained about
the Government's attitude to the Inter-American Press Association.
I dealt with this issue in a public meeting in the University in November, 1957. I wrote an open letter to the Association, and told them of
the *Guardian's* private and speculative interests which they sought to
dignify under the label of freedom of the press. The first thing dealt
with was the notorious Carnival situation, with its discrimination
against coloured girls in the Carnival Queen competition sponsored
by the *Guardian* until the Government took it over.

I dealt similarly with two other private interests of the *Guardian*,
radio licences fees and printing concessions, and I continued in my
letter to the Association:

'I hope that it will be clear that on these three issues – Carnival
Queen, Printing Concessions, Radio Licence Fees – there is no
suggestion whatsoever of any hostility to the freedom of the press,
either on the part of the Party or on the part of the Government
or on my part. The three issues merely involve the special problem
of vested interests in our society.'

And I concluded my dispassionate and restrained discussion of this issue of freedom of the press and the hostility of the leading local newspaper of the time:

'Under the circumstances, I am happy to give you an assurance of our dedication to (*a*) the democratic way of life; (*b*) the spread of political education.

The Press is important to both. But if newspaper democracy conflicts with our programme of political education, we believe that it is in the best interests of democracy in general and of freedom of the press itself that we should, whenever we consider it necessary, defend and proclaim our own freedom as politicians to attack all opposing points of view which we consider inimical to the interests of the people who have placed us in power against the wishes of the *Guardian* and whose confidence after one year in office we are proud to enjoy and to have retained.'

The *Guardian* sought to explain away its hostility and in so doing violated all its previous talk of impartiality and its complaints to the Inter American Press Association. Its alibi, as stated in an editorial on Sunday, December 4, 1960, was as follows:

'In Trinidad the weakness of the Opposition and the divisions in its ranks have resulted in a state of affairs whereby this newspaper has been virtually forced against its will to take the place of an Opposition party. This is not a function any newspaper can welcome, and we do not consider it any part of our normal duties as a public journal to fill a role that is properly one for politicians.'

Whatever the *Guardian* said or did, it could not challenge the hold the PNM had on the population, and eventually sold out to the Thomson interests in 1961.

But the real answer to the *Guardian*'s combination of malice and ignorance – ably seconded by the *Chronicle* until its demise – was not the Press Conference, but our party organ. We rechristened it *The Nation* on December 6, 1958, by which time we had appointed C. L. R. James editor; he had been invited by the Trinidad and Tobago Government as a guest at the inauguration of the Federal Parliament on April 22, 1958, and had stayed on, but many of our good party members on the General Council objected to his admittance into the Party on the ground of his notorious political record.

The Nation got into serious difficulties with the Party. Already, way back in 1957, trouble had started when a quite unnecessary attack was made by the party paper on the Attorney-General, a civil servant, and the party paper demanded a political Attorney-General. The timing was wrong, and the Government, pursuing its way through the murky waters of constitution reform, was considerably embarrassed. James made the situation worse. His comments before Macleod's arrival were deprecated by the General Council which had been summoned to decide on the line to take. He used the Party paper to build up himself and his family, and his personal articles on George Padmore and the James family were widely resented. Whilst party members generally supported his stand that Frank Worrell should be made captain of the West Indies cricket team, more than one looked askance at his methods.

The Fourth Annual Convention appointed a Committee to examine the relationship between the Party and the Publishing Co., and to ascertain the financial position of the Publishing Co. The Committee's report revealed a situation that bordered on chaos. It condemned administrative confusion, and disclosed a very real absence of liaison between Paper and Party.

On October 2, 1960, the General Council appointed its own Committee to report on the PNM Publishing Co., Ltd. The report stated:

'The whole question of management during Mr. James' term of office could be written off quite briefly as a period of mismanagement. Given a free hand, he appeared to use it freely without regard for his own or the Company's responsibilities.'

James was placed before the Disciplinary Committee on two charges. He refused to appear to answer the charges, was found guilty and was expelled from the Movement. His answer was published in a document entitled 'PNM! Go Forward' which subsequently formed the basis of a study by him of party politics in Trinidad and Tobago. In it he claimed that the attack by the Convention on him was a political attack on me, that he should have 'taken' the post of General Secretary of the Party instead of Editor of the Party organ, that the entire General Council should be made to read some study of his, that I was a 'gangster' for refusing to discuss the Convention action with him (I refused to be any party to by-passing the action of the Convention), and that I had sold out to the Americans at the Tobago Conference.

25
INTELLECTUAL PURSUITS

The sixth in the code of responsibilities which I imposed on the Party member at our Fifth Annual Convention was relieving the strain on the Political Leader. The situation was neatly summed up in a famous and popular calypso of the day:

> 'Annabella stocking want patching
> She want de doctah help she wid dat
> Johnson trousers falling
> He want de doctah help he wid dat
> Some want a zephyr motor car
> Others want piece of land
> Dorothy loss she man
> She want to complain to Doctah Williams.'

I turned to my intellectual pursuits whenever I could find, or make, the time. Three major opportunities came my way during the first five-year term of office.

The first was an invitation to write an essay for inclusion in a volume dedicated to my old friend, Fernando Ortiz, by his students, colleagues and friends, on the occasion of the sixtieth anniversary of the publication of his first book. The essay 'The Historical Background of Race Relations in the Caribbean', drew four conclusions, viz.:

1. The recognition of racial equality is a part of the larger world struggle for freedom in general.
2. The attitude of particular individuals to the question of racial inferiority depends on their attitude to social and economic development in general.
3. The Negro will not achieve moral status until he achieves economic and political status.

4. The attitude of whites to race relations in the Caribbean today is conditioned largely by the traditional attitudes of the past.

My second opportunity came with the invitation in 1958 from Alioune Diop of Présence Africaine to write a paper on 'The Political Leader considered as a man of culture' for the Second International Congress of Negro Writers and Artists held in Rome from March 26 to April 1, 1959. The paper was reproduced in *The Nation* on November 20, 1959.

For the best examples in the modern world of the political leader as a man of culture I turned to India – Ghandi and Nehru. And then I turned to the West Indies, comparing the Caribbean unfavourably with Africa and India, and taking Muñoz Marin of Puerto Rico and Aimé Césaire of Martinique as my examples.

I closed my essay with the question, What then is the political leader in the West Indies considered as a man of culture? I saw him as having four principal characteristics, as follows:

'(1) His political outlook and activity are governed by the fact that while he knows his people, appreciates their problems and shares their aspirations, he by formal training, intellectual discipline and practical experience is able to see all of these as part of the larger world problem.

(2) He consciously promotes, supports and encourages all forms and manifestations of culture which, though not indigenous, are based on an adaptation, conscious or unconscious, of their European and American inheritance to their own personality, needs and environment.

(3) He consciously seeks to integrate into one harmonious whole, to weave into an orderly pattern, the disparate strands of culture which constitute the West Indian – the European (whether it be Spanish, French, or British), the African, the Indian, the Chinese, the Syrian – particularly so in Trinidad, the most cosmopolitan, the most 'mixed-up', of all the territories.

(4) And most important of all, in these days of Bandung, Pan Africa, Arab League, British Commonwealth, Pan America, United Nations, European Common Market, he, looking at the history of the past with its isolation (deliberate) of one territory from its neighbours, looking to the history of the future, consciously seeks, with equal deliberation, to break down that isolation and to foster closer association.'

Then in 1961 came my third opportunity – the centenary of the birth of Tagore. The Indian Commissioner asked me to deliver the feature address, as the saying goes in Trinidad and Tobago. On Saturday, May 6, 1961, before a crowded Queen's Hall, I delivered the address. I made my stand clear from the outset, I paid particular attention to the political significance of Tagore's poetry, dramas and novels, though I did not ignore Tagore the poet and the artist. Tagore was born into a world which was dominated politically and economically by the United Kingdom. The United States Civil War was four years off, the rise of Germany ten years off, Japan and Italy were geographical expressions. What was the state of literature in this period? I illustrated this by the poetry of Tennyson, Matthew Arnold, Baudelaire, Rimbaud, and Walt Whitman.

But Tagore was inevitably drawn into India's politics, to protest against the political treatment of India, to oppose the partition of Bengal, to denounce the treatment of political prisoners in the Andaman Islands, to surrender his knighthood against the Amritsar Massacre, to attack the architecture of the new British capital in India.

Tagore was an intellectual nationalist, not a nationalist politician. As such he ran afoul several times of the non-co-operation movement. Magnificent individualist, he blandly went his way, refusing to subordinate his poetry to their politics, glorifying Ancient India's 'Message of the Forest', exalting the individual personality.

I summed up:

'The significance of all this, Ladies and Gentlemen, is that this tremendous outpouring of literature, this devastating attack on materialism, this challenge of Indian ideology to Western thought, all this finds no place in the history of civilisation taught in schools and universities.'

I therefore ended my lecture by calling on the Government of India to endow a chair of Indian Culture and Civilisation at the St. Augustine branch of the University of the West Indian (which has now been done) with a representative collection of the great literature of India.

The lecture was very well received by the audience, which included a large number of non-Indians. It was particularly well received by the Government of India. I was able to put my proposal for a Chair of Indian Culture and Civilisation to Nehru himself, because at the

Lancaster House Conference I received an invitation to visit India after the Conference as the guest of Mr. Nehru.

I arrived in India on June 25, 1961. It was my first visit. I held discussions with the Prime Minister, Krishna Menon, and the Planning Commission. I laid a wreath at the spot where Gandhi was cremated. I established contact with the Congress Party. I visited the Taj Mahal. I renewed contact with Sir Sarvapalli Radhakrishnan, then Vice-President. And I addressed the Indian Council of World Affairs on the Caribbean.

I began with the colonial past, in relation to the problems facing the Federation. That was the historical background out of which had emerged the West Indian people. Thus we started off our independence, 'absolutely naked, with nothing at all – what we have is a European culture, modified, bastardised in some respects'. There was a serious language barrier. From there I proceeded to my favourite theme, multiracialism and the national community. And then I identified the real problem of the Caribbean today – the difference between the Cuban pattern and the Trinidad and Tobago example.

The lecture was received with thunderous applause. I left India to return to Trinidad to report at a long meeting in the University of Woodford Square. I brought back the approval of the Government of India for my proposal for the Indian endowment of a Chair of Indian Culture and Civilisation at the St. Augustine branch in Trinidad of the University of the West Indies and an undertaking to send a planning team to help us with our development planning; the team arrived in Trinidad later in the year.

Race relations, politics and culture, lectures in India, the poetry of Tagore – these were my relaxations from the tension of politics. I wrote a regular column in our party paper. In January 1959 I proposed, for example, a congress of West Indian writers which is to be convened at some future date by the University of the West Indies; President Senghor of Senegal, prophet of *négritude*, has agreed to open the conference. Castro's brief stopover in Trinidad on his way to a Latin American Conference in 1959, provided me with the theme of one of my articles on May 8, 1959.

Thus did I seek to pass on my education to the people of Trinidad and Tobago. Gordon Lewis, writing in *PNM Weekly* on January 13, 1958, put the whole position in a nutshell when he wrote:

'The Education of Eric Williams has become the Education of the West Indies. All that now remains is to carry forward to the federal level this task of thoughtful illumination. . . . We must see the social sciences, not as arid accountants of the way we live now, but as the way we might live, as the handmaiden of power over the material environment, employed to make West Indian man the master and not the slave of the relations in which he is involved.

I suspect myself that half of Dr. Williams' decision to move from scholarship to active politics was a recognition of that truth. He saw, quite simply, that private research is a sterile ivory tower unless it is translated into public policy. What he has seen we can all see. And as we see it it will make us free.'

(b) The Second Mandate

26

THE 1961 GENERAL ELECTION

There were three previews of the General Elections of 1961 – the Federal Elections of March 25, 1958; the County Council Election of February 16, 1959; and the annual elections in the Municipalities to decide five seats in Port-of-Spain, four in San Fernando, and two in Arima. I was heavily involved, necessarily so as Political Leader, in all these election campaigns.

We started off the Federal Election campaign with a bumper meeting in the University on January 24, 1958. I identified the principal issues involved as follows: (1) the economic problem of development, (2) the political problem of the relations between the Federal Government and the Territorial Governments, (3) the problem of the foreign relations of the Federal Government, (4) the Opposition claptrap about socialism and free enterprise.

I have already dealt with the first three issues. On the fourth issue I spoke at length. It again raised the question of PNM's affiliation to a socialist party. I dealt with the large corporations of the USA, the 'Frankenstein monsters' of Justice Brandeis, socialism in India, the Tennessee Valley Authority, the growth of Bookers in British Guiana. I then turned to the West Indies where the Government of Trinidad and Tobago owned a steamer service, a railway, marketing depots, houses and flats, water and electricity services, two banks, until recently operated a bus service, whilst the Government of Antigua owned an arrowroot factory, the Government of Jamaica an ice factory, and the Governments of British Guiana and Jamaica owned railways and controlled the marketing of certain export crops.

The election was a straight fight between the PNM and the DLP with the Butler Party contesting the St. Patrick and Victoria seats. In a total electorate of 342,565 the number of voters was 252,167 – slightly under 75%. PNM won four seats and DLP six. The popular vote was PNM, 117,445; DLP 114,409 – a PNM majority of 3,036.

The Butler Party polled 12,399 votes. As compared with the 1956 election, PNM had increased its popular vote by 12,279 while the DLP vote had declined by 14,309.

I had had myself ninety speeches in twenty-three days all over the country, concentrating on the issues of freedom of movement, customs union, and the imperative need of a federal development programme. What went wrong? I explained it in a speech in the University entitled 'The Danger facing Trinidad and Tobago and the West Indian Nation'.

I said:

'PNM decimation in areas with an overwhelming preponderance of Indian votes reflects the DLP campaign and the DLP appeal that Indians should vote for DLP so as to ensure an Indian Governor and an Indian Prime Minister. Religion figured prominently in their campaign. By hook or by crook they brought out the Indian vote – the young and the old, the literate and the illiterate, the lame, the halt and the blind, men and women. Our opponents even went to the length of distributing by the thousands a letter dated March 28, addressed 'My dear Indian Brother' and signed 'Yours truly, Indian'.

The letter is seditious in intent, offensive, derogatory, an insult to the West Indian nation they claim the honour to represent. From the vicious document I quote only one sentence, the least offensive in terms of language, the most offensive in terms of politics. The sentence reads as follows: "If my dear brother you have realised these occurrences and the shaky position in which our Indian people are placed, woe unto our Indian nation in the next ten years." Just think of that, Ladies and Gentlemen! An election to bring into being a West Indian Nation is fought on one side on the issue of "our Indian nation". The Indian nation is in India. It is a respectable, reputable nation, respected the world over. It is the India of socialism, the India of Afro-Asian unity, the India of the Bandung Conference. . . .

That is the Indian nation talking, not the recalcitrant and hostile minority of the West Indian nation masquerading as "the Indian nation" and prostituting the name of India for its selfish, reactionary political ends.

This, then, is the danger facing the people of Trinidad and Tobago, and the West Indian nation – the deliberate attempt of our opponents to exploit race as the basis of political power.'

An Opposition member subsequently sought to move a motion of censure against me for alleged racialism. I explained to the Legislative Council on May 23, 1958. The member withdrew his motion after my explanation.

I launched the County Council Election campaign on the occasion of PNM's third anniversary meeting in the University on January 26, 1959. In County Council elections each voter has two votes. In this election there were 280,341 electors; 156,516 ballots were cast. PNM won 34 seats, DLP 33, Independent candidates 3, Butler Party 2. In respect of the popular vote PNM received 140,275 votes; DLP 121,435; Independent candidates 19,497; Butler Party 8,344.

The municipalities were PNM strongholds. The scoreboard from 1956 to 1959 read in our favour: three to one in Port-of-Spain, two to one in San Fernando, four to three in Arima.

And so we proceeded to the 1961 General Elections. At the Special Convention of the Party on September 23, I outlined the five dangers that we faced – racialism, communism, the reversion to colonialism, unemployment, and our Party itself which stood out as the symbol of order and discipline and stability in the West Indies.

Through *The Nation* I exhorted the population to vote PNM. In the issue of Friday, December 1, 1961, I wrote that PNM's new society was free secondary education, the emergence of the small man, responsible trade unionism, better housing and higher standards of living, improved sanitation, electricity and pipe-borne water, jobs, orderly and rational economic development. I continued:

'This is PNM's new society. This is the dominant issue in the 1961 General Elections – the self-governing society of PNM versus the old Massa-dominated society of colonialism. . . .

In crucial and eventful days one naturally goes back to and seeks precedents from the heroic past. This crucial election brings to my mind the stirring words of King Henry V of England to his troops before the battle of Agincourt in 1415 on St. Crispin's Day. . . .'

The election was a resounding victory for the PNM. We won 20 of the 30 seats, the DLP winning the remainder. We lost the Fyzabad seat by 126 votes. The popular vote was PNM 190,003, or 56·97%; DLP, 138,901 or 41·66%.

27

INDEPENDENCE

The first positive reaction of the Federal Government to the Jamaica referendum was the appointment of Arthur Lewis as Special Adviser to the Prime Minister. Lewis came to see me and immediately began a tour of the Units to see what could be salvaged of the Federation. His openly stated objective was a Federation minus Jamaica with Trinidad and Tobago in the lead.

On this basis he submitted a report to the Prime Minister on November 9, 1961, which was copied to me. The report made the following proposals for a new Federation of nine Territories:

(1) What had been settled before the middle of 1961 would remain unchanged. Only those points would be opened up where agreement was reached reluctantly, and only in the effort to retain Jamaica. The matters requiring reconsideration were: services to be transferred to the Federal Government; Federal grants to Unit Services; industrial development; customs union; freedom of movement; sources of Federal revenue.

(2) The services to be transferred to the Federal Government should be: customs and excise; inland revenue; audit; postal services; telephones and telegraphs; civil aviation; ports, harbours and wharves; immigration; judicial, including magistrates; police; prisons; broadcasting.

(3) The Federal Government should keep a team of specialists – agriculturalists, doctors, economists – whose services would be available to any Unit on request.

(4) The Federal Government should make grants to the Unit Governments in respect of health and education.

(5) Industrial development should be on the Concurrent List, but it should be made clear that the Federal Government would have no power to legislate to zone industries, while legislation limiting the power of any Unit Government to promote industrial development

should not (unless it concerned income tax concessions) come
into force in a Unit until it was adopted by the legislature of that
Unit.

(6) Full customs union should be introduced as soon as possible, without the delays which had been agreed upon at Jamaica's request.

(7) Freedom of movement should not merely be on the Exclusive
List but should be enshrined in the Federal Constitution. Given such
entrenchment, most of the Governments were willing to concede a
short delay, but others considered that freedom of movement should
come into effect with Independence, as a matter of principle.

(8) All Governments concurred with the proposal in *The Economics
of Nationhood* that the Federal Government should be financed by
taxes on income tax as well as by import duties.

(9) The basis for financing the Federation should be the national
income of the Territories. The contribution of Trinidad and Tobago
would thus work out at 74·6% of the Federal Budget.

(10) Governors and Permanent Secretaries should be abolished in all
Unit Territories. Each Territory should have a maximum number of
two Ministers plus one for each 100,000 of population.

Arthur Lewis advised me that the structure which emerged from
his proposals was stronger than anything which had hitherto seemed
possible. If he had my assurance that the proposals were on the right
lines, he would advise the Federal Government to summon for the
end of 1961 a conference of Unit Governments to agree on final steps
to independence.

My Cabinet would not even discuss the proposals. It rejected them
out of hand. Trinidad and Tobago would be committed to paying
75% of a Federal Budget when it was limited to less than 50% of
Federal representation, notwithstanding the fact that it had over 50%
of the Federal population. Arthur Lewis also argued against a unitary
state on the ground that it was more expensive.

The rejection by the Cabinet was followed by rejection by the Party.
With the announcement that the new Secretary of State for the
Colonies, Reginald Maudling, proposed to visit the West Indies, it
was more than ever necessary for the PNM to take a firm stand on
the question. We did this at a meeting of our General Council on
Sunday, January 15, 1962, when we approved a resolution which
would be put by me before a Special Convention summoned for
January 27–28. After a number of recitals regarding the defunct
Federation, our dominating position in the Eastern Caribbean, our
position *vis-à-vis* other independent countries, trade with non-

British territories in the Caribbean, the resolution as subsequently amended read:

'BE IT THEREFORE RESOLVED that Trinidad and Tobago reject unequivocally any participation in the proposed Federation of the Eastern Caribbean and proceed forthwith to National Independence, without prejudice to the future association in a Unitary State of the people of Trinidad and Tobago with any Territory of the Eastern Caribbean whose people may so desire and on terms to be mutually agreed, but in any case providing for the maximum possible degree of local government.

AND BE IT FURTHER RESOLVED that PNM's Government in Trinidad and Tobago take the initiative in proposing the maximum measure of collaboration among the Units of the disintegrated Federation in respect of such common services as the University and Communications.

AND BE IT FURTHER RESOLVED that Trinidad and Tobago declare their willingness to associate with all the peoples of the Caribbean in a Caribbean Economic Community and to take such action as may be necessary for the achievement of this objective.

AND BE IT FURTHER RESOLVED, that PNM's Government of Trinidad and Tobago take steps to consult responsible organisations in the Territory, political, economic, social, civic, cultural and fraternal, with respect to the above Resolution, in order to implement the Government's pledge contained in His Excellency the Governor's Speech from the Throne on December 29, 1961, to associate the people of the Territory actively with the discussions on independence in the context of PNM's objectives for the achievement of an educated democracy.'

In a long and effective speech, I put the resolution first and foremost in its historical setting. I discussed all the historical attempts at federation, some sort of federation. From there I moved to the Intergovernmental Conference ending with the Lancaster House fiasco, which taught us the lesson of 'the absolute bankruptcy of metropolitan initiative'. From there I moved on to the General Council's resolution which posed the question of the establishment of a common economic community embracing the entire Caribbean area. I again reminded the delegates of the lesson to be learned from the European Common Market, I showed the importance of the entire Caribbean market, with a population of 20 millions, a total import trade of

$3,600 million US and exports of $2,700 million US. I stressed our exports to Curacao, British Guiana, Surinam, Guadeloupe, all outside of the Federation. We must begin by salvaging what we could of the deceased Federation. I referred in this connection to the University, British West Indian Airways, the shipping service, commodity agreements.

I stressed the merits of the unitary state, emphasising that the Philippines and Hawaii were unitary states. Let us move forward, I urged, towards the larger goal:

'There is a great respect for the PNM in the other territories of the West Indies, and we have a great pride in our own achievements and a great respect for ourselves. I think it is fitting that this larger responsibility should be thrown on our shoulders. . . . I know no other party that is as stable in the British area to take that role. . . . It says squarely, we live with Jamaica; we live with British Guiana; we live with Barbados as the leader of an Eastern Caribbean Federation; and we take upon ourselves the solemn responsibility of going to all the West Indian territories and stating – let us go towards the larger goal of a Caribbean Economic Community. . . . We are the undisputed intellectual leaders of the colonial nationalist movement in this part of the world (*Applause*).'

Andrew Rose, our Minister of Communications in the Federal Cabinet, promptly moved an amendment to my resolution calling for participation in an Eastern Caribbean Federation. A full-scale debate ensued, in which delegates representing all the constituencies took part. One after another they spoke in favour of the resolution and against the amendment. Those who sprang originally from the smaller islands but had migrated to Trinidad – there were many – were foremost in their denunciation of the proposal to participate in a smaller federation.

Then we proceeded to our homework at government level. A draft Independence Constitution was prepared, published and discussed at a citizen's meeting before it was taken to the Legislative Council. The Opposition, invited to the meeting, tried to create disorder on points of order and eventually walked out of the meeting before it really got going, to everyone's general disgust; only two delegates followed them out of the room.

On April 16, 1962, I introduced a motion in the House of Representatives, 'that this House approve the appointment of a Joint Select Committee to consider proposals for an Independence Constitution of

Trinidad of Tobago'. We submitted to the members and the House the 141 comments we had received from citizens on the draft constitution we had published.

On May 11, 1962, I moved in the House adoption of the report of the Joint Select Committee. I concentrated particularly on the efforts made by some of the groups which came before the Committee to divide the community on ethnic grounds. I said:

'You will recall, Mr Speaker, that speaking for myself, I had to enquire of one of the Associations, the Indian Association, in respect of its particular proposition for the division of the society into what they call ethnic groups, whether they could define these groups. And you will recall, Mr Speaker, how I received the reply – well, the man-in-the-street has a definition of that, whether it is a Negro, or an Indian, or somebody who is in-between. . . . And I raised the question, you remember, in respect of the defition of the "Indians" – what they called "Indians", I asked them whether they made any provisions in their proposals about Indians for the Dravidians, and the spokesman claimed he did not know what I meant. . . . Another one came in here and said "Africans". . . . I did not know whether he talked about the Mandingos, or the Ashantis, or the Ibos, or which section of Africa he was talking about. . . .

What I was referring to, something that is well known to Members who follow these issues, is that it is only ten days ago, Mr Speaker, since this issue was raised in the Parliament of India – "Separate South Indian State demanded" . . . about which Mr Nehru had this to say eight days ago . . . that if such a thing were attempted it would have to be resisted absolutely and with all one's force! It was inconceivable to Mr Nehru that any such separation could be effected without breaking India up into a thousand pieces! And therefore, Mr Speaker, what we have to keep before us is that any attempt to break Trinidad up into I do not know how many pieces, Sir, (there have been so many suggestions) must be resisted. . . . I was particularly careful to ask the representatives of the Association what was their inspiration. . . . They said, "it was Cyprus". . . . Nothing of the sort, Mr Speaker. Not Cyprus at all. Cyprus was a year and a half ago. This has come up in Trinidad society before. This is not the first time this issue has been raised. This is 40 years old in Trinidad. . . .'

The Indian Association in its presentation before the Select Committee raised another matter – it alleged discrimination against Indians in the public service and the police force. I dealt with this allegation effectively in my speech commending the report of the Joint Select Committee. I said:

'The fact of the matter is, Mr Speaker, that for a section of the community whose proportion of the total population 15 years and over was 33·85 per cent they have more than 33·85 per cent in Civil Aviation. They have more in Agriculture and Fisheries; they have more or are just about equal in postal services; they have more in the Sanitary Inspectorate; they have more in the Magistracy and they are well over 20 per cent in the entire Ministry of Agriculture, 20% in the Ministry of Industry and Commerce, just under their proportion, that is 30%, in the Ministry of Local Government and Community Development; over 20% in the Ministry of Education which includes Culture, Library Services, Archives. Over 23% in the entire Ministry of Works; just under 20% in the Ministry of Housing; over 20% in the Scientific and Allied Staff of the Ministry of Health, Water and Sanitation; 21% in the entire Judiciary, Registrar-General, etc., and in the Magistracy, almost 50% of the Magistrates. . . . And will anybody tell us why is the proportion in the Nursing Services 4·2%? Why? Is it because you are dealing with women there, and the tendency is for them to come out less in the Public Service than where the men are concerned? . . . I cannot give anybody any explanation as to why, between the years 1955 and 1961, there should have been over 2,500 applications for the posts of Stenographer, Probationer-Stenographer, and Typist in Trinidad and Tobago, but just 400 of those were from the Indian community. . . .
In 1961, Mr Speaker, in the Government Scholarship Programme – twenty-one different fields – a total of 75 scholarships were awarded. There were 664 applicants for 75 scholarships. One in every four applicants was Indian. . . .
From 1957 to 1961, both years inclusive, 303 scholarships were awarded – 68 or 22% to people who have Indian names. . . .
The point is that the society last year, under this Government, took a very drastic step forward in the direction of integration, in the direction of the elimination of the conventional discrimination inherited from the colonial régime. That was the free secondary education and the common qualifying examination. . . . A total

of 3,167 pupils were admitted to all types of secondary schools. Thirty-six in every 100 of those, according to names, came from what can be considered the Indian section of the community. Does that say that there is discrimination against the community? . . .

I think we could look forward with a certain amount of pride and confidence to the fact that the secondary school today, with free secondary education and the common qualifying examination, whatever may be said against it by the persons who are familiar with teaching and pedagogy, the fact is that the free secondary school, entrance to which is determined by the common qualifying examination, demonstrates better than anything in this society, now or in the future, the equality of opportunity for all people irrespective of racial origin, irrespective of colour, and irrespective of one of the fundamental considerations in our society, one of the most potent and vicious forms of discrimination in this society, family status. As long as our Constitution does not seek to import into our life any of these prejudices and irrationalities; as long as our Constitution does not seek to turn the clock back; as long as we are on this road to progress; as long as our Constitution does not prevent the free secondary school from being the cradle of the new nationalism of Trinidad and Tobago assimilating all the different cultural stocks and racial strains in this society; as long as it does not do that, then we, as a whole . . . can sit down and argue about the powers of the Prime Minister or the Leader of the Opposition, and let the society go. It is on the right line; let the locomotive of society proceed on that track, knowing perfectly well that it will not be derailed.

Let the secondary school be the cradle of the new society which has one aim in view – the repudiation of the absurd and irrational prejudices imposed on it from above. . . .'

Before proceeding to London, we held the usual mass meeting in the University. I there gave the country the slogan for the age of Independence – 'discipline, production, tolerance'. I dealt again with the allegations of discrimination against Indians in the public service. I showed how Indians represented 40% of the teachers in primary schools, received over 60% of loans from the Agricultural Credit Bank, were 66% of the population in Caroni and had 84% of the daily paid jobs, were 56% of the population in Victoria and had 73% of the daily paid jobs, were 38% of the population in St. Patrick and had 77% of the daily paid jobs, and received 41% of all government contracts in 1962.

The next stage was Marlborough House, where the Independent Conference began on May 28, 1962. I had very little to say at the Conference, leaving the issues to be presented by the Attorney-General, Senator George Richards, and the Constitutional Adviser to the Cabinet, Ellis Clarke. Maudling told me that Macmillan had made it clear that Trinidad and Tobago must be represented in its own right at the Commonwealth Prime Ministers' Conference on the European Common Market scheduled for September.

Slowly but surely Opposition attacks on our draft constitution were beaten down. The suspicions, however, and ill feeling remained, to the point where, after consulting my senior party advisers, I decided to write a letter inviting Maudling to intervene to see what he could do to abate racial tensions. The letter read as follows:

'My party colleagues and I are very deeply distressed and concerned over the possible increase of suspicion and distrust between various sections of the Trinidad and Tobago community. We have given a great deal of thought to it and of the possible ways and means of removing, or at least reducing, both and of promoting the national ideal.

It has occurred to us that the participation of representatives of the two major parties in the Territory in the Independence Conference is an appropriate starting point for a rapprochement in the national interest which cannot be written into a Constitution or protected by constitutional guarantees.

Such a rapprochement will be of value not only to Trinidad and Tobago but also to the Commonwealth. It is for this reason that I now request you to use your good offices to lay the foundations for such a rapprochement by making arrangements for an informal meeting of the representatives of both political parties here in London – if possible, immediately after the conclusion of the Independence Conference – for a full and frank discussion of general issues and problems retarding or which may tend to retard the growth of harmony and tolerance in Trinidad and Tobago.'

It went against the grain, having to involve the metropolitan power in a domestic matter, but there was no alternative. At least so it seemed. It was my intention to present the letter to Maudling at the final sitting. On the last day of the conference, I decided to settle the matter face to face with Dr. Capildeo, Leader of the Opposition. I drew him aside during the tea interval, told him my original intention, indicated that I had abandoned it, and explained that I would make a statement to the conference on the resumption.

I made the statement, to the effect that I intended on my return to Trinidad to raise with the opposition the general question of national integration and national unity with specific reference to (a) Nehru's Integration Committee in India, (b) the promotion of the national culture, (c) the working out of a campaign code on elections, (d) fair employment practices without discrimination on grounds of race, political affiliation, etc.

Capildeo thanked me and withdrew all opposition to the date of independence. The conference ended, catching the British flatfooted, without the reporters and television being on hand. The British never knew what hit them, and I never presented my letter to Maudling.

Before leaving London our top party people had preliminary discussions with some of the Opposition members clarifying procedure, *modus operandi*; etc., and that helped too.

So we proceeded to our date with destiny – August 31, 1962. The Princess Royal represented Her Majesty the Queen. At a children's rally in Port-of-Spain on August 30, I spoke in part as follows:

'You, the children, yours is the great responsibility to educate your parents. Teach them to live together in harmony, the difference being not race or colour of skin but merit only, differences of wealth and family status being rejected in favour of equality of opportunity. I call upon all of you young people to practise what you sing today and tomorrow, to translate the ideal of our National Anthem into a code of everyday behaviour, and to make our Nation one in which "ev'ry creed and race find an equal place". . . .

To your tender and loving hands the future of the Nation is entrusted. In your innocent hearts the pride of the Nation is enshrined. On your scholastic development the salvation of the Nation is dependent. At the birth of our Nation, four of its leading personalities, four of the people with the heaviest responsibility for its guidance, in the Cabinet, Parliament and the Judiciary, are scholarship winners, educated abroad at the expense of your parents, the taxpayers; the Prime Minister, The Chief Justice, the Deputy Prime Minister and Leader of the House of Representatives, and the Leader of the Opposition. When you return to your classes after Independence, remember therefore, each and every one of you, that you carry the future of Trinidad and Tobago in your school bags.'

At midnight the Union Jack was lowered in a dead silence, and our red, white and black flag went up to the deafening roar of the thousands who had assembled to witness the historic ceremony. At the formal opening of the first Independence Parliament, the Princess Royal read the Queen's speech which pledged:

'My Government undertakes to govern the country in the spirit which marked the Independence Conference in London. It will seek the co-operation and invite the participation of all groups in the country in its approach to National questions.'

After the ceremony, I broadcast to the Nation from the Parliament Chamber. I said:

'What use will you make of your Independence? What will you transmit to your children five years from today? Other countries have ceased to exist in that period. Some, in much less time, have become totally disorganised, a prey to anarchy and civil war.

The first responsibility that devolves upon you is the protection and promotion of your democracy. Democracy means more, much more, than the right to vote and one vote for every man and every woman of the prescribed age. . . .'

With the achievement of independence we immediately proceeded, on the application of Grenada, to consider the question of the incorporation of Grenada into the Unitary State of Trinidad and Tobago; we constituted teams of Trinidad and Tobago experts to study the implications of the Unitary State in four major fields; economic, civil service, legal, development.

The teams of experts reported and Trinidad and Tobago transmitted the reports to the Government of the United Kingdom. In all this period we have heard not a word from the United Kingdom, which obviously, as far as we are concerned, has the responsibility of making such economic assistance available to Grenada as would be required to bring up its infrastructure to the level of Trinidad and Tobago.

The next move towards the achievement of a Caribbean Economic Community, once we had set in motion the machinery for appraising and studying the question of the integration of Grenada into the Unitary State of Trinidad and Tobago, was to organise the Conference of Heads of Government of Commonwealth Caribbean Countries. I cleared the way personally for this by private and informal discussions with the Prime Minister of Jamaica and the Premiers of Barbados and British Guiana, and the first Conference was held in Port-of-Spain in July 1963, with Trinidad and Tobago as the host. The second Conference was held in Kingston, Jamaica, in January 1964.

Outside of the British Caribbean area, Trinidad and Tobago took the initiative in respect of discussion with the non-British Caribbean territories. These discussions related to two points in particular: (a) British West Indian Airways, (b) the Federal ships; both in the context of the development of regional communications by air and by sea. We held discussions with the Governments of Puerto Rico, Surinam and the Netherlands Antilles; and we kept in contact with the Government of France in respect of Martinique and Guadeloupe, after overall and general discussions which I had held with the French Foreign Minister in Paris some time before.

All these diplomatic initiatives and discussions, formal and informal, formed the background to the proposal advanced by Trinidad and Tobago in the 1965 session of the Prime Ministers' Conference – that, taking into account the fundamental political and constitutional realities, the United Kingdom should take steps to convene a Conference of all independent states in the area that is to say, the United Kingdom, the United States, France, the Netherlands with Surinam and the Netherlands Antilles, Canada, Jamaica and Trinidad and Tobago to discuss the whole question of regionalism in the Caribbean and promotion of the Caribbean Economic Community.

Within this framework, to which the British reaction was inexplicably timid and unfavourable, we stressed the further point, once more, that Britain, if necessary in collaboration with the United States and Canada, should take urgent steps to promote the economic viability of the smaller territories and should, as consistent with reason, abandon the policy that it has pursued heretofore of making economic assistance dependent on political association in the form of a federation.

At long last a little ray of light seems to have penetrated into the darkness in which the Caribbean area has been left by its metropolitan associates, who have profited so enormously from their connection in previous centuries. The Governments of the United Kingdom, the United States and Canada undertook a survey in 1966 to consider the question of economic viability in the smaller islands, which have now been raised to the status of associated states. The United States nominated in 1968 a Special Ambassador to try and formulate a policy for the entire region.

A further step in the direction of a Caribbean Economic Community was taken when at the end of 1965, Trinidad and Tobago tentatively put forward some new thoughts in the field of association, drawing on the experience of the different forms of association worked out between Northern Ireland and the United Kingdom on the one hand, and between the Netherlands and Surinam and the Netherlands Antilles on the other. The concrete form which this form of association might take may be summarised as follows:

(1) The associated territories will be self-governing in purely local matters, on the basis of a form of self-government somewhat superior to our County Council arrangement; they will have their own elections and will take no part in Trinidad and Tobago elections.

(2) An agreed number of members from each associated territory will sit in the Trinidad and Tobago Parliament when national matters are considered – for example, defence, foreign policy, external relations, the national budget, national economic legislation relating to tariffs, income tax, industrial development, export incentives; and similar questions of this nature.

(3) The associated territories will similarly participate in discussions of the Cabinet of Trinidad and Tobago on such national issues.

(4) For reasons of economy, and to avoid any situation in which the will of the people of Trinidad and Tobago may be frustrated by too excessive a representation from the associated territories, it would be preferable to arrange for such association on the basis of a preliminary grouping of the territories – such as Windward Islands and Leeward Islands.

On the basis of studies by the University of the West Indies and the University of Guyana, the Caribbean Free Trade Association came into effect on May 1, 1968, embracing Antigua, Barbados, Guyana, Trinidad and Tobago. Jamaica and the Leeward and Windward Islands have since joined. The next steps are a common external tariff and harmonisation of incentives for industrial development. Discussions are now taking place about the re-absorption of Guyana into the University of the West Indies fraternity.

28

EXTERNAL AFFAIRS

The dominant question that faced us as we achieved our Independence was an external one – the question of Britain's adherence to the European Economic Community. This was the theme of the Commonwealth Prime Ministers' Conference that started in London on September 10, 1962. We were the only Commonwealth country to support the British case for application to join the European Common Market. We did this on the grounds solely of the national self-interest. I indicated that our export trade with the United Kingdom was worth $143 million and our import trade $137 million, and that 42% of our export trade and 30%of our import trade were with Europe including Britain.

But to go to the Common Market as an associate of Britain under the section of the Treaty of Rome, which made provision for associate status, would require the most precise safeguards. The first related to petroleum and the Common Market's treatment of Curacao and Aruba in the Caribbean. These were refiners of imported Venezuela oil; Trinidad's industry was based on the refining of both local crude and imported oil. The second related to the Commonwealth Sugar Agreement, one of the best of the international commodity agreements. The third safeguard related to economic aid from the European Development Fund. We had had bitter experience with British Development and Welfare Aid. We wanted certain assurances from the United Kingdom.

After the Commonwealth Prime Ministers' Conference I toured all the Common Market countries. I was well received everywhere, if only as a curiosity, the only Commonwealth Prime Minister to support the British application. I also visited the headquarters of the European Economic Community in Brussels, being received by President Hallstein. I was accompanied by a powerful delegation which included the Leader of the Opposition and representatives of the private sector. We submitted to the Community a memorandum on associate status for Trinadad and Tobago which, after dealing with oil, sugar, industrialisation, and economic aid, continued:

> '29 Trinidad and Tobago sees in Associate Status with the European Economic Community . . . tangible advantages.
>
> 30 The first is that Associate Status under the new Convention with its provision of a Ministerial Council including associate members and European members, together with representatives of the Commission, represents a form of political equality between former colonies and former colonial powers which Trinidad and Tobago warmly endorses. . . . Trinidad and Tobago is gratified by the provision contemplated under the new Convention of equality between old Associates and new Associate Members.
>
> 31 The second relates to the Caribbean rather than to Europe. . . .
>
> 33 Two aspects of the contemplated new Convention of Association have powerful implications for the future development of the Caribbean. These are: (1) the rights of an Associate Member to impose discriminatory tariffs on products of the member countries of the Community, (2) the right of the Associates to form a customs union among themselves.
>
> 34 Thus Europe, which for three and one-half centuries has fought over the Caribbean territories and has been responsible for their present division, now has a unique opportunity, through the European Common Market, of bringing them together economically. Associate Status for Trinidad and Tobago with the European Economic Community will ensure greater integration of the economies of the countries of the Caribbean area.'

De Gaulle's veto of the British application created a new situation. We were faced with the increasing threat to the preferences in the British market on which we depended. More and more the tendency grew to link Trinidad and Tobago not with the developing countries of Asia and Africa but with the less developed countries of Europe. Criteria for economic aid tended more and more to emphasise *per capita* national income, aggravating our difficulties as ours was relatively high. The Organisation of American States seemed hostile to Commonwealth independent countries. We could not afford the high cost of diplomatic representation in too many countries, and therefore lacked the opportunity to present our point of view as it needed to be presented. The Geneva Conference on Trade and Development was fixed for March, 1964.

Thus as early as July 1963 the idea was born in my mind that I should undertake a trip to Africa with its 34 votes in the United Nations. I discussed in general terms with Bustamante the idea of seeking to protect West Indian interests by such personal contacts as had been developed by Presidents de Gaulle and Tito in recent tours. He agreed, and we eventually decided that he would take Latin America and I Africa. We further agreed that our two countries would consider the possibility of joint representation in certain key areas.

This was the background to my tour of Africa and other countries. I left Trinidad on February 12, 1964, and returned on May 1. The tour fell into three distinct parts:

(a) visits to African countries, (b) the Geneva Conference followed by visits to Yugoslavia and Iran, (c) visits to United Kingdom, Canada and the USA. On my return to Trinidad from New York, I stopped off in Jamaica to brief the Acting Prime Minister, Donald Sangster – Bustamante was *incommunicado* in Washington, ill – on developments.

My tour of Africa took me to the following countries – Senegal, Sierra Leone, Liberia, Ghana, Nigeria, Uganda, Kenya, Tanzania, Ethiopia, United Arab Republic, Algeria. My original schedule called for a visit to Guinea after Senegal; but some domestic rumpus ensued, and its was suggested that I defer the visit to April. This could not be accommodated in my travel plans, but eventually I was able to chat briefly with Sekou Touré during my visit to Algiers.

The Geneva Conference and the future of preferences dominated my discussions in Africa. I sent home regular reports to my deputy and these all dealt with the Geneva Conference. Liberia, Ghana and Kenya were particularly sympathetic.

The African tour gave me an insight into political realities in Africa. Here, for example, is my comment on Ghana.

'The dominant note in Ghana is the domination of Nkrumah and the Convention People's Party. Nkrumah is everywhere – it is Nkrumah Market, Nkrumah University, Nkrumah House; and Nkrumah's pictures are everywhere, sometimes as many as three in a single room. What is unusual about this is not so much the man as the Party. The CPP Headquarters is a tremendous building, and few countries could boast of such a Party Headquarters. . . .

The Government is merely an arm of the Party. The Party is the State, and Nkrumah is the Party. That is to say, one gets the impression that he is a prisoner of the Party machinery he has created.'

On Nigeria, which was in the midst of a crisis over the census problem on the domination of the Federation by the Northern Region, I wrote as follows:

'Whatever compromise is achieved, ultimately it would seem as if the alternatives before Nigeria lie between (a) the break-up of the Federation into three or more independent states, and (b) revision of the Federal Constitution to remove the relationship between representation and population, possibly by dividing up the Northern Region'.

Anticipating subsequent difficulties in Uganda, I was very impressed with Kenya and its potentialities. I wrote:

'Our visit had an enormous impact with the Kenya Cabinet, the European population, and the Diplomatic Corps. This has been expressed in three ways in particular – (a) a request from the Kenya Government for assistance with stenographers, secondary school teachers, lawyers for the Ministry of Justice, doctors of medicine. . . . (b) a request from the Minister of Agriculture, himself English, for assistance in training Kenya students at the College of Agriculture of the University of the West Indies; (c) the recognition of the influence of Trinidad's multiracial and democratic society on Kenya's integration problems. The Indian High Commissioner specifically raised this point in lamenting to me the slow progress made in the field of the integration of the Asian population. More than one European resident as well as the British High Commissioner stressed the important guidance our multiracialism and formal absence of racial discrimination could wield on Kenya's development.'

I met the heads of State or Government everywhere. I was particularly impressed with Emperor Haile Selassie and President Nasser (whom I had met in 1962). I had three long interviews with Ben Bella of Algeria. Everywhere I discussed the Cuban situation with particular reference to its intervention in Venezuelan affairs and the situation in British

Guiana. Southern Rhodesia figured prominently in the discussions in all countries.

Having sought to the best of my ability to win friends and influence people, I proceeded to join our delegation at the Geneva Conference. The head of the delegation was our Minister of Agriculture, Lionel Robinson. Our speech, after dealing with the general problem of economic decolonisation and the special problems of the West Indian territories, proposed three measures for the protection of small countries.

> '1 A differentiation between preferential arrangements in the interest of a developed country and preferential arrangements in the interest of a small developing country. I suggest as a basis of discussion, that the following criteria should be taken into account in the determination and identification of small developing countries which might qualify:
> (a) the size of its domestic market;
> (b) its economic potential;
> (c) population density and unemployment;
> (d) any of its domestic commodities which represent less than one per cent of total world production of that commodity;
> (e) the historical antecedents of any existing preferential arrangements.
>
> 2 A comprehensive and realistic appraisal by the United Nations of all forms of economic assistance to developing countries, whether bilateral, or multilateral, and the development of appropriate criteria which would take into account the peculiar problems of small countries, especially unemployment.
>
> 3 The study of existing shipping limitations on the possible expansion of the existing marketing arrangements among the developing countries.'

I then proceeded to brief visits to Yugoslavia and Iran to lobby support from these two influential countries for the West Indian position at Geneva. I had discussions with President Tito, who was easily the most impressive Head of State I met on my tour, and with the Prime Minister of Iran (who was later assassinated).

After leaving Geneva I proceeded to London where I had the usual unsatisfactory discussions on British economic aid; Ottawa, where I met Lester Pearson and Paul Martin; Washington, DC, where I held discussions with President Johnson and Secretary of State, Dean

Rusk. The Canadian conversations were particularly satisfactory; Pearson and I agreed on a reconvening of the old Canada–West Indies Conference, even though we had to wait two years before our ideas became reality.

The trip, long and tiring, was well worth while. On my return I found a multitude at Piarco who gave me a tumultuous welcome. Then on June 8 I discussed the tour in a mass meeting in the University in a speech entitled 'A small country in a big world'. The immediate results of the tour were trade missions from the United Arab Republic and Yugoslavia (a trade treaty has since been signed with Yugoslavia), and a grant of economic aid from Canada. It did not subsequently prove possible to arrive at agreement with Jamaica on joint diplomatic representation in Africa, and Trinidad and Tobago subsequently established its own mission in Addis Ababa.

One of the most difficult questions that faced us in our external affairs was the question of British Guiana. My connection with the problem began when I visited British Guiana in March 1963 to seek to persuade the British Guiana Government to reconsider its decision to sever connections with the University of the West Indies and establish its own University of Guyana.

The visit afforded me an opportunity of discussions with political parties in British Guiana, with many organisations, with many individuals, and provided me with the further opportunity of emphasising our stand: (a) in respect of Independence; (b) against Proportional Representation; (c) insisting on adequate safeguards to protect the interests of British Guiana; and (d) suggesting on the basis of our own experience in Trinidad and Tobago the maximum possible community participation in the exercises preceding Independence.

My first thought was to offer the good offices of Trinidad and Tobago at the level of both the Government and the Parliament. After an impression that the atmosphere was not suited to a joint visit by the Prime Minister and the Leader of the Opposition, Dr. Capildeo, with whom I had discussed this idea, I fell back on an alternative, but perhaps even an equally valuable, suggestion of a Parliamentary Mission drawn from both House and Senate and drawn from both parties and including also independent members of the Senate to visit British Guiana. The plan, which was accepted by the Acting Leader of the Opposition, unfortunately could not be carried out because of the intervention of a strike in British Guiana.

I had simultaneously pursued my second line of action in this matter. I sent to the Prime Minister of Jamaica a lengthy communication almost as soon as I returned from my visit to British Guiana, setting out the situation and indicating to him that, in my view, both Trinidad and Tobago and Jamaica, as independent countries, and as independent Commonwealth countries in the Caribbean, had to consider most seriously direct representation in British Guiana at the Commissioner level because, of course, British Guiana was not an independent country. We both felt that, in the light of the strike, in the context of the general chaos and division in the country, we should associate with us the self-governing territory of Barbados.

Thus it was that on April 14 we took the first positive step in Trinidad and Tobago towards developing a joint Caribbean approach – Jamaica, Barbados, Trinidad and Tobago – on the British Guiana question as part and parcel of the policy towards which we were moving to bring together heads of Caribbean Commonwealth Governments, independent or self-governing, for discussing matters of common concern. I suggested a face-to-face meeting between Jagan, Bustamante, Barrow and myself.

The British Guiana Government replied some time later, on May 3, to indicate that the Premier of British Guiana was prepared to send to Trinidad, to discuss with the Prime Minister of Trinidad, the President of the Senate in British Guiana. I thereupon immediately consulted again with the Prime Minister of Jamaica and the Premier of Barbados, suggesting that we go to Georgetown to meet Jagan. Jamaica and Barbados said they agreed with the proposition; and the message was sent to British Guiana.

The Secretary of State for Commonwealth Relations, Mr. Duncan Sandys, in his capacity as Secretary of State for the Colonies, around this time indicated that he would be visiting British Guiana and would like to stop off in Trinidad. I had two meetings with him. I was very careful to indicate to him the broad line of approach that we were contemplating together with Jamaica and Barbados, because, above all things, we wanted to avoid any charge of interference in the domestic affairs of British Guiana, or with what must be accepted as the constitutional responsibility of the United Kingdom. The Secretary of State fully understood our position, showed no disapproval of our attempt to assist in the general problem, and indicated to us that, on the basis of the apparent success that had been reached in Kenya in terms of a coalition of the major parties, that was the solution that he had put forward in British Guiana, and he would give a little time to see how it worked out. We indicated to the Secretary of State, in the light of the fact that within ten days or so after his departure from

Trinidad we were to meet the heads of Governments in Port-of-Spain, that we would like to have another try, because at this meeting we had the Premier of Barbados, the Prime Minister of Jamaica and the Premier of British Guiana all in the same room.

We were aware of the fact that on July 9 the United Nations Committee on Colonies had appointed a sub-committee of five to go into the British Guiana question, with the representative from Mali as Chairman. We were somewhat concerned about the possible effect on this United Nations intervention in the matter. From the very start, we asked our representatives at the United Nations to convey to the United Nations sub-committee dealing with British Guiana that they should give the West Indian leaders a chance to work on the problem.

I worked out with the Prime Minister of Jamaica and the Premier of Barbados the tactics that we should adopt in this situation and we decided that we would approach the Premier of British Guiana and depending on his reaction, we would invite the leaders of the two other political parties in British Guiana to meet privately with us in Trinidad. I remember in one of the approaches we made to Dr. Jagan, Sir Alexander Bustamante saying something like this:

'Look here, Jagan, I do not want to get into any discussions on this matter; I do not want any argument. What we are asking for is this; that Williams, Barrow and Bustamante should meet in the same room with Burnham, D'Aguiar and Jagan and that we would try to work out a constitution in that atmosphere.'

There was at no time any response at all, neither favourable nor unfavourable, to the proposition which was presented to British Guiana – as far as I was concerned, on at least half a dozen occasions, either with the Prime Minister of Jamaica or with the Deputy Prime Minister of Jamaica, or with the Premier of Barbados, or with all of us together, or unilaterally on my own initiative.

The approach to the British Guiana problem that we made throughout our discussions emphasised certain safeguards that should be introduced into the British Guiana Constitution, on the assumption that Proportional Representation was not accepted. Proportional representation was opposed by Jamaica, Barbados and Trinidad and Tobago. But precisely because of this, we concentrated on the discussion of certain essential safeguards to satisfy the general community and to provide the conditions in which the country could proceed to independence.

Some of the safeguards that we worked out were:

(1) A Bill of Rights.
(2) The inclusion of a Senate based on the Trinidad rather than the Jamaican pattern.
(3) The independence of the Judiciary, the Auditor-General and the Public Service Commission.
(4) Consultation with the Opposition to be written into the Constitution as in Jamaica, but even more precisely than in Jamaica – for example, referring specifically to the question of foreign policy.
(5) The system of special entrenchment of particular clauses in the Constitution.
(6) Outside supervision of the elections in British Guiana (the elections to be held under provisions, in so far as boundaries were concerned, broadly similar to those included in the Independence Constitution of Trinidad and Tobago).

At no time was any reply of any sort made to any of these specific propositions. It was therefore impossible for me to suggest that we would continue to hold off the United Nations any longer.

The discussions in New York revolved around the formula that had been put forward by the Secretary of State for the Colonies of a coalition. The Sub-Committee of the United Nations talked also in terms of a Commonwealth Committee. The intention was to include two Asian countries, one African country, one of the older Commonwealth countries – not the United Kingdom, of course, but one of the older Commonwealth countries – and Trinidad and Tobago as a Caribbean country.

We indicated that we would do whatever we could to assist at that late stage in the achievement of some improvement in the British Guiana situation; but it had failed and by the time the Secretary of State for the Colonies announced the resumption of the British Guiana Constitutional Conference, the picture as I saw it was:

(i) Trinidad and Tobago had tried on its own and had failed.
(ii) The West Indian Governments had tried in concert and had failed.
(iii) In so far as the Secretary of State for the Colonies had put up a particular proposition, he had tried and had failed.

(iv) The United Nations had tried, apparently along the same lines
as the Secretary of State for the Colonies had proposed, and
they had failed.

Here the story rested until, in the following year, when I met Jagan to
report on my mission to Africa and Canada, he asked me to intervene.
With the consent of the Cabinet, I agreed, and I invited representatives
of all three parties in British Guiana and of the trade unions to meet
with me and some of my senior colleagues in Trinidad. All, curiously
enough except Jagan, came, but it was clear from our discussions that it
was a hopeless case. I reported as follows to Dr. Jagan on June 13, 1964:

'It is with the deepest regret that I have to record that these discussions and exchanges were at every turn frustrated. Neither your
own actions nor those of your political opponents confirmed the
sense of urgency and gravity on which your request for my intervention had been predicated. If any sense of gravity and urgency
appeared in the discussions, it was limited solely to the question
of the elections – whether they should or should not be held, and
under what procedures they should be held. Where I was able,
with some difficulty, to encourage discussion of the establishment
of a national government to lead the country into Independence,
the conditions proposed were either meaningless or intransigent or
not intended to be taken seriously.

Intemperate remarks by leaders of all the parties during the explo-
ratory efforts did nothing to improve the prospects of those efforts.
The vital importance of appropriate constitutional provisions and
safeguards in the Independence Constitution received perfunctory
consideration, notwithstanding the grim and tragic precedents
which are there today for all to see. There was no readiness on
any side to subordinate sectional interests or personal antagonism
or ideological vagaries to the overriding national interest. What
is most disturbing is that the Ghana Mission, barely four months
ago, going over precisely the ground which I tried to cover, had
appeared to achieve more than ninety per cent agreement between
yourself and Mr. Burnham. Not only, therefore do opinions and
attitudes appear to have hardened in the interim, but, what is more
serious, grave doubts arise as to the value and stability of any accord
that may be reached at any time by any mediator, so long as the
present state of affairs continues. In present circumstances, therefore, I find that there is no basis or reasonable hope for any accom-

modation between the political parties, for any resolution of the political deadlock, or for any agreement on the rational and stable foundation on which the independence of British Guiana must necessarily be built.'

At the Prime Ministers' Conference in July, 1964, I presented to the Commonwealth Secretary 'Proposals for the accession of British Guiana to Independence'. I sent copies to all Prime Ministers. The proposals dated July 7, 1964, read in part:

'There is only one reasonable way out of this dilemma. That is, direct intervention by the United Nations, to which the two principal leaders in British Guiana have repeatedly referred their differences in the past. I propose therefore:

(1) The normal procedures should be set in motion as soon as practicable to enable the United Nations to assume responsibility for the Government of British Guiana.

(2) The Government of British Guiana should be vested in a Commissioner, with appropriate staff, selected by and responsible to the United Nations.

(3) The Commissioner should have full and sole responsibility over the Police, the Defence Forces, all electoral machinery, and the Civil Service.

(4) The Commissioner should be selected from a Commonwealth country (in so far as it is reasonable to expect that British Guiana will achieve its independence within the Commonwealth), which has the minimum connection with or vested interest in the present British Guiana situation. Only one Commonwealth country fits this specification – New Zealand.

(5) The present procedures for election should be suspended, and no elections should be held for a minimum period to be determined.

(6) The immediate responsibility of the United Nations Commissioner must be the disarming of the population and the seizure of all unlicensed arms and ammunition.

(7) The basic responsibility of the United Nations Commissioner is to create a climate in British Guiana in which all citizens irrespective of race or colour or creed can feel reasonably safe in the enjoyment of their human rights and reasonably confident in the operations and practice of political democracy. To this end in due course the United Nations Commissioner should arrange for

a Constituent Assembly of all reputable civic organisations in British Guiana to agree on the terms and conditions and safeguards of the Independence Constitution.'

The Prime Ministers never discussed my proposals, and nothing came of my initiative. The British Government went its way and imposed proportional representation, leading up to independence as the new State of Guyana, with Burnham as Prime Minister.

The Commonwealth Prime Ministers' Conference of 1965 dealt with three issues on which I made some contribution for Trinidad and Tobago – Vietnam, Southern Rhodesia, and the Commonwealth Secretariat. I reported on these to the House of Representatives on July 23, 1965. First, the Vietnam Peace Mission. I reported our position as follows:

'1. Any conference should be essentially a conference of the Vietnamese people and their representatives and the three Vietnamese parties to the dispute should have equal representation – the Democratic Republic of North Vietnam, the Government of South Vietnam, and the National Liberation Front.

2. If at all possible any such conference should be held in Vietnam; if practical considerations of adequate hotel accommodation and appropriate translating facilities cannot be made available and the conference must therefore be held in neutral Geneva, as far as possible committees of the conference should operate in Vietnam itself, in both Hanoi and Saigon, to allow the Vietnamese people to see that it is their conference about their problem.

3. Any such conference should be held within the framework of the 1954 Geneva Conference which set up the temporary dividing line between North and South Vietnam at the 17th Parallel, emphasising however that it was neither a political nor military boundary. . . . Within this context the neighbouring neutral states of Laos and Cambodia would have their place as being essential partners in any settlement of Indo-China as a whole, and France, the former imperial power, whose influence is still very strong in Indo-China, would automatically be included.

4. Any such conference should include as observers the three powers – India as chairman, Canada and Poland – which constitute the International Control Commission set up by the

Geneva Agreement of 1954; their practical experience in the field of international machinery would be of great value.'

On Southern Rhodesia, this is what I had to report:

'Our general line was in support of the unanimous African demand for the implementation of the principles of majority rule and "one man, one vote" as soon as possible, for the convening by the United Kingdom of a constitutional conference to work out the basis on which Southern Rhodesia might proceed to independence, and for the release of detained African leaders so that they could participate in the conference.

We were not able to support the British point of view that Britain had no power to intervene in the internal affairs of Southern Rhodesia which was a self-governing colony. We pointed to the numerous precedents in West Indian history of British intervention in the affairs of self-governing colonies. . . . We took the view that, in the context of this consistent British policy towards the West Indies, any special treatment to potential rebels in Southern Rhodesia threatening a unilateral declaration of independence would be tantamount to downright racial discrimination.'

As the formal proposal for the establishment of a Commonwealth Secretariat came from me, following hints dropped by Ceylon and Ghana, I paid special attention to this question in my report to the House.

Our foreign policy in general was based on the motion I presented to the House on December 6, 1963, as the Minister of External Affairs. The motion read:

'RESOLVED: That this House reaffirms its faith in the United Nations, reasserts the rights of smaller nations; and declares its resolve to support all efforts for the achievement of lasting peace, for the solidarity and stability of the Western Hemisphere, and for the establishment of a pattern of world trade which recognises the rights of developing countries.'

I was particularly careful to differentiate Trinidad and Tobago from Cuba. I dealt with the matter effectively in an article for *Le Monde Diplomatique*, published on the first anniversary of our independence. The article was entitled 'International Perspectives for Trinidad and

Tobago'. As the point of view is still relevant today, I reproduce my conclusion here:

'This, then is the significance of Trinidad and Tobago as an independent country in the modern world, that it represents a confrontation in the Caribbean of the two dominant points of view that face the world today:

(a) Active partnership between government and investors in Trinidad and Tobago as against the state direction of the economy in Cuba;

(b) a direct democracy superimposed upon a parliamentary tradition in Trinidad and Tobago as against Cuba's one party state dominated by its caudillo;

(c) the vision in Trinidad and Tobago of a Caribbean Economic Community with some sort of independent existence as against the submerging of the Cuban personality in the International behind the Iron Curtain.'

In the course of this five-year period, I also had the opportunity of a private audience with Pope John, and I held discussions with Ben Gurion on the occasion of a visit to Israel in 1962.

In our relations with Venezuela, we concentrated from the start on the removal of the unjust 30% surtax imposed by Venezuela since 1886 on the products of the West Indian colonies of the European powers. The tax, in the case of British colonies, was aimed principally at compelling the British to sign a new commercial treaty with Venezuela. PNM objected to being used as pawns in Anglo-Venezuelan commercial rivalry.

In July 1959 a Goodwill Mission from Venezuela toured Trinidad and Tobago and we were able to explore the various difficulties, particularly the surtax and problems of fishermen of both countries in the Gulf of Paria. We reciprocated by sending a follow-up Mission to Venezuela, from August 20 to 27, 1959. I had the honour of meeting President Betancourt, who pledged that the surtax would be removed. I in my turn made it clear that Trinidad and Tobago would not allow its soil to be used as a base for subversive activity against Venezuela. In spite of this, for two and a half years almost, the question of the surtax had not been touched. I made it clear therefore, in moving the adoption of the Speech from the Throne in Parliament on January 12, 1962:

'There will be no discussions with the Venezuelan Government in which I take part, which do not start with the elimination of the surtax; and then we can discuss the question of increased trade.'

A Venezuelan Mission came, headed by the Minister of Finance, and immediately surprised us in conference by requesting compensation for the abolition of the surtax. I was furious. We were penalised by the surtax, not Venezuela, and we were to pay compensation. I immediately retaliated by publishing one of the documents in our possession on the surtax issue. This was a précis of correspondence in 1897, and was published as the second in our series of Historical Documents of Trinidad and Tobago. The document revealed how a former President had promised a former Governor of Trinidad to repeal the surtax, but how Venezuela had demanded in compensation either a large loan or the establishment of a Venezuelan custom house in Port-of-Spain to control contraband!

The conference broke up, and there I let the matter rest, refusing all invitations to go to Venezuela or even to discuss the matters with Venezuela, until in 1966 the Venezuelan Government unilaterally repealed the surtax and so opened the door to healthy and friendly relations between our two countries, which I was able to discuss frankly and fruitfully with President Leoni of Venezuela when we met at Punta del Este in April, 1967. The two Governments have since set up a Mixed Commission to discuss matters of common concern. The first meeting of the Commission was held in Port-of-Spain in November, 1967.

29

DIRECT DEMOCRACY

At home our great contribution to the theory and practice of democracy was our policy of consultation with the widest possible section of the national community.

Our first experiment with direct democracy was the public discussion, initiated with the sanction of the Cabinet, on the draft Independence Constitution. We published the draft, sent it out to civic organisations, urged citizens to buy and to read it, and invited public comments. The procedure was a pronounced success. In forty days we received 136 memoranda; the draft constitution was also a best seller, over 13,000 copies being sold.

We decided to collate all the memoranda and sent the complete analysis to all commentators. The memoranda naturally varied; what one proposed another contradicted. So the Cabinet decided to convene a meeting of all the commentators at which doubts would be clarified, fears removed, and discrepancies eliminated. I spoke at length on this in a broadcast on April 8, 1962. I sought to remove fears on the powers proposed for the Prime Minister in respect of the Chief Justice, the Public Service Commission, the Boundaries Commission and showed how impossible it was to contemplate, as some suggested, transfer of some of these powers to the Governor-General.

On the issue of the communal vote proposed by certain communal organisations I spoke very sharply:

'All that I can say tonight is that I would far prefer to have the Government of Trinidad and Tobago accused of not dividing up the community into racial groups rather than have it accused of constitutional provisions which would establish a Negro President and an Indian Vice President or a Republic with a fixed proportion of seats or places to the various racial groups in the Cabinet, in Parliament, in the Judiciary, in the Police Service and in the Civil Service. As far as I am concerned that way madness lies.'

The meeting of citizens was held at Queen's Hall in Port-of-Spain from April 25 to 27, 1962. It was a great success. The attendance was particularly good. I said at the end of the discussions:

'We have talked a lot about safeguards at this meeting. I think we have found here, in this meeting in Queen's Hall, the greatest safeguard that we could possibly have in Trinidad and Tobago, and one which few countries that I can think of in this part of the world can boast of, and that is an alert public opinion. . . .

The task for the future, as I see it, is to keep that public opinion alert. If we do that, Ladies and Gentlemen, we have found our greatest safeguard.'

Fortified by this heartening experience, we decided to adopt a similar technique in respect of the Second Five Year Development Programme 1964–1968. A draft was published by the Prime Minister's Office in July 1963 and sent to a number of organisations whose comments were invited.

One hundred and forty-seven memoranda were received, a remarkable achievement in respect of so bulky and weighty a document. The Cabinet then invited all the organisations commenting to send representatives to a meeting at Queen's Hall.

The same technique of Queen's Hall meetings was followed sucessfully in respect of village organisations, which met from September 16 to 19, in respect of youth organisations, which met on November 9 and 10, and in respect of the problems on private housing estates, which met in February 1964.

All these meetings were national in scope; I dealt with the citizen body in general. At the same time, together with the Minister of Labour, Robert Wallace, I sought to establish unity in the ranks of both the trade union movement and the business community. Both were badly split. In each case I invited selected individuals to hold informal discussions with me, and then on the basis of these discussions I called for a general meeting.

I invited the trade unions, who were split into three sections, to a two-day meeting on February 8 and 9, 1963, to discuss the following matters of importance to them: (1) the proposed Labour College (eventually established by the Government and formally opened on October 19, 1966); (2) a tripartite seminar with Government and business on industrial relations; (3) steps to expedite the completion of the Labour Code; (4) establishment of an Advisory Council representative of all sections of the labour movement to advise Government on labour matters and on the general economic and social development of the country; (5) the organisation of the labour movement with a view to increasing its effective contribution to the development of our independent country; (6) the organisation of a conference of Trade Unions to discuss matters of common concern and the role of the unions in our independent society; (7) any other matters.

The conference brought out the deep-seated divisions in the trade union movement, but I did succeed in getting the three sections to work together. Out of this emerged a tenuous unity which saw the return to the fold of the Trade Union Congress of the two sections which had separated; thereafter the Congress broke apart again and a rival national organisation was set up, the National Federation of Labour. But the two groups, under pressure from friends outside, have again merged and formed the Trinidad and Tobago Labour Congress.

I next turned my attention to the business community. I invited the following organisations to meet me on March 18, 1963: Chamber of Commerce, Shipping Association, Businessmen's Association, Manufacturers' Association, Employers' Consultative Association, Agricultural Society, Petroleum Association, Junior Chamber of Commerce, Sugar Manufacturers' Association. The agenda was as follows: (1) the proposed Labour Code; (2) the proposed Labour College (it was thought that the College would serve both the trade unions and the business sector and would give courses for management as well); (3) a tripartite seminar with Government and trade unions on industrial relations; (4) the constitution of a Business Advisory Council; (5) the constitution of the National Economic Advisory Council.

Out of these meetings with trade unions and business organisations emerged a National Economic Advisory Council and a Business Advisory Council. A Labour Advisory Council was also constituted representative of the three sections of the movement; but this lapsed with the achievement of unity in the trade union movement, since when the Government normally consults the Labour Congress.

The same pattern of consultation underlay the tripartite conference on unemployment I convened in September 1964 between representatives of the oil and sugar industries, the trade unions in oil and sugar, together with my key advisers in agriculture, petroleum and economic planning.

The essential background to the Unemployment Conference in September was the goal stated in the Second Five Year Development Plan, to provide 44,000 new jobs. This goal, it was recognised, could only be achieved on the basis of full and active collaboration with the Government by the two major industries, oil and sugar. This goal was threatened by the policy pursued by the oil and sugar companies over the past eight years. Both had been responsible for large-scale retrenchment whilst production had increased substantially; wages had also improved.

The leading role in the conference was taken by the Government which was in effect seeking to learn from the companies what assistance they could give towards providing new jobs in industry, agriculture, fishing, tourism, livestock, on the basis of assurances that there would be no further unilateral retrenchment.

The outcome of the conference was the establishment of various tripartite committees to discuss manpower utilisation, agricultural development and industrial development; this broke down when the Oilfield Workers' Trade Union subsequently withdrew.

The highlight of this direct democracy was my Meet the People Tour. Begun on March 22, 1963, it was not completed until January 30, 1964. The tour was intended to bring me into direct contact with village organisations. In all I visited 245 districts, sometimes combining two or more nearby villages. In each area I called for memoranda from the village organisations; a total of 590 memoranda were presented. The tour would have been completed earlier if it had not been for the unexpected interruption of the devastating hurricane in Tobago on September 30, 1963. In all the areas visited I lived among the people.

I reported in a broadcast on the tour to the general population on February 21, 1964. I said:

'It was an experience that I shall never forget and which I would like to share again and again, this community participation in discussions of community problems, and I believe that the tour has achieved, as one of its principal results, a recognition of the value and dignity of community organisations and the importance of community support for these organisations.'

The outstanding problem presented to us in the country as a whole was the problem of community centres in which the community could meet to carry on its activities at various levels. The Government, against the background of the representations made to us by the people, introduced a new policy in respect of community centres. The new policy is that the Government selects the areas in which community centres are to be established, on a priority basis, involving such questions as population and remoteness. The centres are standardised, their size depending on the population to be served. The Government supplies all the materials and the technical supervision required, whilst the community supplies the voluntary labour.

So far over a hundred new community and youth centres have been built and opened at a cost to the Government of some $700,000 in construction grants and over $100,000 in equipment – frigidaires, electric stoves, sewing machines, typewriters in some instances, table tennis facilities, cooking utensils. The centres have become centres of education, particularly in handicrafts, home economics, and sewing, and the Cabinet has recently approved a proposal to make more effective use of them for educational purposes, the Ministry of Community Development (which I took over myself) and the Ministry of Education collaborating in this regard.

A second major field of Government activity arising out of the tour has been the programme for distribution of crown lands, which we have been pursuing as an essential contribution to the problem of unemployment.

The third major result of the extensive tour has been the organisation of the Better Village Programme. With financial assistance provided by Texaco and pledged by Tate and Lyle, we were able to proceed with the programme of community centres and take steps to introduce mobile services in health, libraries, tractors, postal services. The Better Village Programme Committee has also organised a number of additional projects, such as the provision of water pipes to villages which will supply their own labour free of charge; this experiment has been tried out satisfactorily in many villages and emanates from the people themselves. Other matters referred to the Better Village Programme Committee for study included the provision of ambulances and first-aid kits, recreation facilities, including equipment, nursery schools and equipment, school bus system, additional industrial arts and home economics centres to assist in solving the problem of the 11-plus children, cocoa fermentaries and visual aids. The Better Village Programme Committee was also requested to study the question of a national campaign in the field of nutrition utilising the community centres and calling for the co-operation of the Ministries of Community Development, Health, Education and Agriculture.

One of the most important developments which has emerged from the Meet the People Tour is the intensification of interest in handicrafts. This was assisted by the selection of handicrafts as the field for the first of the annual competitions for the Prime Minister's Trophy for the Best Village. No fewer than 114 villages participated in the competition, with a total of 3,864 exhibits. In subsequent years the competition was held in the fields of community concerts, steel-band music, farm production and food preparation, village folklore; in 1968 the competition was to determine the best village and the best-run community centre.

I continued in my broadcast:

'We shall always remember the impact of the tour upon the people themselves. No better medium could have been devised for bringing the Prime Minister close to the people and the people close to the Prime Minister. . . .

What the tour has done more than anything else is to cultivate the nationalist spirit. The people in the communities are conscious that they belong, as they have never been conscious before. . . . The loyalty of the people is beyond question, their confidence is inspiring, their optimism infectious, their dignity in the midst of difficulty heartwarming. I am proud and happy that I was privileged to meet them in their own home surroundings.'

The Meet the People Tour had a gruesome aspect – meeting the people of Tobago after the devastation of the hurricane. I headed the Cabinet Mission sent over to organise the relief and rehabilitation of the island. I spent the entire month of October, 1963 in Tobago, returning to Trinidad only for Cabinet meetings.

I experimented with the direct approach in other directions. I went speaking to sixth formers in all the secondary schools. With the Minister of Education I visited all the Government secondary schools in the country, seeing conditions for myself. I followed this up by convening in December 1965 a conference of the principals of all Government Secondary schools, teacher training colleges, and technical institutes to discuss common problems. I also visited, with the Minister of Agriculture, all the projects which we were developing for the distribution of Crown Lands. The Minister asked me on more than one occasion to distribute farms which had been completed and to say a few words to the farmers. Here is part of my statement at Carlsen Field, one of the returned American bases, on November 2, 1966:

> 'I want to emphasise that everything you do to make your farm succeed reduces the pressure on the amount of money we have to send outside to buy food. . . .
>
> The keys I have given to you are the keys to your houses, they are also the keys to national development in the future.'

30

MEMBER OF PARLIAMENT

During our second term in office I surrendered the portfolio of finance and for the first half of the term I took over the portfolio of external affairs. I retained control of planning and development and responsibility for Tobago Affairs, and I subsequently added to my responsibilities the portfolio of community development. My policy was more and more to leave it to the Ministers involved to do their homework. I restricted my intervention, apart from external affairs (and even this went when I appointed Solomon Minister of External Affairs), to broad national issues.

My outstanding responsibility in Parliament in the second five-year period was the Industrial Stabilisation Act. This was introduced on March 18, 1965, in a situation in which he had had to declare a state of emergency in the sugar areas. The subversive elements in the society, with James in the forefront, were at work; the background was an open attempt to link the trade unions in oil and sugar.

I therefore presented a Bill to provide for the compulsory recognition by employers of trade unions and organisations representative of a majority of workers, for the establishment of an expeditious system for the settlement of trade disputes, for the regulation of prices of commodities, for the constitution of a court to regulate matters relating to the foregoing and incidental thereto.

In the five years, 1960 to 1964, there had been 230 strikes in the country. The number for the year 1962 was 75. The number of workers involved in these strikes in five years was 74,574. The total number of man-days lost for five years was 803,899. The wages lost to workers by the strikes amounted to approximately $4·5 million in five years; and the loss in Government revenue to $4·2 million. The strikes involved issues like recognition and grievances and revision of an agreement, or the agreement on a new agreement, sympathy stoppages, etc.; 10 arbitration tribunals, 9 boards of inquiry and 4 commissions of inquiry had been appointed by the Government.

There were many precedents indeed by which we could be guided, principally the Australian legislation. I spoke as follows in moving the second reading of the Bill:

'The first main feature I should like to emphasise is the aspect of the rule of law and the jurisdiction of the Industrial Court including the fact that agreements, to be valid hereafter, must be registered with the Court. We have avoided the pattern that has developed elsewhere selecting a court with representatives of panels of employers or unions. . . .

The President is to be a High Court Judge, and provision is made for other members: legal practitioner, economist, accountant, and an expert in industrial relations.

The second main feature of the Bill is the provision for the representation of the people of Trinidad and Tobago in all matters coming before the Court. . . .

The Bill sets out certain specific considerations which must guide the Court in arriving at an award and these considerations, as stated in clause 9, are themselves a part of the attempt to protect the national interest, the interest of the people of Trinidad and Tobago.

I should like to say specially, that the attempt to identify such considerations and spell them out in the Bill is perhaps an innovation where the Trinidad and Tobago Bill is concerned. . . .

The considerations as we have spelt them out . . . are as follows:
"(a) the necessity to maintain a high level of domestic capital accumulation with a view to increasing the rate of economic growth and to providing greater employment opportunities;

(b) the necessity to maintain and expand the level of employment;

(c) the necessity to ensure to workers a fair share of increases in productivity in enterprises;

(d) the necessity to prevent gains in the wages of workers from being affected adversely by unnecessary and unjustified price increases;

(e) the necessity to preserve and provide the competitive position of products of Trinidad and Tobago in the domestic market as well as in overseas markets;

(f) the necessity for the establishment and maintenance of
reasonable differentials in rewards between categories of
skills;

(g) the need to maintain for Trinidad and Tobago a favourable
balance of trade and balance of payments;

(h) the need to ensure the continued ability of the Government of Trinidad and Tobago to finance development
programmes in the public sector". . . .

The third principal feature of the Bill . . . is the relationship
between wages and prices. It is not only the trade unionists who
have been very insistent on this, of course; but it is also not only
they who recognise that there must be some relationship. . . .'

The Opposition attacked the bill as totalitarianism, interference with
the rights of trade unions, establishment of a political court. I concentrated in my reply on the attack by our opponents that we were making
political appointments to the Industrial Court:

'In Britain it is the Prime Minister who appoints the Archbishop
of Canterbury; it is the Prime Minister who appoints the Chancellor of the University of Oxford. Somebody has to appoint.
Who is going to appoint?

There are idiots running about Trinidad today saying that the
Senators should be appointed by the Governor-General. Okay.
If you do that then you do not have a Governor-General. Whatever you have it is not a Governor-General. If you have a Governor-General in terms of the Commonwealth, the Governor-
General can act only on the advice of the Prime Minister, who is
the spokesman for the Cabinet. If you do not like it then you can
suggest the Leader of the Opposition; that would put us in an
extremely difficult position in deciding who is the Leader of the
Opposition. . . .

In what country are appointments more political than in the
United States of America? The President is appointing all the time;
somebody has to do the appointing. And in Jordan it is the
Cabinet.'

The measure was passed over the heads of the Opposition. The Court
began to function in the following month. Stability immediately
ensued. Since March 18, 1965, there have been minor strikes in
Trinidad and Tobago; action has been instituted against three unions

for violation of the strike provisions. The Court heard over seventy disputes in its first year; the majority were decided in favour of the Unions. Such has been the pressure on the court – over ninety disputes between May and December, 1966 – that it was agreed in March, 1967, to establish a second division of the Court and increase the number of Judges. The Oilfield Workers' Trade Union went to Court claiming that the act was unconstitutional, bringing in a New Zealand lawyer resident in England for this purpose. The case was decided against the Union, which appealed to the Court of Appeal. The decision has gone against the Union, which has taken the matter to the Privy Council. The fact of the matter, however, is that an oil strike called against the Bill on March 18, 1965, was a total failure, and whilst there were demonstrations around Parliament as the Bill was being debated, the demonstrations were in favour of the measure and not against it. The Court, as a result of a decision in the Court of Appeal, was given in June 1967 specific power to reinstate workers who had been dismissed in harsh and oppressive circumstances.

My second great responsibility in the period under review as a Member of Parliament was the introduction of the Development Plans for Trinidad and for Tobago, in preparation for the 1964 Budget. The combined Plans totalled $320 million during the period 1964–1968.

In presenting the Trinidad Plan I gave priority to the diversification of production. I stressed agriculture and the proposal to distribute 20,000 acres of Crown Lands to small farmers, on whom $4½ million was to be spent on access roads. I stressed the contribution of the citizens' conference to the formulation of the Plan. I dealt with the development of manufacturing industry, and the proposal to set up export promotion industries. I considered education, with particular reference to the vocational school. I paid particular attention to housing. I concentrated heavily on village improvement and community development, with particular reference to the Better Village Programme.

I expressed confidence in the capacity of the country to spend $320 million in five years, an annual average of $64 million. We had spent $53 million in 1961, $61 million in 1962, and expected to spend $61 million in 1963, an annual average of $58 million over the three-year period. I placed great emphasis on local resources: 'The dominant note in the Plan is greater use of local resources, local substitutes for the food and the manufactures now imported . . . The emphasis is on the mobilisation of local savings. . . . And it is in this connection, the greater use of local resources, that I refer to the question of priority to qualified local persons in particular employment, especially at higher level. . . . The revised estimates are here before the House, indicating greater local borrowing, the principle of utilities paying for themselves.'

The Opposition made great play of the fact that there was an uncovered gap in the financing of the Plan, for all the world as if this was not a matter for the Minister of Finance to deal with year by year in his annual development budget. I dealt with this effectively in my reply, referring to Jamaica, India, Nigeria and Pakistan.

On the following day I submitted the Tobago Plan for approval. It had been drawn up by a committee of top civil servants working in Tobago under my direction in the short space of six weeks after the hurricane. Of the total of $320 million, $38 million was to be allocated to Tobago. I dealt comprehensively with all the needs of Tobago - relocation of population, rehabilitation of the forest reserve, acquisition of land for distribution to small farmers, housing and health, community development. Two special features of the Plan related to aliens land-holding and the redevelopment of Lower Scarborough.

All in all, as I said in my presentation of the Plan, 'the hurricane, throughout the history of the West Indies, has been one of the great instruments of land reform and agrarian reform'.

The Opposition opposed the Plan. They saw in it an attempt to eliminate the plantocracy as against the peasant society. They said that the peasant holdings we had in mind were too small. They opposed the concentration on a part only of the national territory. They said we had not consulted the people of Tobago. We had, to the limited extent possible in the time at our disposal. But they, who had sneered at the Queen's Hall Conference in respect of the Trinidad Plan, were full of solicitude for the people of Tobago. They said the plan did not contain certain provisions for land acquisition, which it did, precisely and in some detail. And they accused me of hounding the estate owners in respect of income tax.

My third great responsibility in Parliament was to pilot through the legislation relating to the reorganisation of the public service.

This originated in Working Parties of senior civil servants and representatives of the staff associations which were appointed by the Cabinet in February 1964 – shortly before I left on my African tour – to consider the role of the civil service, teaching service and police force in the age of Independence. The Working Parties reported towards the end of 1964 and the beginning of 1965. Prior to this we had hired an American firm to classify the public service, but its proposals had been resisted by the staff association.

The Working Parties produced valuable reports, but did not re-organise. They said reorganisation would take five years. Cabinet disagreed. It could not accept revised compensation proposals without classification. The matter was then assigned to a Cabinet Committee with myself as Chairman.

Thus it was that on December 6, 1965, I went to the House with the first instalment of reorganisation – a Bill to make provision for the establishment and the classification of the Civil Service, for the establishment of a Personnel Department, for the establishment of procedures for negotiation and consultation between the Government and members of the Civil Service for the settlement of disputes, and for other matters concerning the relationship between the Government and the Civil Service.

The first major point to which I drew attention was the procedure for bargaining between the Government as employer and the Civil Service employees; to this end we set up a Personnel Department attached to the Ministry of Home Affairs. The second principal feature of the legislation was the procedure for the resolution of disputes; we appointed a Special Tribunal of the Industrial Court – the President, the Vice-President, and one other member of the Court selected by the President in his discretion. Awards were to be binding for five years. The third major feature of the legislation was the separation of senior civil servants from trade union activity. We excluded the fire and prison services from the scope of civil service and therefore trade union activities; they were to form their own association. I then dealt comprehensively with the regulations accompanying the act, drawing attention to the fact that there would be regulations governing discipline as well made by the Public Service Commission with the consent of the Prime Minister, as prescribed by the Constitution. But I gave some idea of what those regulations would cover.

It was, as I said in commending the Bill to the House, a good measure, well conceived and well based – a necessary part of the modernisation process in Trinidad and Tobago designed to give statutory protection to the civil servants. The Opposition, however, would have none of it and found all sorts of fault with it. I felt constrained therefore to say in my reply to the debate:

'In so far as anything has been said on the other side, what has been said suggests either the village idiot or the constitutional tycoon.

We heard that a man could be a civil servant today and not to-morrow. We heard that the Government could vary the pay. We heard that the civil servant might have to leave the civil service on the abolition of his office, and this would lead to the spoils system; that the Cabinet could get rid of the office if it wants, and that the Cabinet is to provide jobs for the boys. . . . What surprises me, Sir, is that the Members guilty of these constitutional aberrations pay no attention to the constitution of this country.'

I then dealt with the Public Service Commission and its place in the Constitution of the country. It is responsible for the recruitment, appointment, transfer, dismissal and discipline of civil servants. I quoted from the draft Public Service Commission regulations which I had in my possession. I continued:

'The Commission may remove, the Commission may terminate, the Commission that has exclusive jurisdiction over all matters concerning recruitment, appointment, transfer, promotion, dismissal and discipline of all public servants subject only to one interference with their absolutely exclusive power, and that is the regulations must be made with the consent of the Prime Minister, Either the village idiot or the constitutional tycoon. I myself believe it is a case of village idiocy.'

The Opposition also argued that classification is a technical matter and not a political function. But I reminded them that someone had to take the decisions and bring the matter to Parliament for the funds to be voted: 'technical discussions are not inconsistent with the supervision of the educational qualifications and the application of the criteria that you lay down.'

The next day I dealt with the Police Service Bill, and two days later with the Prison Service and the Fire Service. All these followed in broad outline the provisions of the Civil Service Bill.

On December 8 I presented the Education Bill. Its principal features were: (1) unification of the teaching service, thus removing the traditional discrimination against the primary school teacher, (2) the registration of all teachers, (3) the ban on discrimination against any child in any school on ground of religious persuasion, race, social status or language, (4) the placing of all teachers, including those in assisted denominational secondary schools, under the Public Service Commission, (5) the financial accountability of all assisted schools for Government subventions. The act and the attendant regulations made provision for advisory committees to advise the Minister, including advice on textbooks. The regulations spelled out procedures for admission to secondary schools on the basis of the common entrance examination, and made it clear that even the percentage left to principals of assisted schools for the preservation of their faith must be taken from children who had sat the examination and were on the pass list. The Act laid down a general prohibition against expulsion of a child without the approval of Cabinet or suspension without the approval of the Minister. As I said, the Act was 'a necessary measure of integration of our society, a necessary national system for an independent country.'

On May 28, 1965, I replied for the Government to an Opposition motion calling for the appointment of a committee to investigate urgently the system of education with a view to recommending a system best suited to our needs and to determining how best the denominational bodies could make an even greater contribution to education than they had made in the past.

I took the opportunity to enlarge on our achievements in the field of education: a 30% increase in primary school enrolment and a 140% increase in secondary school enrolment in nine years. Where in 1955, 204 children went to secondary school at Government expense, the number in 1962 was 3,291 and in 1964 was 3,750.

The Opposition Member's general submission, for the appointment of a committee to make recommendations, I opposed, on the ground that we had already had recently an investigation by UNESCO.

On February 26, 1965, another Opposition member called for a Select Committee of the House to make recommendations for the prevention of the further deterioration of rural roads and to report on all aspects of the basic needs of the people in respect to pipe-borne water, lights, footpaths, drains and agricultural traces, many of which were still in a primitive state. It was decided that I should reply on behalf of the Government as the motion involved community development with particular reference to the Better Village Programme. I pointed out the action taken by us in response to the people's representations on my tour.

My only other contribution to the activities of the Parliament was my announcement on April 5, 1963, that the Government had decided to set up an inquiry into the oil industry and another inquiry into subversive activity in the country.

31

THE PARTY IN
THE ERA OF INDEPENDENCE

The five-year period 1961–1966 was a period of intense activity in the life of the Party. It saw three major achievements – the revision of the Party Constitution, the establishment of Party Headquarters, and the celebration of the Tenth Anniversary of the Party.

Article 17 of the Constitution adopted by the Inaugural Conference of the People's National Movement on January 15, 1956, provided that the Constitution shall be subject to automatic review by the Annual Convention only after the expiration of five years from the date of its acceptance by the Inaugural Conference and then on the basis of proposals submitted by the Central Executive.

The Sixth Annual Convention on January 26, 1962, appointed a committee of ten with a chairman drawn from outside the Legislative Group to review the constitution and report to a Special Convention. I was included on the Review Committee.

The principal changes were as follows:

(a) *Aims and Objects:* This section was redrafted to bring it in line with existing political realities.

(b) *Overseas Group:* After prolonged deliberation, the Committee was of the opinion that Overseas Groups should be discontinued, mainly because of (i) difficulty of control, (ii) possible international repercussions.

(c) *Organisation:* It was considered that the Women's League and Youth League should be organised on a Constituency basis, working under the general supervision and control of the Constituency Executive.

(d) *Foundation Members:* The Committee felt by a majority vote that foundation members should be removed as such from the General Council as they could become members thereof as a matter of right rather than privilege, if they show interest in their Party Groups and in the activities of the Movement. Provision was however made to have twelve foundation members selected by the General Council as observers to Party Conventions.

(e) *Officers of the Movement:* Special procedures for the election of the Chairman, the First Vice-Chairman, the Political Leader and the General Secretary were recommended, these posts being held for five years except in cases of resignation or removal. It was recommended that all other Officers should be elected for one year.

(f) *Legislative Group:* It was felt that members of the Legislative Group should be more closely identified with Party activities, and to this end they were given representation at Party Conventions, on the General Council, Constituency Group and Party Group. Membership of the Legislative Group was increased to include Party Members appointed to Statutory County Council Committees who would consequently be better aware of party policy and be subject to party discipline in their role as Party Representatives.

The revised constitution was adopted in Special Convention on January 20, 1963.

The next landmark was a reappraisal by the Party of its origins and fundamentals. On March 15, 1964, the Research Committee of the General Council, headed by A. N. R. Robinson, was directed to prepare a study on 'The Role of the Party in the Era of Independence' and to examine the relationship between the Party and the Party members and other organisations in the society. The Committee's report was adopted by the General Council on July 1, 1964.

In the study the Committee addressed itself to three main questions:

1. Does the Party have a philosophy?
2. Where is the philosophy of the Party expressed?
3. How does the structure of the Party express this philosophy?

In seeking to find answers to these questions the Committee made a detailed study of Party documents and concluded:

'The political philosophy of PNM is abundantly clear. The Party is for independence and democracy. Our concept of democracy is based upon the rule of law, human rights and human dignity. We are against totalitarianism. We are against individualism. We are for political education of the people and their active participation in the conduct of the country's affairs. We are interracial. We are for intellectual freedom. We are for equality of opportunity and a career open to talent. We are against inefficiency. We are for integrity and discipline. We are for planned and rational development, for social security and a higher standard of living.'

The report went on to point out that the Party has eschewed dogmatism or the rigid application of preconceived ideas without reference to environment. In doing so, however, there is no doubt that the Party has evolved a system of ideas that can be the Party's guide in the present and in the future. It went on to emphasise that the Party's avoidance of dogmatism is clearly illustrated in its attitude to the nationalisation issue. Then the report emphatically stated:

'We reject the dogmatism of state enterprise, and we reject the dogmatism of private initiative.'

The report continued:

'It is clear that the traditional philosophical categories such as socialist and liberal are meaningless in the context of a Party such as the PNM; yet it cannot be said that the philosophy of the PNM is contradictory or inconsistent. Independence is not inconsistent with international collaboration. Planned development is not inconsistent with human rights, and social security is not inconsistent with a career open to talent. Public initiative is not inconsistent with private enterprise.'

The report concluded:

'What the PNM has done is to produce a synthesis of ideas both in the liberal and socialist traditions with a strong nationalist and environmental flavour.'

The Committee recommended the translation of the philosophy of the Party into political action culminating in the celebration of the Tenth Anniversary of the Party – January 24, 1966 – to which end the General Council should begin preparations immediately.

The second recommendation of the Committee was that emphasis should be given to the practical expression of certain features of the Party's philosophy during the Tenth Anniversay celebrations. For example its interracialism; its stand on morality in public affairs; on democracy and human rights; on co-operation between the state and private enterprise; and on Caribbean unity.

Thirdly, the Committee recommended that some of the fundamental documents of the Party should be republished on the occasion of the Tenth Anniversary. In addition, the General Council decided that it would publish a collation of the fundamental ideas of the Party in one readable volume as well as a history of the PNM 1956–1966.

In all this the Party was fortified and strengthened by the achievement of our Party Headquarters. The formal ceremony took place on April 22, 1963, before a large number of Party members who had been invited for the occasion. I named the headquarters Balisier House.

Following up my successful Meet the People Tour, about which some Party members had complained that they had been left in the background, I initiated a Meet the Party Tour, to develop direct democracy within the Party itself. My tour began on June 14, 1964, and was suspended on June 5, 1965; I resumed it in September 1967. During the first period I covered twelve of the then twenty-four constituencies, made 75 stops, discussed with representatives of 211 Units of the Party, and received approximately 200 memoranda.

As might be expected, criticisms of the Legislative arm and the officers of the Party figured largely in the discussions with Party Group members. The Party members criticised the lack of a flow of information from Party Headquarters and Party members as undermining the Party structure, and proposed more frequent lectures and discussions by executive members of the Party. Many of the Party Groups were particularly critical of the Party members themselves, many of whom joined the Party for what they could get out of it.

These valuable and important criticisms did not distract attention from the very commendable activities being pursued actively by many of the Party Groups. I was very gratified to note the attention given by Party Groups to the Five Year Development Programme, lectures on Government Bonds and the emerging countries in Africa, the Unitary State with Grenada and the US blockade of Cuba. One Group had appointed a Committee to devise ways and means to attract the 20–30 age group. Party Groups had had discussions on Parliamentary Procedure, Buy Local, Predial Larceny and Unemployment. One Constituency Group had established a Constituency Library. Another Party Group had had lectures on art and its relation to everyday life, and I was very happy to hear that this Group had had a regular series of discussions based on my *History of the People of Trinidad and Tobago.*

I was very happy to see for myself and to hear of the excellent relations maintained with the community organisations by a large majority of Party and Constituency Groups. The Party members for the most part regarded themselves and their Party Groups as the spearhead of the drive for social improvements in the community. As the Party members in one district said, it was they who had for the past seven years been responsible for most of the drive and vitality shown by their Village Council. Many Party members held office in the Village Council, and it was good to see a PNM Constituency Group taking the lead in organising a Community Council while another had developed a promising Youth Movement.

The best testimony to the social consciousness of our Party members was the wide range of national problems to which they drew my attention. Some oustanding examples were National Service, jobs for women over 40, family planning, the rising wave of lawlessness, waste of labour and materials on the job, a National Lottery, the Labour Code, vocational schools, school bus system, re-examination of Pioneer Industries Legislation, Industrial Court, unreasonable wage demands, promotion of National Savings, scrapping of the railway, Caribbean Economy Community.

Arising out of the Meet the Party Tour, acting as chairman of the Legislative Group, I instituted a new programme, whereby each month (*a*) the elected representative reported to his Constituency Group (Senators being delegated to do this in the constituencies not represented by PNM), (*b*) each Minister reported to one of the Constituency Groups in PNM Constituencies, (*c*) senior Party Officials reported to Party Groups, individually or more than one combined, in the constituencies I had visited.

And so we proceeded to our Tenth Anniversary Celebrations. We agreed on a vast programme covering all segments of the national life – a central exhibition of manufactures, products, arts and crafts; a number of concerts, variety and cultural shows; a youth rally in San Fernando; a calypso competition; a fashion show at the Trinidad Hilton Hotel put on by the Women's League; two recitals; a Special Convention of the Party; a reception at Balisier House given by the Legislative Group; a sports meeting. The programme, which covered the entire community, included six public meetings, at which I was the principal speaker, culminating in a mass meeting in the University of Woodford Square.

On January 21, 1966 *The Nation* brought out a huge edition to celebrate 'Ten Years of PNM and Good Government'. The number included articles of historical interest. I sent a Tenth Anniversary message which read as follows:

'It has been Ten Years of hard and relentless work, dedicated always to the public welfare, to political dignity and stability, to the national community, to the political education of our educated democracy.

It has been an uphill fight, which is far from being over. Look outside the PNM and you will see individualism, undiluted and rampant, for all the world as if the PNM had never come on the scene to set a contrary example.

Confusion and chaos will be the order of the day if PNM should disappear or deteriorate. There is still far too much sectional selfishness, every day one hears of another example of corruption in the public service, far too many still put self before NATION. But PNM is there, holding proudly aloft the banner of nationhood, rational economic planning, an integrated national community with equality for all, respect for the rule of law, multi-party democracy, freedom of worship, social security – discipline, production, tolerance.

We have for the past ten years as a Party governed this country which we have taken from crown colony to Independent Nation, with our voices, however small, being increasingly heard in the councils of the world. New industries, farms where there were none before, respectable flats replacing disgraceful shanties, hospital beds and health clinics, new roads, new schools in which education is free – all testify to the power and influence of the PNM, all represent the realisation of the People's Charter of 1956.

I extend my thanks and good wishes as Political Leader to all those Party veterans whose sacrifices, whose dedication, whose loyalty through thick and thin, whose support financial, moral· and ideological, have alone permitted us in the past ten years first to obtain, then to retain, and in the next few months to command once more the support of the majority of the electorate.

In song and dance, in art and agriculture, in literature and painting, in exhibition halls and at public meetings, we and the country have been celebrating the Tenth Anniversary of the PNM.

May we now, fortified by past achievement and public appreciation, rededicate ourselves to the urgent task that lies ahead –

the relentless prosecution of the aims and objectives, the beliefs and fundamental principles with which we set out to conquer ten years ago. As we look back on the ten years that have passed, let us look forward to the ten years that await us, confident always that great is the PNM, and it must and shall prevail.'

The Special Convention was summoned to consider the following resolution moved by me as Political Leader:

'RESOLVED that this Special Convention of the People's National Movement convened this 23rd day of January 1966 on the occasion of the 10th Anniversary of the launching of the Party reaffirms the Party's adherence to the Fundamental Principles set out in the People's Charter and the Party Constitution and rededicates the Party to the task of securing the complete realisation of these principles in every phase of the public and political life of Trinidad and Tobago.'

I showed how over the years we had implemented the People's Charter and had kept our pledges to the Party and the electorate. I placed the greatest stress on Chaguaramas.

The Convention stood up in acclamation to reaffirm their dedication to the People's Charter. Thousands of citizens from all walks of life joined us to celebrate our Anniversary in the University of Woodford Square. We had a battery of top Party speakers. We reviewed the achievements of the Government based on the three policy divisions, Political, Social, Economic, enunciated in the People's Charter.

We followed this up by a quiet celebration, in the form of a cocktail party given by me for the staff, of *The Nation*'s tenth anniversary.

With respect to the liaison between Government and Party, I referred two important matters for consideration by the Party. The first related to family planning, which was discussed by the General Council on January 3, 1965. The Council appointed a Committee to study the issue. The Committee recommended the grant of certain privileges requested by the Family Planning Association, and proposed a Special Convention to deal with the question of family planning. The Special Convention was convened on April 23, 1967 and unanimously agreed that the Government should institute a programme of family planning on a national scale. A Population Council has since been appointed by the Government and aid sought from the International Planned Parenthood Federation.

The second matter referred to the General Council by me was the question of adherence to the Organisation of American States. The matter was discussed at the meeting of the General Council on January 3, 1965. The Council resumed consideration of this matter on January 29, 1967, when it voted unanimously for our seeking immediate admission to the Organisation of American States. The necessary resolution was presented in both Houses of Parliament and the application forwarded on February 9. We were admitted on February 23 at a meeting of Foreign Ministers in Buenos Aires, and as a result I attended the meeting of Chiefs of State at Punta del Este, Uruguay, in April 1967.

I continued to educate and to lecture to the Party whenever time permitted. As an introduction to international affairs, my constituency, for example, organised in February 1962 a week-end school on Africa. I gave the introductory lecture and the concluding lecture on Pan Africanism.

In the field of party schools, we experimented with a National Party school on two occasions, selecting one theme for discussion in all constituencies on the same day. The first of these national party schools, organised on May 30, 1965, dealt with the Industrial Stabilisation Act. To provide a 'textbook' for the school, I wrote seven articles in The Nation. An agenda was prepared for the School, which began with a half hour's address by the representative of the Constituency – Senators and Party officers being deputed to those constituencies not represented by the PNM. Discussion followed on the different articles in The Nation. The school was quite a success.

We followed this up by organising another National Party School on May 15, 1966, on the impending General Elections. The two major themes of the school were (a) ten years of progress under PNM; (b) the Elections Law. The first lecture was principally my responsibility; I had prepared for it by a series over several weeks of Weekly Newsletters to the Party in the pages of The Nation beginning on November 8, 1965, and presenting statistically aspects of progress in many fields. We briefed the lecturers at special briefing sessions before the school was held. The school was a great success, and marked the initiation of our election campaign.

In my leadership of the Party, I was never tired of attacking the social climbing and conspicuous consumption of the population. I warned the population that Independence could collapse, that the road might lead back to colonialism. And I kept before the Party members the difficulty of a small country in a big hostile world.

32
INTELLECTUAL PURSUITS

The pressures on the Prime Minister did not abate with Independence; rather they were intensified – requests for jobs, houses, land, pensions, social assistance, and redress of grievances.

As usual, I deliberately retreated, whenever time permitted, to my intellectual pursuits. This was done publicly, not stealthily. I let the whole population know. I wrote in my column on December 3, 1965:

> 'Finally, the entire West Indian tradition is anti-intellectual. People's lives are bounded by the narrow materialistic considerations of the price of produce or the cost of living or the laziness of the workers or the growth of crime and delinquency or gambling or chasing after women (or men as the case may be) or just plain gluttony and imbibing. Add to that the movies and the radio and in more modern days the equally pernicious television, and fit in somewhere in this schedule sleeping and working or making pretence of working, and the normal individual's day is complete. Cricket and football, a sports meeting, the races – and the normal year is complete. A Head of Government cannot be limited to such narrow and materialistic considerations. So I read deliberately, in silent protest against the bastardisation of so-called West Indian intellectualism.'

In my first five-year term of office I had been content with essays, lectures, articles in our party paper. I thought that I would not have the time for, or be able to give the necessary concentration to, the production of a whole book. Impending Independence posed a challenge – should I allow the country to achieve its Independence without a history of its own? If there was to be one, and one quickly, I alone could write it. I hesitated. It was too big a job. Some of my closest intimates urged me to try my hand at it. I did. The result was the publication, coinciding with Independence, of *The History of the People of Trinidad and Tobago*, the English edition of which appeared in 1964. The book, completed within one month, was conceived as the Declaration of Independence of the People of Trinidad and Tobago.

I had proved that a Prime Minister could write a book whilst he was in office. This opened up untold possibilities for the wealth of research material that I had in cold storage in my files. I followed this up the following year with the first volume of *Documents of West Indian History*, covering the period 1492 to 1655.

My third venture involved bringing back into the light of day my 1944 Atlanta lectures on British Historiography and the Negro question. Amplified and developed, it became *British Historians and the West Indies*, published in Port-of-Spain on the day on which I left on my African tour and published in England in 1966 with a foreword by Alan Bullock.

The long overdue English edition of my *Capitalism and Slavery* at last appeared in 1964, with an introduction by Sir Denis Brogan. My history of the Caribbean, from Columbus to Castro, was deferred until the completion of the autobiography.

Throughout the five-year period I kept in close touch with universities – here at home in the West Indies, in Canada, in the United Kingdom, and in Africa. I was appointed Pro-Chancellor of the University of the West Indies. My *alma mater* honoured me first with an Honorary Fellowship at St. Catherine's College, and then with the Honorary Degree of Doctor of Civil Law. Then followed the Honorary Degree of Doctor of Laws at New Brunswick and the Honorary Degree of Doctor of Letters at the University of the West Indies.

I delivered the Address to the graduating class at the University of the West Indies on February 16, 1963. Some of the students were themselves from Trinidad and Tobago. I stressed to them their responsibilities – to defend the national independence and to read.

I delivered the Encaenia Address to the graduating class at New Brunswick on May 20, 1965, on the occasion of my Honorary Degree. My theme was 'The Developing Nation in the Modern World'. I dealt principally with international issues.

On my African tour I made it a point to speak at as many universities as possible. I spoke at Dakar, Fourah Bay, Monrovia, Lagos, Nsukka, Ife, Ibadan, Addis Ababa and Cairo, and I had valuable discussions with the Faculty at Accra, Makerere, and Dar-es-Salaam. I also held discussions with the Ministry of Education in Algiers and with University professors at Zagreb in Yugoslavia. My principal theme was intellectual decolonisation, and I was concerned with interpreting West Indians and the West Indies to my African audiences. On my return journey to Trinidad I spoke to dons at Queen Elizabeth House in Oxford, to West Indian students at McGill in Montreal and at Howard in Washington, and on my return I addressed the students at St. Augustine on my African tour.

I lectured in French on West Africa and the West Indies' at the University of Dakar. I was very glad to be in Senegal because it was my first introduction to the African heritage in the West Indies, and a thoughtfully prepared official programme allowed me to see the historical data preserved at Goree. I interpreted West Indian society for them, and especially Trinidad's multiracialism. I went on to quote freely from President Senghor's writings to show the difference between West Africa and the West Indies – his analysis of the position of women in African society, the African family, the African village, and finally socialism.

On March 4, 1964, I paid a brief stop at the University of Ife in Nigeria. The students met me on the campus outside and read an address of welcome. In my brief reply I dealt with the question of Southern Rhodesia.

At Haile Selassie I University in Addis Ababa on March 16, 1964, I made a major address. My theme was the role of African Universities in the development of African Unity. I dealt principally with four problems. The first was the lack of co-operation between the African Universities. I then proceeded to deal with the introduction of basic survey courses in West Indian studies and in the social sciences and humanities which I had helped to originate at the University of the West Indies. Problem three was the outstanding gap in the period of slavery and the slave trade in Africa, and I called on the African scholars to fill it. The fourth problem was the lack of attention being paid in Africa to the influences exercised by Africa through slave migrations – in the West Indies, Brazil, Cuba, Haiti.

At McGill and St. George William Universities in Montreal, I spoke on the community of interest between Africa and the West Indies, and I told them of my mission to Africa. I dealt particularly with the modern scramble for Africa. At my old school, Howard, in Washington, I spoke on April 29 on intellectual decolonisation. I dealt particularly with the question of African studies and the part African Universities were playing – or not playing – in this field. When I returned to Trinidad, the St. Augustine branch of the University of

the West Indies asked to speak to them on Africa. I dealt among other
things with the question of African socialism.

In June and July 1965, after the Prime Ministers' Conference, I
toured a number of British Universities to discuss common problems
and try to work out details of technical assistance in one form or
another as well as to make arrangements for subsequent collaboration.
I went as Pro-Chancellor, and was accompanied by the Vice-Chan-
cellor, Sir Philip Sherlock, and the Principal of the Barbados Campus,
Mr. Sidney Martin. We visited the following universities in a tour
kindly arranged for us by the Inter-University Council for Higher
Education: Sussex, Reading, Manchester, Bradford, Leeds, Oxford,
Edinburgh, Glasgow, Strathclyde, Wales (at Swansea and Aber-
ystwyth), Bristol, Cambridge, London. I was able to renew acquaintance with Sir Kenneth Wheare and Lord Franks at Oxford, and with
Sir Denis Brogan at Cambridge. I was able to meet for the first time
such striking University personalities as Sir John Fulton at Sussex
and Sir Roger Stevens at Leeds. A bad attack of hay fever prevented
me from visiting Wales, to my great regret, and reduced my effectiveness at Glasgow. A report of the visit has been published by the University of the West Indies. I reported on the aims and purposes of the
Mission to the House of Representatives on July 23, 1965.

All these university visits and contacts gave me a valuable opportunity to improve the scope of my library, both in quantity and
quality. The African documentation and the literature on university
developments were particularly useful in this regard.

For the rest I continued to write my weekly column in *The Nation*.
Between August 29, 1964 and December 17, 1965, I wrote no fewer
than sixty-seven articles. Several were series of articles – the Prime
Ministers' Conference, our Industrial Stabilisation Act, Reflections on
the Caribbean Economic Community, Reminiscences of the Prime
Minister (which remained incomplete), The Reality of Independence.
I would write on British West Indian Airways one week and a progress
report on education another week; the public ownership of bus transport one week and Meet the Party another week; the community
centre one week and Oxford revisited another.

I was given a special page in *The Nation*, 'The Political Leader's
Page'. In addition to the article, the page carried a book review. I
wanted our party members to read. They lacked the money to buy
books, or the time or inclination to read them. So I did their reading
for them and reported back to them, my reviews being deliberately
distinguished by copious quotations from the original. This was one

way of keeping up with my reading – in order to review I had to read; and as I gave priority to external affairs, I kept myself as a Minister responsible *au courant* with what was going on in the world. This was particularly the case with Vietnam and Castro's Cuba. Several of the reviews were done in four parts, if the book was particularly relevant to Trinidad and Tobago's problems. Between August 28, 1964, and December 17, 1965, I reviewed forty-five books.

One of my best articles in *The Nation* was an appreciation of Leopold Senghor, President of Senegal, written on September 25, 1964, shortly before he arrived in Trinidad on an official visit.

I lectured to the Economics Society of the University of the West Indies in Jamaica on 'Some Thoughts on Economic Aid to Developing Countries'. Under the auspices of the Extra Mural Department of the University I lectured in British Guiana on 'The Future of the West Indies and Guyana'. On November 14, 1964, on the occasion of the 75th anniversary of the birth of Nehru, I gave a lecture, at the invitation of the Indian High Commissioner, entitled 'A Tribute to Nehru'. I saw in Nehru principally a historian turned politician. I dealt firstly with his analysis of British imperialism in India. On his letters written to his daughter, now following in her father's footsteps as Prime Minister, whilst he was in prison, I said:

'*Glimpses of World History* is a classic in the literature of intellectual decolonisation. It sets out to do two things. The first aim is to place Asian culture and history in its world context and therefore to place in its true perspective the dominant European history, written of Europe and for Europe, to impress colonials in particular. . . .

The second purpose of Nehru's analysis of world history is to place the history of India in true perspective. . . .'

(c) The Third Mandate

33
THE 1966 GENERAL ELECTION

During the five-year period the DLP split into three parts. Four Members of the House, claiming that it was not possible for Capildeo to operate the party by remote control (he was acting as a lecturer at London University), seceded to form the Liberal Party. The Industrial Stabilisation Act split the party down the middle. The Acting Leader broke with the party on the Industrial Stabilisation Act which he had opposed, whilst two other members of the DLP supported. He sought to use his power to remove the four DLP Senators who had voted for the Act. The remaining DLP members in the House got together to advise the Governor-General that the acting leader was no longer acting Leader, and so the Governor-General removed him. He thereupon formed the Workers and Farmers Party. There was also the skeleton of the Butler Party interested in the St. Patrick County seats, and there were several independent candidates in the election race. Thus for the 36 seats provided in accordance with the Constitution provision prescribing one seat for every 12,000 electors, there were 156 candidates in the election on November 7.

The PNM fought the election campaign on its ten-year record of service, progress and achievement. We never let the country forget what we had done. We did not hesitate, however, to warn the country of the dangers ahead. As we put it in our Election Manifesto, the country faces three principal problems: the rapid growth of population, the balance of payments, the high recurrent costs of government.

The principal issues in the election campaign were: (1) the WFP pledge to take away the land from the sugar companies; (2) our agricultural programme; (3) the DLP education proposals; (4) the question of economic independence with particular reference to foreign investment; (5) subversive activities in the country. All of these were debated openly and publicly on the platform.

The WFP claimed that it would expropriate the lands of the sugar companies and divide them up among tens of thousands of small farmers. I selected the Special Convention of September 11, called to approve our election manifesto and our candidates, to reply to this as follows. Trinidad and Tobago, with 94% of total holdings under 50 acres and embracing 48% of the total acreage, and with the Government the biggest single owner of land, is a paradise for the small farmer as compared with Latin America. The three sugar companies control 84,825 acres. The effective acreage in cane cultivation is 57,892. But there are 16,400 sugar workers. Divide acres by farmers and you get a holding of 3½ acres. There are already thousands of cane farmers producing small quantities of cane who are not making a living. Those producing up to 5 tons of cane have a gross annual income of $24·52; those producing from 6–20 tons of cane have a gross income of $163·17; and those producing 21–50 tons of cane have a gross income of $360·36. You cannot get efficient cane farmers, therefore, on 3½ acres of land.

By contrast, studies made in the Prime Minister's Office have demonstrated that from five acres of yams, pumpkins, pigeon peas and corn the effective gross family income per year is $4,178. This income is $2,258 from five acres of dasheen, eddoes, tannia, corn and beans; $5,849 from five acres of tomatoes, patchoi, cabbage and pepper; $4,990 from three acres of melongene, lettuce, mustard and cabbage. The net income from a 15-acre dairy farm is $3,031 and from a 5-acre pig farm $1,922. But there is not enough land to give all sugar workers five acres for pigs and food crops or fifteen acres for dairy cattle. 'You can't, in other words, have it all ways at the same time. Either you break up the land and you get tens of thousands of inefficient cane farmers. Or you substitute food crops for cane and you satisfy only a section of the sugar labour force.'

This immediately raised the issue of our agricultural programme. All the opposing parties opposed it, and I dealt with it comprehensively. I began by discussing three of the basic realities we face in Trinidad and Tobago – the search for jobs, the large imports of food, and the necessity to conserve our balance of payments. They were responsible for the Government's agricultural programme, which fell into three parts.

The first part concerned the settlement of new farmers on 20,000 acres of government lands, in three types of schemes – 15-acre dairy farms, 5-acre pig farms, 5-acre food plots. We had spent $6 million on this programme since 1964, $½ million on access roads in the food plots. The second part of the programme was assistance to the established farmers – tractor pools, agricultural credit, roads of which we had built 64 miles in the last five years, guaranteed prices. The third form of assistance was assistance to the small sugar farmers whom we had encouraged to form the Cane Farmers Association – loans for fertiliser, buying a headquarters, subsidies for ploughing and control of froghopper, representation on appropriate boards, a Commission of Enquiry into the price of farmers' canes. I ended up with the *pièce de resistance*: a few days before the International Bank for Reconstruction and Development had announced a loan of $8½ million for our agricultural programme.

All the opposing parties sneered at our Independence. They said it was not 'genuine'. Especially the WFP claimed that we were stooges of foreign investors. I asked my audience, if American capital could be invested in oil refining in Britain and West Germany, why could it not be invested in oil production in Trinidad to provide additional jobs? I asked them, if the whole world could be dependent on American capital investment, why should Trinidad and Tobago, lower than Canada, France, Germany, Japan, United Kingdom, Italy, in terms of gross domestic product *per capita*, seek to make American capital investment difficult?

The DLP attacked our education achievements. Apart from resurrecting the outworn slogan 'education before sewerage' (the sewerage scheme had in any case been completed), they pointed to the fact that 30,000 children sat the Common Entrance Examination and only 6,000 were found free places in secondary schools; so that, they claimed, for every child being admitted, five were left stupid.

The Minister of Education and I gave the principal replies to this propaganda. We showed that it was PNM's egalitarian policies which were responsible for such a large number of entrants to the common entrance examination. We pointed to the fact that there were many hundred children who repeated the examination in the second year; so that the proportion of one in six was not correct. And we stressed that, if the child reverted to the primary school because of the absence of a place in the secondary school, a new syllabus had been introduced into the eleven-plus classes of the primary school, incorporating some features of the secondary syllabus.

The DLP claimed that it would set up 40–50 comprehensive secondary schools going right up to the external degree of London University. This curious hybrid of secondary school and university college would be very costly. We reckoned that the increased expenditure would be $140 million over some years in capital costs, and anything between $8 and $100 million a year in recurrent costs, depending on how many of the eleven-plus children would be admitted under the DLP scheme. As usual with these visionaries, the DLP never said where the money would come from.

The other great issue in the election was subversive activity. Many of the WFP members had been prominent in the trade union activities which had led to the declaration of a state of emergency in 1965 and the passage of the Industrial Stabilisation Act. Some were referred to by name in the report of the Mbanefo Commission on Subversive Activities. Two of their candidates had attended the Tricontinental Conference in Havana in January 1966. Gerard Montano, as Minister of Home Affairs, made this attack on subversive elements and the WFP his principal theme. He thundered at a meeting in Fyzabad on June 21, where I was on the platform:

'There are some people who have just returned from Cuba who are saying what a fine country it was.

If I could have persuaded the Prime Minister I would advise him to pay their passages and send them to Cuba, that wonderful land they are boasting about. Only one condition I would impose: when once they go there, let them stay there.'

On September 14, speaking in San Fernando, I issued my own warning to the Castroites. I said:

'Go out and finish up with this Marxist ideology, which goes to Havana, Cuba and dares to sit down and take part in subversive resolutions against the lawful Government of Trinidad and Tobago. To hell with Castro.

San Fernando put PNM in power, not Castro. Castro has no right to interfere with Trinidad and Tobago Affairs. We don't interfere with Castro's affairs, and Castro has no business setting up any revolutionary organisation in order to interfere with and disrupt the normal development of Trinidad and Tobago.'

The Opposition assiduously circulated the story that I was not interested in the election campaign; I would be proceeding to New York to take over U Thant's job. I dismissed the allegation in my speech in San Fernando.

My greatest scoop in the election was the dissection of the Liberal Party manifesto forty-eight hours before it was officially presented to the public. I ridiculed the manifesto from start to finish as a mere copy of the PNM's. The biggest laugh was when I read out their pledge to organise adequate bus transport for school children; I had inaugurated the service on September 12. I showed how they had copied PNM's programme on the Caribbean Economic Community, Tobago, agriculture, low cost housing, public transport, tourist travel facilities, encouragement of investment in hotel development. Their programme was entitled 'Straight Forward to New Horizons' and had a picture of a beautiful yacht. I laughed at it, 'riding to PNM horizons in a POPPG yacht' (the POPPG was the conservative party of big business in 1956). I poked great fun at the whole programme. They promised to support carnival. But they had voted year after year against any appropriation for carnival. I concluded that the Liberals were 'twisting to PNM's manifesto'.

My election campaign was, as usual, a hard one. Between May 1 and September 9, before the selection of candidates at our Special Convention, I organised with the Senior Ministers fifty-five pre-election meetings at which we spoke on the Party's achievements in the ten-year period. With the selection of our candidates and the ratification of our election manifesto, the campaign began in real earnest. It started in the University of Woodford Square on September 12, when we presented our candidates, and ended at the University on November 6 at the end of a day of spot meetings all over the five Port-of-Spain Constituencies. In all I held 184 election meetings, and reached, according to my staff, an estimated total audience of 308,015.

Election Day, November 7, produced many difficulties. It was clear that the enumeration left much to be desired – we had had to extend the period of registration of voters. Many returning and presiding officers, according to numerous complaints, behaved as if they were appointed to discourage people from voting. A few of the voting machines developed minor faults which took time to correct.

In the face of all these discouragements, two-thirds of the estimated electorate cast their votes. The Liberals and WFP were obliterated, failing to win a single seat; all the WFP candidates were among the eighty-two candidates who lost their deposits (no PNM candidate lost his deposit). James, repeating himself, in Lawrence's phrase, like the flushing of a WC, ran with the rest. PNM won 24 seats and DLP 12. In terms of the popular vote PNM received 52%, DLP 34%, Liberals less than 9%, WFP slightly more than 3%. It was another great victory, third in a row, for the PNM. Victory night in the University, on November 9, was the usual mammoth affair.

I set out at once to organise the victory. I organised a series of lectures to bring the new members up to date on basic legislation. I assigned backbenchers to work on Cabinet Committees. I directed each MP to report to his constituency group once a month. I arranged for each Minister and Parliamentary Secretary to lecture once a month to a constituency group in one of the PNM's twenty-four constituencies. I arranged for consultation with the Party on important Government legislation: rent restriction, amendments to the Industrial Stabilisation Act and the Trade Unions Ordinance, divorce, petroleum legislation, social security, a new education plan.

The Nation had done a magnificent job during the election campaign; under its young editor Irwin Merritt, it had brought political reporting to heights never before achieved in Trinidad and Tobago. It had kept the issue of subversion before the electorate, challenging the WFP week after week. It had dissected, to the point of damning them, the parliamentary records of the leaders of the Liberal Party and the WFP. I set out to work to give *The Nation* a home of its own, with improved equipment. The new headquarters was opened in June 1967.

Since the election the PNM has had to deal with the tactics of the DLP Opposition. Claiming that the voting machines were rigged, they opted for a policy of silence in Parliament and pledged not to contest any election under the voting machine system, whilst Capildeo resumed his teaching assignment in London, until he forfeited his seat. The by-election in January 1968 was won by Bhadase Maraj, seeking to resurrect the PDP; the DLP Opposition advised the population not to vote, but 43% disobeyed the injunction. Maraj promptly broke the policy of silence, and the DLP thereupon decided to contest the local government elections with the voting machines. The elections, held on June 24, 1968, resulted in PNM winning 68 of the 100 seats – 10 of the 12 seats in Port-of-Spain were unopposed – and controlling all three municipalities and four of the seven County Councils.

34
THE REALITY
OF INDEPENDENCE

Our Independence was part of the world movement against colonialism – the colonial peoples disinclined to tolerate it any longer, the imperialists unable to carry on. On the achievement of Independence we took the conventional decisions – joining the United Nations, remaining in the Commonwealth, providing for limited external representation, establishing a small Defence Force.

Independence did not bring us a clean slate. Apart from the deteriorating terms of trade, we found ourselves with a particular economy and specific economic issues generated by the many centuries of colonialism. I summarise some of the particular aspects of the economy bequeathed to our independent nation by the antecedent colonialism.

Our economy was essentially in foreign hands, the capital coming from outside, the profits being repatriated outside. This was essentially true of the oil and sugar industries and the banks. The normal steps taken to encourage industrial development and attract foreign capital for investment, in the interests of import substitution, tended to strengthen foreign control of the economy; whilst the incentives offered to those industries, especially income tax remission and duty-free imports of machinery and raw materials, tended to reduce the government's share.

The economy was essentially undiversified, with oil dominating the exports and government revenues, and export agriculture, principally sugar, dominating the agricultural scene. We remained tradionally dependent upon imports, particularly food. Here we have on the one hand the traditional aversion to agriculture because of its association in the minds of the citizens with the forced labour of slavery and indenture; and on the other hand the large expenditures which are necessarily associated with any properly conceived programme of land reform – access roads, housing, the utilities, credit.

We inherited also inadequate social services in the form of poor housing and of a deficient education system – this is another result of centuries of slavery and indenture. The report on the 1937 disturbances in Trinidad in the colonial period emphasised the irresponsibility of the employer class in relation to improved housing. Our colonial history is replete with contempt for education and for the profession of teaching. Everything was imported into the West Indies, complained Père Labat at the beginning of the eighteenth century, except books. Charles Leslie, in his description of the Jamaica of 1739, indicated the contempt with which the teacher and the teacher's profession were viewed. Baron de Wimpffen, in his travels in 1789 through what later became Haiti, stressed the insipid nature of the conversations of the planters. The Guadeloupe poet, Léonard, at the end of the eighteenth century commented on the general absence of books and the limitation of the interests of the planters to trade and rural administration, in which they blindly followed routine.

Our independent society inherited the sectionalism and individualism bred by colonialism. The essence of the colonial system was internal disunity – evidenced by the attempts to segregate African tribes, the separation of African freedmen from Indian immigrants, the contrast between countryside and town, the confusion of racial origins among the labouring section of the population, the deliberate imposition of colour distinctions and gradations, the conflict between metropolitan flags in the area, the emphasis on the differences between island and island.

But the gravest problem inherited from the colonial régime was unemployment aggravated by the enormous increase of the population in a period when the death rate from tropical diseases was conspicuously on the decline. The unemployment rate has been increasing in recent months and stood at December 31, 1967, at 15% of the labour force – in absolute numbers, 57,200 persons, an increase of 6,400 in one year. This problem is made worse by the fact that unemployment is particularly high among young persons, and especially so among young females. One out of every three persons in the labour force 15–19 years of age is unemployed, and one out of every four of the labour force 20–24 years of age. Of the males 15 years old and over, 88% are in the labour force, as compared with only 40% in the case of females. In the midst of the labour unrest generated thereby, we have had an upsurge of the young people calling for 'young power' under the stimulus of international developments.

All this poses serious issues for the future which are currently being considered in connection with our third 5-year Development Plan to come into effect in 1969.

The first and most important issue is the foreign control of the economy. There are the precedents before us of developments or anticipated developments in Canada, Mexico, Chile and Zambia. Our banks, insurance companies, hire purchase arrangements, advertising, external telecommunications and mass media are all in foreign hands, together with a large portion of our lands, especially the lands devoted to sugar cultivation. We have to think in terms of some form of control of this arrangement, by restricting the sale of lands to foreigners, by opposing exclusive beach rights (and casinos) in tourist development, by the control of work permits to expatriates, by the requirement that foreign companies must re-invest a portion of their profits in local enterprise, by establishing a commercial bank of our own and a National Petroleum Company, by assuming some control over radio and television, by encouraging private companies to go public and issue shares to the Trinidad and Tobago community, and by government partnership in industry and tourism where the national community is not yet prepared or ready to participate. All this will raise in an acute form the problem of management. We have also to think in terms of the Government itself taking the initiative in respect of certain types of industry, for example, stockfeed – the country's remarkable achievement in establishing self-sufficiency in the poultry and pork industries has been marked by the creation of an even worse problem for the balance of payments in terms of imported stockfeeds, especially corn. Side by side with this we must continue our programme of agricultural diversification, with special reference to the diversification of the sugar industry, where too many small farmers are growing sugar cane and are being exposed to all the vagaries of the uncertain world market.

Our principal concern remains the question of finding additional jobs for the increasing population. From the long-term aspect, this is a question of the family planning programme that we have instituted. From the short-term aspect, it involves the question of accelerating industrial development with particular reference to labour-intensive industries such as electronics and garments. We also have to emphasise even more the provision of additional tourist facilities, including the modernisation of our two airports to take into account the anticipated increase in the size of jet planes in the 70's. Looking at developments in Shannon in Ireland and in Taiwan, we are considering the establishment of a free port at our major airport. But it is to housing that we look for the immediate provision of additional jobs, whilst paying attention to one of the principal amenities needed to satisfy the revolution of rising expectations.

In this context of additional job opportunities we are paying particular attention to the youth of the country. A vast programme of youth camps under the auspices of the programme for Community Development has recently been approved to provide training for the young boys principally in agriculture and animal husbandry, but also in the basic trades such as welding and plumbing. In carrying out this programme we keep our eyes on the possibility of emigration which itself requires the possession of some basic skill by the emigrant.

Two basic problems have arisen in respect of this programme of economic development and jobs. The first is foreign aid. By the time we achieved our independence in August 1962, all the techniques and procedures that might have paid off had already been tried repeatedly in other parts of the world, and when Trinidad and Tobago raised the issue in principle we found a hardening of opinion and a general disillusionment with the experience in other places. The United Kingdom for example, made such an unsatisfactory offer to us that we were, forced to decline; its principal concern at the Independence Conference was to ensure the heavy entrenchment of the monarchical system. As I said to students at the London School of Economics, Britain had sucked the orange dry and was merely nervous about slipping on the orange peel. Canada has come to our rescue, providing some limited aid that is very satisfactory in respect of terms and conditions on which it is offered; the conventional limitation of this aid to services provided by the donor country is less onerous where we are able to buy cattle for our Crown Lands Distribution Programme in order to achieve our goal of self-sufficiency in milk production, factory shells for industrial development, and materials for rural electrification. Now that we have joined the Organisation of American States we look to the Alliance for Progress and the Inter-American Development Bank for some of the aid we need, andassistance has already been forthcoming in the field of housing and agricultural credit, whilst the International Bank for Reconstruction and Development, after its initial loans for electricity development and the Crown Lands distribution programme, has agreed to provide assistance to our new education plan.

The second problem that we face in respect of this programme of economic development and jobs is the question of markets. The

Caribbean Free Trade Association launched on May 1, 1968, and expanded on July 1, will be of invaluable assistance in providing a larger base for our industries and agriculture. We are at this moment studying the question of participating in the Andean community of the Latin American Free Trade Association, comprising Venezuela, Bolivia, Colombia, Chile, Peru and Ecuador. In making this study we are considering the possible alternative of the Central American Common Market. This, however, will not solve the problem of Britain's entry into the European Common Market which could jeopardise not only our basic agricultural exports like sugar and citrus but also our petroleum and petrochemicals. Whilst Associate Status in the European Common Market will not solve the agricultural problem, it is possible that some special treaty could be worked out with the European Economic Community.

And finally, high up on the agenda for the next few years, is our new Education Plan for the period 1968–1983. This involves cutting off Primary School education at the age of 11, elimination of the Common Entrance examination for the 11-plus children and their automatic movement from Primary School to a new Junior Secondary School, which will take in 90% of the eligible population. At age 14 the students will take an examination to decide what level of higher secondary education they will pursue – whether at the secondary Grammar School or at the secondary Comprehensive School with its large infusion of technical education. At this level the Plan calls for taking in 38% of the population. To avoid throwing so many of the 14-plus children on to an overcrowded market, we are now pursuing with friendly foreign governments the question of assistance for the provision of a number of trade schools to increase the percentage of children studying in school after age 14. The new Plan calls for the introduction on a large scale of the modern media of education, radio and television. One measure of our difficulty is afforded by the fact that the capital cost of this programme – with all of its limitations – is estimated at $171 million in fifteen years, while the recurrent costs are estimated at $1,140 million.

This is the Reality of our Independence. We lack the tribal animosities of Nigeria or the religious passions of India or the economic difficulties of Ceylon or the political difficulties of Israel. By and large we have an interracial harmony, disturbed at election periods, which many will envy. Indians are not repatriated as in Burma, Ceylon, Kenya. We have no 'Quebec nation'. Our economic and social difficulties are not more formidable than those faced by other emerging countries. Our army is not a Latin American one. We have no Red Guards on the rampage.

But with the pressures from individual citizens and sectional interests, I understand why Gandhi used to retire to his ashram, and why Dr. Radhakrishnan insisted, as he told me, that, if he accepted Mr. Nehru's invitation to take up the post of Ambassador to Moscow, he should be free to spend six months of the year in the quiet of his rooms at All Souls, Oxford, where he was a Fellow. I unfortunately can look for relief in neither of these directions, and have to make do with my private study upstairs, turning off the lights downstairs, taking the telephone off the hook. Achieving peace at the price of air and sunlight, I deliberately leave the files and reports and grievances and read and write as a private citizen, maintaining his sanity and seeing the daily chores, stresses and strains in clearer perspective, determined to prove that, like Dante's Ulysses, I

> Could conquer the inward hunger that I had
> To master earth's experience, and to attain
> Knowledge of man's mind, both good and bad.

Port-of-Spain,
Trinidad and Tobago,
July 6, 1968.

INDEX

Achimota College, West Africa, 102
Adams, Grantley, 125, 202, 224
Addis Ababa, 294, 329
Adult education campaign, 113–17
Agricultural Credit Bank, 283
Agriculture, 13–14, 333–4
  See also Sugar industry
Alexander, Wilfrid, 163, 245
Algeria, 291
All Souls, Oxford, 44, 45, 343
Alliance for Progress, 341
American Committee of the International
  Women's League for Peace and Free-
  dom, 74
American Council of Learned Societies,
  79; conference on Negro Studies, 73
Amery, Julian, 170, 203, 236
Amritsar Massacre, 271
Anglo-American Caribbean Commission,
  81ff., 96–100, 105, 107–8, 112–13, 118–
  127, 131–2
  See also Caribbean Research Council
Anglo-American destroyer-base deal.
  See Leased Bases Agreement
Ankylostomiasis, 18, 19
Antigua, 69, 92, 94–5, 212, 240, 288;
  emigrants from, 179
Antigua Public Library, 95
Antigua Star, 69, 71, 84–6, 94
Arden-Clarke, Sir Charles (Chairman,
  Chaguaramas Joint Commission), 208,
  229
Arima, 165, 220, 276
Aristotle, 133, 263, 264
Armstrong, Hamilton Fish, 76
Aruba, 92, 289
Asquith, H. H., 15
Association for the Study of Negro Life
  and History, 74
Atlanta University, Georgia, 77
Australia, 150, 154, 162
Azikiwe, Dr., 100–1, 142

Bahamas, 212
Balankura, Chamkad, 54
Baron, Hon. F. A., 205
Barbados, 115, 179, 288, 295, 296; its
  assembly, 13; and Federation, 173–4,
  177, 184; emigrants from, 179
Barbados Advocate, The, 71, 88
Barbados Public Library, 95
Barbados Workers Union, 138
Barrow, Mr., 165, 296

Beetham, Sir Edward (Governor of Trini-
  dad and Tobago), author's letter to,
  227–30
Belgium, 150
Ben Bella, 292
Ben Gurion, 302
Benevolent Societies. See Friendly Societies
Benitez, Jaime, 66
Berle, Adolf, 61
Bermuda, 212, 213
Betancourt, President (of Venezuela), 302
Better Village Programme, 308–9, 318
Bevan, Aneurin, 255
Birth rate, increase during 1901–11, 16
Blanco, Ramos, 65
Blanco, Tomás, 66
Bolivia, 342
Boston, Mass., 73
Boundaries Commission, 253–4, 304
Bradshaw, C. E., 37, 38
Bradshaw, Hon. R. A., 205
Brandeis, Justice, 274
Brazil, 221
Bridgetown, Barbados, 165
Brierre (poet), 67
British Caribbean Union of Teachers, 124
British Guiana (late 1966 Guyana, q.v.), 92,
  138–9, 177–8, 199, 212–13, 274, 280,
  292–3; self-government issue, 247, 252,
  294–300
British Development and Welfare Organi-
  sation, 82, 289
British West Indian Airways, 280, 287
British West Indian University. See West
  Indies, University of the
Brogan, D. W. (Sir Denis), 48–9, 71, 81,
  169, 328, 330
Brown, Sterling, 61
Brussels, 139, 141, 142, 143, 289
Bryan, V., 120
Buenos Aires meeting of OAS foreign
  ministers (1967), 326
Bullock, Alan, 328
Bunche, Ralph, 61, 63
Burma, 15, 342
Burnham, Mr., 165, 296, 298
Bus concessions, 252
Business Advisory Council, 306
Bustamante, Sir Alexander, 165, 291, 296
Butler Party, 161, 164, 274–6

Cabinet Day, 170
Campos, Albizu, 67

Canada, 16, 173, 175, 180, 208, 293–4, 300, 334, 340, 341; sugar imports, 14; and the Caribbean Economic Community, 287–8

Cane Farmers Association, 334

Capildeo, Dr. Rudranath (Leader of the Opposition), 252, 258, 285, 294, 332, 337

Car loans, 254–5

Carenage constituency, 162

Caribbean Commission. *See* Anglo-American Caribbean Commission

Caribbean Economic Community, 286–8, 336

Caribbean Economic Review, 106

Caribbean Free Trade Association, 288, 342

Caribbean Historical Review, 72, 109

Caribbean National Labour Party, 164–5

Caribbean People's Democratic Party (PDP), 164, 165, 337

Caribbean Research Council, 90, 92, 105–7

Carlsen Field, 226, 310

Carnegie Corporation, 108

Caroni, 165, 253–4, 283

Caroni Swamp, 206, 257

Castro, Fidel, 272, 331, 335

Central African Federation, 176

Central Tenders Board, 250

Central American Common Market, 175, 342

Césaire, Aimé, 142, 270

Ceylon, 98, 168, 301, 342; University of, 102

Chachas, the, 76

Chaguaramas Naval Station, 84, 168, 170–172, 186, 194, 202, 203; the London Conference, and appointment of a Joint Commission, 207–9; the 1941 Agreement, 209–13, 217–18, 231, 233–4, 238–9, 242; the public campaign, 213–25; negotiations with the new American Consul-General, 225–7; the demonstration in Woodford Square, 227; Chief Minister's letter to the Governor, 227–230; the march to Port-of-Spain, 230–5; the Tobago Conference and the new agreement, 235–45

Chatham, Earl of, 40

Cheap labour, 16

Chicago, 74; University of, 99

Chicago University Press, 77

Chile, 340, 342

Chinese, in Trinidad, 13, 18

Christ Church, Oxford, 40

Christophe, Henri, 65

Churchill, Winston, 15, 65, 211, 255

Cipriani, Mr., 173, 235

City of Port-of-Spain, SS, 254, 256

Ciudad Trujillo, Santo Domingo, 66

Civil service: in colonial period, 16, 24–5; limits on their political expression, 153;

the Public Service Commission, 304, 316–17; reorganisation of, 315–17

Civil Service Act (1965), 153

Clarke, Ellis (Constitutional Adviser to the Cabinet,) 284

Cocoa, 13–15

Cocoa Planters Association, 14

Codrington, Christopher, 40

Codrington College, Barbados, 39

Colonial Development Finance Company, 182

Colonial Development and Welfare Funds, 249

Colombia, 342

Columbus, Christopher, 11, 66

Columbus, Ohio, 74

Comma, Carlton, 93

Commager, Henry Steele, 71, 77, 79

Common Market. *See* Central American Common Market; European Economic Community

Commonwealth Prime Ministers' Conferences: (1962), 284, 289; (1964), 299–300; (1965), 300

Commonwealth Secretariat, 300, 301

Commonwealth Sugar Agreement, 289

Communist Party, French, 142

Community Development, 307–8, 341

Concepción, Gilberto, 67

Congo, 186

Conservative Party (U.K.), 153

Constitution reform. *See* under Trinidad and Tobago

Cordero, Rafael, 66

County Council Elections: (1959), 262, 274; (1968), 337

Coupland, Reginald, 49, 50

Courier-Journal, Louisville, Ky, 166

Cramer, Mr., 19

Creoles, 25

Crime, in 1911, 19–21

Crown lands, distribution of, 308, 314, 333, 341

Cuba, 63–5, 71–2, 76, 81, 185, 244, 292, 322, 331

Curacao, 92, 107, 208, 289

Customs Union, proposal, for 181, 195, 278

Cutteridge, J. O., 37–9, 49

Cyprus, 281

D'Aiguiar, 296

Daily Gleaner, Jamaica, 165

Daily Star, Toronto, 166

Dakar, University of, 329

Daniel, E. W., 38, 49

Danish Virgin Islands, 109

Daunt, Achilles, 37

David, Prudhomme, 25

Davies, R. Trevor, 41

Democratic Labour Party (DLP), 233, 252, 254, 257, 263–4, 274–6, 332, 334–5, 337

Descartes, Sol, 66
Dessalines, J. J., 65
Deutsch, André, 70
Development and Welfare Grants, 182
Development Programme. *See* Five Year Development Programmes.
Dewey, John, 97–9, 117
Diarrhoea, 18
Diop, Alioune, 270
Disease, 18–19
DLP. *See* Democratic Labour Party
Doctors, 25
Dominica, 115–16, 191, 249; emigrants from, 179
Dominica Conference (1932), 173, 175
Dominican Republic (Santo Domingo), 66, 107
Dominion Status, 144, 181–2
Donnan, Elizabeth, 69, 71
Doorly, Stokely, 37
Douglass, Frederick, 80
Duke University Press, 72
Durham University, 98
Dysentry, 18

Economist, 165
Ecuador, 342
Education and Small Scale Farming Conference, 105–6, 122
Education: in colonial period, 21–4, 35–6, 339; Commission on higher education in the West Indies (1944), 96–9; PNM attitude to denominational education, 156; secondary schools, 251, 283, 334; Premier's visit to secondary schools, 309; Education Act of 1965, 317–18; Plan for 1968–9, 342
Eisenhower, President, 207
Electoral procedure, reform of, 247, 253–4
Elias, Dr. T. O., 169, 178
Elton, Godfrey (later Lord), 41
Englund, Dr., 88
Enteritis, 18
Erickson, Professor Edgar, 109
Ethiopia, 291
European Development Fund, 289
European Economic Community, 175, 178, 249–50, 256, 279, 289, 342

Family Planning Association, 325
Farm Foundation, New York, 74
Farrell, Arthur, 39
Federal Elections (1958), 274
Federal Labour Party. *See* West Indies Federal Labour Party
Fire Service, 317
Fisk University, Nashville, Tenn., 77
Five Year Development Programmes: first, 246, 247; second, 305, 307, 314–15, 322
Foot, Sir Hugh, 143
Foreign Affairs, 76, 85

Foreign aid, since independence, 341
Foreign Policy Association, 63
Fort de France, Martinique, 68, 142
Foundation of International Research, 100
France, 90, 108, 156, 287, 300, 334
Franks, Lord, 330
Fraser, Hugh, 186
Frazier, Franklin, 61
French West Indies, 12–13
Friendly Societies, 17
Fulton, Sir John, 330
Fundamental Education Centre of UNESCO (CREFAL), 107
Fyzabad constituency, 276, 335

Gandhi, M. K., 52, 343
Gaulle, President de, 11, 290–1
Gee, Wilson, 71
General Agreement on Tariffs and Trade (GATT), 124–5
Geneva, 139, 141; Conference on Trade and Development (1964), 291, 293
George Washington University, Washington, 63
Georgetown, British Guiana, 165, 295
Germany, 334
Ghana, 182, 265, 291–2, 301
Gleaner, Jamaica, 71
Gold Coast, 142
Gomes, Albert (leader of the POPPG), 141, 151, 164–5
Goree, 329
Government Training School for male teachers, 25, 39
Grenada, 173, 179, 191–2, 286–7, 322
Guadeloupe, 92, 94, 280, 287
Guérin, Daniel, 142
Guerra y Sanchez, Ramiro, 64–5
Guillén, Nicholas, 65, 67
Guinea, 291
Guyana (*see also* British Guiana), 288; University of, 288, 294

Haile Selassie, Emperor, 292
Haile Selassie I University, Addis Ababa, 329
Haiti, 65, 107, 339
Haldane, Lord, 98
Hallstein, President, 289
Hanke, Lewis, 69
Harlow, Vincent, 49, 50, 52, 63, 81, 169
Harris, Abe, 61, 63
Harvard Educational Review, 99
Hastie, William, 61
Havana, Cuba, 64, 66, 71–2; Tricontinental Conference at (1966), 335
Hawaii, 280; University of, 102
Hebrew University of Jerusalem, 98
Hindus, 22
Hitler, Adolf, 48, 59, 163, 215
Hoare-Laval plan, 45, 50

Hochoy, Sir Solomon (Governor-General, Trinidad and Tobago), 171, 238
Holland. *See* Netherlands
Home Affairs, Ministry of, 246, 316
Housing, in 1911, 17
Howard University, Washington DC, 52, 57–62, 73, 86, 96, 99, 329; public lectures by Division of Social Sciences, 73
Howard University Press, 73
Huggins, Sir John, 81–5

Iceland, 213, 218, 221
I.C.F.T.U. and the Plantation Worker, The, 141
Ife, University of (Nigeria), 329
Illegitimacy, 17–20
Illiteracy, 20, 21, 23
Immigration, 246; of Indians, 14, 19, 76 *See also* Migration
Immorality, 17–18
Imperial College of Tropical Agriculture, 96
Imperial Preference, and the sugar industry, 115
Independence, 196, 200, 230–1, 277–84; Marlborough House Conference (1962). and attainment of, 284–6; results and hopes, 338–43
Indenture, 16, 19, 70, 265
India, 156, 162, 182, 208, 265, 270, 274, 300
Indian Association, 281, 282
Indians, 13, 174; immigration of, 14, 19, 76; social conditions in 1911, 19–22
Industrial Court, 312–14
Industrial Stabilisation Act (1965), 311–14, 326, 332, 337
Inniss, W. D. ('Billy'), 36–9, 92
Institute of Commonwealth Studies, 169
Institute of Colonial Affairs, proposal for, 101–2
Institute of Race Relations, 77
Inter-American Development Bank, 341
Inter-American Press Association, 266–7
Intergovernmental Conferences on the Federal Constitution. *See under* West Indies Federation
International Bank for Reconstruction and Development, 334, 341
International Confederation of Free Trade Unions (ICFTU): Caribbean Area Division, 138–9; conference in Brussels, 139–42
International Co-operation Administration, 251
International Institute of Differing Civilisations (INCIDI), 107
International Labour Organisation, 139–40
International Planned Parenthood Federation, 325
International Standards for Plantation Workers 141
Inter-University Council for Higher Education, 330

Iran, 291, 293
Ireland, 340
Irois Bay, 209, 214, 226
Irvine, Sir James, 96–7, 99
Italy, 271, 334

Jagan, Dr., 295, 298
Jamaica, 76, 82–3, 107, 143, 212, 240, 274, 295; its house of assembly, 13; constitution of 1944, 83; universal suffrage introduced, 96; and Federation, 174, 177, 182–4, 186–7, 195, 197, 199–203, 277–8; and the Caribbean Economic Community, 287–8; education in colonial period, 339
Jamaica Conference on Federal Capital Site (1957), 171, 174, 204
Jamaica Institute Library, 95
Jamaica Progressive League, 73
James, C. L. R., 77, 143, 151, 267–8, 336
Japan, 271, 334
Jefferson, Thomas, 263
Jenks, Leland, 63
Jerningham, Sir Edward (Governor of Trinidad and Tobago), 22
John, Pope, 302
Johnson, Charles S. (President of Fisk University), 77, 79, 101–2; *Bitter Canaan*, 77
Johnson, Gerald W., 70–1
Johnson, President, 293
Johnson, Dr. Samuel, 40
Jones, A. Creech, 101
Jones, E. M. Hugh, 47–8
Joseph, Roy (Minister of Education and Social Services), 151
Journal of Negro Education, 74
Journal of Negro History, 74

Kandel, Mr., 99
Kennedy, President, 244
Kenya, 100–1, 140, 291–2, 342
Kingston, Jamaica, 165

Labar, Père, 339
Labour Party (U.K.), 146, 153
Lamming, George, his tribute to PNM, 156–9
Lancaster House Conference. *See under* London Conferences
Laski, Harold, 48, 159
Latin American Economic Institute, 74
Latin American Free Trade Association, 342
Laventille, 248, 253–4
Lawyers, 25
League of Nations Mission of Educational Experts, 98
Leased Bases Agreement (1941), 65, 68, 81, 205–6, 209–13, 217–18, 231, 233–4, 238–239, 242
See also Chaguaramas Naval Station

Lee, Jennie, 143
Lee, Ulric, 164
Leeward Islands, 92, 177
Le Hunte, Sir George Ruthven (Governor
  of Trinidad and Tobago), 11
Léonard (Guadeloupe poet), 339
Leoni, President (of Venezuela), 303
Leprosy, 19
Leslie, Charles, 339
Lethem, Sir Gordon (Governor of the
  Leeward Islands), 218
Lewis, Arthur, 69, 143, 246, 277–8
Lewis, Professor Gordon, 169, 178; tribute
  to PNM, 159–60; tribute to the author,
  272–3
Liberal Party, 332, 335–7
Liberia, 77–8, 291
Libya, 215, 217–18
Literature, Caribbean, 116
Locke, Alain, 61, 63, 68, 75
Logan, Rayford, 61
London Conferences: (1941), 214; (1956),
  173; (1957; on Chaguaramas), 206–7,
  211, 214, 217; (1961; Lancaster House),
  196–201, 272, 279; (1962; Marlborough
  House), 284
London University, 98
Low, A. M., 37

Mbanefo Commission on Subversive
  Activities, 335
McDavid, Sir Frank, 125
McGill University, Montreal, 329
Macleod, Iain, 171, 186–7, 196, 237, 254,
  268
Macmillan, Harold, 136, 186, 203, 207, 284
Macpherson, Sir John, 86, 112
Macqueripe, 217, 226
Macqueripe Club, 217
Makerere College, East Africa, 102
Malaria, 18, 19
Malaya, 166, 168–9, 175, 180, 182, 193
Mali, 296
Manley, Norman W. (Prime Minister of
  Jamaica), 62, 73, 91, 120, 125, 143, 165,
  202–3, 206, 217; author's letter to, 112–
  113; and Federation, 174, 186–8, 190
Maraj, Bhadase (Leader of the Opposition),
  257–8, 337
Marin, Muñoz, 66–7, 76, 270
Mars, Jean Price, 65
Marti, José, 64, 134
Martin, Paul, 293
Martin, Sidney, 330
Martinique, 92, 287
'Massa Day Done', 264–5
Mathieson, W. L., 50
Matos, Pales, 66, 67
Maudling, Reginald, 278, 284
Medical Department, expenditure in 1911,
  21
Menon, Krishna, 272

Meet the Party Tour, 322
Meet the People Tour, 307, 309, 322
Merritt, Irwin, 337
Mexico, 107, 340
Migration, 179, 191–2, 199
Milk supply, a factor in disease, 18
Mitchell, J. J., 36–8
Molasses, 13
Moline, Edwin, (American Consul-
  General), 225–7
Monde Diplomatique, Le, 301
Montano, Gerald (Minister of Home
  Affairs), 335
Montego Bay, Jamaica, 173
Montserrat, 92, 179, 191
Morocco, 221, 237
Mortality, statistics for 1911–12, 18
Moscoso, Teodoro, 246
Moyne Commission, 210
Murder, 19, 20
Muslims, 22

Naparima College, San Fernando, 110
Nasser, President, 292
Nation, The (formerly PNM Weekly, q.v.),
  53, 152, 224, 244, 270, 276, 330, 337; its
  'Open Letter to Dr. Williams', 196, 225;
  PNM Tenth Anniversary edition, 324–5
National Economic Advisory Council, 306
National Oil Company, 340
National Party Schools, 326
National Workers Union, 143
Nationalism, West Indian, taks of build-
  ing, 113–17
NATO, 215
Nehru, Jawaharlal, 143, 271–2, 281, 285,
  331, 343
Netherlands, 90, 109, 208, 287–8
Netherlands Antilles, 287–8
New Brunswick University of, 328
New Deal, 81
New York, 73, 74, 297
New Zealand, 98
Newfoundland, 213
News Chronicle, 166
Newton, A. P., 49
Nigeria, 100–1, 142–3, 168, 175, 180, 193,
  291–2, 342
Nkrumah, Dr., 229, 291–2
North, Lord, 40
North Carolina, University of, 70, 99
Northern Ireland, 288

Oglethorpe, J. E., 40
O'Halloran, Mr., 236
Oil Industry, 13–15
Oilfield Worker's Trade Union, 307, 314
Old age pensions, 248
Opposition. See under Trinidad and
  Tobago
O'Reilly, Sir Lennox, 88

Organisation of American States (OAS), 290, 326, 341
Ortiz, Dr. Fernando, 62, 64, 134, 269
Otero, Morales, 66

Padmore, George, 69, 77, 85, 143, 268
Pagan, Bolivar, 69
Pakistan, 140
Panama Canal Zone, 237
Pan-American Havana declaration, 68
Pandit, Madame, 143
Pares, Richard, 49
Paria, Gulf of, 214, 247, 257
Paris, 142
Party of Political Progress Groups (POPPG), 151, 164, 336
Party Schools. See National Party Schools
Patzcuaro, Mexico. See Fundamental Education Centre.
Pay As You Earn system (PAYE), 247-8, 258
PDP. See Caribbean People's Democratic Party
Pearson, Lester, 293, 294
Pembleton, E. S., 90, 91
Penn, William, 40
People's Charter. See under People's National Movement
People's Charter for Economic Development. See Five Year Development Programmes
People's Education Movement, 131
People's National Movement (PNM), 54, 171, 174, 228, 229, 249, 254,; its foundation, 133-4; Inaugural Conference, 144; the People's Charter, 144-6, 325; constitution, 146; units of the movement, 146-7; the General Council, 147; the officers, 147; Central Executive, and Legislative Group, 148; organisation of women and youth, 148; the Annual Convention, 148; launched, 149-50; opposition to, 150-2; first Annual Convention, 153, 155-6, 159; tributes to, 156-60; wins 1956 General Election, 161-7; and the Federation, 174, 179-80, 278, 279; affiliated to West Indies Federal Labour Party, 202; and Chaguaramas, 214, 220, 224, 227, 230-6, 237, 244-5; and British Guiana, 252; reappraisal of 1958, 260-8; and its Publishng Company, 268; wins 1961 General Election, 274-6; and Venezuela, 302; ¹1963 revision of constitution, 319-20; reappraisal of 1964, 320-3; Tenth Anniversary celebrations, 323-5; the Special Convention, 325; and the Organisation of American States, 326; and Party Schools, 326; wins 1966 General Election, 332-7; wins 1968 County Council elections, 337

Perham, Margery, 96
Perth, Lord, 249
Peru, 342
Philippines, the, 221, 237, 280; University of, 102
Piarco, 219, 226, 235, 294
Picó, Rafael, 66
Pilgrim, G. E., 37-9
Pitch Lake, Trinidad, 13
Pitman, Frank, 50, 63
Plague, 19
Plantations Trade Union Movement, 142
PNM. See People's National Movement
PNM Publishing Co., Ltd., 268
PNM Weekly (later The Nation, q.v.): editorials quoted, 152-5; George Lamming's article, 157-9; Gordon Lewis' article, 272-3
Poland, 300
Police, expenditure in 1911, 21
Police Service Bill, 317
Political Science Quarterly, The, 72
POPPG. See Party of Political Progress Groups
Population: increase during 1901-11, 16; proportion of Indians in 1911, 19; of some of the islands, 191
Population Council, 325
Port-au-Prince, Haiti, 65
Port-of-Spain, Trinidad, 16, 17, 27, 165, 174, 186, 237, 252, 257, 276, 285; the Indians in, 19-21; Public Library, 20; the march to, 230-5; road to Chaguaramas, 242, 244; the constituencies 253, 336-7; Prime Ministers' Conference in (1963), 287; Queen's Hall meeting (1962), 305
Port-of-Spain Gazette, 26, 71
Porter, Professor Kenneth W., 79-80
Portuguese, in Trinidad, 13, 18
Premier's Press Conference, 266
Prest (economist), 247
Priestley, Raymond, 96
Prime Ministers' (West Indian) Conference (1965), 287
See also Commonwealth Prime Minister's Conferences
Prison Service, 317
Privy Council, 255, 314
Prostitution, in Puerto Rico, 66
Public service. See Civil service
Public Service Commission, 304, 316-17
Puerto Rico, 12, 66-7, 82, 92, 107, 127, 134, 156, 217, 287; University of, 66, 98, 102, 108; racial discrimination in, 76, 84
Punta del Este (Uruguay), meeting of OAS Chiefs of State at (1967), 326

Queen Elizabeth House, Oxford, 329
Queen's Royal College, 23, 31-2, 36-7, 39, 41, 92, 124

Rabies, 19
Race relations: in Puerto Rico, 76, 84; historical background, 134–5, 269–70; editorial in *PNM Weekly*, 154–5
Radhakrishnan, Sir S., 52, 53, 272, 343
Raffles College, Malaya, 102
Ragatz, Lowell, 50, 63, 69, 70
Randolph, Philip, 74
Rangoon, University of, 102
Reid, Ira, 79
Richards, Senator George (Attorney-General), 284
Roads, 242, 244, 318
Roberts-Wray, K., 122
Robinson, A. N. R., 320
Robinson, Lionel (Minister of Agriculture), 293
Roebuck, J. A., 94
Roosevelt, Eleanor, 61
Roosevelt, F. D., 65, 81, 264
Rosario, José, 66
Rose, Andrew (Minister of Communications, Federal Cabinet), 280
Roseau, Dominica, 173
Roumain (poet), 67
Rum, 13, 191
Rusk, Dean, 293–4
Russell and Russell (publishers), 70

St. Catherine's College, Oxford, 51, 63, 328
St. George, 162, 165, 253
St. George William University, Montreal, 329
St. James, Port-of-Spain, 21
St. Kitts, 92, 115–16, 199; emigrants from, 179
St. Lucia, 140, 179, 212, 249
St. Mary's College, 23
Saint Mery, Moreau de, 94
St. Patrick constituency, 165, 274, 283
St. Vincent, 179, 249
San Fernando, 110, 132, 164–5, 223, 244, 257, 261–2, 276, 335
Sandys, Duncan, 295
Sangster, Donald (Acting Prime Minister of Jamaica), 291
Santo Domingo. *See* Dominican Republic
Sartre, Jean Paul, 142
Savings Banks, 17
School and Society, 99
Senegal, 291
Senghor, Leopold (President of Senegal), 272, 329, 331
Sewell, W. J., *The Ordeal of Free Labour in the British West Indies*, 109
Shenfield, Mr. (economic adviser, Trini- and Tobago Government), 110–11
Sherlock, Sir Philip, 96, 330
Shipping service, 280, 287
Sierra Leone, 291
Singapore, 166

Slavery, slave trade, 16–17, 49–50, 64, 69–72, 93–4, 110
Smith, Adam, 14
Solomon, Dr. (Deputy Chief Minister), 171, 233; Minister of External Affairs, 311
South Africa, 98, 265
Southern Rhodesia, 140, 293, 300–1
Spain, 64, 72, 108, 215
Sparrow (calypso writer), 201, 248
Springer, Hugh, 96
Stevens, Sir Roger, 330
Stevenson, Adlai, 225
Stock, Leo, 69
Stockdale, Sir Frank, 88
Strikes, 311–14
Subversive activity, 333, 335
Sugar industry: formerly a British interest, 13, 14; connexion with slavery, 64, 68, 74, 76; and Imperial Preference, 115; economic aspects, 138–40; International Sugar Agreement, 182; and the American sugar quota, 254; Commonwealth Sugar Agreement, 289; question of sugar companies' lands, 332–3
Sunday Guardian, 163
Surinam, 140, 280, 287–8
Survey Graphic, 75
'Susu', the (informal bank), 17
Swiss Bank, 254–7
Switzerland, 161

Tagore, Rabindranath, 271–2
Taiwan, 340
Tannenbaum, Professor Frank, *Slave and Citizen: The Negro in the Americas*, 72
Tanzania, 291
Tate and Lyle, 308
Taussig, Charles, 81–2, 86, 120
Tawney, Professor R. H., 81
Taxation, 15–16; proposals in 1958 budget, 247
Teachers' Economic and Cultural Association, 99, 131
Teachers Education Movement, 144
Telephone company, 250–1
Tenders Board. *See* Central Tenders Board
Texaco, 308
Thant, U, 335
Thompson, Dean Charles, 74
Times, India, 166
Times Educational Supplement, 165
Times Literary Supplement, 71
Tito, President, 291, 293
Tobago, 164–5, 185, 191, 252, 257, 336; development programme for, 248–8, 315; Independence Movement, 248–9; hurricane devastation, 309
Tobago Conference (1961), 235–41, 268
Town and Country Planning, 246–7, 251
Trade Promotion Conference, 125

Trade unions: and affiliation to PNM, 146, 149; divisions amongst, 305–6; and the Industrial Stabilisation Act, 313–14
See also International Confederation of Free Trade Unions
Tricontinental Conference, Havana (1966), 335
Trinidad Chronicle, 217, 248, 267
Trinidad Guardian, 110, 115, 233, 263–4, 266–7
Trinidad Labour Party, 164
Trinidad Leaseholds Ltd., 152
Trinidad Lake Petroleum Company, 14
Trinidad Public Library, 93, 113–14
Trinidad and Tobago: political, social and economic structure as a crown colony, 11ff.; Chamber of Commerce, 125; reconstruction of Legislative Council, 166–167; constitution reform, 168–72; internal self-government, 172; and Federation, 173ff. (*and see* West Indies Federation); chosen as site of Federal capital, 178; and migration, 179, 191–4; the disunited Opposition in the Legislature, 257–9; achieves independence, 284–6, 338–43; and the Caribbean Economic Community, 286–8; joins United Nations, 338
See also Chaguaramas Naval Station; People's National Movement; West Indies Federation; Williams, Eric
Trinidad and Tobago Historical Society 109
Trinity College, Dublin, 98
Trujillo, President (of Dominican Republic), 66
Tuberculosis, 18
Tucker Valley, 207, 226, 236
Turnbull, Richard, 71

Uganda, 140, 291
Unemployment: conference on (1964), 306–7; legacy from colonial period, 339
UNESCO, 106–7, 122
United Arab Republic, 291, 294
United Kingdom, 168–9, 186, 205, 249–50, 255–6, 334, 341,; and Cuba, 64, 71–2; destroyer-base deal with U.S.A., 65, 68, 81, 205–6, 209–13, 217–18, 231, 233–4, 238–9, 242; and immigration, 179, 193–194; and the Chaguaramas base, 206–9, 215, 227ff.; and the Caribbean Economic Community, 287–8; and the EEC, 289; and British Guiana, 295
United Nations, 291, 296–9
United States, 161–2, 186, 205; cocoa imports, 14–15; and Cuba, 64; destroyer-base deal with U.K., 65, 68, 205–6, 209–213, 217–18, 231, 233–4, 238–9, 242; and the Chaguaramas base, 206ff.; and the Caribbean Economic Community, 287–288

University College of the West Indies, 102, 110, 242–3
Usine Ste. Madeleine, 14

Venezuela, 162, 194, 210, 235, 292, 342; goodwill mission to Trinidad and Tobago, 302–3
Vietnam, 300–1, 331
Vila, Herminio Portell, 64
Virgin Islands, 76, 84, 92

Wages, colonial period, 16
Wages Council for Agricultural Workers, 216
Walcott, Frank, 138
Wales, 330
Wallace, Robert (Minister of Labour), 305
Waller Field, 206, 222–3, 226, 239
Warburg (publisher), 53
Washington DC, 96, 132, 293
Water Riots of 1903, 25
West India Club, London, 15
West India Committee, 14, 69, 71
West Indian, The, 94
West Indian Conferences, 92, 106, 119–23
West Indian Crusader, St. Lucia, 88
West Indian Independence Party, 165
West Indies, University of the, 239, 244, 271–2, 288, 294, 328–31; projected, 79, 96–9
West Indies Federal Labour Party (WIFLP), 202
West Indies Federation, 68, 115–17, 136–7, 168, 234; first proposed, 173; agreement on at London Conference (1956), 173; Jamaica Conference on Federal capital site, 174, 204; question of type of federation, 175–7; question of economic aid from U.K., 177–8; federal capital site chosen, and the economic and social results, 178–9; failure of Intergovernmental Conference (1959) on the constitution, 181–6; Intergovernmental Conference of 1961 and the aftermath, 185–95, 277–83; Lancaster House Conference, 196–201; breaks up, 201–3
West Virginia University, Negro History Week, 74
Wheare, Professor Sir Kenneth, 169, 330
Wight, Sir Gerald, 263–4
Wilkinson, A.M., 37
WILLIAMS, ERIC: early years, 26–9; wins college exhibition and scholarships, 30–31; at Queen's Royal College, 31–3; at Oxford, 33–5, 39–49; teachers who influenced him, 36–9; denied a Fellowship, 45–7; decides on historical research, 49–51; thesis on slavery, and receives Ph.D., 51; awarded Senior University Studentship, 51–2; Assistant Professor at Howard University, 52, 57–62; study on West Indian developments, 52–3; travels

WILLIAMS, ERIC:—(cont.)
in Europe, 53–4; research on West
Indian history, 63, 68–72; elected to
Julius Rosenwald Fellowship, 63; travels
in West Indies, 63–7; and Federation, 68,
115–17, 127, 136–7, 173ff., 277–83; lec-
turing, articles, and university contacts
(1943–7), 73–80; and the Caribbean
Commission, 81ff., 112–13, 118–27, 131–
132; lectures at Queen's Royal College
and Trinidad Public Library, 92–4; visit
to Antigua, 94–5; evidence to Commission on higher education, 96–9; and
John Dewey, 97–8; research on British
Empire problems, 100–2; Deputy Chairman of Caribbean Research Council,
105–7; research on Caribbean history,
108–9; and the Historical Society of
Trinidad and Tobago, 109–10; replies to
attack by Mr. Shenfield, 110–11; adult
education campaign, 113–17; forms a
political party (PNM), 131–7; direct contact with workers, 138–9; at ICFTU
conference, 139–42; meets Aimé Césaire,
142; addresses meeting in House of
Commons, 143; launches PNM, 144,
149–50; and opposition to PNM, 150–2;
editor of, and editorials in PNM
Weekly, 152–5; speech at first PNM
Annual Convention, 155–6; and the
1956 General Election, 152–5; forms a
Government, 166–7; and constitution
reform, 168–72; and the Chaguaramas
base, 204 ff.; demands independence,
234–5; responsibilities and burdens in
the Legislative Council, 246; introduces
Development Programme, 246–7; his
1958 budget, 247–8; and Tobago, 248–9,
309, 315; and the Common Market,
249–50; and the telephone company,
250–1; and town and country planning,
250–1; and bus concessions, 252; and
British Guiana, 252, 294–300; and reform of electoral procedure, 253–4; and
morality in public affairs, 254–7; and the
Opposition in the Legislative Assembly,
257–9; and the PNM organisation, 260–
268; and Sir Gerald Wight and the
Trinidad Guardian, 263–6; intellectual
pursuits during first term of office, 269–
273; visit to India, 272; and the 1961
General Election, 274–6; and achievement of independence, 283–6; and the
Caribbean Economic Community, 286–
288; and EEC, 289–90; visit to Africa,
291–3, 328–9; in Yugoslavia and Iran,
293; in Ottawa and Washington, 293–4;
and Vietnam, 300–1; and Southern
Rhodesia, 301; and the Commonwealth
Secretariat, 301; and Venezuela, 302–3;
and direct democracy, 304–10; and the
Industrial Stabilisation Act, 311–14; and

the second Development Plan, 314–15;
and the public service, 315; initiates
Meet the Party Tour, 322–3; and the
tenth anniversary of PNM, 323–5; intellectual pursuits during second term of
office, 327–31; Pro-Chancellor of the
University of the West Indies, 328;
honorary degrees conferred on, 328;
visits universities, 330; articles for The
Nation, 330–1; and the 1966 General
Election, 332–7; on the reality of inde-
pendence, 338–43
WRITINGS
British Historians and the West Indies, 72,
79, 328
British West Indies in World History, The,
93
Capitalism and Slavery, 69–73, 93, 112,
328
Colour, The Unfinished Business of Demo-
cracy, 75
Documents of West Indian History, 328
Economic Aspect of the Abolition of the
West Indian Slave Trade and Slavery, 51
Economic Future of the Caribbean, The, 73
Education in the West Indies, 99, 112, 131
'Historical Background of Race Rela-
tions in the Caribbean, The', 269–70
History of the People of Trinidad and
Tobago, 323, 328
'In support of Textbooks with a Carib-
bean Flavour', 106
'International Perspectives for Trinidad
and Tobago', 301–2
Negro in the Caribbean, The, 52, 68, 69,
73, 81, 84–6, 94, 112
PNM Weekly editorials, 152–5
'Political Leader considered as a man of
culture, The', 270
'Reflections on the Aristotelian Revolu-
tion in Trinidad', 115
Wilson, Woodrow, 154
Wimpffen, Baron de, 339
Windward Islands, 173, 177
Women's League, in PNM, 146, 149, 319,
323
Woodford Square, Port-of-Spain, 131–3;
University of, 133, 135–6, 143, 148–9,
154–5, 157–8, 161–3, 167, 170–1, 196,
227, 230–5, 256, 262, 266, 323, 336
Woodson, Carter, 71
Workers and Farmers Party (WFP), 332–
333, 335–7
Worrell, Frank, 268
Wright, Richard, 142

Youth League, in PNM, 146, 319
Youth centres, 308
Yugoslavia, 291, 293–4, 329

Zambia, 340
Zurich, 113

CPSIA information can be obtained
at www.ICGtesting.com
Printed in the USA
LVHW010856130920
665859LV00001B/8